FORGING FREEDOM

FORGING FREEDOM

The Formation of Philadelphia's Black Community, 1720–1840

GARY B. NASH

Harvard University Press
Cambridge, Massachusetts
London, England

Copyright © 1988 by the President and Fellows of Harvard College
All rights reserved
Printed in the United States of America
10   9   8   7   6   5

First Harvard University Press paperback edition, 1991

Library of Congress Cataloging-in-Publication Data

Nash, Gary B.
   Forging freedom.

   Includes bibliographical references and index.
   1. Afro-Americans—Pennsylvania—Philadelphia—History.
2. Philadelphia (Pa.)—History.   3. Philadelphia (Pa.)—
Race relations.   I. Title.
F158.9.N4N37   1988   974.8′1100496073   87-23696

ISBN 0-674-30933-2 (paper)

For Cindy

Acknowledgments

MANY PEOPLE and several institutions gave me valuable help in preparing this book. I gratefully acknowledge the assistance of the many librarians and archivists at the Library of Congress; National Archives; Pennsylvania State Archives, Harrisburg; Presbyterian Historical Society, Philadelphia; Methodist Historical Society, Philadelphia; University Research Library, University of California, Los Angeles; American Philosophical Society, Philadelphia; and Van Pelt Library, University of Pennsylvania. My special thanks go to Linda Stanley, Historical Society of Pennsylvania; Philip Lapsansky, Library Company of Philadelphia; and Ward Childs, Archives of the City and County of Philadelphia. Many research grants from the Academic Senate at the University of California, Los Angeles, and a Research Professorship at the Philadelphia Center for Early American Studies provided time and subsidies without which I could not have completed this work. My gratitude goes also to two friends at Harvard University Press. Aida Donald, who knows the ways of authors, provided encouragement and valuable criticism while waiting patiently. Ann Hawthorne, nonpareil in the underappreciated art of copyediting, took infinite care with the manuscript and improved it immeasurably.

In researching and writing this book over the last nine years, I have been assisted by many talented graduate students who eased the strain on my microfilm-wearied eyes, tracked down countless bits of information, analyzed statistics, searched newspapers for scraps of information, recorded and collated data from manuscript censuses and city directories, checked notes, and thus enabled me to complete this study. In these tasks I gratefully acknowledge the contributions of Margaret Clark, Rachelle Friedman, Thomas Ingersoll, Daniel Johnson, Mark Kleinman, David Lehman, Carla Gardina Pestana, Rosalind Burnam, Cynthia Shelton, Ronald Schultz, and Billy Smith to the pages that follow.

Another set of friends, by their criticisms and emendations of the manuscript, challenged, amused, and inspired me in such a variety of instances and ways that this book inevitably reflects their scholarly collaboration. Parts of the manuscript were read by Margaret Creel, University of California, Los Angeles; William Gravely, University of Denver; Susan Klepp, Rider College; Billy Smith, Montana State University; Jean Soderlund, Swarthmore College; members of the Seminar of the Philadelphia Center for Early American Studies, University of Pennsylvania; and members of the Los Angeles Labor History Study Group, including Hal Barron, David Brundage, Roberto Calderon, Nancy Fitch, Jacklyn Greenberg, John Laslett, Steven Ross, Alexander Saxton, Dorothee Schneider, Frank Stricker, and Devra Weber. Jon Butler, Yale University; David B. Davis, Yale University; Graham Hodges, Colgate University; Eric Monkonnen, University of California, Los Angeles; and Michael Zuckerman, University of Pennsylvania, read the entire manuscript and made many useful suggestions. My greatest debt is to the deep reading and searching comments of Ira Berlin, University of Maryland; Emma Lapsansky, Temple University; Peter Wood, Duke University; and my wife, Cynthia J. Shelton, who sustained the spirit in which the book is written.

Chapter 4 is a recast version of "'To Arise Out of the Dust': Absalom Jones and the African Church of Philadelphia, 1785–95," in my book *Race, Class, and Politics: Essays on Colonial and Revolutionary Society* (Urbana: University of Illinois Press, 1986).

Contents

Illustrations

Maps

What poor despised company
Of travellers are these
That's walking yonder narrow way,
Along that rugged maze?

Why they are of a royal line,
They're children of a King;
Heirs of immortal Crown divine,
And loud for joy they sing.

Why do they then appear so mean,
And why so much despis'd?
Because of their rich robes unseen
The world is not apprized.

Richard Allen
*A Collection of Hymns
and Spiritual Songs* . . .
Philadelphia, 1801

Introduction

IN THE HEAT of an August afternoon in 1793, an unusual medley of Philadelphians gathered under shade trees at the edge of the city to share a ceremonial banquet. Scores of construction tradesmen, several merchants, and the city's most renowned doctor sat down at long plank tables and feasted on a bounteous dinner, concluding with melons and liqueurs. They were served by about fifty free black residents of the city. Then the whites stood, yielding their chairs to the black Philadelphians, who were served by six of the "most respectable" of the whites. The occasion for this display of racial reciprocity was the raising of the roof beams of the African Church of Philadelphia, the first free black church in the northern states of the new American republic. "Peace on earth and good will to men," toasted the ebullient Benjamin Rush. "May African churches everywhere soon succeed to African bondage," he continued, making explicit the connection between Christian conscience and antislavery commitment. One of the black leaders, William Gray, attempted to express the gratitude of the small black community for the help they had received from white Philadelphians in building the church; but he "was checked by a flood of tears." The day ended with much clasping of hands and feelings of "virtuous and philanthropic joy," Rush reported to his wife. The warmhearted doctor must have spoken for nearly all those who attended the interracial, cross-class breaking of bread when he wrote, "To me it will be a day remembered with pleasure as long as I live."[1]

Almost four decades later, in June 1832, the *Julius Pringle,* with ninety-two former slaves from North Carolina aboard in the care of a Quaker abolitionist, eased toward the Delaware River wharves in Philadelphia. Hundreds of free blacks in the South, living in debt peonage and fearing reprisals from incensed white southerners in the aftermath of Nat Turner's bloody insurrection, were heading north, and Philadelphia had been known for two generations as a city of refuge. But as the ship prepared to land in the City of Brotherly Love, an angry horde of whites on the dock brandished guns and vowed to repel the sojourners. A prominent Quaker in the throng, momentarily forgetting his pacifist principles, called out that if a landing was attempted, "he should not think [it] strange if they shared the fate of the Boston tea." Fearing wholesale violence, the dismayed captain veered away from shore and turned the ship downriver. The disappointed black passengers watched the Philadelphia skyline, dominated by church steeples, disappear. When a second debarkation was attempted a few miles south at Chester, the migrants were similarly repulsed by an armed crowd.[2]

This book recounts how the optimistic spirit of racial harmony, dramatized in the banquet of 1793, came to be transformed into the militant antiblack sentiment of the 1830s. This explanation in turn serves a larger story—the formation of the free black community in Philadelphia in the period between the American Revolution and the 1830s. For two generations after the Revolution, Philadelphia was the largest and most important center of free black life in the United States, and it continues to this day to be one of the vital urban locations of black Americans. But black Philadelphia was created in an atmosphere of growing Negrophobia in the early nineteenth century. This surging racial hostility shattered the hopes of postrevolutionary reformers that those who had been held in bondage would become respectable and respected citizens of the new nation. Equally, it compromised their belief that a biracial society would emerge to fulfill the ideals expressed in the Pennsylvania Constitution of 1776, which proclaimed that "all men are born equally free and independent, and have certain natural, inherent and inalienable rights."[3]

The Enlightenment ideals expressed in this language undergirded what many Philadelphians, both black and white, of the revolutionary era believed would be an epochal transformation of a people brutalized under slavery in the New World. Much was at stake here; many American and European observers were regarding the fate of Pennsylvania's free blacks as a litmus test of environmentalist theory regarding racial differences. Most whites during the eighteenth century believed that Africans were by nature inferior, occupying the lowest rung of the human ladder, and had been so degraded under slavery that they were unfit for freedom. Even the minds of early antislavery advocates such as Benjamin Rush had been tinctured by this belief. As late as 1782, Rush wrote that slaves had acquired so many "habits of vice" under slavery that to free them now in the South "would be to injury them and society."[4] A few reformers in the revolutionary era had demurred, agreeing with the unswerving Quaker abolitionist Anthony Benezet that slavery alone was responsible for the degradation of Africans in America, and hence that in different circumstances the scars of slavery would heal and freedmen and freedwomen would take their place among those who had been better advantaged from birth.

Three years after expressing doubts that slaves could become citizens, Rush concluded that in the North emancipation was working well. The several thousand free blacks in the city, he observed, "are in general more industrious and orderly than the lowest class of white people."[5] To white abolitionists who subscribed to environmentalist theory in the late eighteenth century, such evidence of the capacity of freed slaves to overcome the twin disabilities of a heathen background and the marks of oppression came as welcome news. On the other side of the Atlantic, those who were working to abolish slavery and the slave trade eagerly awaited reports of "the Philadelphia experiment," for after the war the capital of American Quakerism was home to the largest urban concentration of free blacks of any place where slavery had been established in the English-speaking parts of the Western Hemisphere. The Pennsylvania Abolition Society, established by white Philadelphians in 1775, was quick to publicize its optimistic conclusions. Writing in 1787 to the London Society for the Abolition of the Slave Trade, its members offered evidence that the men and women just emerging from bondage could function as orderly and useful citizens. Including "vouchers and testimonials" regarding the "industrious, orderly & moral deportment" of a large number of manumitted slaves, they echoed Rush's judgment that these Afro-Americans had outperformed whites of the same economic stratum. Such defects as were visible in those rescued from thralldom, they ventured to suggest, were caused entirely by the lack of education and religious instruction denied them as chattels.[6]

The vital role of Philadelphia in the transatlantic campaign to abolish the slave trade and slavery was apparent to the free black community. Free blacks had flocked to the city from every point on the compass because of its reputation for benevolence and more particularly for its dedicated abolition society, the first formed in America. Since the 1790s, the *Encyclopaedia Britannica* had called Philadelphia the world's leading city in the struggle to improve the human condition.[7] If free blacks did not know that specific fact, they knew generally of the unusual commitment to antislavery that existed among the ethnically and religiously mixed population of William Penn's town. Proofs of this commitment were the abolition law passed in 1780, the first in the new nation; the steadfast work of the abolition society; and the many meetings of the interstate American Convention for Promoting the Abolition of Slavery, first convened in the city in 1794. Black Philadelphians knew that they faced scoffing remarks and downright hostility from the many whites who could not overcome a legacy of prejudice against dark-complexioned men and women formerly encountered only as slaves. But the first generation of emancipated slaves also knew that they were beginning life anew in a city that was the center not only of Quaker humanitarianism but also of the new ideology of manufacturing, which stressed free labor and free trade, and subscribed to the view of Adam Smith that slavery was incompatible with an expanding commercial, manufacturing society.

Philadelphia's free blacks also understood that they occupied a unique place in the postrevolutionary struggle to fulfill the ideals upon which the new republic had been established. Black struggles to expand the sphere of liberty were in fact an important, if largely unrecognized, part of nation building in the new American republic. Moreover, hanging on the ability of free blacks to perform as virtuous citizens rested the fate of millions of other blacks—those still enslaved and countless others yet unborn. For black newcomers in the Delaware River port city who were not aware of the community's historic mission, the Pennsylvania Abolition Society and black leaders issued frequent reminders. Not only did Philadelphia's free blacks have their own welfare at risk, but upon their shoulders, cautioned their white abolitionist friends, weighed the responsibility of proving to "the enemies of your liberty" that they were mistaken in justifying the continuation of slavery by "loudly and constantly assert[ing] that you are not qualified to enjoy it." It fell to the black community to disprove such "calumnies and thus to contribute your part towards the liberation of such of your fellow men as yet remain in the shackles of slavery."[8]

Mindful of what hung in the balance, Philadelphia's free black citizens pursued their goal of a dignified and secure existence. This book describes a generation of noteworthy accomplishments in an atmosphere of relative racial harmony from the end of the Revolution to the beginning of the nineteenth century. It argues, however, that from the beginning free black Philadelphians understood that the only secure foundation upon which to fashion their lives was one constructed of independent organizations embodying their sense of being a people within a people and relying on their own resources rather than on white benevolence. It follows a second generation of black Philadelphians who had to carry on their struggles for freedom amid mounting white hostility and traces the ways in which they adapted to a growing, industrializing city and created intricate systems of self-support as a way of coping with northern urban life. This story is partly one of leaders—some inspired, others frail; but it is also a reckoning of ordinary people making choices, searching for solutions to their own problems, and determining the course of their lives as best they could. Recognizing the obstacles they faced, and maneuvering within boundaries that most of them had only limited resources to redefine, they tested, contested, sometimes transcended, and sometimes succumbed to the power of white Philadelphians above, among, and around them. Always their lives were intertwined with those of their white fellow residents, for urban society in Philadelphia was biracial and multiethnic from the beginning, and even the most Negrophobic whites lacked the ability to separate the races physically. Thus the history of racial relations, which is intimately bound up with the history of the developing black community, involved a continuously changing set of human boundaries, an ever-shifting pattern of reciprocal relationships and influences.

The dual themes of this book—tragedy and triumph—warrant a few more words of explanation. The tragedy lay in the unfulfilled promise of a racially equal and harmonious society. By the 1820s, such hopes were collapsing. Thereafter racial conflict and discrimination intensified, as if unstoppable once unleashed. As devoted as some white Philadelphians were to the cause of antislavery and racial justice, they proved impotent to control their society at large. Played out in Philadelphia in the first half of the nineteenth century was a demonstration of the core difficulty of liberal reform—the "inferiority of the morality of groups," as Reinhold Niebuhr phrased it, "to that of the individuals who compose the group."[9] Not until the latter part of the twentieth century would Philadelphians and the generality of other Americans work their way back to where they had stood two centuries before—perceiving the possibility of a society undivided by race. The failure of "the Philadelphia experiment" thus prefigured the course of race relations in the last century and a half, and race relations have been the most searing and enduringly tragic part of this country's history.

This failure of race relations, however, was not accompanied by a disintegration of the black community. Quite the opposite occurred. Although increasing white hostility ushered in a long period of violent racial conflict, the black community continued to grow and developed its own mechanisms for coping with a hostile environment. The successes of black Philadelphians were sufficiently large to convince Frederick Douglass in 1848 that Philadelphia, "more than any other [city] in our land, holds the destiny of our people."[10] Douglass was not mistaken, for in the aftermath of the American Revolution there emerged in this mid-Atlantic port town a free black community of a size and strength to build the institutional foundations of modern Afro-American life, to provide leaders for the growing antislavery struggle in the 1830s and thereafter, and to supply the crucial links between the slave past and the free future.

It has not been easy for historians to recognize how vibrant and multifaceted were the northern urban centers of black life in the antebellum period. Mostly they have focused on what happened *to* black communities, not what transpired *within* them. The traditional approach to black urban history has been to see the cities as venues of discrimination and impoverishment where an almost pathological disintegration of black family and social life occurred.[11] Although none of them deals fully with the post-revolutionary formation of northern black communities, newer studies have begun to alter this view, demonstrating that alongside a history of discrimination and oppression must be placed the internal history of a people striving to live life as fully, as freely, as creatively, and as spiritually rich as their inner resources and external circumstances allowed. A community *was* forged in Philadelphia—not only a geographic clustering of former slaves but also a community of feeling and consciousness. Once formed, it could not be obliterated, whatever the magnitude of hostility toward its members. It is no coincidence that from black Philadelphians came the most vigorous protests against the white movement, beginning in 1817, to recolonize free blacks in Africa. Nor was it happenstance that this city was the home of the first African Protestant Episcopal church, the first African Methodist church, the first African Presbyterian church, and the first African Baptist church in the North and the first fully independent black religious denomination in the hemisphere—the African Methodist Episcopal Church. From Philadelphia's narrow alleys and cramped courtyards came men and women who established many of the first northern black schools; literary, musical, and historical societies; and black newspapers. Here the first national Negro convention met in 1830. In this southernmost of the nation's northern seaports, enmeshed through trade with both the slave South and the free North, there grew a corps of men and women activists who would advance the cause of racial equality and racial concord, both before and after the Civil War. It is this dialectic between oppression and achievement, racism and race consciousness, external structures of power and internal consciousness and experience that the following pages attempt to demonstrate.

1. Slavery and Antislavery in the Capital of Conscience

IN LATE NOVEMBER 1684, just three years after the first Quaker settlers arrived in Pennsylvania, the *Isabella,* out of Bristol, England, sailed up the Delaware River and docked at the infant settlement of Philadelphia. Clambering down to the wharf to greet the ship, the villagers discovered that the *Isabella* carried no new immigrants from England or Ireland or English woolens, metal implements, or finished household goods, but 150 Africans in chains. Merchant William Frampton, the Philadelphia agent of a Bristol firm, negotiated the sales of the dark-skinned, foreign-speaking men and women brought up from the ship's hold, and it took him only a few days to dispose of the human merchandise. So eagerly did the pacifist Quaker settlers snap up the newly arrived laborers, whom they set to work clearing trees and brush and erecting crude houses in the budding village, that most of the specie they had brought to Philadelphia from England departed with the *Isabella* when it sailed down the Delaware the next spring.[1]

The introduction of 150 slaves into a population of about one thousand white settlers in 1684 marked the beginning of an intermingling between white and black Philadelphians that has continued ever since. The friction that has accompanied this interaction was also present from the start. One Philadelphian who purchased four newcomers from the decks of the *Isabella* wrote a few weeks after his acquisition that his two best Africans had run away, and he had "no tithings of them at all."[2] At the outset of their "holy experiment" the pacifist Quakers had ensnared themselves in a troublesome institution, for slavery by its very nature involved coercion and violence to extract labor from its unwilling victims.

For a half-century after 1684, as Philadelphia grew to a river-front town of 8,000, slaves continued to arrive in the city. The market for slaves was never large enough to require more than an occasional shipload, and almost always the slaves came from the West Indies or South Carolina, where they received their introduction to English culture.[3] A cluster of West Indian Quaker merchants who had been attracted to William Penn's colony, such as Samuel Carpenter, Isaac Norris, and Jonathan Dickinson, directed this minor traffic and were themselves the largest slave-owners.[4] Extensive mercantile contacts in the sugar islands sustained the traffic in enslaved black workers whenever the local economy demanded them. Among deceased Philadelphians whose estates were inventoried before 1750, nearly half held slaves, and within the wealthiest echelon—those with estates worth £200 sterling or more—nearly six out of ten had acquired human property. Philadelphians did not rely so heavily on enslaved labor as their urban counterparts in New York City; but rapid economic development in the first half of the eighteenth century created a demand for labor and generated enough capital to encourage merchants, lawyers, doctors, shopkeepers, ship captains, tavernkeepers, and artisans to import sizable numbers of slaves and white indentured servants. By the 1740s about 15 percent of all male laborers along the wharves and in the shops of artisans were slaves, while in the kitchens black women tended children, scrubbed, cooked, and served; by the early 1760s, this share grew to at least 20 percent.[5]

Throughout the colonial period the arrival of black laborers in the Philadelphia region ebbed and flowed in rhythm with a number of factors. A slave conspiracy to burn the town of New York in 1712 temporarily chilled the desire of Philadelphians for more Africans in their midst and led the Quaker-controlled assembly to impose a prohibitive £20 per head import duty on slaves, though the Crown promptly disallowed the tax. When Philadelphia recovered from its first serious economic recession in the late 1720s, the traffic in human flesh resumed with a vengeance. "We have *negroes* flocking in upon us since the duty on them is reduced," wrote the early Quaker abolitionist Ralph Sandiford.[6] A few years later, when Irish and German indentured servants began pouring into the colony, the slave traffic tapered off. But when the outbreak of the Seven Years' War in 1755 suddenly dried up the supply of indentured white servants and induced many unhappy servants to flee their masters for service in the British army, Philadelphians turned their eyes once more to black slaves. "All importation of white servants is ruined by enlisting them," wrote one of the most active of the city's traders in 1756, "and we must make more general use of Slaves."[7] For the next nine years, despite the mounting protests of some Quakers against the slave trade, merchants imported Africans in unprecedented numbers. In 1762, when the traffic apparently peaked, some 500 slaves arrived, many of them directly from Gambia.[8] A few years later the number of slaves in Philadelphia reached its apogee—about 1,400 in a city now grown to about 18,000.[9]

Just as suddenly as it had expanded, the slave trade withered a few years after the Seven Years' War. British recruiting sergeants no longer beat their drums for white servant enlistees, and the influx of Irish and German indenturers resumed. Free to choose between white and black bound labor, Philadelphians with capital to invest imported fewer than thirty slaves a year by 1770. Three years later, Anthony Benezet, the unwavering Quaker abolitionist, noted that more slaves were exported than imported in Philadelphia. The involvement of Philadelphians with slavery was far from over, but even before the outbreak of violence with England the slave trade was dead, the casualty of a growing revulsion at trafficking in human beings and of a preference for white servants and free wage laborers.[10]

From the earliest years, the slaves brought together in Philadelphia were a polyglot population. Almost all came from the kingdoms on the west coast of Africa, although until the Seven Years' War most had been "seasoned" first by the wretchedness of sugar cultivation in the West Indies. Others were obliged to migrate with their masters from other mainland colonies, especially from Delaware and Maryland, which in the colonial era supplied Philadelphia with a steady flow of aspiring planter-merchants, lawyers, shopkeepers, and artisans. Not until the late 1750s did Philadelphia merchants import Africans directly in substantial numbers; but as many as a thousand of these arrived between 1759 and 1766, about half of them in 1762, and through those who were sold to city dwellers came the greatest infusion of African culture in Philadelphia's history.[11]

Differences in language and culture among West African subgroups, as well as the importance of varying experiences in the Americas, gradually faded among slaves living in the Quaker city. Nevertheless, some subgroup idiosyncrasies persisted, and even as late as the mid-nineteenth century these differences in background and outlook could spark conflict within the black community.[12]

One reason slaves rapidly absorbed elements of European culture was that they lived in intimate contact with white families, most of whom owned only one or two slaves and seldom more than four. A few Philadelphians, usually merchants, owned ten, twenty, or even thirty slaves, but they generally hired out many of them, keeping only a small number for household service and common labor in their warehouses and stores.[13] In Philadelphia no equivalent existed to the gang labor used on southern tobacco, rice, and indigo plantations. Rather, the urban slave toiled alongside a master who was a sailmaker, baker, cooper, carpenter, or tailor; sailed with a seagoing master as cabin boy or deckhand; worked for a small manufacturer in a brickyard, ropewalk, shipyard, brewery, or tannery; performed domestic service in the house of a merchant or professional master; or cleaned the stables and performed common labor for a tavernkeeper. Throughout the colonial era about two-fifths of Philadelphia's slaves worked for mariners, artisans, and proprietors of small manufactories. Hence, nearly as many slaves acquired artisan skills as performed domestic service.[14]

Urban slavery in the North was decidedly milder than plantation labor in the South. Slaves were better fed, clothed, and housed, were often less confined, and had less physically debilitating labor, greater access to intellectual stimulation in a more cosmopolitan setting, and marginally better prospects of obtaining freedom. Nonetheless, harsh treatment and violence frequently accompanied human bondage in the city. Years after the Revolution a longtime city resident recalled that the brickmaker John

Figure 1. Portrait of Black Alice (1803), who died in 1802 at age 116. She was apparently born to one of the first slaves brought to Philadelphia in 1684. She remembered having often lit the pipe of William Penn.

Coates, who relied on slave labor in his brickyard, fastened iron collars on the necks of his slaves, "with projecting hack[le]s to prevent their escape in the woods—no rarity in those days in the neighborhood of Philadelphia."[15] Records of slave suicides in the city in 1743, 1748, 1759, 1761, and 1764 provide further reminders of the despair that slavery engendered in its victims.[16] Far more often slaves deprived their masters of their labor by running away—"a persistent, irremediable problem" for slaveholders in Pennsylvania as in all other colonies.[17]

Crimes committed by slaves against their masters, ranging from theft and arson to murder, studded the newspaper accounts of the colonial period and served as daily reminders of the discontent of slaves. Even so gentlemanly a figure as James Logan, Philadelphia's leading scholar, jurist, and proprietary official in the early eighteenth century, felt the wrath of his black bondsman. In 1737 his slave Sampson, charged with burning a house owned by Logan, made "a long, artful and pathetick defense" before a special court. Fearful of the "ill consequences" of "so heinous a crime," especially in the context of "the insolent Behaviour of the

Negroes in and about the city, which has of late been so much taken notice of," the white court sentenced Sampson to death.[18] Such severe punishment of enslaved blacks—far greater than that meted out for similar crimes by whites—was common. In 1762, for example, a slave convicted and sentenced to death for burglary was refused a pardon even though twenty-seven white petitioners asked the court for leniency, citing the slave's exemplary record and his recent service in the Seven Years' War, during which he had served in two campaigns and been held prisoner for five years.[19]

Although they were vastly outnumbered by white inhabitants and most lived in white households containing only one or two slaves, black Philadelphians in bondage managed to form families, perpetuate some of their African heritage, and create at least a general feeling of group identity. As early as 1699, slaves were protesting that they could not secure time from work to bury their dead during daylight hours—a poignant complaint among a people whose long tradition of reverence for ancestors made proper burial rites highly important. A separate section of the Strangers' Burial Ground was set apart for blacks, perhaps not so much in response to white separatist sensibilities as to the strongly expressed desire of the city's black bondsmen to preserve the remains of their friends and kin in an area that was theirs alone. Regarding this place of burial during the colonial era, one old lady remembered seeing slaves from Guinea "going to the graves of their friends early in the morning, and there leaving them victuals and rum." Throughout the prerevolutionary period, the Negro burial ground was the gathering place of the city's slaves and the small number of free blacks. On Sundays, holidays, and fair days they could be seen dividing into "numerous little squads," "dancing after the manner of their several nations in Africa, and speaking and singing in their native dialects."[20]

Slaves also found ways to form sexual liaisons and networks of friends in the city. To do so they needed different strategies from those available on a tobacco estate in Virginia or a rice plantation in South Carolina. Such large agricultural operations, sometimes involving scores of servile workers, contained by definition a slave community with all the attendant possibilities for companionship and family life—as well as for personal antagonism, competition, and hierarchical sorting by gender, age, skill, and function. Seaport towns such as Philadelphia contained no dense collections of slaves living alongside one another in separate quarters and working collectively. Yet the northern colonial ports generally provided a more favorable place for slaves to develop social networks and family life. The cities were geographically compact, and slaves had considerable latitude to move about in them. They were also of a size to permit multiple personal contacts. With a population of more than 13,000 by 1750, Philadelphia remained small enough that one resident could claim "he not only knew every gentleman in town, but every gentleman's black servant and dog."[21] By 1767 about 1,400 slaves lived within no more than about twenty blocks of developed urban space. Only blacks on the largest southern plantations were more densely settled, and in such a "walking city" a greater variety of intimate relationships was available than on the more thinly populated and often geographically isolated southern plantations and farms.[22]

Living in hundreds of different households rather than in segregated quarters, Philadelphia's slaves resorted to the city's public spaces for social interaction after the day's labor was done. Besides the burial ground, which served as the center of festive activities on Sundays and holidays, the courthouse provided the main meeting place for after-hours socializing and conviviality. As early as 1693, white citizens protested the "tumultuous gatherings" of slaves. Their protests led to restrictive legislation that required masters to jail and whip at their own expense any blacks who congregated there on Sundays without passes from their owners. Nine years later the Philadelphia grand jury was still complaining about "the great multitude of Negroes" who gathered on Sundays "in a Riott & tumultuous manner." Calls for the suppression of such boisterous Sunday meetings recurred in 1717, 1726, 1738, 1741, 1750, and 1751. These complaints testified both to whites' fear of what might happen when large numbers of slaves gathered together and to blacks' desire to maintain a social life outside their separate places of residence.[23]

Although no systematic records of marriages and births remain, it is still possible to glimpse urban slave family life. Because most enslaved Philadelphians found themselves isolated in white house-holds, they typically had to go beyond the property lines of their masters to find marriage partners of similar background and status—across the street, in the next block, or on the other side of town. Of twenty-seven slave marriages between 1745 and 1776 performed in Christ Church, St. Paul's Church, and St. Michael's and Zion (German) Lutheran Church, twenty-one involved part-ners owned by different masters or mistresses.[24] This greater difficulty in contracting marriage was often compounded after the nuptials by the sale of one black spouse.[25] In the city, where a slave might be sold to a new master living only a few blocks away, this did not necessarily shatter a slave marriage, as often occurred in the South when masters sold their slaves into a different county or even a different colony.[26] But slave children in Philadelphia rarely grew up in the same household with both their mother and father, and their masters often hired them out to families outside the city when they reached ten or twelve years of age.[27] If financially pressed, slaveowners often broke up families by selling the man or woman they owned, sometimes with the children, to a rural farmer, while the slave's spouse, the property of another master, remained in the city. Many of Philadelphia's slaveowners were merchants and professionals with family ties and close connections in Delaware and Maryland, and it was to these nearby plantation colonies that many slaves were sold. All of this meant that slaves had to nurture family life under great duress, although they had some advantages over enslaved persons in the South or in the rural North.[28]

One case in which the entire family was sold together was the slave family owned by Benjamin Chew, a wealthy lawyer and colonial official in Delaware, who moved to Philadelphia in 1754, bringing with him a number of slaves from his Dover plantation. About 1766, suffering financial reverses like so many others in the economic slump that hit Philadelphia after the Seven Years' War, Chew sold six of his slaves—a married couple and their four children—to a small plantation owner near Dover. Twenty years later the youngest child of this slave family, by then bearing the name of Richard Allen, would return to Philadelphia to become a leader of the emerging community of free blacks.[29] All his life

Chew bought and sold slaves, shuttling them between his Dover and Philadelphia homes. He leased one young boy in 1762 for seventeen years to a farmer outside Philadelphia, bought a Negro boy in 1772 without reference to any mother or father, and hired a slave woman and her child to a neighboring planter in Delaware in 1775.[30]

WHILE FRESH DRAFTS of Africans arriving in Philadelphia in the 1750s and 1760s kept alive the cultural practices of various parts of West Africa, the preponderant pressure on Philadelphia's slaves was to adapt to the culture of the master class. This tendency was increased by the everyday experience of living in white households as the only black or with one other black adult and a child or two. In Philadelphia, however, the master class itself was far from culturally homogeneous. English, Scots-Irish, and Germans made up the majority of the population, but sprinkled among them were Swedes, Dutch, French Huguenots, and Sephardic Jews—a mosaic of people who worshiped at a dozen different churches by the late colonial period. Throughout the eighteenth century, a polyglot African people were thus enmeshed in a heterogeneous European society.

Among slaveholders, however, the great majority were English; hence most slaves quickly learned that language. A minority, however, spoke German and other European languages. Cuffy, the runaway slave of David Frank, spoke French and Spanish as well as English. Thomas Bartholomew's twenty-three-year-old slave Joe, born in Guadaloupe and previously owned by masters in New York City and Charleston, South Carolina, was fluent in English, French, Spanish, and Portuguese.[31] Philadelphia's German Lutheran minister, Henry Melchior Muhlenberg, encountered one slave outside the city in 1763 who spoke a mixture of his Gambian native tongue, French, Spanish, and English. Taken from Africa to the French West Indies in 1761, he had been captured by the English and carried to Philadelphia, where he was purchased by a German innkeeper.[32]

Acculturation began in the small living units where slaves resided with their master's family, often no more than a four- or five-room house. By the 1740s it was also occurring in the churches, and somewhat later in church-related schools. Because Pennsylvania is thought of as a Quaker colony and the Society of Friends has been so consistently identified with American abolitionism it is easy to imagine that this tutelage of slaves was primarily the work of Quakers in their New World capital. But in fact Quakers, as early as the 1730s, owned only about one-third of the slaves in Philadelphia, and they rarely brought their slaves to their own religious devotions.[33]

It was the Anglican church that led the way in educating blacks, in exposing them to Christian doctrine and rituals, and in encouraging them to marry and baptize their children in the church. The Anglicans did not take the lead very early, and when they did, it was at the initiative of a wayfaring outsider, George Whitefield, who had taken Anglican orders in England but became the nemesis of most of colonial America's Anglican clergy.

From the beginning of the eighteenth century English Anglicans had expressed a desire to spread Christian doctrine among both Native Americans in the colonies and the Africans enslaved by European settlers. The Church of England established the Society for the Propagation of the Gospel (SPG) in 1701 as its missionary arm for just that purpose. The SPG had put its agents in the field in many American colonies by the first decade of the eighteenth century, and some of them worked Philadelphia's hinterland. They consistently faced the stubborn opposition of masters who feared, as one missionary put it, "the untoward haughty behavior" of slaves who had learned the precepts of Christianity. Such slaves, once baptized, conceived that they were entitled to freedom, for they knew that Christian doctrine sanctioned only the enslavement of heathens, not that of fellow Christians. No amount of chastising that the purpose of Christian instruction was to save their souls while making them more obedient servants could erase this notion entirely.[34]

None of the Anglican ministers in Philadelphia before 1739 showed any interest in the growing slave population, and few masters voluntarily brought their slaves to church. The first recorded black marriage united Samuel Francis and Violetta Bone at Christ Church in 1728, but it is likely that both Francis and Bone were free, since it was rare at this time for slaves to bear surnames. Not until 1745 would another black marriage be recorded at Christ Church; nor was a single baptism performed before 1741.[35]

The advent of black Christianity in Philadelphia can be dated to November 1739, when the spellbinding young George Whitefield, the generalissimo of the Great Awakening that would sweep the colonies in the 1740s, arrived in Philadelphia on his second American tour. Many of the city's approximately one thousand slaves must have heard his daily sermons preached in Christ Church and also outdoors from the gallery of the courthouse, where at six o'clock on one evening six thousand auditors "stood in an awful silence to hear him."[36] For a people whose ancestral religion was grounded in an understanding of nature as indwelling and whose eschatological vision provided no sharp distinction between the secular and sacred, Whitefield's emotional message and mellifluous voice had a powerful appeal. The highly literate and rational Protestant religion, sanitized of its mystical elements and supervised by a professionally trained clergy, had only limited power to render intelligible the strange and repressive world in which slaves found themselves. But revivalists such as Whitefield preached a personal rebirth, used music and body motion, and asked for the dynamic participation of each individual in an intense emotional experience. His religious outlook shared enough with traditional African styles and beliefs such as spirit possession and ecstatic expression—in the form of dancing, shouting, rhythmic clapping, and singing—to allow for an interpenetration of African and Christian religious beliefs.[37]

When Whitefield returned to Philadelphia in April 1740, and again in May, slaves were numerous in the huge crowds that thronged to hear him. Their receptivity to his message of redemption was almost certainly heightened by Whitefield's announced plan to establish two schools for Negroes in Pennsylvania, one of them in Philadelphia, and by Benjamin Franklin's publication of the evangelist's appeal to southern slaveowners for humanitarian treatment of their chattels. After his last exhortation, in a week of daily preaching in April 1740, Whitefield recorded in his journal that "many of the negroes were . . . much affected." In May, as he prepared to leave the city after another visit, he recorded that "near fifty Negroes came to give me thanks, under God, for what has been done to their Souls." Some of them, he noted, "have been effectually wrought upon and in an uncommon Manner."[38]

Whitefield's concern for the bondage of slaves was for their souls, not their bodies. He never attacked slavery itself; in fact he sanctioned and participated in it. Nonetheless, his interest in the souls of American slaves led to the first attempt in Philadelphia to provide education for them—a prerequisite for substantial Protestant religious indoctrination.[39] One previous attempt had been made in Philadelphia to teach slaves to read and write English when the bearded mystic, Samuel Keimer, just arrived from England in 1722, offered to provide free instruction to slaves in reading the scriptures. White Philadelphians met his offer with ridicule, perhaps mixed with apprehension.[40] Now, under Whitefield's inspiration, a far different schoolmaster appeared. None other than Philadelphia's dancing master, Robert Bolton, whose dancing assembly and musical concerts catered to Philadelphia's upper crust, came forward as Whitefield's instrument. Deeply affected by the evangelist, Bolton astonished the elite in the spring of 1740 by renouncing his role in providing them with "devilish diversions." Locking up his dancing school, he opened a school for children to which black youths were specifically invited. Within a few weeks fifty-three "black Scholars" were enrolled—a sufficient threat to notions of the proper role for slaves to get Bolton arraigned on charges of breaking the colony's law limiting the rights of slaves. Bolton's defense was adequate, however, to gain a dismissal of the charges before the city's grand jury.[41]

When Whitefield returned for a fourth visit to the city in November 1740, Philadelphia's blacks had further occasions to explore their interest in evangelical Protestantism. Whitefield preached sixteen times in the still roofless "New Building," a huge tabernacle built by his admirers as a nondenominational place of worship.[42] Between his May and November visits thousands of Philadelphians also turned out to hear a battery of Whitefield's American lieutenants, including Gilbert and William Tennent, Samuel Blair, James Davenport, and John Rowland, who preached fourteen sermons to a five-day synod of the Presbyterian church.[43]

Philadelphia's slaves, like so many other dispossessed people in colonial America, were apparently deeply moved by their exposure to spiritual leaders who minimized the importance of rank, emphasized the special virtue of "Christ's poor," and called for the participation of the individual in his or her own salvation.

The seeds broadcast by Whitefield and his followers among Philadelphia's blacks sprouted further in 1741 when Aeneas Ross, an SPG missionary, arrived to replace temporarily the stricken Archibald Cummings, rector of Christ Church. At this point the city's blacks had been drawn not so much to the Anglican church as to evangelical Christianity, and to its concern for the religious condition of slaves that Whitefield and some of his American subalterns had proclaimed. Cummings, in fact, had denied the pulpit of Christ Church to Whitefield in April 1740 and was neither a friend of the Awakening nor interested in Christian instruction of slaves. Ross, on the other hand, had already converted many slaves in Delaware, and he used his temporary appointment, which lasted only until Cummings's successor could be appointed in 1742, to open the doors of Christ Church to the city's slaves and a handful of free blacks. During his short tenure he baptized about one hundred persons; among the eighteen adults, twelve were blacks, "who appear'd publickly before the Congregation & were examined in, & said their Catechisms to the Admiration of All that heard them." Ross baptized nine young blacks—seven men and two women, all between twenty-one and twenty-six years old—in one mass baptism on January 17, 1742. "The like sight never [had been] seen before in [a] Philadelphia Church," he wrote.[44]

Cummings's permanent successor, Robert Jenney, continued Ross's work after he arrived in 1742. Jenney was no friend to the Awakening, but he had previously catechized slaves in New York City's Anglican church, and he continued his efforts among Philadelphia's slaves. He noted in 1744 that "Our Negroes are numerous & many of them inclined to be religious."[45] A year later, Jenney reported that since his arrival he had baptized many Negroes "and never administer[ed] the Lord's Supper (every month) without several of them [present]." The register book of baptisms shows that Jenney baptized twenty-one blacks between his arrival and the end of 1745. The "generality" of the city's blacks had "a disposition towards [Christian] religion," but many of them "run after the vagrant factious preachers." Jenny argued that blacks, "if properly instructed," would "keep steady to the Church."[46]

Jenney's reference to the appeal of the itinerant evangelists, made in November 1745, takes on more meaning when it is remembered that Whitefield had preached in Philadelphia throughout that summer and had set up a prayer society for blacks there.[47] Blacks may also have been attending the new evangelical Presbyterian church established in 1743 by Whitefield's followers and led by his friend Gilbert Tennent.[48] Philadelphia's slaves and a few free blacks had found new meaning in life through these evangelists. Sensing their identification with evangelical Protestantism, Whitefield had earlier contrived a sermon on "The Ethiopian's Conversion." He had learned, according to one account of his second visit to Philadelphia, to "invite the poor Negroes to touch Jesus Christ by Faith, whereby they would gain Freedom from the Slavery of Sin and Satan."[49]

Evangelical Christianity offered slaves the prospect of moving from the doctrine of liberation from sin to a religion of personal liberation. One vivid example, well known in the city, was Preaching-Dick, the slave of Robert Grace, who ran away in August 1745, was recaptured and sold, and then fled his new master, the butcher Thomas Rutter.[50] Many Anglican slaveowners, like their minister Jenney, were greatly bothered by the leveling and liberating implications of the radical awakeners. It appears to have been this nervousness about slaves imbibing notions of equality that led Christ Church to implore the SPG to send a "catechistical lecturer" to Philadelphia to rescue the city's blacks from the clutches of "the vagrant preachers of faction & schism," as Jenney called them. Masters hoped they could reach an accommodation with their slaves whereby the rising black interest in Christianity might be redirected from evangelical notions of equality and the brotherhood of all mankind into more respectable channels that stressed the ideal of the obedient Christian servant.[51]

After a year's delay, the SPG responded to the request from Philadelphia by creating a position for an instructor of "Negroes and others" in the city. A young Yale graduate, William Sturgeon, accepted the post in 1747, about a year after Whitefield had spent another month preaching in Philadelphia. Sturgeon's success in recapturing Philadelphia's slaves and free blacks from "vagrant factious preachers" was considerable. By April 1749 he reported that fifty blacks were attending his Sunday evening services, and he had baptized seven adults and four children after proper instruction.[52] Sturgeon labored diligently at tutoring black children and adults. By 1752, when twenty-eight blacks were baptized at Christ Church, he seems to have successfully neutralized the dangerous evangelical connection. The task was made easier because Tennent, a slaveholder himself, apparently made little attempt to attract slaves to his evangelical Presbyterian church, and Whitefield, after his departure in 1746, did not return for eight years.[53]

The ties of the black community to the Anglican church were strengthened in 1758 when the Bray Associates, an Anglican philanthropic society associated with the Church of England, launched a school for blacks in the city. This was no easy task, for most white Philadelphians still opposed the education of blacks. Benjamin Franklin, who as a young journeyman had witnessed Samuel Keimer's failed attempt to offer free education to slaves, wrote the Bray Associates in 1758 that the opposition to black education stemmed "partly from a prejudice that reading and knowledge in a slave are both useless and dangerous; and partly from an unwillingness in the masters and mistresses of common schools to take black scholars, lest the parents of the white children should be disgusted and take them away, not chusing to have their children mix'd with slaves in education, play, etc."[54] However, with Sturgeon in charge and a white mistress doing the teaching, the school soon enrolled thirty-six pupils, including Othello, the house slave of Benjamin and Sarah Franklin. The school accepted both free black children and the children of slaves, thus further blurring the line between the free and slave Negroes in the city.[55]

Although the Anglican church used education and religion to counteract the social dynamite implicit in the message of the radical Awakeners, many black Philadelphians retained their commitment to evangelical Protestantism. In 1761, after the evangelical Anglican William McClenachan led a group of enthusiasts out of Christ Church to form a new congregation of St. Paul's, many of Sturgeon's students defected to the black classes set up by McClenachan in opposition to Sturgeon's school.[56] But the controversial McClenachan, under attack by more sedate Anglicans, abandoned his church four years later. No successor could be found until 1768, and when William Stringer arrived from England, he quickly indicated his lack of interest in ministering to Philadelphia's blacks.[57]

In Christ Church, St. Paul's, and St. Peter's, built in 1763, Anglican efforts to educate and Christianize blacks created links to Philadelphia's black people, slave and free, that would last for many decades. From 1745 to 1776 more than 250 blacks, about one-fifth of them free, were baptized at Christ Church, and 45 couples were married there. Some were the slaves of the colony's governors, some of merchants and lawyers, some of artisans and ship captains. They came to the church to unite in marriage, and they brought their children for instruction and baptism. Some bore African names, such as Quam, "an old Negro man" belonging to Widow Green, who was baptized in 1769. Some carried the names of their masters, such as Sharper Tuttle, "near 80 years of age," who was baptized in 1770, forty years after his master, James Tuthill, freed him. And some went by names they gave themselves after gaining their release from bondage, such as the slaves Cuffe and Ruth, who took the last name Anthony after they were freed; or Abraham and Margaret, who adopted the surname Smith after their manumission.[58]

Beginning in the late 1740s, a few slaves and free Negroes married and baptized their children at other Philadelphia churches—St. Mary's and St. Joseph's Catholic churches, St. Michael's and Zion Lutheran Church, Gloria Dei Swedish Lutheran Church, the First and Second Presbyterian churches, and the Moravian Church. The numbers involved were very small, however, in comparison with the scores of slaves and free Negroes who came to the city's handsome Anglican brick churches.[59] Among those black Philadelphians who were drawn to Christian services—and especially among the small number of free blacks—the Anglican church was *the* church from 1740 until the Revolution. This might not have been so if the more evangelical churches had opened their doors to the city's blacks. But they did not; hence blacks went where they were welcomed and where schooling was available, worshiping in ways that were not altogether to their satisfaction and biding their time for the advent of a structure that more closely matched their innermost yearnings.

WHILE THE ANGLICANS DREW many slaves and free blacks into their fold, Philadelphia's Quakers maintained an anomalous position toward the Afro-American inhabitants in their midst. From the beginning of the settlement Quakers had alternately embraced and recoiled from the institution of chattel bondage. Their founder, George Fox, on a visit to Barbados in 1671, had warned against the oppression of Africans and advised Quakers to Christianize their servants, treat them humanely, and release them from bondage after thirty years of service.[60] But, eager to develop their colony, Quaker settlers with capital to invest in human labor purchased lifetime slaves as enthusiastically as did colonists of other religions. The Quaker elite dominated the assembly that legislated slave codes in 1700, 1705, and 1726 for controlling the growing number of slaves in Pennsylvania and also for restricting the small number of blacks who gained their freedom through manumission, usually after the death of their master. Ideally, Quakers hoped they might fit African slaves into a system of Christian servitude where familial relations would prevail—a "fraternal relationship of unequals." The reality of the matter proved to be very different.[61]

Quaker consciences were sorely trammeled by their involvement with slavery, for in Pennsylvania a succession of persistent critics pointed out the contradictions of the institution among a people who professed that Christ died for all mankind. Only six years after the first Quaker settlers disembarked on the banks of the Delaware, a group of German petitioners called for cleansing the colony of the abominable practice on the simple ground that it violated the Golden Rule. Periodically thereafter men such as William Southeby, John Farmer, Ralph Sandiford, and Benjamin Lay embellished this argument. They protested that slavery was incompatible with the Quaker credo, which pronounced the unity of all mankind, the evil of any form of violence in human affairs, and the sinfulness of ostentation and pride, all of which the ownership of fellow human beings unambiguously signified.

Most of these antislavery advocates were regarded by diligent white entrepreneurs as dangerous disturbers of the peace—a charge that was easy to make given the radical behavior and dramatic symbolic gesturings of some of them. The vegetarian hunchback Benjamin Lay, for example, practiced a severe asceticism that mocked well-to-do Quakers and took to sitting outside the Quaker meetinghouse on winter Sunday mornings with one unclothed leg and foot plunged in the snow. When Friends voiced their concern, he directed their attention to the sufferings of their half-clothed slaves. Often ejected from meetings for what orthodox Quakers regarded as disruptive behavior, Lay would lie in the dirt in front of the door, obliging Friends to step over his body as they left the meeting. In Burlington he burst in upon the Yearly Meeting of the Quaker elders bearing a sword and a sheep's bladder full of pokeberry juice. After lecturing the Quaker leaders for slaveowning, Lay plunged the sword into the bladder, spattering the shocked leaders, whom he called "old rusty candlesticks," and shouting that God's reward for slaveowners who similarly were plunging daggers into the hearts of their slaves would be the sheathing of God's almighty sword into the bowels of Pennsylvania.[62]

Such protests almost always led to the disownment of protesting Friends, as was the case with Farmer, Sandiford, and Lay. Even when the Yearly Meeting heard the more moderate appeals of country Friends, such as those from Chester County, they equivocated. Four times between 1711 and 1730 Chester Friends called for steps to end the purchase of slaves, but the Yearly Meeting would do no more than issue cautions against the practice, as it did in 1716 and 1730. When the Yearly Meeting's advice was ignored, the elders took no further action, hoping that in time conscience would prevail.[63]

But in the 1750s, amid the reforming impulses of the Great Awakening, a fresh generation of Quaker leaders emerged at the

Yearly Meetings who responded differently to new antislavery advocates. Concerned with the growing affluence of the Quaker community and the ostentation and pride displayed in the houses, clothing, and demeanor of Friends, they began a reform program that promoted the "root-and-branch correction of Friends' lives." Hundreds of members were disowned for infractions of the Quaker discipline in next few decades as the old testimonies of asceticism and pacifism gained new strength.[64]

Heavily involved in this reform movement were two new trumpets of antislavery whose voices resonated with a timbre that in the day of Lay and Sandiford would not have registered. Anthony Benezet and John Woolman were self-deprecating and totally determined men who possessed the radical perfectionism of some of the earlier reformers. But they substituted quiet appeals to their fellow religionists for the confrontational outbursts of Lay and Sandiford. Through their efforts and those of established leaders such as the merchant Israel Pemberton and the visiting English Quaker Samuel Fothergill, the Yearly Meeting adopted the uncompromising stance that other Friends had been scorned for advocating in earlier years. In 1755, a year after Woolman and Benezet confronted the Yearly Meeting with a sharp attack on slaveholding, accompanied by a call for educating those held in bondage to prepare them for eventual emancipation, the Yearly Meeting warned Friends against importing slaves or purchasing them locally. At the epic Yearly Meeting of 1758, with the spirit of "the Christ-like Woolman" much in evidence, leaders of the Society, after warm debate, called upon all local monthly meetings to end the buying and selling of slaves and to exclude from positions of authority in their monthly meetings Friends who refused to conform. It would take another sixteen years for the Philadelphia Yearly Meeting to make disownment the penalty for selling or buying slaves. Two years after that, in October 1776, the Yearly Meeting directed local meetings to "testify their disunion" with any Friends who did not entirely clear themselves from "holding mankind as slaves."[65]

Throughout the long period from the 1680s to the year of independence, when the Quakers took the final steps to extricate themselves from the snare of slavery, they also struggled with their responsibility for the education and moral guidance of slaves. The resulting intimate relationship with their black chattels strongly conditioned the interplay of the two groups in the post-manumission years.

The destiny of no religious group was more closely interwoven with American slavery and its abolition than that of the Society of Friends. Yet, paradoxically, the Quakers were the least prepared to forge intimate bonds with, or even to accept into close Christian fellowship, those whom they struggled to rescue from thralldom. Quaker humanitarianism was never founded on a deep sense of the "likeness among all persons." From their earliest experiences in England in the mid-seventeenth century, Quakers held themselves at arm's length from the rest of the world. "They kept themselves apart," writes Sydney James, "by the special qualities they expressed in their distinctive language and clothing, their conviction that they gave more resolute obedience than others did to the divine will and commands, and by their solicitude for the reputation of Truth, even when they required practical demonstrations of the brotherhood of man."[66]

The mid-century crisis within the Society of Friends reinforced and somewhat extended this distancing of Quakers from their fellow colonists. For two generations Philadelphia Quakers had not been holding the world at arm's length but eagerly embracing it. In response to this waning of the original Quaker identity, reformers such as John Churchman, Samuel Fothergill, Daniel Stanton, and John and James Pemberton led an internal crusade aimed at moral revitalization. At the same time a smaller group of reformers, led by Anthony Benezet and John Woolman, strove to abolish slavery and promote the welfare of its victims. The success of these "conscience reformers" in convincing the Quaker leadership to adopt a tougher antislavery stance rested largely on the degree to which the idea of abolition could be made to fit into the larger movement to purify the Society and to separate Friends from the corrupt world around them. Woolman and Benezet did convert the leaders of the larger movement to the idea that slaveholding was a form of sinful social ostentation. And in time, several of these "more tribalistic Friends" accepted abolitionism, "but only as a part of a more general effort to purify the Society."[67] In the meantime, Benezet, Woolman, and a few others were left to carry the burden of moving the Society of Friends from the principle of preparing slaves for freedom to practical plans for accomplishing this.

The revival of the Quaker sense of exclusiveness, which dominated the Society of Friends from the 1750s until the Revolution, nurtured abolitionist sentiment, but its success in preparing blacks for freedom by teaching them the principles of Christian religion was much more limited. As early as the 1690s, William Penn had urged Quakers to acknowledge their religious duty to slaves by establishing separate monthly meetings for them. These early meetings quickly languished because most masters would not send their slaves. Nor did Quaker masters take their slaves to their own Sunday meetings. The idea of special religious meetings for Negroes was revived after John Woolman pressed the idea of preparing slaves for freedom at the 1754 Yearly Meeting of Friends in Philadelphia. However, even Woolman's appeal was not to include slaves in the Quakers' Christian fellowship or admit them to the Society, but rather to ready them for roles as free people in society at large.[68]

In 1756 the Yearly Meeting proposed instituting special quarterly religious meetings for "the Negroes in this city," and in the remaining years before the outbreak of the Revolution these seem to have been held. But Quaker masters remained unenthusiastic about sending their slaves to meeting, and their failure to do so led to frequent complaints that the religious education of blacks "is too little attended to."[69] The institution of special quarterly meetings for blacks reflected the Quakers' ambivalence and stand-offishness toward black Philadelphians. Duty required that masters attend to the religious instruction of their slaves, but the Quaker concept of church was far less suited than that of other Protestant churches to accommodating blacks. Few attempts were made to include them in the worship meetings of white Quakers. There was much in the contemplative Quaker manner of worship that, in any event, would have limited the attractiveness of Quakerism to most of Philadelphia's black residents. But the few who were drawn to the Quaker religion, at a time when marriages and baptisms of blacks were being performed at most of Philadelphia's churches, found themselves quietly but firmly discouraged from participation in the weekly Quaker religious fellowship. Few were ever married by the Society of Friends.[70]

The notable exception to the diffidence of prerevolutionary Philadelphia Quakers to working intimately with slaves and free blacks toward their religious and educational improvement was Anthony Benezet, a Huguenot who immigrated to Philadelphia in 1731 and, after a disastrous attempt at following his father's mercantile career, found his calling as a teacher of young children. Benezet was to emerge after 1760 as the most prolific antislavery writer and the most influential advocate of the Negro's rights on either side of the Atlantic. Devoid of worldly ambition, he dressed plainly, lived a spartan life, and devoted himself to the classroom, following a profession that for a man whose only two children had died in their youth perhaps provided an outlet for all his parental yearnings. A small man with a face that according to an early nineteenth-century biographer "beamed with benignant animation," he regarded himself as homely. When asked to sit for a portrait, he demurred: "O no, no, my ugly face shall not go down to posterity."[71]

About 1750, seven years before the Bray Associates' school for blacks opened in Philadelphia, Benezet began tutoring free Negroes and slaves at night in his simple brick house on Chestnut Street. Teaching the same subjects he taught in his day school for Quaker children, he continued this informal instruction for twenty years. It was in these classes that Benezet discovered ("beyond his own expectation," according to his first biographer, writing in 1817) that black children were as capable as white children both in learning to read and write and in "moral and religious advancement."[72]

Benezet is best remembered for his important contributions to the antislavery movement through the stream of pamphlets he published from 1759 until his death in 1784 and for his unflagging energy as a member of visiting committees sent by the Philadelphia Monthly Meeting after 1774 to persuade footdragging Friends to free their slaves. But to the black population of Philadelphia his greatest contribution lay in his frontal challenge to the deeply rooted belief in black inferiority. As early as 1762, he ar-

Figure 2. "Benezet Instructing Colored Children" (1850). Anthony Benezet argued as early as the 1760s that blacks were no different from whites in mental endowment. His devotion to the black community brought a concourse of black mourners to his funeral in 1784.

gued that the African environment had produced notable cultures and was falsely construed as a place of jungle barbarism. He taught his black students that it was the conditions of slavery, not innate inferiority, that turned Africans in America into degraded and disheartened human beings. "A. Benezet," he wrote of himself in 1767, "teacher of a school established by private subscription, in Philadelphia, for many years, had opportunity of knowing the temper and genius of the Africans; particularly of those under his tuition, who have been of many different ages; and he can with truth and sincerity declare, he has found amongst them as great a variety of talents, equally capable of improvement, as amongst a like number of whites."[73] After visiting the Bray Associates' school in 1762, Benjamin Franklin reached the same conclusion, writing of the black children that "their apprehension [is] quick, their Memory as Strong, and their Docility in every Respect equal to that of the White Children."[74] But this remained a minority view.

Most Philadelphia Quakers were probably grateful to Benezet for taking on the task of educating blacks. Subject to the admonitions of leading Quakers that they should shun the world and withdraw to the purer realm of Quaker simplicity and spirituality, they may have found it odd that Benezet mixed so readily with the city's benighted blacks. He was "unwearied in collecting statistics and facts from the negroes themselves," wrote his first eulogist in 1817; "he would often be seen on the wharves surrounded by a group of these people, whose story afterward served as a basis for an argument or a touching appeal in one of the almanacs or papers of the day."[75] But if they regarded Benezet as eccentric, other Quakers acknowledged that he served a need that they did not much relish confronting themselves. Something of a "let-Anthony-do-it" attitude seems to have shown itself in 1770, when Benezet pushed for the establishment of a Society-supported school for free blacks. The proposal gained general acceptance, but he supplied most of the energy required for raising money, building a structure, and hiring a teacher. The school was intended to encourage slavemasters to free their human property by assuming responsibility for the education that they regarded as necessary to prepare former slaves for freedom. The schoolhouse was built in Willing's Alley in 1773, and slave children were also accepted when not enough free black children could be found to fill the classes. About 250 students gained at least the rudiments of education there in the next six years, including several who would become leaders of the free black community after the Revolution.[76]

BY 1770, six years before the Philadelphia Yearly Meeting issued its epochal edict vowing disownment of all members who did not free their slaves, the abolitionist movement in Pennsylvania was in full flood. It is well known that Quakers led the way in this process, and recent studies have added to our understanding of its inner workings.[77] What remains historically obscure, however, is the degree to which other white Philadelphians—Presbyterians, Baptists, Moravians, Anglicans, Lutherans, and German Reformed—participated in the growing conviction that slavery was immoral, uneconomical, discouraging to laborers who had to compete with slave labor, and, in the context of the growing rift with England in the 1760s and 1770s over American liberties, inconsistent with the ideology of freedom and equality upon which the colonial argument against England was based. What has also gone unrecognized is the extent to which these Philadelphians of other religious convictions were freeing their slaves from the 1740s onward. It was this bundle of individual decisions to manumit slaves—not always made as a matter of conscience—that brought into being in the city a community of free blacks that grew steadily in the second and third quarters of the eighteenth century.

The best sources for tracing the advance of the manumitting urge are the wills of Philadelphians, since it was through the death of the master that most freed persons escaped bondage. Individual Philadelphians had been manumitting slaves since the beginning of the eighteenth century if not earlier, but the number released before 1730 was insignificant. In the 1730s, however, one of every seven Quakers whose wills mentioned slaves gave them their freedom—a testimony, perhaps, to the inroads on conscience that Lay and Sandiford had made in spite of their unacceptability to their Quaker brethren. In the 1740s more than one of every three slaveowning Quakers released their slaves by will. By the 1760s, when Woolman, Benezet, John and James Pemberton, Thomas Harrison, and others were making personal appeals to Friends to cleanse themselves of the sin of slaveholding, 43 percent of their Philadelphia coreligionists who still owned slaves complied. The Quaker records of manumissions in Philadelphia, begun in 1772, show that scores of Friends resisted these appeals, freeing their slaves only when threatened with disownment. Even without this coercion, however, the releasing of slaves had advanced significantly.[78]

As rising moral objections to slavery coincided with a growing preference for free labor in the economic slump of the early 1760s, entrepreneurial Philadelphians of other religious persuasions also gave their slaves freedom or sold them (as the Quakers could not do without fear of disciplinary action) in order to wash their hands of the institution. One-third of the Presbyterian slaveowners dying in the 1760s freed their slaves, and the proportion of Anglicans and Swedish Lutherans who did so was nearly as high.[79] The enthusiastic young doctor Benjamin Rush, whom Anthony Benezet had persuaded to write an antislavery tract in 1773, proved to be overly sanguine in his report that the "spirit of liberty and religion with regard to the poor Negroes" was "spreading rapidly thro' this country." He was even less foresighted in predicting that "the emancipation of slaves in America will now be attended with but few difficulties except such as arise from instructions given [from England] to our Governors not to favor laws made for that purpose."[80] Nonetheless, by the eve of the Revolution the structure of slavery in the seaport towns had been weakened. In 1767, the first year for which extant tax lists make it possible to draw an accurate picture of slaves and slaveholders in the city, Philadelphia was the home of about 590 slaveowners and nearly 1,400 slaves in a total population of 18,600. Eight years later, when the city had grown to about 25,000, the number of slaveholders had declined to 376 and the slave population to less than 700.[81]

This halving of the slave population between 1767 and 1775 can be accounted for only partly by the manumission of slaves because the reduction was by no means equaled by a comparable increase in the free black population. Between 1766 and 1775 at least 124 slaves were manumitted in the city by will or given outright release.[82] Undoubtedly other slaves were sold out of the city, though this was strictly forbidden by the Society of Friends. But most important in the plummeting slave population was the inability of the black population as a whole to reproduce itself in a period when slave importations had virtually ceased. Benezet, who knew the black people well, observed in 1773 that black mortality in Philadelphia, as throughout the northern colonies, was so severe, especially among infants, that only new arrivals could prevent the black population from gradually dying off.[83] The annual bills of mortality published by the Anglican church confirm Benezet's judgment. They show that 679 black Philadelphians were interred between 1767 and 1775—an average of 75 per year.[84] Thus each year about 7 of every 100 blacks in the city died—a crude death rate about 50 percent higher than that for the white population.[85]

An abnormally low fertility rate also contributed to the rapid decline of the black population as the colonial era ended. The contributing factors were the shortage of marriage partners for women in a racially segregated culture and the fragmented nature of family life that occurred when so many marriage partners lived in different households. Evidence of this low fertility rate appeared when Philadelphia's constables conducted a house-by-house census of the city in 1775, listing slaves and servants by gender and age for each householder. The constables found fewer than 100 black children born since 1766 who had survived infancy, hardly half of what might be expected in a population of about 1,400 in the mid-1760s.[86] As a result of such high mortality and low fertility, Philadelphia's black population declined rapidly as the Revolution approached. Never since the first shipload of Africans had arrived in 1684 was the ratio of blacks to whites so low as when the Second Continental Congress gathered in the city in 1775.[87]

While the total black population declined, the number of blacks who were free grew steadily in the early 1770s. Manumissions in the city and the arrival of blacks released from bondage in other parts of the Delaware River Valley swelled the small free black community in these years. Breathing free air for the first time, these newly independent men and women had to fit themselves into a white society that had for generations strictly controlled the small number of free blacks and, in the 1770s, was in a state of economic and political disruption.

Free blacks had lived in Philadelphia almost as long as slaves had existed there, and they had always caused concern. Many white householders viewed them only as a public burden and most white Philadelphians feared the blurring of the lines of racial division that they represented. In 1722 the colonial assembly considered a bill discouraging the manumission of aged slaves, who it was believed would require public poor relief, and in 1726 the same body passed a comprehensive "Act For the Better Regulating Negroes in This Province," whose restrictions upon free blacks would remain in force for the remainder of the colonial period.[88]

The attitude of the legislators, who were reacting to white fears and prejudices, were manifestly clear in the preamble, which stated that " 'tis found by experience that free negroes are an idle, slothful people and often prove burdensome to the neighborhood and afford ill examples to other negroes [slaves]." To remedy such perceived problems, the law provided that all manumitting masters must post a £30 bond to defray any maintenance charges that the freed person might incur if "rendered incapable of self-support." Furthermore, the magistrates received authority to bind out to willing employers, on a year-to-year basis, all "slothful" free black adults and any free black children until they reached the age of twenty-four if male and twenty-one if female. The law also specified heavy fines for free blacks who harbored runaway slaves or entertained slaves without the consent of their masters or mistresses, or who traded or dealt with slaves. The most severe penalty, however, was reserved for sexual crossing of the racial boundaries. Cohabitation of white and black partners was punishable by seven years of servitude by the black participant and the usual punishment for fornication or adultery for the white participant. Interracial marriage carried a penalty of reenslavement for life for the black partner and a £30 fine or up to seven years of servitude for the white partner. Mulatto offspring of interracial liaisons were to be bound out until the age of thirty-one. As had been the case since 1700, free blacks, like slaves, were subject to summary justice in special courts that functioned without juries and could impose heavier penalties for particular crimes than those to which white offenders were subject.

The threat posed by free blacks to the racial hierarchy and the social order continued to concern white Philadelphians after mid-century. In 1751, at the request of concerned citizens, Benjamin Franklin reprinted the entire racial code, as set down in the 1726 law, in his *Pennsylvania Gazette*. The code was prefaced with the warning that "frequent complaints have been lately made to the magistrates . . . that Negroes, and other Blacks, either Free, or under Pretence of Freedom, have resorted to, and settled in the

City, and that Slaves, contracting to pay certain Sums of Money to their Masters, or Owners, have been permitted to wander abroad, and seek their own Employment, and wandering Slaves, have taken Houses, Rooms, or Cellars, for their Habitations, where great Disorders often happen, especially in the Night time."[89] Slaves living without masters, slaves pretending to be free, and free blacks mingling with "Servants, Slaves, and other idle and vagrant Persons" who were "entertained, corrupted and encouraged to commit Felonies, and other mischievous Offences" challenged the authorities' definition of acceptable social order.

Even as white Philadelphians expressed such concern in 1751, the number of free blacks was growing considerably. Several dozen received their freedom by will in the 1750s and some 70 more in the 1760s. Forty-five free black children were baptized at Christ Church between 1750 and 1769. By 1768, 8 free black children were attending William Sturgeon's school, and two years later the Quaker school for free blacks enrolled 36 free black children. From such scattered and incomplete evidence, it appears that the free black population had reached 200 or 300 by 1770.[90] In the remaining six years before the outbreak of revolution, this free black population probably doubled. At least 175 slaves in Philadelphia received their freedom between 1771 and 1776 and many free blacks probably moved to Philadelphia from outlying areas, where Quakers were freeing their slaves in large numbers after this became mandatory in 1776.

Not a single document remains to inform us how Philadelphia's slaves and free blacks might have viewed their world as the colonial era drew to a close. However, we can surmise what they might have felt by summarizing the events and movements they had experienced in the previous decades. Many of them had been born in Africa, and because the largest importations of slaves had occurred during the Seven Years' War many of them had lived in the British colonial world for only ten to fifteen years. Yet they had adapted quickly to English ways, though retaining some of their African heritage, which exhibited itself in funeral customs, music, dance, dress, and hairstyles. Many had buffered themselves against the agony of slavery by forming families and networks of friends, by gaining a rudimentary education, and by adopting

Christianity. Others had resisted bondage by attacking their master's person and property, committing other crimes, running away, and even taking their own lives. Almost all had acquired a deep familiarity with their physical environs and had developed a partially autonomous existence through attending church and school; gathering with fellow slaves and free blacks at funerals, celebrations, and days off; and performing a multitude of tasks that took them away from their master's residence. Now, as their masters and mistresses debated how to cope with what they perceived as English attempts to enslave white colonial subjects in the early 1770s, black Philadelphians began to witness fissures in the slave system that entrapped them. They saw the Quaker-led abolitionist movement gain momentum; they no doubt rejoiced that many of their kind were being released from bondage; and they noticed that almost no new slaves entered the city. Here were reasons for black Philadelphians to believe that they were about to experience momentous opportunities for changing their lives.

2. The Black Revolution
in Philadelphia

WHEN WHITE PHILADELPHIANS were furiously debating the Stamp Act in 1765, their city contained about 100 free blacks and 1,400 slaves. Only a handful of Quakers were working actively to abolish the slave trade and slavery, and only occasionally did slaveowners feel moved to free their chattel property. By 1783 a revolution—or half a revolution at least—had occurred among black Philadelphians. In less than twenty years the number of slaves had fallen to about 400, while the free black population had grown to more than 1,000. Hundreds of slaveowners had released their human property, hundreds of other blacks had secured their freedom by making their own declarations of independence, and the revolutionary government of Pennsylvania had passed the first gradual abolition act in America. Amid the complex interplay of events during the wartime years, black Philadelphians waged their own American Revolution and in the process laid the foundations for the new nation's largest and most active free black community.

PHILADELPHIA'S BLACKS, most of them slaves, were not affected directly by revenue stamps, sugar duties, or tea parties; nonetheless, they were caught up in the events leading to revolution and were politicized by the language and modes of protest.[1] As early as 1765, while white colonists remonstrated against the Stamp Act, blacks had participated in street protests. Two black drummers, one the slave of wealthy alderman Samuel Mifflin, had "beat thro all parts of the City with Muffled Drums" as the bells pealed at Christ Church and the State House on October 5, 1765, calling a huge assembly of Philadelphians to the State House yard to intimidate John Hughes from taking up his post as stamp distributor.[2] Through another decade of protest by urban crowds, black Philadelphians were present in the streets and on the waterfront, where the rhetoric of white patriots protesting the oppressive acts of a corrupt and unresponsive colonial master could not help but have reached their ears.

When the language of protest overflowed its initial boundaries and confronted the relationship between American liberty and domestic slavery, black Philadelphians must have listened intently and talked arduously among themselves. Dozens of writers in all the major northern seaports were pointing out the hypocrisy of arguing for God-given natural liberties while domestic slavery flourished in the colonies.[3] Although no direct statements from Philadelphia slaves have survived, their later actions show that they would have heartily subscribed to the sentiments of Phyllis Wheatley, the young African-born slave in Boston, who wrote in 1774 that "in every human Breast, God had implanted a Principle, which we call love of freedom; it is impatient of Oppression, and pants for Deliverance; and by the leave of our modern Egyptians I will assert, that the same Principle lives in us."[4]

In Philadelphia attacks on slavery circulated freely, and blacks living in white households would have been quick to learn of their existence and share rumors about their contents. As elsewhere, pamphleteers labeled the institution a grotesque contradiction of the freedoms that white Americans argued were being infringed by *their* colonial masters. Many of the pamphleteering opponents of slavery were Quakers.[5] But others, such as the young Presbyterian doctor Benjamin Rush, joined the campaign. The son of a slaveowning Philadelphia gunsmith, Rush studied as a boy under the New Light evangelical Presbyterian Samuel Finley. Later he matriculated at Princeton (then the College of New Jersey), which was headed by Samuel Davies, another Presbyterian infected by the evangelical fervor of the Great Awakening. It may have been from Davies that the young Rush first gained the compassion for enslaved Africans that later caused him to involve himself extensively with the black community. Before accepting the presidency of Princeton in 1759, Davies had been the most important evangelical preacher in Virginia and the first to convert large numbers of Old Dominion slaves to Christianity. From him Rush may have imbibed his view of the essential capability rather than the innate inferiority of Africans. "Your Negroes may be ignorant . . . as to divine things," preached Davies, "not for want of capacity but through your negligence."[6]

In 1773, after he had returned from medical studies in Edinburgh and begun a practice among the laboring poor of Philadelphia, Rush was prevailed upon by Anthony Benezet to write a pamphlet attacking the slave trade. At stake was a bill before the legislature for raising the import duty on slaves so high as to tax the odious traffic out of existence. Twenty-seven years old at the time, Rush produced a pamphlet in a few evenings and titled it *An Address to the Inhabitants of the British Settlements in America, upon Slave-Keeping*. The pamphlet attacked not only the slave trade but slavery itself, and it picked up the theme of the hypocrisy of American patriots who protested English tyranny while keeping in chains one-fifth of the colonial population. Rush urged the Pennsylvania assembly—"ye ADVOCATES for American liberty"— to excise the cancer of slavery from the American body politic while they fought for their own freedom, warning that God would punish the Americans for their inattention to the sin of slavery. Rush also argued, as had his mentor Samuel Davies and Anthony Benezet, that the vices commonly assigned to Africans by whites, who regarded them "as an ignorant and contemptible part of mankind," were actually "the genuine offspring of slavery."[7]

Black Philadelphians also came to know a pamphleteer remembered mostly for a sizzling attack on monarchical tyranny but whose first Philadelphia essay concerned the black inhabitants of the city. Two years after Rush penned his antislavery pamphlet, he met a young immigrant named Thomas Paine while browsing in Robert Aitken's bookstore. The unkempt man with fire in his eyes had just arrived from England with a letter of introduction from Benjamin Franklin and with hopes that in Philadelphia he could repair his broken career. Aitken had hired Paine to edit his *Pennsylvania Magazine*. From his room above Aitken's store, Paine

Figure 3. Portrait of Benjamin Rush, by Charles Willson Peale (1783). After Benezet's death, Benjamin Rush became the most important liaison between the black community and its white supporters, most of them members of the Pennsylvania Abolition Society.

looked down on the marketplace where slaves were auctioned. Shocked by the trading in human flesh, Paine published an attack on slavery in one of Philadelphia's weekly newspapers. Like many other such indictments, the essay drew upon natural rights philosophy. It warned Americans that by enslaving multitudes of Africans—and in "shed[ding] much innocent blood in doing it"— they risked retribution from on high. "With what consistency or decency," queried Paine, could American slaveholders "complain so loudly of attempts to enslave them, while they hold so many hundred thousand in slavery?"[8]

Antislavery pamphlets authored by partisans of the resistance movement such as Rush and Paine surely heartened Philadelphia's slaves; but their anticipation of a new era must have been further increased when more conservative inhabitants, who could not be accused of a radical cast of mind, raised their voices against slavery. The most important in Philadelphia was that of Richard Wells, a recently arrived merchant and eventual Tory who delivered a biting attack on his fellow city dwellers in 1774. How could Americans "reconcile the *exercise of* SLAVERY with our *professions of freedom*," he asked? By what right did Americans in every city and colony hold slaves? In England, Wells declared, Lord Mansfield had ruled in the Somerset case in 1772 that a slave was free as soon as he or she set foot on English soil, for there was no law legitimating bondage in England. Would Americans who argued for the rights of Englishmen declare as much for slaves on their soil? "Were the colonies as earnest for the preservation of liberty, upon its true and genuine principles, as they are opposed to the supremacy of an English Parliament," chided Wells, "they would enter into a virtuous and *perpetual* resolve, neither to import, nor to purchase any slaves introduced amongst them after the meeting of the [Continental] Congress."[9]

By the spring of 1775 Philadelphians—black as well as white— had been exposed to a spate of pamphlets and newspaper articles attacking slavery, and the Society of Friends was on the verge of a dramatic declaration that its members must cleanse themselves of slaveholding or face disownment. Adding to the changing consciousness of what might be possible was an event that occurred in April, just five days before the firefight at Concord and Lexington. Meeting at the Rising Sun Tavern, ten white Philadelphians founded the Society for the Relief of Free Negroes Unlawfully Held in Bondage. Though not explicitly an abolition society at first, it would flower after the Revolution into the first corporate group in the English-speaking world dedicated to the eradication of slavery. In 1775, however, it was simply a small group of men, mostly Quaker artisans and small retailers, who had imbibed the humanitarian message of Woolman, Benezet, and others.[10] They assumed the task of redeeming freedom for blacks in the city who claimed to be free persons but who had been snatched back into bondage by unscrupulous slave traders.

The attention of these men had initially been drawn to an Indian woman, Dinah Nevill, and her three children, whose New Jersey master had sold the family to a Virginian who intended to pick them up in Philadelphia. After being taken to the city, Nevill declared herself a freeborn person who had been illegally enslaved. Israel Pemberton and Thomas Harrison, both Quakers who for years had been quietly aiding blacks in purchasing their freedom, entered a suit on Nevill's behalf, asking the Court of Quarter Sessions to overturn buyer's claim. Meanwhile, the mayor of the city committed Nevill and her children to the workhouse while the case was decided. The court ruled against her, but Miers Fisher, a Quaker lawyer, appealed the decision and prevented the buyer from claiming his purchase. After years of wartime delays and disruptions in the legal proceedings, Thomas Harrison purchased Nevill and her children in 1781 and set them free.[11]

The Society for the Relief of Free Negroes met only four times in 1775, although its lawyers intervened in four other cases involving blacks who claimed they had been illegally enslaved. But late in 1775, as Philadelphia became deeply embroiled in the resistance movement, the society disbanded, not to be revived until 1784, and then in a different form and with much broader purposes.[12] Nonetheless, for black Philadelphians held in slavery the formation of an antislavery group was an additional indication that a new day might be dawning.

The appeals to conscience and to natural rights philosophy and the activities of the Society for the Relief of Free Negroes could hardly have passed unnoticed by Philadelphia's slaves, who lived on virtually every street in the city, worked in the taverns and coffeehouses, eavesdropped on their masters' dinner-table conversations, and in some cases must have actually read the newspapers and pamphlets. As tension with England grew in 1774–75, slaves in the city must have heard of rumored slave insurrections and of black petitions for freedom in other colonies. They also had opportunities to hear of British plans, in the event of a war that many now thought inevitable, to proclaim freedom for slaves and indentured servants who would flee their masters and join the British forces stationed in America. Late in 1774, Philadelphia printer William Bradford heard from the young James Madison, a member of the Committee on Public Safety in Orange County, Virginia, that some slaves were conspiring to escape to the British when the king's forces arrived in the vicinity, understanding that they would receive their freedom. A few weeks later Bradford reported to Madison that "a letter from a Gentleman in England" had been read aloud in the Philadelphia coffeehouse that told of the plan in London, if a final rupture occurred, to declare "all Slaves & Servants free that would take arms against the Americans." "By this," wrote Bradford, "you see such a scheme is thought on and talked of."[13]

The restiveness of Philadelphia's slaves, living in the city where the Continental Congress met during September and October 1774 and almost continuously after May 1775, could only have been heightened by the knowledge that some black Philadelphians were being freed by their masters. With appeals to conscience growing more effective amid an increasing preference for free labor, which in uncertain economic times could be hired and discharged at will, Philadelphia masters began to manumit significant numbers of slaves in 1774. Owners had occasionally liberated their slaves since as early as the 1690s, but only twice before 1774 had the number obtaining freedom each year exceeded a dozen. In that year fourteen slaves gained release from bondage or were promised freedom. In 1775 the number rose to twenty-two, and in the following year it climbed to ninety-seven.[14] More than two-thirds of the manumitters were Quakers, but dozens of non-Quakers, facing no religious compulsion to free their slaves, also severed their connection with the system of bondage. The ebullient but politically naive Benjamin Rush grossly overestimated the abolitionist sentiment in 1773 when he assured an English correspondent that whereas Benezet had "stood alone a few years ago in opposing Negro slavery," now three-quarters of all Philadelphians "cry out against it."[15] Yet enslaved Philadelphians had reason to believe that the end of their servitude might be near at hand.

Consciousness of the possibilities for freedom were not long in leading to concrete action by enslaved blacks. In the South, where slaves outnumbered whites, the threat of internal subversion loomed largest, especially after Lord Dunmore, the royal governor of Virginia, issued his dramatic proclamation on November 17, 1775, that guaranteed freedom to slaves and indentured servants escaping their masters and reaching the king's forces. By early December Dunmore's proclamation had thrown white Virginians into a frenzy of fear, and enough slaves had reached his troops to form the Black Regiment, "whose soldiers wore on the breast of their uniform the chilling inscription 'Liberty to Slaves.'"[16] Even in Philadelphia, where residents knew that their strategic location would bring war to their doorsteps, the possibility of black insurgency was on many people's minds. Those who assumed otherwise, that the city's slaves were docile and relatively contented, must have been shocked by an event that occurred shortly after Dunmore formed the Black Regiment of escaped Virginia slaves. This news reached Philadelphia in less than a week. A few days later, the *Evening Post* reported that a white "gentlewoman" walking near Christ Church was insulted by a black man. When she reprimanded him, he shot back, "Stay you d[amne]d white bitch 'till Lord Dunmore and his black regiment come, and then we will see who is to take the wall." Two white men, hearing the outburst, chased the bold slave, but he escaped into the night, leaving his pursuers to wonder at the speed at which news traveled from Virginia and leaving readers of the *Evening Post* to ponder how many such aggressive rebels resided in their city.[17]

White Philadelphians had many opportunities to contemplate black rebellion in the remaining months before the war came to their doorsteps. In neighboring New Jersey, rumors of black insurrection were rife.[18] Many white Philadelphians were vividly reminded of the creation of Dunmore's Black Regiment in one of the scenes of *The Fall of British Tyranny,* a play written by Philadelphia silversmith John Leacock. Published in the city during the summer of 1776, Leacock's drama included "A very black scene between Lord *Kidnapper* [Lord Dunmore] and Major Cudjo [an escaped slave]." The play was full of invective against Dunmore, who was portrayed as a degenerate who dallied with his prostitutes Jenny Bluegarter and Kate Common in his cabin while promising to invert the social order by making all escaped slaves officers with "money in your pockets [and] good cloaths on your backs." Cudjo, speaking in dialect, promised to shoot down his old master and any other rebels available.[19]

THE MENACING BEHAVIOR of the anonymous black man near Christ Church in December 1775 displayed the political consciousness of a single individual who chose to threaten a structure of authority firmly controlled by white inhabitants of the city. Twenty-one months later, in September 1777, all black Philadelphians, slave and free, found greatly enlarged opportunities for changing their lives as a result of the impending British occupation of the city. For the previous year the city had seethed with apprehension. General William Howe's defeat of Washington's army in and around New York and Washington's retreat across New Jersey toward the Delaware River left white revolutionaries trembling at the prospect of the redcoats reaching their city. On December 12, 1776, the patriot general Israel Putnam arrived to assume command of the city as military governor. Philadelphians began fleeing the city, while Putnam commandeered all wagons, horses, arms, and supplies and began preparing public buildings for military use. "This city was, for days," reported the wealthy merchant Robert Morris, "the greatest scene of distress that you can conceive; everybody but Quakers were removing their families and effects, and now it looks dismal and melancholy."[20]

Stung by Washington's surprise attack at Trenton the day after Christmas, Howe's army did not, as expected, veer south from New Jersey toward Philadelphia. Instead, it retreated to winter quarters. Eight months later, however, Howe mounted the anticipated attack, this time from a different direction. Sailing from New York to Virginia waters in late July, his forces made their way up the Chesapeake Bay and landed at Head of Elk, Maryland. Howe's troops then pushed northward toward Philadelphia and mauled Washington's army in a bloody battle at Brandywine on September 11. From there a part of Howe's army, under the generalship of Lord Cornwallis, moved to occupy the city. While Washington's battered and ill-equipped forces withdrew to the west, Philadelphians fled to the countryside. About one-third of the residents departed, many of them white males who might be impressed by the British or imprisoned for treasonous activity. Their departure stripped the city of many who traditionally controlled the behavior of slaves. Sarah Logan Fisher, whose Quaker husband had recently been exiled for Loyalist activities, described "wagons rattling, horses galloping, women running, children crying, delegates flying, and altogether the greatest consternation, fright and terror that can be imagined."[21]

A few days later, 3,000 British and Hessian troops marched into the city through the Northern Liberties. For the next nine months Philadelphia remained an occupied city, with as many as 10,000 troops and 2,000 cavalry garrisoned there. In the manner of most occupying armies, they used the city harshly.[22] But for the city's black inhabitants the British occupation offered unusual opportunities to break the bonds of slavery. A slave did not have to flee by night and negotiate many miles through patriot territory to reach the English army on the coast, as in Virginia, but merely had to leave the master's house and report to the occupying British army billeted on every block. Foreseeing such circumstances, many owners no doubt took their slaves with them when they left Philadelphia, or, if they remained in the city, sent their slaves into the countryside. They knew, as the Lutheran minister Henry Muhlenberg wrote, that the slaves "secretly wished that the British army might win, for then all Negro slaves will gain their freedom."[23]

In a situation of such flux slaves had to reckon their chances carefully. Some hedged their opportunities by running away on the eve of the British occupation and hiding out until the enemy army arrived. Hero, a slave of merchant Robert Morris, took flight twelve days before Cornwallis led his troops into Philadelphia. Morris advertised for him in the remaining days before he fled the city with his own family, describing how his slave "plays well on the violin, whistles remarkably well, and has an excellent ear for music" and detailing his "handsome suit of light blue clothes, brown coat, red cape."[24] Hero made good his escape until seven months later, when Thomas Willing, Morris's business partner, found him. Though sick and tattered, Hero resisted Willing's promises of "cloaths & every indulgence"; "he says you were a good Master," Willing wrote Morris, "but he don't like the Country & cannot consent to go out."[25] This was telling testimony to what one Philadelphian pointed out a few years later— that even in the Quaker capital, where slavery was practiced in its mildest form, slaves were to their masters as the English colonists to the king: "internal enemies" and unwilling subjects. "Some persons would have denied this, before the British army invaded Pennsylvania," wrote a correspondent to the *Pennsylvania Packet,* but "the defection of the Negroes [to the British], [even] of the most indulgent masters . . . shewed what little dependence ought to be placed on persons deprived of their natural liberty."[26]

The odyssey of Adam, the slave of house carpenter Jedidiah Snowden, provides an example of how the flight for freedom, amid revolutionary turmoil, sometimes boomeranged painfully. Snowden had owned Adam for fifteen years before the war and was chagrined when he ran away just before the British arrived. Adam hid himself in the city and then passed himself off as a free man. Like many other blacks, he left with the British when they evacuated Philadelphia in June 1778, sailing with the departing army to New York and then signing on the British brig *Bixon.* As fate would have it, the brig was captured and brought into Philadelphia by a ship of the Pennsylvania navy, the *General Greene.* Getting wind that Adam was a member of the *Bixon*'s crew, Snowden applied to the captain and had his runaway slave restored to him.[27]

Many Philadelphia slaves, whether they were taken to the countryside or remained in the city, found ways to escape and join the British ranks and fight against the Americans. This was not only a way of escaping bondage but, equally important, provided a means of contributing to the British victory, which many slaves thought would bring about a general emancipation. The belief that the British would free all slaves after defeating the Americans, reported the judicious Reverend Muhlenberg in 1777, "is almost universal among the *Negroes* in America."[28]

The desire to fight with the British must have been heightened by the presence among Cornwallis's occupying troops of the Black Guides and Pioneers, a company raised in Virginia that fought under white officers throughout the war. A muster list of the Guides and Pioneers, taken at Head of Elk on September 5, 1777, as the British troops were marching north toward Philadelphia, showed 172 men, 2 women, and 2 children. Three months later, another muster taken in Philadelphia showed 200 men and 8 women, suggesting that the numbers had been swelled by escaping slaves in and around the city.[29] These "irregular" troops epitomized for whites the alienation and danger of those denied their freedom, for, as Muhlenberg warned, they were "fitted for and inclined toward barbarities, are lacking in human feeling, and are familiar with every corner of the country."[30]

Advertisements in the Philadelphia newspapers provide evidence of the variety of slaves who sought freedom through flight to the enemy during the nine months of British occupation and the range of strategies they used. Some slaves escaped their masters in the nearby countryside, such as the two mulatto girls Phyllis and Poll, ages twenty-two and fourteen, with their hair self-consciously styled "very much in the negro fashion," who fled from a Haverford Township farmer just outside the city in February 1778. Some sought refuge among free blacks in Philadelphia, such as Charles, a mulatto boy of about fifteen, who in the same month ran away with the keys to his master's house and "was seen the same afternoon in the market house among the negroes, drinking coffee, [where] it is supposed that they inticed him away and now secret him."[31] Others, such as Dick and Farmer, the twenty-year-old slaves of Adam Hubley and Dougall Forbes, and the country-bred slave Gabriel, tried to pass as free Negroes and make their escape on ships leaving Philadelphia.[32] Even the slaves of British army officers in Philadelphia ran away, such as George, "a negro boy . . . with recent marks of the small pox on his face" who belonged to Captain Smyth of the Queen's Rangers.[33]

For some who had fought futilely for their freedom through legal channels, the British occupation provided an immediate resolution to their struggle. One such case involved Harry, claimed by widow Ann Humphries as her slave. Harry had sought the aid of the Society for the Relief of Free Negroes in the spring of 1775, claiming that he had many witnesses to the fact that he had been promised freedom by his master, Jonathan Humphries. Yet after his master's death, Widow Humphries seized Harry and "detained him in Bondage as her slave." The society's visiting committee pleaded with the widow but "met with a very unpleasant Reception." More than two years later, with rumors flying of a British invasion, his mistress, according to Harry, tried to sell him to a purchaser who would carry him out of the state. With the aid of Thomas Harrison and Cadwalader Dickinson, Harry appealed to the Supreme Executive Council, which ordered Mrs. Humphries not to sell Harry until the court decided the case. She defied the order, however, selling Harry to a Captain Berry and then locking him up for delivery to the buyer. While being carried to Captain Berry, Harry escaped, hid in the city while a guard of armed men searched for him, and then, after the British entered the city, took refuge with them. Harry escaped during the British occupation of the city and left with them for New York in June 1778.[34]

Not all slaves were determined or fortunate enough to make their escape, and no doubt many obediently served their owners. The fact that dozens of Philadelphians were individually liberating their slaves must have given hope to many that freedom would soon be theirs, and the slaves of Quakers knew that freedom could not be denied them much longer unless their masters were willing to face expulsion from the Society of Friends (as indeed some were). In 1777 and 1778 Philadelphians freed at least 148 slaves, with the date of freedom of 62 of these, mostly children, deferred from one to nineteen years.[35] Such expectations of freedom probably kept many slaves faithful to their owners, at least for a while. John Dickinson, the Philadelphia lawyer and revolutionary pamphleteer, apparently had no qualms in using Cato and Mingo, two of his many slaves, to carry letters between Philadelphia, Trenton, and Kent County, Delaware, at a time when they had to pass through British lines.[36] In another case, family legend maintained that one of Philadelphia's stateliest mansions was saved by a dutiful black servant during the Battle of Germantown. British troops were positioned to the west of Philadelphia to guard the city, and they had made Stenton, the home of William and Hannah Logan, their headquarters. When the Americans attacked on October 4, 1777, two British soldiers prepared to burn the house. When they went to the barn to get straw to set the fire, a British officer rode up, sword drawn, and inquired of Dinah, the old family slave who had been freed at her own request in 1776, if she had seen any deserters. "She promptly replied," recounted a family member many years later, "that two such had just gone to secret themselves in the Barn." The officer rode to the barn, drove the two protesting soldiers away, and Stenton was saved.[37]

For slaves who held no hope for manumission the prospect of freedom depended mostly on fleeing to the British. But a small number of Philadelphia's black inhabitants, most of them free but a few who were slaves, reckoned to improve their status by serving with the American forces. Such patriotism found an outlet primarily in maritime service, where slaves of mariners and merchants had served for decades. A handful went to sea in the small Pennsylvania navy, which recruited heavily from Philadelphia.[38] Others served on privateers, such as James Forten, later to become one of the most respected members of Philadelphia's free black community. According to family history, Forten's great-grandfather had been brought in chains from Africa to the Delaware even before the English Quakers arrived, and his grandfather had been one of the first slaves in Pennsylvania to purchase his freedom. Forten's father, born free, was a sailmaker who lived only seven years after James's birth in 1766. When he was old enough, James was sent to Anthony Benezet's school, where he learned to read and write and imbibed many of the kindly Quaker's principles about the universality of humankind. Two years after his father's death in 1773, Forten left school to help support his mother by working in Benezet's grocery store.[39]

In 1781, at age fifteen, Forten signed on Stephen Decatur's twenty-two-gun privateer the *Royal Louis* as a powderboy and began a career of heroic acts that would gain him fame in Philadelphia. "Scarce wafted from his native shore, and perilled upon the dark blue sea," wrote William C. Nell, the country's first black historian, "than he found himself amid the roar of cannon, the smoke of blood, the dying, and the dead." This was the bloody engagement of the ultimately victorious *Royal Louis* with the British ship *Lawrence* in which Forten was the only survivor at his gun station. But Forten's colors showed even truer on the next voyage, when his ship was captured by the British after a battle at sea. Forten was befriended by the British captain's son and offered free passage to England and the patronage of the family. "NO, NO!", Forten replied to the offer, according to Nell, "I am here a prisoner for the liberties of my country; I never, NEVER, shall prove a traitor to her interests." His offer spurned, the British captain consigned Forten to the *Old Jersey,* the rotting death-trap prison ship anchored in New York harbor where thousands of Americans died. Released seven months later as the war was drawing to a close, the sixteen-year-old Forten made his way shoeless from New York to Trenton and from there to Philadelphia, where great things lay in store for him.[40] At the time, however, his exploits were notable primarily for their atypicality, for few Philadelphia blacks had reason to be infected by the patriotic fever.

In addition to the small number of seagoing black patriots, a few black Philadelphians were probably among the thirty-five blacks in the Second Pennsylvania Brigade of the Continental Army, and at least one served with the Philadelphia militia. But blacks were generally unwelcome in army units. One Philadelphian remarked that "to persons unaccustomed to such associations" the presence of Negroes in the New England regiments that came south to Pennsylvania had a "disagreeable, degrading effect."[41] Only after 1779, when recruiting officers had great difficulty enlisting white men, were blacks grudgingly accepted in the army, and free blacks in Philadelphia were never drafted into the Philadelphia militia.[42] In some cases, however, they were sentenced to a stint in the military as a form of criminal punishment. Daniel Stevens, for example, from a "very reputable poor free Negro family" in the city, won remission from a £2,000 fine for stealing 400 gallons of rum from Robert Morris in 1780 by agreeing to serve in the Pennsylvania Line without receiving the usual enlistment bounty.[43]

Figure 4. Portrait of James Forten. Forten's great-grandfather was brought to the colonies as a slave. His grandfather purchased his freedom and became one of Pennsylvania's first free blacks and the progenitor of a long line of distinguished black activists in Philadelphia. This watercolor portrait is assumed to be of Forten.

It is not surprising that so few of Philadelphia's free blacks, whose numbers were swelling rapidly after 1776, chose to risk their lives for the patriot cause. Several generations later abolitionist writers would focus attention on the heroic contributions of isolated individuals such as James Forten in order to convince white Americans that slaves and freedmen had contributed faithfully to the "glorious cause" of independence. It was thought that this might "stem the tide of prejudice against the colored race," which was one of the obstacles to a general emancipation.[44] But in fact men like Forten were highly unusual. Many slaves no doubt would have enlisted in the army or navy in return for freedom, but this was never offered in Pennsylvania. For those who were free, only American privateers offered more than skimpy wages in return for risking one's life. If risks were to be taken, black recruits were better placed with the British, who promised them the same benefits after the war that they extended to other Loyalists— provisions, land, and the protection of the English sovereign.[45] In addition, any free black who joined the Americans took the risk that when his regiment or ship moved away from the place of his manumission, where witnesses to the event could be summoned, he might be spirited back into slavery.

The picaresque tale of Emmanuel Carpenter vividly illustrates the dangerous zone between freedom and slavery that most free blacks struggled to avoid during the turbulent war years by eschewing service with the Americans. Carpenter had been born free in Jamaica, probably about 1745, and had served aboard a British man of war during the Seven Years' War. At the end of that conflict he signed an indenture to a British officer, who took him to Ireland. Then in 1765, he shipped as an indentured servant to Philadelphia, where his passage was paid by Andrew Colville, who trained him as a cooper. When the Revolution erupted, Carpenter signed aboard a Pennsylvania gunboat in the Delaware River; but, like James Forten, he was taken prisoner by the British and removed to New York. When he was released in 1783, Carpenter returned to Philadelphia and found cooper's work with William Hamilton. When the unscrupulous Hamilton obtained the job of vendue master in New York City in 1784, he promptly swore that Carpenter was a runaway slave and had him arrested.

For ten months, until he could get word of his case to the newly reestablished Pennsylvania Society for the Abolition of Slavery, Carpenter languished in jail under the imminent threat of lifetime servitude—hardly an appropriate veteran's benefit for revolutionary service.[46]

AMONG THE CITY'S BLACKS who had not been manumitted or promised release from slavery by the spring of 1778, an agonizing moment of decision arrived when it became known in May that the British forces intended to evacuate Philadelphia and return to New York. The choices were to flee to the British, trusting to be evacuated with them, or to remain with one's master, in or outside the city, hoping for eventual emancipation. The question was complicated by the fact that the British had proved themselves less avid in their support of black freedom than American slaves had been led to expect by Dunmore's proclamation in 1775. Throughout the war, the British desire to exploit the disaffection of black Americans was much greater than their intention to offer anything more than a limited freedom to escaping slaves. The British formed some of the fleeing slaves into black regiments such as the Black Guides and Pioneers. But far more often they were relegated as body servants to British officers, as camp laborers, stevedores, and cooks. Where they would go or be sent when the war ended nobody said or knew. In the early years of the war blacks widely believed that the emancipation of slaves was a British war policy, but by 1779 Afro-Americans had reason to doubt that a British victory would bring the abolition of slavery in America.[47]

The ambiguities that Philadelphia blacks confronted in choosing a strategy for securing freedom were highlighted a month before the evacuation of Philadelphia, on June 18, 1778, when the occupying British officers staged an extravaganza in the city for General Howe, who had been pressured to resign his command. The estate of the wealthy loyalist merchant Thomas Wharton, located on the southern border of the city, provided the scene for a lavish *meschianza,* as the invitations billed it. The guest list included the Bonds, Shippens, Chews, Redmans, and other prominent Philadelphia families who had collaborated and socialized with the British during their nine-month occupation of the city.[48]

The fête was designed as a recreation of English medieval festivities, but it was modernized in one peculiar way, as if to incorporate England's two-hundred-year history in the New World and its construction of an empire based on racial slavery. The festivities began with a regatta along the Delaware with festooned boats carrying British officers and their wives and prominent Philadelphia Tory couples up the river to the Walnut Street wharf. Disembarking between columns of British grenadiers, they paraded up Walnut Street to the Wharton estate, where they entered the grounds beneath a magnificent arch erected for the occasion. From there they proceeded to the mansion's ballroom, where twenty-four slaves "in Oriental dresses, with silver collars and bracelets" performed "the submissive grand salam as the Ladies passed by." The ranking British officer, mounting a "maneged horse," appeared as chief of the knights attended by "two young black slaves, with sashes and drawers of blue and white silk, wearing large silver clasps round their necks and arms, their breasts and shoulders bare," who held his stirrups. British officers arrived costumed as medieval knights, and the Philadelphia ladies appeared dressed as Turkish maidens. A mock medieval chivalric tournament amused the guests until dinner, at which twenty-four slaves served courses almost beyond count. Fireworks and dancing followed, keeping some of the celebrants away from their beds until six the next morning. The twenty-three British staff officers who gave the party were 3,312 guineas the poorer for the affair.[49]

From such knightly spendor, with slaves displayed conspicuously as symbols of subordination and aristocratic privilege, a bondsperson might have glimpsed the limitations of the British offer of freedom to American slaves. Yet the alternatives were equally dubious. So when the British evacuated the city in June 1778, a month after the *meschianza,* scores of runaway slaves crowded onto the ships that sailed from the Delaware docks with several thousand Philadelphia Loyalists, some of them with servants and slaves at their sides. Exactly how many blacks fled with the British is uncertain, but the number was large. Eighteen months later Philadelphians were publicly reminded that "by the invasion of this state, and the possession the enemy obtained of this city, and neighbourhood, [a] great part of the slaves hereabouts, were enticed away by the British army."[50] Five years later, when the British evacuated some three thousand former American slaves from New York City to Nova Scotia at the end of the war, sixty-seven among them were listed as having fled from masters in the Philadelphia region, most of them in 1777 and 1778.[51] Many others no doubt died while with the British, fled from their service in the five-year interval between the evacuation of Philadelphia and the end of the war, or made the decision in 1783, as the English fleet prepared to embark, to remain in America and take their chances on preserving their status as free persons.

The biographical details appearing on the 1783 embarkation lists provide further insights concerning those who evacuated Philadelphia with the British. Among them were twelve blacks who claimed they were born free or had been freed by their masters shortly before the British occupation of the city. If these twelve were truly free when they joined the British, then they demonstrated the alienation of many blacks, even when free, from American society and the belief that their rights as British subjects would be greater than those as American subjects. Moses Thompson, only twenty years old in 1783, swore that both his parents were born free. John Vans joined the British in 1777, shortly after his master, Samuel Barker, freed him. Simon Ganway got his freedom at age twenty-one from Jenkins Philips, served him a year more on wages, and then joined the British army. Lucy Hart was freed by merchant Sampson Levi in Philadelphia and then joined the redcoats. It can be surmised that these free blacks perceived a bleak future for themselves in Philadelphia and believed that life would be better elsewhere in the British realm, wherever the fortunes of war might carry them.

Many blacks who fled from the Philadelphia area—twenty-three of sixty-seven on the evacuation register in 1783—were women. Most of them were single and young. Of those whose ages were specified, only one was over thirty-five, and whereas the average age of the males was twenty-seven, that of the women was twenty-two. Elderly and married slaves generally resisted the opportunity to declare their independence. The only two slaves over thirty-five at the time of joining the British were Venus Williams, who at forty-four escaped her master George Gibson, and Amos Thomas, who at forty-eight fled Philip Dickinson in Philadelphia. Only two married couples were among the Philadelphians evacuated from New York, and they may have married in the five years after leaving Philadelphia.[52]

The composite profile of Philadelphia slaves who staked their future with the British—generally single blacks in their prime years, two-thirds of them male—can be supplemented by a picture of slaves who did *not* seek refuge with the British. In late 1779, about seventeen months after the British evacuation, the city's constables conducted a household census that listed 442 slaves still in the city. Many of them had probably been removed by their owners when the British occupied Philadelphia in 1777 and had returned when the enemy retreated. Of those whose ages were given (about 72 percent), four out of ten had been sixteen or younger at the time of the British occupation and another quarter were forty-five or older. Therefore, only about one-third (roughly 150) of the city's 442 slaves in 1779 had been between seventeen and forty-four when the British seized the city, and many of them were undoubtedly married, with children of their own and hence constrained by family ties from fleeing.[53]

Taken together, the two sets of data indicate that a large proportion of the slaves who were not immobilized by family or old age and were old enough to risk the future by joining the British seized the opportunity when it presented itself. Those too aged, too young, too sick, too encumbered with family ties, or too cautious to take the chance were left with the hope that the revolutionary principles of freedom and equality would fortify the abolitionist campaign that Quakers and others had begun to wage on the eve of the Revolution.[54] They, along with several hundred free blacks who had decided to remain in the city, were among those who looked so pathetic to refugee Philadelphians returning to the capital after the British retreated. "If you had seen their bodies," wrote the amazed Robert Morris in June 1778, "you wou'd not be surprised at their timidity. You cou'd know a Country refugee from a Citizen [who remained in Philadelphia] the whole length of the Square by the difference of their looks."[55]

THE BRITISH ARMY that evacuated Philadelphia in 1778 never returned. The war moved southward in 1779, and for the next four years Philadelphians were left to solve the problems of inflation, food shortages, high taxes, and internal friction. While arguing over these difficult matters, they also confronted the issue of slavery. The legislature that met in Philadelphia in 1779–80, little more than a year after the enemy had left the city, passed the first abolition law in the Western world at a time when the most dedicated opponents of slavery, the Quakers, were at the nadir of their power in Pennsylvania. A coalition of Philadelphia radicals and backcountry Scots-Irish Presbyterians had gained control of the legislature as the Revolution began, and they fashioned a state constitution that, despite its radically democratic features, was entirely silent on the matter of slavery. Philadelphia Quakers stood in great disrepute for the remainder of the war, not only because of their disavowal of all military service but also because of the well-known British sympathies of many of their wealthiest members. The revolutionary state government exiled some Quakers for collaborating with the enemy and confiscated much Quaker property, and anti-Quaker hostility led to mobbing and property destruction on several occasions.[56] Under these conditions, Quakers withdrew almost entirely from political affairs, knowing they would only hurt the abolitionist cause by actively supporting it.

Black Philadelphians did not draft petitions to the legislature during the war years calling for the abolition of slavery, as their counterparts did in Massachusetts and other states.[57] Possibly they reckoned that the abolitionist momentum that had been gathering since 1775 would soon produce legislative action and consequently they should not press the issue too hard. They would not have been unaware that other Philadelphians, not associated with the Society of Friends, took up the cause of abolition when they gained the reins of government. These men had been influenced by the Quaker appeals to conscience, by the natural rights ideology of the Revolution, and by their own quasi-enslavement when the British occupied Philadelphia. In August 1778, only two months after the occupying army had withdrawn, a member of the assembly submitted a bill calling for gradual abolition. The bill was tabled, but three months later the Supreme Executive Council endorsed the idea of manumitting infant slaves and promising freedom to any children born of slaves. "No period seems more happy for the attempt than the present," the council advised the assembly, to set slavery on the road to extinction, "as the number of [slaves] . . . had been much reduced by the practices & plunder of our late invaders." By erasing this "opprobrium of America," Pennsylvanians would regain the respect of "all Europe, who are astonished to see a people eager for Liberty holding Negroes in Bondage."[58]

In early 1779 the assembly drew up another abolition bill and ordered it printed for public discussion.[59] The preamble contained a trenchant history lesson, calling attention to the peculiar retrogression of human progress in the New World. It pointed out that "the practice of domestic slavery, so highly detrimental to morality, industry, and the arts, has been, in the instance of the natives of and their descendants, in modern ages revived among christians." Contrary to the vision of a utopian New World, America had been "made the scene of this new Invasion of the rights of mankind after the spirit of Christianity had abolished it from the greater part of Europe."

The bill itself called for the emancipation of all children born to slaves in the future but required them to serve, with privileges equivalent to those of indentured servants, until age eighteen if they were female and age twenty-one if male. All slaveowners must register their slaves so there would be a legal record for determining whether a child had been born before or after the effective date of the law and hence was entitled to freedom upon reaching maturity. Any slave not registered by the specified date would automatically be entitled to freedom. Congressmen and foreign ministers who brought personal slaves into the state were to be exempt from the law; but any slaves carried into Pennsylvania by other visitors or incoming residents were to be freed at the end of six months, although during that time masters could indenture their slaves until age twenty-eight or for seven years if the slave was no longer a minor. The bill also prohibited slave importations and repealed the slave code, while retaining the colonial prohibition of mixed marriage and the old practice of binding out free blacks if they proved unable to support themselves.

Caught up in a storm of controversy over spiraling inflation, food shortages, price fixing, and the Fort Wilson riot, which brought Philadelphians into mortal conflict with each other, the assembly of 1778–79 never voted on the abolition bill but carried it over to the next assembly.[60] This new legislature, convening in late October 1779, was perhaps the most radical ever convened in eighteenth-century America. Among the Philadelphia representatives was George Bryan, an immigrant from Ireland in 1752 who had become an important proprietary officeholder in Philadelphia before the Revolution. By the onset of hostilities Bryan had been radicalized—a Philadelphia Tory sneered that he identified himself "with the *people,* in opposition to those who were termed *well born*"—and adamantly opposed slavery. Bryan took charge of the abolition bill, serving on the committee to redraft it and bringing it to a vote early in the session.[61]

The new bill contained a much longer preamble replete with ringing phrases about the revulsion Pennsylvanians felt at the tyranny threatened by England, the tremendous blood sacrifice they had made to hurl back this threat of enslavement, and the new sympathy for the plight of slaves that their struggle had produced. Having looked oppression in the eye and endured nine months under the heel of an occupying army that starved prisoners, desecrated churches, and laid waste much of the Northern Liberties of Philadelphia, many of the legislators were persuaded to view black slavery in a new light.[62] "When we contemplate our abhorrence of that condition, to which the army and tyranny of Great Britain were exerted to reduce us," the preamble pronounced, "we are unavoidably led to a serious and grateful sense of the manifold blessings which we have undeservedly received from the hands of that being, from whom every good and perfect gift comes. Impressed with these ideas, we conceive that it is our duty . . . to extend a portion of that freedom to others, which hath been extended to us, and a release from that state of thralldom, to which we ourselves were tyrannically doomed."[63] Though unstated in the preamble, the legislators may also have been willing to reduce "the sorrows of those who have lived in undeserved bondage" because the economic viability of slavery had diminished in the preceding generation and because the surprising rebelliousness of slaves in the Philadelphia region during the war provided a new perspective on the costs of maintaining slave labor.[64]

Despite the elevated rhetoric of its preamble, the new version of the abolition bill retreated from the first bill in several important particulars. Partially the retreat was meant to satisfy slavemasters such as "A Citizen," who argued that the children of slaves should not be freed until age twenty-eight or thirty so that their masters could recapture the costs of rearing them. Thus the assembly extended the period of servitude of those born after the passage of the act to twenty-eight years, adding ten years of bound labor for females and seven for males in the prime of their lives.[65] This extension transferred the costs of gradual emancipation from slaveowners to the slaves and their children. By allowing masters to keep their slaves and to hold in servitude the children of slave women until these offspring had worked a substantial part of their productive years, gradual emancipation offered Pennsylvania slaveowners who had been touched by natural rights principles "the opportunity to engage in philanthropy at bargain prices."[66] "Phileleutheros," who advocated the immediate abolition of slavery, argued that twenty-eight years was an "unreasonably long" servitude because most people "used to hard labour without doors begin to fail soon after thirty, especially if they have been obliged to live on poor diet."[67]

Although the revised abolition bill doubled the number of productive years that the children of slaves owed their masters, it also made two concessions to free blacks and to those with white spouses. The threat of binding them out if they became too poor to support themselves was dropped and so was the ban on interracial marriage.

The abolition bill of 1780 was notable as the first passed in America, and it has attracted much praise as exemplifying the spirit of Enlightenment reform in the revolutionary era. The first historian of the Pennsylvania Abolition Society writing in 1847, called it a law "which for justice, humanity, and philanthropy, has seldom been equalled, and which raised the State of Pennsylvania to a high position amongst the nations of the earth."[68] Less enthusiasm is warranted in historical hindsight, however, for the law was in fact the most severe of the five gradual abolition laws enacted by northern states between 1780 and 1804.[69] The 1780 law freed not a single slave; it held in slavery for life all children born up to the day the law took effect; and it consigned to twenty-eight years of bondage every child born of a slave after March 1, 1780. Hence it was hypothetically possible for a female child, born of a slave on the last day of February in 1780, to live out her life in slavery and, if she had children up to her fortieth year, to be bringing into the world in 1820 children who would not be free until 1848. In fact total abolition did not come in Pennsylvania until 1847.

The watered-down abolition law was still too liberal for many Pennsylvanians, and when the political tide turned conservative in the 1780 elections, sweeping out of office many who had voted for it, pressure mounted from slaveholders and others to repeal or amend the bill. Pressure was especially intense to reenslave freed blacks who had gained their freedom by proving to the courts that their masters had not registered them by the November 1, 1780, deadline. Many slaveowners, especially those with pregnant slaves whose offspring would be enslaved for life or freed at age twenty-eight according to whether their birthdate fell before or after March 1, 1780, may have believed they could outwit the law by not registering their slaves before the deadline and then pleading ignorance. But blacks proved their knowledge of the 1780 law and often prevailed over their masters. When they knew they had not been registered, they applied to the courts for their freedom and frequently won it. "Great numbers in this state [who] have derived freedom from that clause," a group of black petitioners told the assembly in September 1781, were now in danger of being cast back into slavery.[70]

By March 1781 the assembly was considering an amendment to the law of 1780 that would extend to January 1, 1782, the registration date for slaves and consequently return to slavery those who had gained their freedom because their masters had not registered them. When the bill passed narrowly on the first reading, free black Philadelphians reacted immediately. In one of their first collective political acts, "divers Negroes" petitioned the legislature to defeat the amendment.[71] Six months later, as a second vote on the bill loomed, free blacks presented another petition to the assembly. It, along with a plea from Cato, a black who had gained his freedom because his master had not registered him, was published in one of the city's newspapers.[72]

The black petitions, which bear the mark of Anthony Benezet's assistance, were styled in what would become virtually a formula used by free blacks who negotiated with whites in the early years of freedom. First expressing gratitude for what had already been done for them and acknowledging their inferior status, the petitioners proceeded to make their case forcefully and to hold up before their superiors the inconsistency of their actions. Thus the supplicant Cato addressed the legislature as "a poor negro, who with myself and children have had the good fortune to get my freedom, by the means of an act of assembly." He then besought the legislature not to amend the law. "To make a law to hang us all would be merciful, when compared with this law," he pleaded, "for many of our masters would treat us with unheard of barbarity, for daring to take advantage (as we have done) of the law made in our favour." Cato went on to quote liberally from the natural rights preamble of the 1780 act in order to point out the trampling of principle that would occur if those entitled by birth to freedom were cast back into slavery after they had finally been rescued from it.[73]

In the petition of "divers Negroes" a similar tone of deference was struck, but a powerful appeal then followed. "We are fully sensible, that an address from persons of our rank is wholly unprecedented, and we are fearful of giving offence in the attempt," it began. But "the great question of slavery or liberty, is too important for us to be silent. It is the momentous question of our lives. If we are silent this day, we may be silent for ever." With deft phrases and invocations of the language adopted by the assembly in the gradual emancipation bill, the city's petitioning blacks put their case: "not having by any act of ours deprived our selves of the common rights of mankind, we were happy to find the house sympathizing in our distress, and declaring that we had hitherto 'lived in undeserved bondage' &c. We cannot persuade ourselves to believe that this honourable house, possessed of such sentiments of humanity and benevolence, will pass an act to make slaves of those whom they have freed by law, and to whom they have restored 'the common blessings they were by nature entitled to.'" If they did so, the assembly would plunge "into all the horrors of hateful slavery, made doubly irksome by the small portion of freedom we have already enjoyed," those who had been "raised to the pinnacle of human happiness by a law unsought and unexpected by us."[74] On the same day the petition was received the legislature voted against amending the gradual abolition act of 1780, and five days later it defeated a final attempt to reenslave those who had gained their freedom.[75] Black Philadelphians, many of them only recently freed from slavery, must have taken satisfaction that their collective action in petitioning the legislature had not been in vain.

IN 1783 about four hundred Philadelphia blacks remained in slavery, but more than twice that number had gained their freedom in the city during the years of bloodshed or had drifted in from the hinterland after obtaining their release from thralldom there.[76] This was the first gathering in one American community of a large number of former slaves. Perhaps more important than their numbers, however, was the latent power of a new group self-consciousness, as evidenced by the petitioning of the legislature and the increased willingness of individuals to assert their desires and rights. Now, individually and collectively, black Philadelphians faced the momentous task of completing the passage from bondage to freedom. Legally free, they next had to forge an autonomous existence. That meant obtaining employment, finding places of residence, forming or reconstructing families, and, underlying all these basic requirements of life, negotiating the crucial psychological passage from dependent bondspersons to independent citizens. It was a task, moreover, that had to be accomplished in a social climate dominated by white Philadelphians, who, for the most part, presumed that blacks, by nature's vagaries as well as through the damaging effects of slavery, were probably incapable and undeserving of independent citizenship.

3. Becoming Free

OUT OF THE WARTIME CHAOS that decimated and scattered Philadelphia's black population, a community of free blacks gradually coalesced in the early 1780s. The black population had declined sharply from the late 1760s to the early 1780s; many families had been shattered by death and flight; new families formed infrequently; and no black leaders had emerged in the port town.[1] Yet within a single generation the city would contain the largest urban free black population anywhere in the new nation, and its black residents would be laying the foundations for the country's emerging free black churches, schools, and beneficial societies. This happened with a rapidity that might have stunned most white Philadelphians, who harbored severe doubts that former slaves could make the conversion to free citizens at all. The pilgrimages of two former slaves who gained their freedom in the city after the war illustrate the variety of ways in which the Philadelphia black community began to take form between 1781 and 1786.

When the Revolution began, Moses Johnson was a slave of a brutal master in Virginia. Like many other southern slaves, he seized the opportunity to escape "the severity of his treatment" by joining "the British standard" sometime after Dunmore's proclamation in November 1775. During the war he served on an English privateer. But after the ship was captured by the twenty-six-gun *Revolution,* an American privateer sailing out of Philadelphia, Johnson was imprisoned in Gloucester, New Jersey. American state governments cared little about the claims of escaped slaves that they were free British subjects. While white British sailors were held for prisoner exchange, black sailors were taken to the auction block, which is where Johnson found himself, at Trenton, New Jersey, in 1782.

Sold at a marshal's sale to Matthew Irwin, the Philadelphia merchant and official who owned the *Revolution,* Johnson became a slave once more. Two years later he appealed to the newly reestablished Pennsylvania Abolition Society for aid in securing his freedom, for he had learned that under the gradual abolition act of 1780 any slave brought into Philadelphia after March 1, 1780, was legally free after six months. Within a year Johnson secured his freedom and found employment as a laborer for Thomas Attmore, a Quaker hatter. When Attmore had no further work for Johnson, he paid him his wages and discharged him. A few days later Johnson came to Attmore's door, a Spanish dollar in his hand, to tell the hatter he had overpaid him by that amount. Impressed by this honesty, the Quaker hired Johnson "for several years at a time" and found him so faithful and honest that he started leaving him in charge of "his most valuable effects" during absences from the city. In the meantime, Johnson married another ex-slave, established a residence, and began a family in the city.[2]

Like Johnson, Absalom Jones had been a slave on a southern plantation before the war. Born in 1747 into the prominent family of merchant-planter Abraham Wynkoop in Sussex County, Delaware, he was taken from the fields into his master's house when he was very young. Removed from the world of debilitating field labor, he gained on opportunity for learning. "I soon bought myself a primer," he later recalled, with pennies given to him from time to time, "and begged to be taught by any body that I found able and willing to give me the least instruction." Literacy probably increased the distance between him and those of his age who did not live in the master's house, and hence Absalom became introspective, or "singular," as he put it. Then in 1762 his master, Benjamin Wynkoop, decided to leave the Delaware plantation that had been willed to him by his father nine years before and move to Philadelphia. Having little use for a large family of slaves in the city, he sold Absalom's mother and his six brothers and sisters, arriving in Philadelphia with only the fifteen-year-old slave boy.[3]

The move to Philadelphia, though it broke up his family, provided Absalom with new opportunities. He now found himself in the center of the nascent abolitionist movement in America and in a city where several schools for blacks had formed in the years before the Revolution. Although he had to work in his master's store from dawn to dark, Absalom soon prevailed upon Wynkoop to allow him to attend a night school for blacks.

In 1770, at age twenty-three, Absalom married Mary, the slave of his master's neighbors Thomas and Sarah King. The slave couple took their vows at St. Peter's Anglican Church, where the masters of both black partners worshiped. Soon after the nuptials, encouraged by the abolitionist sentiment that was spreading in the city, Absalom put the tool of literacy to work. Drawing up an appeal for his wife's release from slavery (whose freedom would allow their children to be born free) he carried it, with his wife's father at his side, to "some of the principal Friends of this city," asking for their support. "From some we borrowed, and from others we received donations," he later recounted.[4]

Thereafter, as war came to Philadelphia, Absalom "made it my business to work until twelve or one o'clock at night, to assist my wife in obtaining a livelihood, and to pay the money that was borrowed to purchase her freedom." By 1778 he had paid the debt and was pleading with his master to allow him to purchase his own freedom. Wynkoop would not consent. Unlike many of the slaves they knew, Absalom and his wife decided to bide their time rather than attempt to escape with the British when they evacuated the city in the summer of 1778. Already they had saved considerable money, which Absalom used to purchase a lot and sizable house in January 1779, just seven months after the British withdrawal. Now this half slave and half free black couple became the immediate neighbors in southern Dock Ward of the wealthy merchant Joseph Stamper; of Cyrus Griffen, a delegate to the Continental Congress from Virginia; and of Thomas McKean, chief justice of Pennsylvania.[5]

Five more years elapsed before Wynkoop, after a series of humble but persistent requests from his slave, permitted Absalom Jones, now thirty-eight years old, to purchase his freedom.[6] His liberty secured, Jones behaved as though he bore his master no

Figure 5. Portrait of Absalom Jones, by Raphaelle Peale (1810). A property owner while still a slave in Philadelphia, Absalom Jones was finally allowed to purchase his freedom in 1784. Within a few years he was leading the effort to establish the African Church of Philadelphia. Like so many others in the city's black community, Jones had roots in Delaware.

grudges. Forbearing, even-tempered, and utterly responsible, he continued to work in Wynkoop's store. Like Moses Johnson, he was dependent upon white Philadelphians for employment and patronage; but Jones was shortly to take steps in a new direction.

Johnson and Jones, two among hundreds of former slaves who were converging in Philadelphia immediately after the Revolution, were entering a world filled with both barriers and opportunities. To understand the situation they faced, and how they began the work of creating a community of free blacks, it is necessary to comprehend the condition of Philadelphia at the end of the war and also white sensibilities regarding those released from bondage. The limits of the possible in the world that black Philadelphians were trying to construct were always dictated to some extent by the white majority around them.

THE OVERRIDING CONCERN of most Philadelphians in the early 1780s was to repair their war-torn society and secure a place for themselves in the new republican order. Philadelphia had not been the scene of vast military destruction, nor did it suffer the devastating fires that ruined British-occupied New York City during the Revolution. Rather, it suffered from a much disordered economy and a badly shredded social fabric. Economic recovery rested on rebuilding the prewar commerce on which the city depended for its prosperity and halting the runaway inflation that hit hard at the budgets of householders, especially those in the lower and middle ranks. Social recovery depended on healing the deep split between radical and conservative revolutionaries that had continued from the fight over the radical constitution of 1776 into issues of the early 1780s, such as repealing the test act that disqualified Quakers and Loyalists as voters, establishing a Bank of Pennsylvania, and revising the populist constitution of 1776, which in the conservative view conferred far too much power on the people at large.[7]

All of these issues loomed far larger in the minds of most Philadelphians than the problem of taking further action on slavery or providing opportunities for recently freed slaves to find a niche in the city's social structure. Benjamin Rush's opinion in November

1783, that the prevalent attitude toward blacks in Philadelphia had changed remarkably since before the war, must be weighed cautiously, for Rush was a perpetual optimist and politically artless. Those who had been "advocates for the poor Africans" before the Revolution, he opined, were regarded as fanatics and disturbers of the peace, but "at present they are considered as the benefactors of mankind and the man who dares say a word in favor of reducing our black brethren to slavery is listened to with horror, and his company avoided by every body."[8] To be sure, the legislature had passed a gradual abolition law in 1780 and white Philadelphians were becoming accustomed to the idea of a small free black population residing among them. But Rush badly misconstrued the situation in suggesting that his white neighbors conceived of ex-slaves as "our black brethren."

A few individuals aside, the only white groups in postwar Philadelphia that actively involved themselves in continuing the abolitionist cause, in policing the gradual abolition act, and in easing the passage of slaves to freedom were the Society of Friends and the Pennsylvania Society for the Abolition of Slavery (PAS), which was revived in 1784. But even among Quakers, who made up most of the Abolition Society's membership in the mid-1780s, the concern for blacks was complicated by the difficult situation of the Friends themselves. Reviled for their pacifism and Tory leanings during the war, they had suffered the loss of much property when they refused to pay fines for not serving in the militia, and they were still thoroughly on the defensive as the 1780s began. Thus the free blacks who gathered in Philadelphia after 1783 began reconstructing their lives in a world strewn with obstacles—and in a city where, as of 1790, 95 percent of the inhabitants were white.

The nucleus of the free black community that emerged in the postwar era was composed of the black Philadelphians who had been freed before or during the Revolution and who, like Absalom and Mary Jones, had remained in the city, resisting the chance to join the British. However, such persons could hardly have numbered more than a few hundred. Swelling their ranks were blacks whose masters voluntarily released them from slavery, though not obligated to do so by the gradual abolition law of 1780. With doubts growing about the morality and economic viability of slavery, Philadelphia owners manumitted at least 269 slaves from 1781 to 1790.[9] Several hundred more slaves secured their freedom through the work of the PAS in these years. Both of these assaults on slavery, the one by an organization and the other stemming from individual decisions, increased Philadelphia's free black population by reducing its slave population. However, the fourfold increase in the city's free black population from 1783 to 1790, by which time it had reached about 2,000, owed even more to the arrival of slaves freed in the rural hinterland. Much as Philadelphia had attracted hundreds of young white men such as Benjamin Franklin at the beginning of the century, it now proved a magnet for scores of newly freed blacks at the end of the century. They had obtained their independence in the rolling hills of Chester, Bucks, Lancaster, and York counties; in the flat, sandy farmlands across the Delaware River in New Jersey; in neighboring Delaware, where Quaker influence was very strong; in the upper South, especially the eastern shore of Maryland, where the shift to grain crops was reducing the economic viability of slave labor; and even in southern New England, where an inhospitable climate convinced many ex-slaves to migrate southward. By 1790 this rural migration had drawn more than one-fifth of Pennsylvania's black population to the capital city, whereas less than one-tenth of the state's white citizens lived there.[10] Thus the free black community that blossomed in the 1780s represented a convergence of people from different regions and with different experiences. A very small number of freeborn residents of the city mingled with a larger number of manumitted Philadelphia slaves and with a still more numerous conglomeration of migrants for whom Philadelphia held an irresistable attraction.

It was a reckoning by former slaves of where opportunities for economic survival and a decent life were greatest that brought thousands of rural migrants to the coastal towns after the Revolution. Lacking capital, they must have felt that their chances to become independent farmers were dismal. For those not prepared to work as agricultural laborers, with all the seasonal unemployment that plagued such work, or to farm for shares, the maritime towns seemed most likely to provide a living. Men might find work on the coastal and transatlantic vessels where slaves had long been employed, and in other niches in the city's economy, and women could hope for domestic service in genteel urban homes.

The appeal of the city as a likely place of employment was magnified by the many attractions of black community life. In northern rural areas, where they were often uninterested in or ostracized from white social life, freed Afro-Americans found themselves living in isolation. With only a few other black people in their locale, they felt relatively defenseless against the frequent coldness or competition of whites. But in the cities the concentration of free blacks promised some security against a hostile world. Equally important, the city offered greater chances to find a marriage partner, to establish a family, and to participate in social and religious activities with other former slaves.

Once the exhilaration of freedom had been savored, one compelling necessity stood above all others for freedpersons: finding a livelihood. During the war some free blacks solved the problem of maintenance by military service, either with the American or the British army. At war's end, the necessities of life could no longer be procured through membership in a large white-directed organization; now every freedman was on his own. Compounding the challenge was the fact that black city dwellers in the 1780s faced a fluctuating economy. A prolonged slump struck the northern cities in the mid-1780s, caused by the collapse of overseas demand for farm products and the closure of the English West Indian ports to American commerce. The resulting unemployment among laboring Philadelphians was compounded by the postwar influx of job-seeking freedmen and ex-soldiers. In 1788 Benjamin Rush noted that one thousand houses were lying empty in the city and that construction tradesmen and laborers were suffering greatly. "Scarcely an artificer of any sort can at this time meet a decent support," wrote Phineas Bond, the British consul in the city, and many who could find no work "are left destitute and distressed." The economy began recovering by 1790, but even a year later the *Pennsylvania Gazette* reported the extensive "sufferings of the poor in the City."[11]

Although the dawn of freedom coincided with a period of economic stagnation, free blacks were remarkably successful in securing employment—the foundation of an independent existence. A

PAS subcommittee formed in 1790 to assist blacks in finding jobs reported that "the negroes have been so universally employed that the committee has had little to do," and a year later the group noted that they had been contacted by "many persons wishing to employ colored in preference to white children." In the same year, reporting to his friend Granville Sharp in England, Benjamin Rush observed of free blacks that "such is their integrity and quiet deportment that they are universally preferred to white people of similar occupations."[12]

Although no systematic records exist to trace black occupations in the first decade after the war, it appears that by far the largest number of free blacks found work as mariners, day laborers, and in domestic work. But former slaves availed themselves of a variety of other work opportunities. Historians have often assumed a degradation of black skills in the emancipation period, perceiving that former slaves of artisans, now cast free of a master's protection and patronage, were forced as freemen into menial labor.[13] But many more free blacks than is recognized carved out new occupational niches for themselves, including substantial numbers who launched their own small enterprises that served a predominately black clientele. Also vital to their quest for material security was the labor of black women. Far more than among white families, which were spread fairly evenly along the social spectrum, the black family constituted an economic partnership at the poorest end of the social continuum, so the income of both husband and wife became indispensable.

Some indications of the occupational diversity of the initial generation of free blacks can be found in the Philadelphia directory of 1795, the first in any of the port cities to designate black heads of household. The directory, which lists only 105 blacks, 83 men and 22 women, is biased in the direction of the better established families. It does, however, show that even at this early stage a group of skilled and entrepreneurial blacks of middling rank was forming. Among those listed were 4 black teachers and preachers, 10 artisans, and 17 retailers and proprietors, including carters, grocers, fruiterers, and boardinghouse keepers.[14]

Finding work meshed with forming families in the early years of freedom. Again the sources are limited, but some indications of

Figure 6. "Pepper pot, smoking hot" (1810). Black female street vendors, here selling pepper-pot soup, a Philadelphia favorite, contributed to the family economy and were among the many free blacks whose small entrepreneurial roles made them a familiar part of urban street life.

the roots of free black family life are contained in the Abolition Society records, the federal census of 1790, the indenture records of the city's House of Employment, the massive indenture books kept by the PAS, and the marriage records of the city's churches. Together these data show that newly freed slaves began to repair the wartime wreckage of family life as soon as the fighting moved south in 1779. Many existing slave families had been broken during the war, and the number of marriages and births had declined; but the release of several hundred slaves from bondage and the flow of migrants into the city after the war led to the largest number of black marriages in Philadelphia's history. An average of only six black marriages a year had occurred in the city's churches from 1775 to 1778, but eighty-four were recorded from 1779 to 1786, doubling the number per year. Forty-five of the marriages occurred in the city's three Anglican churches, continuing the close connection of blacks with that denomination that reached back to the 1740s. The other black marriages were split evenly among Gloria Dei Swedish Lutheran Church and St. Michael's and Zion German Lutheran Church.[15]

The minutes of the Society of Friends' women's Committee to Inquire into the Condition of Freed Slaves, established in 1781, give additional glimpses into the beginnings of officially sanctioned family life among those recently released from slavery. In 1783, for example, the committee visited Fannie, who rented quarters in Moore's Alley, where she lived with her mother and a woman named Chloe, who had been manumitted by Dr. Cadwallader Evans in 1774. "They all live together . . . [and] go out and take in washing and appear to live neat and clean," the committee reported. Some families in Elbow Lane "appear to live poor," the committee recorded, but most black families visited were "orderly and industrious" and "appear to live comfortable."[16]

By 1790, when the first federal census takers made their rounds in Philadelphia, they counted 183 independent black households containing 950 persons. It is not surprising that these households, averaging just over 5 persons, were smaller than those of white Philadelphians, for free blacks were still in the early stages of family formation. Of those for which the name of the head of household was recorded, 14 percent were headed by women— only fractionally higher than the rate of female-headed white households. The other half of the free black population—947 persons—lived in white households.[17] One year later, when the PAS conducted its first household survey of free blacks, it found that the number of independent households had grown to 250, with about 1,000 members, including 400 minor children.[18]

For many black adults just emerging from slavery the struggle to find work, establish a residence, and provide for their children tested the limits of endurance. For parents unable to make ends meet the most common solution was to bind out their children to white families on long-term indentures. Of the 947 free blacks living in white households in 1790, at least one-fourth were such children who had been indentured out for long-term service. About one-third of these indentures were made by the House of Employment when black parents sought relief there. Beginning in 1782, as many freed blacks began migrating to Philadelphia, the number of such indentures rose sharply from an average of one per year from 1779 to 1781 to an average of twenty-one per year from 1782 to 1785. The managers of the almshouse directed a steady stream of black children into white homes: two-year-old Eleanor was assigned to grocer John Dorsey to serve for twenty-two years; eighteen-year-old Nancy and her mulatto children of nine months and three years were bound to merchant William Smith, each of them to serve until they were twenty-eight; four-teen-year-old Ned was indentured to river pilot Michael Davidson for ten years.[19]

Binding out poor children was a common expedient on both sides of the Atlantic for keeping down the costs of poor relief and inculcating the offspring of the laboring poor with the requisite habits of industry and morality. Poor white children whose parents could not support them had been indentured in this way for generations, and most of the indentures made by the House of Employment in the 1780s were for white children. Genteel thought held that the children of the poor would benefit from being raised in a respectable white family where the labor contract required the master or mistress to teach them to read and write, train them in a skill (housewifery in the case of almost all girls), provide moral instruction, and discharge them at the end of their term with "freedom dues"—usually two suits of clothes. What distinguished the black indenturers was not their form but their length. By law, the authorities bound out white children until they reached their majority—eighteen for girls and twenty-one for boys. But the almshouse managers, drawing on prerevolution-ary custom, and perhaps responding to pressure from white em-ployers, indentured most black children until they were twenty-eight, with only about one-sixth of the indentures from 1778 to 1790 running until ages eighteen and twenty-one and another sixth until age twenty-four or twenty-six.[20] If George Bryan, the leader of the wartime movement to legislate slavery out of exis-tence, was correct in believing that only one in three black chil-dren survived to the age of twenty-eight, then this was primarily a system of providing cheap labor for white masters rather than a means for training youths for citizenship.[21]

Some black parents, who were not so destitute as to repair to the almshouse, voluntarily indentured their children, although this occurred in only thirty-nine cases from 1778 to 1790, and these parents were usually willing to indenture their children only to age eighteen or twenty-one. Another fifty-five blacks who had reached adulthood indentured themselves in the same period, usually for seven years or less.[22]

Why did so many recently freed slaves reluctantly return to the limbo between slavery and freedom by consigning themselves or their children to servitude? The answer lies primarily in the conception of freedom held by the first generation of ex-slaves. For white Philadelphians, all the more so because of the wrenching wartime experience, slavery and freedom were polar opposites— contradictory and mutually exclusive. Slavery was the denial of freedom and freedom was the escape from slavery. With far more limited opportunities, blacks necessarily understood the terms more subtly, perceiving a continuum where slavery and freedom stood at the terminal points but with a vast number of intermediate positions. Understanding that to be legally free carried no guarantee whatsoever of economic freedom, many former slaves had to reconcile themselves to intermediate stations on the road to a fully autonomous existence.[23] The first historian of Pennsylvania's blacks, writing seventy-five years ago, took note of this condition of half-freedom that many blacks occupied for years: "There was no instantaneous creation of a great body of freedmen," wrote Edward Turner. "In the course of his slow rise from complete servitude to complete freedom the negro occupied successively two distinct intermediate positions; he was generally a servant before he became a free man; sometimes he was an apprentice . . . The ascent was slow and laborious, and the negro was compelled to halt for long periods on his way up."[24] Many more blacks in the first generation than Turner recognized leaped the boundary separating slavery from freedom and never looked back. Others, however, had to bide their time.

While perhaps one-fourth of the blacks living in white households in 1790 were serving indentures, a far larger number were hiring out their labor as domestic servants. For many blacks, especially those who were single and young, this was the best strategy available for building toward the future. Working for wages and receiving room and board, they could save for tomorrow while sharing a social life among people of their own kind in the evenings and on days off.[25]

FOR NEWLY FREED BLACKS, moving to the city was a logical way to obtain work, to find friends and sociability, to begin or perpetuate a family—in short, to build for the future. In the process ex-slaves had to create a new identity for themselves. How were they to fit into a society that in Philadelphia was overwhelmingly composed of white residents? Individually and in groups they had to develop a consciousness of place among white Americans, who were themselves groping in the postrevolutionary period to define their identity as a new nation. Were these newly freed and dark-skinned people to regard themselves as Africans in America who might best return to the lands of their ancestors, if that possibility presented itself? Were they Afro-Americans whose future rested where they had toiled most of their lives but whose cultural heritage was distinctly African? Or were they simply Americans with dark skin, who, in seeking places as free men and women, had to assimilate as quickly as possible to the cultural norms and social institutions of the dominant white society?

Probing the consciousness of this first generation of free men and women in Philadelphia is difficult because they left behind hardly a scintilla of literary evidence. But one thing that every slave recorded, as did every other man and woman in the society, was his or her name and the names they gave their children. Names are filled with social meaning, reflecting in many cases, as one anthropologist has put it, "personal experiences, historical happenings, attitudes to life, and cultural ideas and values."[26] Especially in the absence of a rich documentary record, which exists for white Philadelphians of the postwar generation, black names give us particularly valuable insights into the world that recent freedpersons saw around them and the world they wished to create for their children.

In addition to names, a few documents from the 1780s have survived that show how Philadelphia's free blacks referred to themselves collectively and how they named their first community organization. Taken together this evidence indicates that from the very beginning of the era of freedom most black Americans, as W. E. B. Du Bois wrote of later Afro-Americans, were possessed of "a peculiar sensation," a "double-consciousness." The black American, Du Bois argued, "ever feels his twoness—an American, a Negro; two souls, two thoughts, two unreconciled strivings; two warring ideals in one dark body, whose dogged strength alone keeps it from being torn asunder."[27] In the early days of freedom, this double consciousness manifested itself in the sharply contrasting names they gave themselves and their institutions.

In the matter of naming, the first generation of freed slaves was truly unique. They not only chose the names of their children, a right that in large degree they had already claimed under slavery, but they had the opportunity—in fact they felt a strong compulsion—to give themselves surnames while simultaneously jettisoning their slave forenames. To choose a first name for one's children and to name oneself are quite different matters. Naming one's children is an ordinary act, although "group patterns of nomenclature," reflecting "a folk flavor in a fashion similar to language," allow the use of children's forenames as evidence of the particular experiences and values of a group.[28] But inventing a family name for oneself is an extraordinary act that few people experience. For those emerging from slavery, it was a far more conscious act than for whites giving forenames to their children, and surely one of the most satisfying aspects of the transition from bondage to freedom. As Ira Berlin has written, "A new name was both a symbol of personal liberation and an act of political defiance; it reversed the enslavement process and confirmed the free Negro's newly won liberty, just as the loss of an African name had earlier symbolized enslavement."[29]

Analysis of the forenames and surnames of slaves and freed blacks in Philadelphia reveals, even if imperfectly, two stages in the process of cultural self-definition: first, the symbolic obliteration of the slave past; and second, the creation of a unique Afro-American identity.

For two generations before the Revolution, when slave importations were high, a rich mixture of names prevailed among black

Philadelphians.[30] African names or Anglicized versions of African names were common. Of 258 slaves manumitted in wills before 1750 or appearing in church records before 1775, about 11 percent had African names—Cuffee, Cajoe, Quash, Juba, Quame, Phibbe, and the like. Most of these names signified the day of the week on which they were born, a customary naming practice in West Africa. A somewhat larger number, about one-sixth, bore classical names. Caesar was by far the most popular, but Cato, Scipio, Diana, and Chloe were often used and an occasional Dionysus, Jupiter, Mars, Pundis, Septimus, Daphne, Dirander, Parthena, and Sabina could be found. Another sixth had biblical names. The most frequently used were Dinah, Hagar, Hannah, Hester, Judith, Ruth, and Rachel for females and Adam, Jesse, Jacob, Immanuel, and Isaac for males; but lesser-known first names such as Caleb, Hezekiah, Ishmael, Obadiah, Titus, Shadrach, Dorcas, Cyrene, Tamer, and Tabitha were also assigned. Place-names such as London, York, Hanover, Edinburgh, Warwick, Glasgow, and Bristol were also used for males in about one of every twenty instances, though never for women. Typically they reflected the master's origins or places where he did business. Among males, derisive or fanciful tags such as Robert Neverbegood, Mistake, and Moody were also found.[31]

But the most common names before 1775, accounting for more than two of every five slave names assigned by masters or used when slaves were brought to Philadelphia from other places in the colonies or West Indies, were Anglo-American. The most popular were Elizabeth, Sarah, Phyllis, Susannah, and Ann for women, and James, Richard, William, John, and Peter for males. Often these English names appeared in a shortened or diminutive form, as if to connote the half-person status of slaves. Studding the record books are names such as Dick, Tom, Toby, Ben, Will, Betty, Fanny, Jenny, Lucy, Polly, and Nelly.

As slaves adjusted to life in colonial Philadelphia, formed conjugal relationships, and bore children, they quickly adopted Anglo-American cultural ways, especially compared with slaves in the plantation colonies, where large living groups and the steady influx of fresh slaves created more favorable conditions for preserving African customs. Strong evidence of this urban acculturation can be found in the forenames given to slave children as they were brought to the Anglican and Lutheran churches in Philadelphia for baptism. It is no surprise that black parents eschewed derisive names altogether and rarely repeated geographic names. But neither did they more than occasionally perpetuate African or classical names. English names, on the other hand, appeared far more frequently, especially after about 1760. In 1749, Bristol and Daffy christened their son Dionisius when they took him to Christ Church for baptism, and London and Juba baptized their daughter Juba in 1751. Caesar and Amy named their first son Caesar in 1755. But in subsequent years, when numerous Philadelphia slaves had been attending church services for some time and many had received catechistic lessons, African and classical names almost disappeared in naming patterns. Thus Mistake and Dirander, taking their infant daughter to Christ Church in 1759, baptized her as Margaret. Caesar and Phoebe, bearing classical and African names, baptized their first son Caesar in 1755 but named their next three children, baptized in 1762, 1764, and 1771, Elizabeth, Peter, and Mary. Likewise, Cuffee and Metee Jackson christened their son James at Christ Church in 1766, and Cuffee and Hester Jones christened their son Charles in 1770.

Biblical names also increased somewhat as black parents attended the city's Protestant churches and took over the naming process. But the biggest change came in the more frequent assignment of English names. As indicated in Table 1, whereas 44 percent of the forenames of adults in the prerevolutionary church and manumission records were English, two-thirds of the children's names were.

Although the master may have exerted some influence in naming slave children, the parents appear to have borne most of the responsibility. To the extent that slaves assumed the right to name their own children, the disappearance of classical, geographic, derisive, and fanciful names represented their desire to rid themselves of absurd invocations of the classical past or names that connoted the master's attitudes or background. By the same token, the increasing frequency of biblical and Anglo-Saxon names provides evidence of adaptation to the culture in which their children were being raised and would presumably spend their lives.

Table 1. Forename patterns of blacks in Philadelphia, 1698–1790

Origin of name	Parents 1698–1774		Children 1747–1774		Parents 1775–1790		Children 1775–1790	
	No.	%	No.	%	No.	%	No.	%
African	28	10.8	3	1.9	13	4.6	1	1.4
Geographic	7	2.7	3	1.9	5	1.8	—	—
Classical	42	16.3	4	2.5	35	12.4	—	—
Derisive or whimsical	13	5.0	3	1.9	7	2.5	1	1.4
Biblical	44	17.0	30	19.0	38	13.5	10	13.2
English	114	44.2	105	66.5	170	60.1	57	81.6
Other	10	3.8	10	6.3	14	5.0	2	2.6

Sources: Register Books of Christ Church: Marriages, Christenings, Burials, I (1719–1750); II (1750–1762); III (1763–1810), Historical Society of Pennsylvania; transcripts of marriage and baptism records for Gloria Dei Swedish Lutheran Church, Pennsylvania Genealogical Society; slave names from wills provided by Jean R. Soderlund, Swarthmore College.

Thus the slaves of Philadelphians often passed their own names along to their children if their names were Elizabeth, Sarah, Benjamin, Richard, or John. But they rarely perpetuated such names as London, Toss, Christmas, Sharp, Cato, Othello, and Dirander; and such African names as Quasheba and Quam disappeared altogether. Only Cuffe and Phoebe, especially the latter, which had a biblical as well as African derivation, persisted. As for the diminutive forms used so commonly by masters, in a linguistic structure that emphasized the dominant and subordinate roles prevailing in a white household containing slaves, they were traded in for full English praenomens: Ben became Benjamin, Betty became Elizabeth, Will became William, Dick became Richard.

Upon gaining freedom, Afro-Americans took complete possession of the naming process. Of first importance, perhaps, was adopting a surname. Just as the absence of surnames symbolized the fact that slaves were only half-persons, the creation of a full name signaled the emergence of a complete person. Even before gaining their freedom, some slaves, as early as the 1750s, were adopting surnames, such as the runaway Jack, "who calls himself John Powell," his owner noted, or a "mulattoe fellow, who calls himself Joe Leek."[32] The importance of adopting a surname to those who were emerging from slavery is evident in the nearly universal practice of inventing a surname immediately or soon after gaining freedom. Only 7 of 182 black heads of household enumerated in the 1790 census lacked surnames, and from 1775 to 1790 very few black men and women came without surnames to the city's churches to be married.[33]

In many cases the surviving records indicate precisely the names that ex-slaves took for themselves. When he was manumitted in 1766, Oronoko Royal, the slave of James Dexter, kept his forename. It may have been bestowed by a master or parent familiar with the late seventeenth-century novel by Aphra Behn or the tragedy by Thomas Southerne concerning "Oroonoko." In any case, it commemorated the fabled grandson of an Angolan king who was sold into slavery in Surinam and led an insurrection there. While keeping this forename, however, Oronoko Royal substituted his master's surname for Royal, thus becoming Oronoko Dexter. Some time later, long after his former master had died, Dexter assumed the forename James, apparently wanting to rid himself entirely of his slave past. In another instance, Jammy, probably a shortened form of Jamaica, whence his master brought him to Philadelphia, renamed himself Samuel Stephens when he was manumitted in 1783, thus shucking his slave name altogether and declaring his identity with a thoroughly Anglo-American name.[34] Cicero turned his slave name into a surname and preceded it with James. So did William Scipio and Joseph Caesar. More frequently the slave name was retained as a forename and a surname was chosen to follow it. Thus Caesar became Caesar Godfrey, Moody became Moody Jackson, Cuffy became Cuffy Jordan, Cato became Cato Wilkes, and Rutland became Rutland Moore. But most frequently the slave name was discarded altogether. Jacob became William Trusty, Caesar became Samuel Green, Moses became William Johnson, Susanna became Elizabeth Howell, and Pompey became James Jones.[35]

A few freed Afro-Americans used the choice of a new name to make unmistakably clear their transition from slavery to freedom. Freemans and Newmans, who wore their names like advertisements, are scattered through the church, census, and tax records. In Philadelphia such names were most frequently taken by former slaves who had migrated north from Delaware after being freed. Manumitted in an area where slavery continued long after the Revolution, they wanted to declare their liberation unequivocally in a land where kidnapping of recently freed slaves for shipment south was common. Somersets, commemorating the judge who ruled against slavery in England in 1772, also appeared. Other names suggesting artisans' skills were taken regularly—Cooper, Mason, and Carpenter, for example—although sometimes this may have been a coincidence.

Occasionally a former slave would celebrate freedom with etymological flourish, as did Julius Caesar and Alexander the Great in Philadelphia after the Revolution. Others took names commemorating turning points or moments of high drama in their lives. The previous name of the slave-born West Indian sailor who turned up in Philadelphia during the Revolution and signed aboard John Paul Jones's *Bonhomme Richard* remains unknown. But this black mariner, who fought lustily in the epic battle against the English ship *Serapis,* losing a leg during the fray, sometime thereafter renamed himself Paul Jones.[36]

While these individual examples show a variety of orientations, ranging from identification with the former master to proud assertion of newly won independence, only the massed evidence of hundreds of surnames taken in the early years of freedom shows the larger picture of free black consciousness in the process of formation. Two hundred seventy free black males who emerged from slavery from 1776 to 1790 can be traced from the church records, the tax list of 1789, the records of manumission, and the census of 1790. The patterning of their names represents, in effect, the collective consciousness, so far as names can reveal it, of the pioneering generation of free black Philadelphians.

Aggregate statistics thus gathered demonstrate dramatically the psychological importance that northern blacks attached to affirming freedom through the choice of names that wiped away reminders of the slave past. In this selection process there was an unmistakable effort to make complete the break with former masters by avoiding their surnames. Of 270 slaves manumitted from 1770 to 1790, only 19 chose names that appear among the given names of 197 slaveholders who manumitted slaves in this period, and in many of these cases the new name taken by the former slave was not that of his or her own master but coincidentally that of a different white family that had owned slaves. Thus when Charles Willson Peale freed his slave in 1786, the freedman took the name of John Williams, which had no apparent connection to the Daniel Williams who had freed three slaves in 1783. Conspicuously absent in the list of freedmen's surnames were the prominent slaveowning families of Philadelphia—the Cadwaladers, Mifflins, Prestons, Plumsteads, Walns, Logans, Markoes, Shutes, Whartons, and Wistars.[37]

Instead of names of former masters, these pioneering free blacks chose names of their own making. In reaching a decision, they had an enormous pool of names available to them in an ethnically diverse city of 30,000. Two characteristics stand out in the pattern of their choices. First, a large majority of the names chosen were familiar English names such as Alexander, Bennett, Carpenter, Jackson, Johnson, Moore, Morgan, Richards, Roberts, Taylor, and Turner. To some extent these choices may have reflected their sense of their vulnerability in a white-dominated world. A name was a certificate of entry into Philadelphia society, and Anglo-Saxon names might ease the process. Second, freedmen ranged widely in their choice of surnames. Among the 252 who have been traced, there were 210 different surnames—an indication that they felt a strong desire to express their individuality, an essential part of an autonomous existence, in these early years. Only 3 surnames—Brown, Jones, and Williams—were chosen by more than 3 of the 252 males. Many others, moreover, had little or no currency in Philadelphia. Israel Burgaw, Joseph Tunch, John Teebo, James Lanty, Moses Hocal, John Debrick, Charles Golden, George Grenish, Caesar Cranchell, James Dancer, Josiah Emmester, James Funney, Harry Gooseberry, Richard Limehouse, Humphrey Sharper, Thomas Truxman, Benjamin Paulk, and John Yorrick were some of those whose surnames had no counterpart among white Philadelphians of the period.[38]

This pattern of inventing surnames with which to launch a free life contrasts sharply with the situation in the rural South, where freedmen frequently took the names of their former masters in order to cultivate their patronage.[39] In the urban North, by contrast, freedmen in the early years of the republic apparently felt no need to curry favor with those who had manumitted them. Consequently, they chose family names that bore no reminders of the slave past.

The choices of first names also reveal a strong desire to obliterate the memory of slavery. It is not surprising that slaves who had been tagged derisively should abandon such names as Plug or Lucky. But in the rapid abandonment of geographic, classical, and African names evidence exists of a consciousness of starting anew as people who would make their lives in America as Americans (Table 2). Affia, Cutcho, Ozmior, Venus, Hercules, Spinage, Quansheba, Cubit, Accro, Hamlet, Dingo, Newcastle, and Sedgefield were not to be tolerated by those who looked to the future. William, Elizabeth, Thomas, Mary, John, and Alice were more fitting for men and women embarking on a journey into freedomland.[40]

How rapidly slaves completed the process of discarding their former names and adopting new ones can be seen in a comparison of the male forenames of 270 slaves freed from 1770 to 1790 and

Table 2. Forename patterns of black males in Philadelphia, 1770–1790

Origin of name	Manumitted slaves 1770–1790		Free blacks 1794–1795	
	No.	%	No.	%
African	7	2.6	2	0.8
Geographic	15	5.6	7	2.7
Classical	28	10.4	16	6.2
Derisive or whimsical	9	3.3	3	1.2
Biblical	34	12.6	38	14.7
English	170	63.3	186	72.1
Other	7	2.6	6	2.3
Total	270		258	

Sources: Manumission Book A, Papers of the Pennsylvania Society for the Abolition of Slavery, microfilm ed., reel 20, Historical Society of Pennsylvania; *Heads of Families at the First Census of the United States Taken in the Year 1790: Pennsylvania* (Washington, D.C., 1908); Edmund Hogan, *The Prospect of Philadelphia and Check on the Next Directory* . . . (Philadelphia, 1795); William Douglass, *Annals of the First African Church in the United States of America, Now Styled the African Episcopal Church of St. Thomas* (Philadelphia, 1862), pp. 107–110.

the 258 forenames that appear in the 1790 census, the 1795 city directory, and on lists of black congregants in 1793–94 at Bethel and St. Thomas's African Episcopal churches. Just as Afro-American parents in the revolutionary period were avoiding African, geographic, classical, and whimsical first names for their children, choosing biblical and English names instead (Table 1), so they renamed themselves to a striking degree as they achieved the status of freed persons. Many, of course, kept the old slave name or turned it into a surname. But many more discarded the slave name and began life as free persons with a wholly new identity, so that by the 1790s nearly nine of ten declared themselves to fellow Philadelphians with English or biblical forenames (Table 2).

WHILE PHILADELPHIA's rapidly growing number of free blacks individually forged the rudiments of an independent existence in the postwar years, the city's Quakers emerged from a searing wartime experience that led many of them to look at their social obligations in a different light. For a generation before the Revolution, moral reformers of the Society had preached a return to the old Quaker asceticism, warning that Friends would ultimately be punished for their material indulgence and moral laxness. The war fulfilled the most drastic prophecies of suffering, and Quakers emerged from it morally rearmed: having witnessed the rectitude of the reformers' position, they now better understood the road they must travel. To some extent that road led to plain living and continued abstinence from a world of power and politics. But it also led to a renewed concern for wrongs perpetuated in the world around them.[41]

In particular, the matter of slavery and the condition of liberated slaves commanded the attention of Philadelphia Quakers. During the war the radical revolutionaries, driven by their own compelling needs, had trampled on the pacifist principles of Friends. "Liberty" became one of the watchwords of the Revolution, but for some of those living in the capital of American Quakerism it seemed a much dishonored concept. Thus were Quakers emotionally driven by the severity of their wartime experience to identify with the oppressed blacks and to strengthen their commitment to them. This sympathy was made easier and more appropriate by the fact that the Friends had recently and publicly cleansed themselves of slaveholding.

The first signs of this renewed moral fervor came even before the war ended. In October 1778, the Philadelphia Yearly Meeting urged all quarterly and monthly meetings to promote "the spiritual and temporal welfare of such Negroes and their children who have been restored to freedom," specifically by promoting religious instruction and "pious education" for black children.[42] The Meeting for Sufferings issued a long condemnation of the slave trade in January 1780 and expressed its "lively concern . . . for the discharge of christian duty towards the oppressed Africans."[43] Throughout the late 1770s and into the 1780s the Quakers convened special meetings for blacks.[44]

Much of the work in promoting the welfare of the freed slaves fell to the Committee to Inquire into the Condition of Freed Slaves, established in 1781. Composed mostly of the wives of prominent Friends, the committee embodied the newly felt obligation to "reform" those who had been degraded and brutalized under slavery and fulfilled the Yearly Meeting's pledge in 1776 to "assist and advise . . . [the former slaves of Friends] both for their spiritual & temporal good."[45] The women of the committee seem mostly to have visited their own former slaves, advising them of the importance of attending church, avoiding bad company, keeping the children "to school," and indenturing out their young "to such families as would attend to their religious improvement and teach them industry." For four years the women continued these visitations before disbanding in 1785 with the explanation that "the business for which this committee was nominated [is] now nearly gone threw."[46]

The philosophy underlying these Quaker actions—that they must not only free slaves but also provide reparations for years of injustice—was entirely consistent with the argument promoted by Woolman, Benezet, and others that much work remained after manumission to prepare blacks for citizenship. Because slavery bred ignorance and moral insensibility, those released from bondage would never be able to live satisfactory lives until these defects had been remedied. This paternalistic attitude was shared by no other religious group. Predictably, the Quaker commitment was not always welcomed by former slaves. They probably would have accepted with alacrity the cash reparations that the Delaware Quaker Warner Mifflin believed his slaves were entitled to, but they often begrudged the moral guardianship that Friends thought themselves obliged to extend.[47] Yet they could hardly afford to express this resentment, for Quakers were their best allies in an otherwise indifferent, if not hostile, world.[48] Quakers sighed when their offers of help were turned away, but some free blacks who were visited beginning in 1779 continued to show "backwardness" in accepting advice in the following years.[49]

While the Quaker monthly meetings charged women of prominent families with acting *in loco parentis* toward former bondsmen and bondswomen, individual Quaker men proved less willing to commit themselves to aiding the former slaves of other Philadelphians or the growing number of free blacks who found their way to the city after 1780. In the early 1780s neither Quakers nor any other white Philadelphians heeded the pleas of Anthony Benezet to revive the Pennsylvania Abolition Society, which had met a few times before he war.[50] It was left to Benezet, to the Quaker tailor Thomas Harrison, and to a few others to carry forward, as best they could with meager resources, the work of abolitionism and aid to former slaves. Quakers kept their African School open, largely through Benezet's efforts, and schoolmaster John Haughton taught about two hundred fifty students during the war years. When Haughton's health failed in 1782, Benezet assumed the teaching duties.[51]

Benezet also kept peppering the public with appeals to end slavery and the slave trade, which was reopening in the early 1780s. In June 1782 the *Pennsylvania Evening Post* carried his letter to the Abbé Raynal, the radical French reformer, calling for an abolition of slavery, and Raynal's approving reply. Two months later the *Pennsylvania Packet* printed a moving appeal for abolition, probably written by Benezet, that quoted extensively from Raynal's essay on the subject. In Benezet's fashion, the author asked Philadelphians to consider whether the epic words about equality and inalienable rights that had justified the revolutionary cause were consonant with the "situation of the Negroes, still kept in slavery on this continent."[52] Such appeals had an effect in 1783, when more than five hundred Friends attending the Philadelphia Yearly Meeting signed a ringing petition to the Continental Congress to "discourage and prevent so obvious an Evil" as the revival of the slave trade by those "prompted from avaricious motives" in contradiction of "the solemn declarations often repeated in favour of universal liberty."[53]

Despite these appeals, it took two dramatic cases of black suicide to bring the Pennsylvania Abolition Society back into existence in 1784. Anthony Benezet, only nine months from the grave, recounted that blacks came to him "almost daily & sometimes more" to solicit help. Sometimes they were the body servants of delegates to the Continental Congress, who, having seen freedom dawning for Philadelphia's slaves, found the idea of returning to slavery in the South unbearable. Such was Billey, the slave of James Madison, whom the southern leader described candidly to his own father as "merely . . . coveting that liberty for which we have paid the price of so much blood, and have proclaimed so often to be the right . . . of every human being." With regard to Billey, Madison was "persuaded his mind is too thoroughly tainted to be a fit companion for fellow slaves in Virginia"; yet the legislator could not bear to sell him into another slave state.[54]

But few slaves were fortunate to have a master of such a mind. Many were victimized by owners who defied the Pennsylvania law of 1780 by selling their slaves south, often tearing families apart in the process. Benezet reported that the situation seemed so hopeless to some Philadelphia slaves, and to freedmen about to be reenslaved, that when redress of their grievances was refused or delayed, they took their lives rather than be returned to slavery or sent south. One "sensible" black, "who from the most clear evidence was a freeman" but could not obtain a writ of habeas corpus to prevent his forced departure from the city, despite Benezet's request to the court, "hung himself to the great regret of all who knew him." Another, "having pressingly, on his knees, solicited a friend, without success, to prevent his being sent away to the southward" from his family, threw himself into the Delaware River from the deck of a departing ship and drowned. Benezet's repeated efforts to obtain assistance from the Friends' committee for assisting free blacks, he related in October 1783, had met with little encouragement in these cases.[55]

Four months later, however, a group of Philadelphians, including six survivors of the short-lived Abolition Society founded in 1775, met to reestablish the organization. Its members, like their prewar predecessors, were staunchly in favor of gradual abolition everywhere but knew that in their region their principal contribution would be using existing laws to rescue blacks illegally held in slavery.[56] The initial group of eighteen who met in February 1784 was almost entirely Quaker. But after the first few meetings, the core group, probably recognizing the advantages of building a cross-denominational organization, reached out for additional members to every neighborhood and church in the city and even into the countryside. By the end of the second year of operation, a bare majority of the Abolition Society's eighty-two Philadelphia members were Quakers.[57]

Once reorganized, the PAS found business enough to do. A single case will indicate the complexity of their work—and the intricate process by which many enslaved Philadelphians achieved freedom. In May 1784 the society learned that Christopher Elliot, who operated a large plantation just outside the city in Kingsessing, was holding in slavery thirteen children of several slave women he had inherited before the Revolution. Elliot's father and uncle had provided in their wills that these slave women should be held only until they were thirty years old and then freed. Before reaching thirty, however, the two women had given birth to nine children, all born between 1768 and 1780. Four of the children had been sold in Chester County as slaves for life, and Elliot had duly registered the other five in 1780, as the abolition act required. By Elliot's reasoning, the children were slaves for life since the mothers were still slaves when the children were born. By the reasoning of the Abolition Society, the mothers had been promised freedom at age thirty by their masters before the Revolution, and from the time of their masters' death, when the will promising freedom was executed, these women "could only be considered as servants until they respectively arrived at the age of thirty"; hence their offspring were born "altogether free."

Threatened with lawsuits by the PAS, Elliot and three Chester County farmers to whom he had sold four of the children came to terms: three of the children were released outright to their parents and the other six, with their parents' consent, were indentured to their purported slave masters until age eighteen in the case of the girls and age twenty-one in the case of the boys.[58] The time of several members and the *pro bono* work of friendly attornies over a period of seventeen months had secured freedom for nine blacks who otherwise would have spent their lives in slavery.

As the PAS scored successes of this kind, word of its work spread rapidly to the households of free blacks and to black migrants entering the city. They came in a steady stream for help, especially to the shop of tailor Thomas Harrison on Third Street near Walnut. Described by a contemporary as "a lively, bustling man, with a roguish twinkle in his eye," Harrison would involve himself more than any other member in the individual cases taken up by the Abolition Society over the next thirty years.[59]

With Harrison a mainstay, the PAS worked to secure freedom for blacks whose masters had not registered them as the 1780 law required, or who had been brought into the state as slaves and not freed after six months as required, or who had fled to Philadelphia in hopes of breaking slavery's bonds. In 1784 the Abolition Society investigated at least twenty-two cases of slaves brought in by migrants from many locations in Philadelphia's trading orbit, including New England, South Carolina, and the West Indies. Abraham Butter, who had been sold seven times and served eight masters in New England, Virginia, Delaware, rural Pennsylvania, and Philadelphia, was one of many who found his way to the PAS. Another was James Daniel, who as a free black had fought with Nathanael Greene during the Revolution and then indentured himself in 1782 to a Lancaster County farmer, who shortly sold him into slavery across the Pennsylvania line in Cecil County, Maryland. Fleeing to Philadelphia with his master in hot pursuit, he too sought the protection of the PAS. In another case, John Gardiner recounted how, when sailing with his master from Virginia early in the Revolution, he had been captured by the British and sold to a Frenchman who lived in Hispaniola. At the end of the war, when his French master gave him his freedom,

Gardiner took passage, freedom papers in hand, with Captain Peter Anderson from Port-au-Prince to Philadelphia. Reaching Philadelphia, Anderson was convinced by an unnamed person that Gardiner was an escaped slave and had him confined to the workhouse. Through the intercession of the Abolition Society, Gardiner was released by the court after four weeks of confinement.[60] Through such interventions the reorganized society "restored to liberty," as its secretary phrased it, "upwards of one hundred persons" from 1784 to 1787.[61]

In April 1782, with the Revolution not yet quite over, six Philadelphia free blacks penned a petition to the state government in which they "humbly craveth liberty to fence in the Negroes Burying ground in the Potters field."[62] Embedded in this one-sentence petition were further signs of a rising consciousness among recent freedpersons that they were a distinct people who must work collectively to secure a place of dignity and security in white American society. Speaking for "the Black people of the City and Suburbs," the six petitioners—John Black, Samuel Saviel, Oronoko Dexter, Cuff Douglass, Aram Prymus, and William Gray—showed that free black leaders in different parts of the city were already stepping forward to take collective action on behalf of the growing population of freedpersons.[63] It was of special significance that this first act concerned the treatment of the dead. White churches did not permit the mortal remains of black worshipers to be interred in their cemeteries but instead consigned blacks to the Potters' Field, or Strangers' Burial Ground, as it was tellingly called. This extension to the dead of the racial inequalities among the living may have been especially grievous to Afro-Americans, whose African religious heritage emphasized dignifying the dead. Now, in 1782, blacks wished to delineate their own area in the Potters' Field, where they had gathered since before the Revolution to celebrate their dead and reaffirm their cultural identity.

Two years after the burial ground petition the city's blacks again showed themselves as a collectivity when they gathered, several hundred strong, to testify their gratitude for Anthony Benezet's lifework in their behalf. On May 4, 1784, the old Quaker schoolmaster, who knew most of the city's blacks and had taught several hundred of them, died in his seventy-first year. According to the French visitor Jean Pierre Brissot, four hundred blacks followed the funeral procession to the grave, paying homage to a man who said on his deathbed that he wanted no posthumous testimonies to his life. If anything was to be said, asked Benezet, let it be noted only that "Anthony Benezet was a Poor Creature and through divine favor, was enabled to know it." Benjamin Rush hoped that Benezet's epitaph would read: "He went about doing good."[64]

Though a heavy loss to the fledgling black community, the death of the gentle Quaker may have spurred further self-generated activity among blacks. That possibility was distinctly advanced by the arrival in the city two years later of a young man who had once been a slave in the family of one of the city's wealthiest and most prominent citizens. Richard Allen, as he would name himself after gaining his freedom, had been born in 1760 to a slave who belonged to Benjamin Chew, a conservative lawyer who had become one of the most important proprietary officials in Pennsylvania. Chew had moved to Philadelphia in 1754, but he kept his plantation in Delaware, where he had many slaves. It is possible that Allen, living with his parents and siblings, was raised partly in Philadelphia and partly in Delaware. Sometime in the 1760s or early 1770s Chew sold the slave family to Stokely Sturgis, a middling farmer who owned a neighboring plantation outside Dover. It was here, as a seventeen-year-old slave in about 1777, that Allen experienced a religious awakening at the hands of itinerant Methodists. No small part of his conversion may be related to the loss of his parents and younger siblings, whom the financially pressed Sturgis sold shortly before this. Left with his older brother and sister, the desolate young man may have found comfort and a new reason for existence in a religion that emphasized the experience of rebirth and promoted the idea of a family or community of redeemed sinners.[65] The antislavery pronouncements of those he heard, especially the silver-tongued circuit rider Freeborn Garretson, may also have moved Allen. It was Garretson who had convinced Allen's master that slaveholders at Judgment Day would be "weighed in the balance and found wanting." Shortly thereafter, just before Allen's twentieth birthday in 1780, his master, himself touched by the Methodist flames that were kindling in Delaware, proposed that Richard and his older brother buy their freedom.[66]

Taking a surname to signify his status as a free man, Allen spent the next six years interspersing work as a sawyer and wagon driver with months of riding the Methodist circuits from South Carolina to New York and even into the Appalachian Indian country. Riding horseback with some of the leading early Methodist sojourners, he learned to preach with great effect to black and white audiences alike. One of the white Methodists he encountered was Francis Asbury, who would soon become the first bishop of the American Methodist-Episcopal church. Much later a Methodist chronicler related that Asbury, struck by the strength of Allen's emotions and "jealous of his power," "embargoed him to locate and become stationary," deciding that Philadelphia was the best place for the young black Methodist.[67] Whether or not under Asbury's orders, Allen arrived in the Philadelphia area full of zeal early in 1786. By this time he seems to have completed the crucial psychological middle passage by which those who gained freedom in a legal sense procured as well the emotional autonomy that enabled them to overcome their dependence upon whites.[68]

Early in 1786, when Allen was preaching to a racially mixed group of Methodists in Radnor, twelve miles west of Philadelphia, the Methodist elder in the city sent for him to preach to the small group of blacks who were coming to St. George's Methodist Church, a poor, dirt-floored structure in a German part of the city. Allen was asked to preach at 5:00 A.M. so as not to interfere with white services. Nonetheless, "several souls were awakened," he recounted years later, "and were earnestly seeking redemption in the blood of Christ." Noting the large number of free blacks arriving in the city, and aware that "few of them attended public worship," Allen began supplementing his predawn services at St. George's with daytime meetings on the commons in adjacent Southwark and the Northern Liberties, where many black families were taking up residence. While supporting himself as a

Figure 7. Portrait of Richard Allen. Another Delawarean born into slavery. Allen was a pivotal figure in Philadelphia's black community from 1786 to 1831. The abolitionist paper *Genius of Universal Emancipation* reported an "immense concourse of coloured people . . . exceeding perhaps any thing of the kind ever witnessed in this country" in attendance at his funeral in March 1831.

shoemaker, he soon had established black prayer meetings and "raised a Society of forty-two members."[69] Among them was Absalom Jones, who had abandoned Anglican services at St. Peter's Church, where his former master still worshiped, in favor of St. George's. Like taking a surname, choosing to attend the services of a black minister became a step in forging a new identity.

Within months of Allen's arrival in Philadelphia, Absalom Jones and several other recently freed slaves had joined the black Methodist preacher to discuss forming a separate black religious society. Religion and literacy had helped all these men achieve freedom, so it was natural that, when they looked around them to find the majority of former slaves illiterate and unchurched, they "often communed together upon this painful and important subject in order to form some kind of religious society."[70]

It was not a church that Allen, Jones, and the others established, however. They were still too few in number and too varied in their religious sensibilities. Instead they launched the Free African Society, formally establishing it in April 1787. Possibly the first black organization of its kind in America, the society was designed in the manner of white benevolent societies, which had originated in craft or ethnic consciousness. It has often been seen simply as a black mutual aid organization. In his classic study, *The Philadelphia Negro,* W. E. B. Du Bois described it more generously, calling it "the first wavering step of a people toward an organized social life."[71] But even this designation is too limited. Although mutual aid was its purported goal, the society was quasi-religious in character from the beginning. Moreover, it was an organization in which the people emerging from bondage could gather strength, develop their own leaders, define themselves as a group, and independently explore strategies for hammering out an existence that went beyond formal legal release from thralldom.

The articles of incorporation of the Free African Society made clear the sharp racial identity that its members felt. It began with the words: "We, the free *Africans* and their descendants, of the City of Philadelphia." Among its first members were Moses Johnson, the former Virginia slave whom we met at the beginning of the chapter; Cato Freeman, who proclaimed his new status in the surname he added to his old slave name; Richard Allen; Absalom

Jones; and Caesar Cranchell. Meeting monthly, the founding members of the Free African Society gathered new recruits in 1787, assumed a guardianship role over the conduct of its members, and began planning for the future.[72] In that future, they believed, the work of the Pennsylvania Abolition Society, the fulcrum of white benevolence toward former slaves, would play a welcome part. But the future must also be shaped by ex-slaves themselves, operating within organizations of their own making. It was an American future, as the naming patterns of postrevolutionary blacks reveal; yet it was also, as the title of the first independent black organization tells us, the future of Africans in America. With this "double consciousness" free black Philadelphians approached the 1790s.

4. "To Arise Out of the Dust"

THE YEAR 1787, known in American history primarily for the deliberations of the Constitutional Convention, was a crucial one for the growing community of former slaves in Philadelphia. In this year Absalom Jones and Richard Allen emerged as spokesmen among the city's blacks; the Pennsylvania Abolition Society reorganized itself, soon to establish what in effect became the first freedmen's bureau in the new nation; and Philadelphia's free blacks pondered the first of what would be a continuing series of proposals to repatriate former slaves to their African homelands. While America's political theorists gathered in the State House to begin the epic debate on reorganizing the national government, hundreds of humble former slaves were considering their place in the new republic and their relationship to Africa. Caught between accepting their adopted country, which was not yet ready to accept them, and returning to a native land that they had been told by many whites was a heathen jungle awaiting Christian redemption, they began the work of forging a visionary collective consciousness upon which to build a viable future.

At the center of this process of molding a public self-identity stood the Free African Society of Philadelphia (FAS). By September 1787 it had gathered several dozen members and had instituted a visiting committee to inspect the conduct of fellow city dwellers through house visits. Such a Quakerly method of exercising stewardship reflected the Friends' early influence on the FAS. In fact the society's articles of incorporation, written when the aura of the influential Anthony Benezet still prevailed, specified that "it is always understood that one of the people called Quakers . . . is to be chosen to act as Clerk and Treasurer of this useful institution." In May 1788, when the society became too large to meet at Richard Allen's house, it rented a room in the house of Sarah Dougherty, one of Benezet's former students and a teacher at his school for blacks. By January 1789 the society was meeting in midcity at the Quaker African School House, founded by Benezet, in Willing's Alley.[1]

While still taking the first steps to organize the free black community, the FAS unexpectedly found itself faced with an extraordinary proposition that obliged its members to clarify their thoughts about who they were and where their future lay. Into Philadelphia in 1787 came William Thornton, an urbane, wealthy Quaker physician originally from Antigua, where his father had owned a large sugar plantation. Thornton had studied medicine in Edinburgh during the American Revolution and had come under the influence of a circle of fashionable, humanitarian reformers in London who had been mounting opposition to the slave trade. By 1785, when Thornton inherited his father's sugar plantation—and a small army of slaves with it—he had joined those in London who were attempting to establish a free black commonwealth on the west coast of Africa, where thousands of impoverished blacks in London, many of them former American slaves, might begin a new life. Embarrassed by his new inherited role as slaveowner, he planned to contribute his own slaves in Antigua to the experiment.[2]

Coming to the United States in 1786 to promote the African colonization scheme, Thornton asserted that "there can be no sincere union between the whites and the Negroes," even if free blacks conceded all political rights.[3] In New England he found fertile ground for his ideas about colonization. In Boston and Newport, where such schemes had already been broached, he encountered numerous Afro-Americans ready to return to the ancestral lands. Convinced they would never achieve equality and a decent life in America, scores of Boston's blacks were petitioning the legislature for funds to "return to Africa, our native country, which warm climate is much more natural [and] agreeable to us . . . and where we shall live among our equals and be more comfortable and happy, than we can be in our present situation."[4]

Gathering endorsements from leaders such as Samuel Adams and James Madison, Thornton made his way to Philadelphia, convinced that there too he would find numerous blacks "very desirous of reaching the coast of Guinea"; there they could live peacefully in a commonwealth where "their own laws are alone to be regarded . . . and where a man that Nature cloathed with a white skin, shall not, merely on that account, have the right of wielding a rod of iron."[5]

However, in Philadelphia, by now the largest free black community in the United States, Thornton's plan met a distinctly chilly reception, despite the fact that many black residents had been born in Africa. Talk of colonization had been in the air since before the Revolution, when both Anthony Benezet and Thomas Paine had suggested an all-black settlement beyond the Allegheny Mountains.[6] But when Thornton appeared before one of the meetings of the Free African Society, his efforts to sell his plan failed abysmally. He described the expedition already under way from London to establish the free black colony of Sierra Leone, where a former black Philadelphian, Richard Weaver, was to become an important local leader. Thornton promised that land would be granted outright to black American pioneers, and he painted a glowing portrait of the majestic mountains that formed a backdrop to the area of settlement, the freshwater brooks, and the "noble Forests of all kinds of Timber" that stood nearby.[7] Reading from the "General Outline of a Settlement on the Coast of Africa" that had been drawn up in London, he promised a land of freedom, self-government, schools and churches, and free trade with Great Britain, France, and the United States. Thornton also argued that the free black colony would eventually stop the barbaric slave trade by making Sierra Leone a haven for thousands of slaves each year who would be rescued from slave traders plying the coast. Such redeemed souls would thus be adopted "into a Family of Peace on Earth, and taught the Doctrines of him the King of Kings who has promised peace to his followers in heaven."[8]

Almost fantastical in what it promised—a combination of landowning security for former American slaves, the Christian redemption of pagan Africa, and the end of the slave trade—

Thornton's plan convinced nobody in Philadelphia, as it had farther north, to sign the articles of agreement to emigrate. But it did occasion a debate among black Philadelphians about where their destiny lay and galvanized their thinking about how they might shape the future. Some months after Thornton's appeal, the Free African Society sent one of its members, Henry Stewart, to Newport and Boston to confer with African societies there about colonization. Stewart returned in 1789 with letters from the Free African Union Society in Newport describing the "calamitous state" of free blacks in that city, who were "strangers and outcasts in a strange land, attended with many disadvantages and evils which are likely to continue on us and our children, while we and they live in this country."[9] Similar messages came from Boston. But Philadelphia's blacks remained convinced that although the path to acceptance and accomplishment in America was strewn with obstacles, it was the road to be taken. Breathing the spirit of Christian redemption, they advised that, as found in the "holy writ . . . the race is not to the swift, nor the battle to the strong; but that one who has on the shield of faith, shall chase a thousand, and two put ten thousand to flight. Here is encouragement for us of the African race."[10]

Although other factors may have been involved, a main reason for the unenthusiastic reception that Philadelphia's free blacks gave Thornton was the considerable support they had been receiving from the Pennsylvania Abolition Society and especially the promise that a reorganization of the PAS seemed to hold for them. In its letter to the Free African Union Society of Newport, the FAS spoke of the "persons who are sacrificing their own time, ease, and property for us, the stranger and the fatherless, in this wilderness."[11] This was almost certainly a reference to the Abolition Society, which in the spring of 1787 had reorganized under a new name that for the first time stressed abolition as a primary goal: the Pennsylvania Society for Promoting the Abolition of Slavery and for the Relief of Free Negroes Unlawfully Held in Bondage and for Improving the Condition of the African Race. The organization now revised its constitution, broadened its membership, adopted an aggressive strategy of litigation on behalf of free blacks, explicitly embraced abolitionism, and reached out to the FAS to work cooperatively for the benefit of the growing population of ex-slaves.[12]

Personifying the new energy of the Abolition Society was Benjamin Rush, who was still a slaveowner himself.[13] Rush joined the PAS in 1784 but attended few meetings. One of Philadelphia's most influential citizens, the widely connected, opinionated Rush suddenly threw himself into the cause of Philadelphia's blacks in 1787. During the next decade he became the Anthony Benezet of the late eighteenth century to the free black community, although his personality contrasted sharply with that of the self-effacing Quaker.

In fact it was the ghost of Benezet that galvanized Rush into action in 1787. In a poignant example of transatlantic influence, Rush became an avid abolitionist after a disturbing dream occasioned by his reading of Thomas Clarkson's recently published *Essay on the Slavery and Commerce of the Human Species,* which in turn had been inspired by Benezet's *Historical Account of Guinea.*[14] Rush recounted how, after he had read Clarkson's essay, the figure of the saintly Benezet pursued him into his sleep. Transported nocturnally to the shores of a distant country, Rush found himself standing on a sandy beach in a country of surpassing beauty. Approaching a grove of trees, he came upon a group of Africans gathered for religious observances. The natives fell into panic at the sight of the white man because, as one of them, a venerable old man, told him, the color white, "which is the emblem of innocence in every creature of God," was to Africans "a sign of guilt in man." The old African informed Rush that he was standing in the paradise that God had given to Africans who had been wrenched from their homeland after a shattered family life and ghastly brutality under slavery. Then, after a number of fellow Africans poured out tales of the horrors they had experienced under slavery, all eyes turned down the beach, where an ancient, decrepit white man was seen approaching. Coming closer, his face appeared "grave, placid and full of benignity." He carried a petition in one hand and in the other a pamphlet on the unlawfulness of the slave trade. Then the throng of blacks rushed to meet the "venerable figure" and began applauding. "And I awoke from my dream," recounted Rush, "by the noise of a general acclamation of—ANTHONY BENEZET!"[15]

So thoroughly was Rush converted to the free blacks' cause after this guilt-drenched vision, through which he identified himself with the saviorlike Benezet, that he became one of the Abolition Society's most active members. He helped write the society's new constitution in 1787, was elected its secretary, and in the next year promised freedom to his slave William Grubber.[16] In the same year he wrote Jeremy Belknap, Congregational minister of Boston's Federal Street Church and friend of free blacks in that city, that "I love even the name of Africa, and never see a Negro slave or freeman without emotions which I seldom feel in the same degree towards my unfortunate fellow creatures of a fairer complexion . . . Let us continue to love and serve them, for they are our brethren not only by creation, but by redemption."[17] After a long hiatus, Rush had returned to the avid support of abolitionism and the succoring of former slaves that had prompted him much earlier to predict that within a generation people would "behold and admire the finished TEMPLE OF AFRICAN LIBERTY IN AMERICA."[18]

Few Philadelphians were so earnest about reform as Benjamin Rush—"Mr. Great Heart," Jeremy Belknap of Boston called him, after the character in Bunyan's *Pilgrim's Progress* who battled every hydra, hobgoblin, and giant who blocked the way to the Celestial City.[19] But the reorganization of the PAS in 1787 brought a new wave of converts to the cause. Like Rush, many of them were prominent Philadelphians who had largely avoided the society in its early postwar years. Among those who joined were the aged Benjamin Franklin, triumphantly returned from a decade of diplomatic exploits in Paris; Tench Coxe, the herald of entrepreneurial capitalism in Philadelphia; and James Pemberton, a wealthy and venerable leader of the Society of Friends. Many important Quakers who had kept to the shadows until the revolutionary animus against the Friends subsided in the mid-1780s, and many other men who had previously seen abolitionism as too radical a cause or believed slaves incapable of functioning responsibly as free persons, now joined the middling artisans and shopkeepers who had formed the core of the PAS from 1784 to 1787. Among the new recruits after the reorganization of 1787, merchants, professionals, and government officials now far outnumbered artisans and retailers.[20] Not all these men would prove to be genuine friends of the free black community, but for the moment they were attracted to the transatlantic reform movement, especially against the slave trade, which seemed the most objectionable blot on the national conscience.

If Philadelphia's free blacks could take heart from the expansion of the Abolition Society, they could find further grounds for optimism in its aggressive work in the very years when William Thornton and free black organizations in New England were counseling a return to Africa. In 1787 the PAS petitioned the Constitutional Convention, meeting in Philadelphia, to ban the slave trade, which it labeled a "part of the obloquy with which foreign nations have branded our infant states" and "a Commerce that can only be conducted upon Rivers of Human tears and blood."[21] It also lobbied the city's newspaper editors to refuse advertisements for slave sales and convinced the sheriff to forbid the public sale of slaves.[22] In addition, in an effort to promote the idea that the international crusade against the slave trade and slavery was gaining momentum, the society kept the newspapers and magazines filled with news of the campaign against the slave trade in England, of antislavery activity in other states, and of the progress of free blacks in Philadelphia and elsewhere.[23]

Part of the campaign to create conditions in which freed slaves could fulfill their potential involved combating generalized notions of black inferiority. One influential treatise, published by a member of Philadelphia's American Philosophical Society just a few months before the Constitutional Convention gathered, made the strongest case to date against such ideas. Soon to become president of Princeton, Samuel Stanhope Smith placed before the public in early 1787 his *Essay on the Causes of the Variety of Complexion and Figure in the Human Species,* the first systematic American inquiry into physical and mental variations among humans. Smith argued that humanity composed a unitary species and all human variation within this single species arose from climate or factors of social environment. If widely accepted, such a belief in the fundamental kinship of all human beings could have inspired commitment to abolitionism and an empathy among whites toward those among their brethren now emerging from slavery.[24]

Two extraordinary men of the period, James Derham and

Thomas Fuller, provided publicists with opportunities to show that innate ability in blacks could survive the psychic destruction that slavery often wrought and hence to prove Smith's argument that environment alone caused variation among humans. Benjamin Rush happily publicized the talents of the black physician James Derham, who had been born in Philadelphia in 1762 and sold to a Quaker doctor, who taught him the rudiments of medicine. After passing through the hands of at least four other masters, including a British officer during the Revolution, Derham had been freed in New Orleans, where he was practicing successfully in the late 1780s. On a visit to Philadelphia in 1788 he was baptized in Christ Church and talked knowledgeably about medicine with Rush, who saw to it that his accomplishments received public notice.[25]

Even more newsworthy was Fuller, the "African Calculator." African-born, the illiterate Fuller, a slave in Virginia, could perform spectacular arithmetic calculations. When tested by doubting whites with the problem of figuring the number of seconds a man has lived after 70 years, 17 days, and 12 hours, he reflected briefly and answered 2,210,500,800 seconds. When his white interrogators charged him with a small error, he stunned them by pointing out that they had forgotten to account for leap years. Fuller topped off the performance by tackling in his head the problem of how many sows a farmer would have if he started with six and each sow had six female pigs in the first year "and they all increased in the same proportion to the end of eight years." After a few minutes' reflection, he produced the correct answer of 34,588,806. Fuller's feats were publicized in Philadelphia's magazines, and when he died at eighty in 1790, the *General Advertiser* proclaimed that if average opportunities had come his way, "neither the Royal Society of London, the Academy of Sciences at Paris, nor even a Newton himself, need have been ashamed to acknowledge him as a brother in science." His case, it was pointed out, demonstrated "the genius, capacity and talents of our ill fated black brethren" and gave reason to deplore prejudiced white conduct based on "a supposed inferiority of their intellectual faculties; sentiments as ill founded in fact, as they are inhuman in their tendency."[26]

Although Philadelphia's free black residents must have understood that neither learned treatises refuting ideas of inherent black inferiority nor concrete cases of black genius could do more than begin to melt white prejudice, they could take heart in specific actions by those whites who did embrace the idea of the brotherhood of all mankind. In 1788 the Abolition Society, working in conjunction with the Society of Friends, gave further evidence to the city's free blacks that they might find in America rather than in Africa the promised land of freedom. Gathering nearly two thousand signatures in Philadelphia, they petitioned the legislature to amend the gradual abolition act of 1780 so as to make illegal the fitting out of slave ships in Philadelphia's shipyards and to plug loopholes that unscrupulous men were using to avoid the 1780 law. Chief among the evaders of the law were a growing number of Pennsylvania slaveholders who transported children born of slaves after 1780 into slave states, thus depriving them of their liberty, and who carried pregnant slave women south where their children would be born in bondage. Acting with unusual dispatch, the legislature amended the 1780 law in the spring of 1788 to prohibit sending slave children or pregnant women out of state. The law also imposed heavier fines for slave kidnapping, made illegal the separation of slave families by more than ten miles, and prohibited building, outfitting, or sending ships from the state to traffic in slaves.[27]

Engaging the *pro bono* services of four distinguished Philadelphia lawyers—William Lewis, Meirs Fisher, John D. Coxe, and William Rawle—the PAS kept the courts humming with suits brought to obtain freedom for slaves, especially those brought into Philadelphia and held by their masters beyond the six months allowed under the 1780 law.[28] Then, in 1789, the society heightened its efforts both to oppose slavery and to aid free blacks. Appealing to the public for support for the first time, it issued a moving address signed by its new president, the aged Benjamin Franklin, that attacked slavery as "an atrocious debasement of human Nature" and announced a "Plan for Improving the Condition of the Free Blacks."[29] A Committee of 24, with four subcommittees, would administer what in effect was a freedmen's bureau—obtaining employment for free blacks, establishing schools, and conducting house visitations to inculcate the virtues of frugality, industriousness, and morality.

WHILE BENEVOLENT WHITE PHILADELPHIANS worked on be-half of the city's growing black community, free blacks were themselves beginning to seize control of their destiny. Sometimes they worked in close conjunction with white patrons, as in May 1790, when the Free African Society entertained a committee of the Abolition Society to discuss a plan for improving "the condi-tion of the free blacks." Out of this meeting came a joint commit-tee of the two societies that canvassed the city and obtained a list of black families.[30] But the FAS also took independent action. In May 1790 it attempted to lease the Strangers' Burial Ground in order to turn it into a black cemetery under the society's control. In the next month the FAS established "a regular mode of proce-dure with respect to . . . marriages" and began keeping a book of marriage records. Having assumed quasi-ecclesiastical functions, the society took the next logical step in September 1790, when a special committee recommended the initiation of formal religious services, which began on January 1, 1791.[31]

Richard Allen, who had played a leading role in the Free African Society up to this point, viewed the Quakerly drift of the society with concern. He made no objections when the black organization adopted Quakerlike visiting committees in late 1787 or instituted the disownment practices of the Friends the next year. But in 1789, when the FAS adopted the Quaker practice of beginning meetings with fifteen minutes of silence, Allen led a withdrawal of "a large number" of dissenters whose adherence to Methodism had accustomed them to "an unconstrained outburst of the[ir] feelings in religious worship.[32] Allen stopped going to meetings of the African Society and privately began convening some of its members in an attempt to arrest the drift of the organization to-ward the practices of a religious group whose "detachment and introspection were not without value, but . . . did not seem to speak to the immediate needs of black people as Allen saw them."[33]

The appeal of Methodism for many free blacks is not hard to

Figure 8. In this depiction of interclass, interracial dialogue a black peddler dressed in cutaway and top hat calls on a wealthy Quaker couple (c. 1799).

understand. Leading austere lives, itinerant Methodist preachers reached out to the humble folk of city and countryside with a message of redemption and an ideal of a reformed community in which plain living, self-discipline, and mutual support would bring salvation and escape from poverty. As the first black historian of the African Church of Philadelphia wrote in 1862, the new Methodist preachers "made no pretensions to literary qualifications, and being despised and persecuted as religious enthusiasts, their sympathies naturally turned towards the lowly, who, like themselves, were of small estimate in the sight of worldly greatness."[34] Methodism also provided far more participatory and stirring experience than did other denominations. Advocating lay preachers and lay societies, simplifying the liturgy of the Book of Common Prayer, and holding meetings in fields and forests or, in the city, in sail lofts and homes, the Methodists grew rapidly in

postrevolutionary Philadelphia, recruiting heavily among laboring city dwellers of both races.[35] Also commending Methodism to
former slaves were the well-known antislavery views of its founder, John Wesley. Moreover, the Methodist discipline and polity,
formulated in America in 1784, attacked slavetrading and
slaveholding and barred persons engaged in these practices from
holding church offices. No other religious group except the Society of Friends assumed a stronger antislavery posture.[36] In Philadelphia, the inherent appeal of Methodism, complemented by the
passionate preaching of Richard Allen, had drawn many blacks to
St. George's Church, near the waterfront in the northern part of
the city.

Hence, several conflicting religious influences operated within
the Free African Society. Some of the early members had been
educated by Anthony Benezet and continued to be influenced by
Friends after his death. Others had been reared in the Anglican
churches of the city and were at the moment attracted to the
evangelical Joseph Pilmore at St. Paul's Church. Still others were
recent converts to Methodism—the one denomination in Philadelphia in which a black man actually led some religious services.

Attempting to overcome these differences in religious temper-
ament, Jones and others tried repeatedly to bring Allen back into
the bosom of the Free African Society. When he proved unyield-
ing in his criticism of their Quakerly innovations, they followed
the Friends' procedure of censuring him "for attempting to sow
division among us." When this had no effect, they reluctantly
declared in August 1789 that "he has disunited himself from membership with us."[37]

Now the mantle of leadership of the Free African Society fell to
Absalom Jones. It was the mild-mannered but persistent Jones
who made the crucial connections in the white community that
led to plans for building a black church. The ties with the Society
of Friends were wearing thin by the summer of 1791 because
many Quakers objected to the Sunday psalm singing by blacks in
the Quaker schoolhouse.[38] But Jones, perhaps understanding the
limits of the Quaker connection, had been cultivating new lines of
patronage to Benjamin Rush, who by this time was full of zeal for
the cause of blacks.

Jones and a small group of emerging black activists had by now fixed their sights on building a community, or "union," black church. It was to be formed, Rush wrote the English abolitionist Granville Sharp, from "the scattered and unconnected [black] appendages of most of the religious societies in the city" and from an even larger number of blacks "ignorant and unknown to any religious society."[39] Lacking denominational affiliation, it would not be tied to creeds or ordinances governing most white churches. Its goals were black unity in Christian fellowship and the general welfare of the city's blacks. In fact Jones and his group proposed to build a black school first and then a church, though the two enterprises were hardly separable in their minds.[40] Their formula was to become the classic one for the emergence of the black church in the United States, "a pattern of religious commitment," writes Gayraud S. Wilmore, "that has a double focus—the free and autonomous worship of God in the way Black people want to worship him, and the unity and social welfare of the Black community."[41]

The plan for a union church flowed naturally from the religious services that the Free African Society had been holding. Rush described how "two or three of their own colour conduct the worship, by reading the Scriptures, praying, singing, and occasionally exhorting." The minutes of the FAS reveal that "the religious meeting" had been ecumenically defined so that approved ministers of all denominations could be invited to conduct services.[42] One who led services frequently—with results that could not have been predicted at the time—was Joseph Pilmore, an English follower of Wesley who had served the newly formed Methodist congregation in Philadelphia before the Revolution. Beginning in 1769, the popular Pilmore had attracted many blacks to his worship services in the fields and sail lofts of Philadelphia. After a ten-year absence in England, from 1774 to 1784, he returned to Philadelphia and was ordained in the American Protestant Episcopal church. When the Free African Society began holding religious services in 1790, Pilmore was serving as assistant rector at St. Paul's Episcopal Church, the most evangelical of the three Anglican churches in the city, and had recently married the niece of Anthony Benezet, the revered benefactor of Philadelphia's black community. Pilmore's personal warmth and his indifference to color brought thirty-one black couples to St. Paul's for marriage from 1789 to 1794.[43]

Aided by Rush, Jones and his cohorts drew up a plan for the separate black church early in 1791. Attempting to cast their appeal broadly, they adopted articles of association and a plan of church government "so general as to embrace all, and yet so orthodox in cardinal points as to offend none."[44] The church was to be named the African Church of Philadelphia, and it was under this title, openly announcing their sense of a distinct identity but devoid of denominational reference, that the work of raising subscriptions went forward for the next three years. Jones and his group drew Richard Allen back into the fold, and they, along with six others, were selected to act as the "representatives" of the African Church. Included were William Wiltshire, a mulatto who had been freed only five years earlier after the Methodist merchant, Lambert Wilmore, purchased him from his owner in order to manumit him; Cato Collins, a nineteen-year-old former slave of a Philadelphia Quaker; Henry Stewart, the African Society's emissary to blacks in Newport and Boston; and William White, freed seven years before by the Anglican merchant Jacob Giles and a founding member of the FAS.[45]

In a ringing broadside appeal for support, the founding trustees argued that a black church would gather hundreds of those who worshiped in none of the white churches of the city because "men are more influenced by their moral equals than by their superiors . . . and . . . are more easily governed by persons chosen by themselves for that purpose, than by persons who are placed over them by accidental circumstances."[46] This democratic argument was accompanied by another, which indicated that already in these early years of freedom, as one historian has written, "black religious sensibilities [could not] be contained within biracial, Euroamerican structures."[47] "Africans and their descendants" needed their own church, the black leaders advised, because of the "attraction and relationship" among those bound together by "a nearly equal and general deficiency of education, by total ignorance, or only humble attainments in religion" and by the color line drawn by custom. All of this argued for the "necessity and propriety of separate and exclusive means, and opportunities of worshiping God, of instructing their youth, and of taking care of their poor."[48]

Such a decisive act of self-assertiveness by Philadelphia's black leaders signaled the pivotal role in the life of emancipated slaves that the black church would assume in an era when the centrality to community life of the white churches, disestablished and fragmented by the Revolution, was diminishing. Black religion, writes Gayraud S. Wilmore, was "never so much a matter of social custom and convention as it has been for white people. It was a necessity." Even at the beginning it was seen that the black church would be "the one impregnable corner of the world where consolation, solidarity and mutual aid could be found and from which the master and the bossman—at least in the North—could be effectively barred."[49]

The first black historian of the African Church, writing in the 1860s on the basis of earlier oral interviews "with many of the old members now gone to their final account," described just this creative striving for dignity and self-generated power. It was, wrote William Douglass, an "age of a general and searching inquiry into the equity of old and established customs," a time when "a moral earthquake had awakened the slumber of ages" and caused "these humble men, just emerged from the house of bondage . . . to rise above those servile feelings which all their antecedents were calculated to cherish, and to assume, as they did, an attitude of becoming men conscious of invaded rights."[50]

The boldness of the small group of men, led by Absalom Jones, who pushed ahead with plans for a black church, can be appreciated fully only if one understands the climate of opinion within which they operated. Despite the staunch support that free blacks were receiving from the Society of Friends and the Pennsylvania Abolition Society, they were maneuvering within a slaveholding republic where the prevailing sentiment, in the North as well as the South, was that blacks were either innately handicapped or had been irreparably degraded by the experience of slavery. Even in the center of American antislavery thought, only a minority of white Philadelphians believed that recently freed slaves could overcome these marks of birth and oppression.

The members of the Abolition Society, presumably those whites in the city most benevolently disposed toward free blacks, were themselves dubious of the possibility of reconstructing slaves into free citizens. In a broadside *Address to the Public* in 1789 they expressed their views on the lingering effects of slavery:

> The unhappy man who has long been treated as a brute Animal too frequently sinks beneath the common standard of the human species; the galling chains that bind his body, do also fetter his intellectual faculties, and impair the social affections of his heart; accustomed to move like a meer Machine by the will of a master, Reflection is suspended; he has not the power of Choice, and Reason and Conscience have but little influence over his conduct, because he is chiefly governed by the passion of Fear. He is poor & friendless, perhaps worn out by extreme Labour Age and Disease. Under such circumstances Freedom may often prove a misfortune to himself and prejudicial to Society.[51]

Although not all blacks were "governed by fear," as the Abolition Society put it, former slaves no doubt did carry into freedom many scars of oppression and an acute understanding of the tactics of survival, which included an almost instinctive wariness. Moreover, they had to face the dominant culture, which was far from ready to treat them as equals and continued to demand compliant comportment from them. We can infer from the fact that almost all the early black institutions in the North described themselves as "African" rather than "Negro" or "coloured"—the Free African Society, the African School, the African Church of Philadelphia— that these ex-slaves identified positively with their ancestral homelands and did not subscribe to the common white characterizations of Africa as a dismal, cultureless environment. But white racism impinged on their lives at every turn; and, though not of the virulent form it would assume early in the nineteenth century, it led many blacks to adopt a diffident posture. Yet the will to plan rationally, to strive for an independent and dignified existence, to confront racial prejudice, and to work for the future of their children depended upon throwing off the incubus of slavery, an institution that had perpetuated itself by exacting a terrible price for attempts at independent or self-reliant black behavior.

Having enunciated the concept of a racially separate, nondenominational and socially oriented church, Jones and the seven other trustees began the practical work of financing its construction. Rush's suggestion for circulating a broadside appeal with subscription papers—a proven method of raising money in Philadelphia—had been received by the black leaders, he wrote, "with a joy which transported one of them to take me by the hand as a brother."[52] A few days later Rush received poetic thanks from "J. B.," who assured the doctor that "Afric's muse" would never forget the name of Rush:

> For from thine youth, thine eyes has wish'd to see
> The day when Afric from her chains would go,
> To test the sweets of gen'rous liberty
> And feel no more of slavery's grief and woe
> For well thou knowest that if matur'd aright
> Their gen'us equals that of skins that's white.[53]

Flattered in verse, Rush now enlisted the aid of Robert Ralston, a prominent Presbyterian merchant, who agreed to act as treasurer of the group. The work of circulating the subscription papers began in the fall of 1791. Rush tried to stay in the background, convinced that "the work will prosper the better for my keeping myself out of sight."[54] But he was hardly capable of self-effacement, and word of his role in the plans soon circulated through the city. William White, rector of Christ Church and recently appointed bishop of the Protestant Episcopal Church of Pennsylvania, accosted Rush in the street and "expressed his disapprobation to the proposed African church" because "it originated in pride." Leading Quakers also conveyed their displeasure to Absalom Jones, and the Methodist elder John McClaskey threatened to disown any black Methodist who participated in the undertaking.[55] Paternalistic Philadelphians revealed that helping their black brothers provided more satisfaction than seeing them help themselves.

Such disapprobation from Episcopalians, Quakers, and Methodists, some of whom had been active in the Abolition Society, drove home the lesson that even whites who claimed to want to befriend free blacks were unwilling to see them move beyond white control. An early historian of black Methodism, reflecting in 1867 on the final separation of Richard Allen from the white Methodist church in 1817, dwelt on precisely this point. "The giant crime committed by the Founders of the African Methodist Episcopal Church," wrote Benjamin Tanner, "was that they dared to organize a Church of men, men to think for themselves, men to talk for themselves, men to act for themselves: A Church of men who support from their own substance, however scanty, the ministration of the Word which they receive; men who spurn to have their churches built for them, and their pastors supported from the coffers of some charitable organization; men who prefer to live by the sweat of their own brow and be free."[56]

The opposition of white church leaders partially undermined the appeal for building funds. Some modest contributions were garnered, including donations from George Washington, Thomas Jefferson, and the Free African Union Society of Newport. Rush's appeals to Granville Sharp to raise money in England brought in a small amount, and Rush himself contributed £25.[57] But after six months, with money only trickling in, Jones and Allen decided to take to the streets themselves. Believing "that if we put our trust in the Lord, he would stand by us," Allen recounted, "we went out with our subscription paper and met with great success," collecting $360 on the first day.[58]

Thereafter the going got harder, and some of the early optimism began to fade. The initial subscriptions proved sufficient, however, to buy two adjacent lots on Fifth Street, only a block from the State House, for $450. But most blacks had only small amounts to contribute from their meager resources, and ten members of the African Society, including influential men such as William Wiltshire, Moses Johnson, and Caesar Cranchell, withdrew in protest at using the society's funds to purchase land for a church.[59] Most whites seem to have snapped their pocketbooks shut at the thought of an autonomous black church. White church leaders, who had initially responded to the idea of a separate black church as a piece of arrogance on the part of a people so recently released from slavery, now began calculating the effect on their own churches. "The old and established [religious] societies," Rush confided to a friend, "look shy at them, each having lost some of its members by the new association." Still, Rush did not waver in his conviction that "the poor blacks will succeed in forming themselves into a distinct independent church."[60]

Despite early difficulties, the resolve of black Philadelphians to form a separate church grew mightily in the fall of 1792 after one of the most dramatic confrontations in early American church history. A number of black leaders were still attending services at St. George's Methodist Church, where the congregation had outgrown the seating capacity. When the elders decided to expand their house of worship, black Methodists contributed money and labor to the effort. Then, on the first Sunday after the renovations were completed, the elders informed the black worshipers who filed into the service that they must sit in a segregated section of the newly built gallery. Allen later recounted:

> We expected to take the seats over the ones we formerly occupied below, not knowing any better. We took those seats; meeting had begun, and they were nearly done singing, and just as we got to the seats, the Elder said, "Let us pray." We had not been long upon our knees before I heard considerable scuffling and loud talking. I raised my head up and saw one of the trustees, H____ M____, having hold of the Rev. Absalom Jones, pulling him off his knees, and saying, "You must get up, you must not kneel here." Mr. Jones replied, "Wait until the prayer is over, and I will get up, and trouble you no more." With that he beckoned to one of the trustees, Mr. L____ S____, to come to his assistance. He came and went to William White to pull him up. By this time prayer was over, and we all went out of the church in a body, and they were no more plagued by us in the church.[61]

Many historians, assuming that the incident at St. George's took place in 1787, before the Free African Society was formed, have seen the discriminatory and insulting treatment by the elders of St. George's as the catalyst that drove Jones and Allen away from an assimilationist position within biracial churches and toward the creation of a separate black church. The black church, it is argued, had its origins in the racial segregation imposed by whites. But recently it has been shown that the confrontation at St. George's took place in late 1792, more than five years after the Free African Society was established, several years after separate black religious services were first held, and many months after Absalom Jones and others had launched the subscription campaign for a black church.[62] The St. George's incident did confirm, however, what many blacks must have suspected—that there would be no truly biracial Christian community in the white churches of the city. Allen recalled that after the incident the black leaders renewed their determination "to worship God under our own vine and fig tree" and "were filled with fresh vigor to get a house erected to worship God in."[63]

By late 1792, with money coming in only slowly, the black leaders faced the prospect that they would not be able to raise sufficient money to build their African church on the lots they had purchased. To their rescue came the unlikeliest of figures—the Welsh immigrant John Nicholson, who had blazed meteorically onto the Philadelphia scene after the war as state comptroller and high-flying speculator in western lands and wartime loan certificates. Not wholly accepted in polite Philadelphia circles and not involved in the work of the Abolition Society, Nicholson provided what none of the established Philadelphia elite would offer—a large loan to begin construction. "Humanity, charity, and patriotism never united their claims in a petition with more force than in the present instance," Rush wrote Nicholson in a letter hand-carried by William Gray and Absalom Jones. "You *will* not—you *cannot*—refuse their request for the sake of Religion & Christianity and as this is the first Institution of the kind."[64]

It took two months more to execute the mortgage and another to draw up building contracts.[65] Finally, in March 1793, with reports of black rebellion in the French West Indies reaching Philadelphia, the city's free blacks and some of their white benefactors gathered to see earth turned for the church. Allen remembered the day vividly a quarter of a century later. "As I was the first proposer of the African Church, I put the first spade into the ground to dig the cellar for the same. This was the first African Church or meeting house to be erected in the United States of America."[66]

Before the two-story brick building on Fifth Street could be completed, its humble founders had to endure additional difficulties. Like most visionaries, Jones and his cohorts had planned expansively, designing a church spacious enough to seat 800. The

Figure 9. "A Sunday Morning View of the African Episcopal Church of St. Thomas in Philadelphia" (1829). The African Church of Philadelphia, renamed the African Episcopal Church of St. Thomas, boasted a congregation of nearly 500 within a few years of opening its doors in 1794.

cost estimates for the building ran to $3,560. Even with a $1,000 loan from Nicholson, more money had to be raised. Ironically, another kind of black movement for independence undermined this attempt. With hundreds of French planters fleeing the Afro-French rebellion in Saint Domingue and streaming into Philadelphia with French-speaking slaves, many white city dwellers reneged on their pledges to the African Church in order to help the destitute slaveholders now taking refuge in their city. When Benjamin Rush sent William Gray to Baltimore to raise money from the parishioners of a church shepherded by a cousin of Rush's wife, Gray was similarly rebuffed because of the heavy claims made on white philanthropy by the influx of French sugar planters. Philadelphia's free blacks, witnessing the collection of $12,000 in a few days for the refugee slave master class, learned that even the most sympathetic white men placed the distress of white slave-owners, even those from outside the United States, ahead of the aspirations of those who had been slaves.[67]

Nicholson again came to the rescue, loaning another $1,000 in mid-August.[68] Ten days later, on a sultry afternoon, the black leaders staged a roof-raising banquet in an open field on the edge of the city. About one hundred white construction tradesmen and two of Philadelphia's most important citizens sat down at long tables "under the shade of several large trees" and consumed a sumptuous dinner complete with excellent liqueurs and melons for dessert. A company of Philadelphia's free blacks served the white diners. Then the white guests arose. About fifty blacks took their places and were waited on at a second sitting of the banquet by "six of the most respectable of the white company." In this early display of the separate-but-equal doctrine, Rush toasted "Peace on earth and good will to men" and "May African churches everywhere soon succeed to African bondage." Describing to his wife the outpouring of emotion on that hot afternoon, he wrote: "Never did I witness such a scene of innocent—nay more—such virtuous and philanthropic joy. Billy Grey in attempting to express his feelings to us was checked by a flood of tears." After dinner all the blacks converged on John Nicholson and clasped the hand of the city's helpful entrepreneur. One old man "addressed him in the following striking language: 'May you live long sir, and when you die, may you not die eternally.' " Rush vowed "it will be a day to be remembered with pleasure as long as I live."[69]

Even as glasses were raised in toast, ill fortune struck again, delaying the completion of the church for nearly a year. It came in the form of the worst outbreak of yellow fever in the history of North America. The first victims succumbed late in July 1793; within a month the fever had reached epidemic proportions. With twenty Philadelphians dying daily of the putrid fever, shopkeepers began closing their doors, and all who could afford it commandeered horses, wagons, and carriages to carry their families out of the city. Hardest hit were the laboring poor. Living in crowded alleys and courts where the fever spread fastest, they were too poor to flee, usually too poor even to pay for a doctor.[70]

By early September the social fabric of the city was disintegrating. The work of tending the sick and burying the dead exceeded the capacity of the doctors and city authorities because most nurses, carters, and gravediggers, regarding the disease as contagious, refused to go near the sick, dying, and dead. Husbands left wives of many years who were in the throes of death, parents abandoned sick children, masters thrust servants into the streets. Mathew Carey, the main chronicler of the catastrophe, wrote that "less concern was felt for the loss of a parent, a husband, a wife or an only child than, on other occasions, would have been caused by the death of a servant, or even a favorite lap-dog."[71] Hundreds perished for lack of treatment, "without a human being to hand them a drink of water, to administer medicines, or to perform any charitable office for them." By mid–September the poor were starving and the dead lay everywhere in the streets, while thousands of middle- and upper-class Philadelphians took refuge in the countryside.[72]

Into this calamitous breach stepped Philadelphia's free blacks. Benjamin Rush, who played generalissimo of the relief forces, implored Richard Allen in early September to lead his people forward as nurses, gravediggers, and drivers of the death carts. Assuring Allen that the malignant fever "passes by persons of your color," he suggested that this God-bestowed exemption from the disease laid blacks "under an obligation to offer your services to attend the sick."[73]

The Free African Society met on September 5 to consider Rush's request. Much of what had transpired in the last year might have inclined them to spurn the requests for aid—the humiliating incident at St. George's, the opposition to establishing their own church, and, most recently, the readiness of many who had signed their subscription lists to beg off in order to aid slaveowning French planters who arrived with their chattel property in tow and then attempted to overturn the state law requiring manumission within six months of any slave brought into the state. But much had also transpired that argued for committing themselves to alleviating the white community's desperate plight—the encouragement they had received in planning their church, the considerable aid of the Abolition Society, and the personal solicitation of Rush, their closest adviser.

A pamphlet written by Absalom Jones and Richard Allen after the epidemic indicates that they saw this as a God-sent opportunity to prove their courage and worth and to show that they could drive anger and bitterness from their hearts. Perhaps they could dissolve white racism by demonstrating that in their capabilities, civic virtue, and Christian humanitarianism they were not inferior, but in fact superior, to those who regarded former slaves as a degraded, hopelessly backward people. The "God who knows the hearts of all men, and the propensity of a slave to hate his oppressor," they wrote, "hath strictly forbidden it to his chosen people." Philadelphia's black Christians would act as Good Samaritans, reenacting the drama of the despised man who aided a fellow human in desperate need when all the respected men of the community turned their heads. They would succor those who reviled and opposed them because "the meek and humble Jesus, the great pattern of humanity, and every other virtue that can adorn and dignify men, hath commanded to love our enemies, to do good to them that hate and despitefully use us."[74]

On September 6, 1793, Jones and Allen offered their services to the mayor, who immediately placed notices in the newspapers notifying citizens that they could apply to Jones or Allen for aid. "The African Society, intended for the relief of destitute Negroes," writes the historian of the epidemic, "suddenly assumed the most onerous, the most disgusting burdens of demoralized whites." They nursed the sick, carried away the dead, dug graves, and transported the afflicted to an emergency lazaretto set up outside the city. Jones, Allen, and William Gray, under instructions from Rush, acted as auxiliary doctors, bleeding patients and administering purges. By September 7, wrote Rush, Jones and Gray were "furnish[ing] nurses to most of my patients." Before the epidemic ran its course, Rush's black assistants had bled more than eight hundred persons, making notes on each case for Rush as they worked through the day. At night they drove the death carts to the cemeteries.[75]

Working closely with the free blacks amid the terrifying fever,

Rush's psychological attachment to their cause reached its peak. On September 10, in a letter to his wife, he wrote of "my African brethren" and recounted how he "met a good woman of their society a few days ago at the foot of a pair of stairs. 'Hah! Mama,' said I, 'we black folks have come into demand at last.' She squeezed my hand, and we parted."[76] But within two weeks Rush's claims that blacks were immune to the infectious fever had proved a ghastly error. Seventy Philadelphians were dying each day of the sickness transmitted by the *Aëdes aegypti* mosquito, and now blacks were numerous among them. "The Negroes are everywhere submitting to the disorder," Rush wrote disconsolately on September 26, "and Richard Allen who had led their van is very ill."[77] The immunities of those descended from Africans provided only frail rather than total protection, so blacks were stricken and died at only a slightly lower rate than whites.

In the first weeks of October the disease raged through the half-abandoned city. On one day alone 119 died. Still convinced "that it was our duty to do all the good we could to our suffering fellow mortals," Jones, Allen, and the other blacks carried out their gruesome tasks. By the end of the month nearly 20,000 whites, along with the national and state governments, had fled the city, and nearly 4,000 persons, including about 240 blacks, had succumbed to the fever.[78] Not until early November, when cold weather killed the transmitting mosquitoes, did the epidemic pass.

In soliciting support in the white community, the black leaders may have expected to draw on the credit they had accumulated through their heroic efforts during the terrible autumn days of 1793. But even this altruism had to be defended, for Mathew Carey, the Irish immigrant publisher in the city, publicly vilified the free blacks for opportunistically charging exorbitant fees to nurse the sick and remove the dead. Carey's pamphlet, *A Short Account of the Malignant Fever,* itself provided a lesson in deriving profit from mass misery. Selling briskly, it went through four editions between November 14 and December 20. Carey rendered a narrative account of the holocaust, discussed the origins of the epidemic (a subject on which Philadelphia's doctors argued vociferously, in private and in print, for the rest of the decade), and appended lists of the dead.[79] But the city's saviors in Carey's account were the rising immigrant merchant Stephen Girard and other whites who organized an emergency hospital just outside the city, where they selflessly tended the sick and dying. For the black Philadelphians who drove the death carts, buried the dead, and nursed the sick in the back streets and alleys of the city Carey had few good words.

Carey's *Short Account* drew a shocked response from Jones and Allen.[80] They did not deny that some opportunistic persons "in low circumstances," both white and black, charged extravagant prices to nurse or remove the infected. This was to be expected, "especially under the loathsomeness of many of the sick, when nature shuddered at the thoughts of the infection, and the task was aggravated by lunacy, and being left much alone" with the sick. But Philadelphians should balance such stories, they argued, alongside those of the many blacks who asked no recompense at all, content to take whatever the patient thought proper to give. One old black woman, when asked her fee, answered, "A dinner master on a cold winter's day." Caesar Cranchell, a founding member of the African Society, swore he would not "sell my life for money," even though he should die, which he did in the process of tending sick whites.[81] Jones, Allen, Gray, and most other blacks had remained in the city throughout the biological terror, while nearly twenty thousand whites, including Carey, had fled. Before cold weather ended the scourge, nearly one-tenth of the black population had died, proportionately nearly as many as whites. "Was not this in a great degree the effects of the services of the unjustly vilified black people?" asked Jones and Allen.[82]

Perhaps Carey's cruel remarks on the role of the free blacks derived from the Irishman's advocacy of the large number of Hibernian immigrants flooding into Philadelphia and their lively competition with former slaves for unskilled and semiskilled jobs.[83] In the end, Carey's views did not convince the city's church leaders. On the contrary, by the time the epidemic had passed, the opposition to the African Church, except among the Methodists, seems to have dissolved.

WORK ON THE AFRICAN CHURCH, suspended for nearly three months during the yellow fever crisis, resumed in December 1793. By the end of the year workmen had enclosed the building and completed the exterior.[84] It took further fundraising and another six months to complete the interior. As workmen finished the church in the spring of 1794, Philadelphia's blacks gathered to make a momentous decision about denominational affiliation, apparently now convinced that without such a connection they would violate the canons of Christian culture. They may also have believed that affiliation was necessary to guarantee state recognition of their corporate status—without which their church property would be insecure. Whatever the reasons, a "large majority" of the black elders and deacons favored uniting with the Episcopal (formerly Anglican) church, with only Jones and Allen opting for the Methodists.[85]

The majority view is understandable for several reasons. The Methodist church had insulted Philadelphia's blacks less than two years before, and the presiding white elder remained opposed to a separate black church; he "would neither be for us nor have anything to do with us," remembered Allen.[86] Moreover, Methodism, though an evangelical and popular movement, operated under an autocratic ecclesiastical structure that permitted its congregants no voice in the pastoral affairs of their church or in the church's annual policymaking conferences.

The Episcopal church, on the other hand, had much to commend it. Its worship in Philadelphia had been theologically flexible and tinged with evangelicalism since before the Revolution, and its authority structure was more fluid than that of the Methodists. Many black Philadelphians, both slaves and free persons, had married, worshiped, and christened their children in the city's three Episcopal churches since the 1740s.[87] Furthermore, their two closest white supporters were Episcopalians—Benjamin Rush, who had converted from the Presbyterian church in 1787, and Joseph Pilmore, the former Methodist who, after returning to Philadelphia as an Episcopal priest, had ministered to the Free African Society's religious meetings.

Steadfast in his conviction that "there was no religious sect or denomination that would suit the capacity of the colored people as well as the Methodist," Allen withdrew again. He could not accept the invitation to be the minister of the church. "I informed them," he wrote later, "that I could not be anything else but a

Methodist, as I was born and awakened under them, and I could go no further with them, for I was a Methodist, and would leave them in peace and love."[88]

With Allen declining to lead them, the deacons and elders turned to Absalom Jones. He lacked Allen's exhortatory gifts, but his balance, tenacity, education, and dignified leadership all commended him. His ministrations to the sick and dying during the terrible days of the yellow fever epidemic had also brought him wide recognition in the black community. "Administering to the bodily as well as the spiritual wants of many poor sufferers, and soothing the last moments of many departing souls among his people," it was later written, "he became greatly endeared to the colored race."[89]

With Jones leading them, the elders and deacons of the African Church of Philadelphia began to formalize the union with the Episcopal church in July 1794. The black Philadelphians agreed to "commit all the ecclesiastical affairs of our church to the government of the Protestant Episcopal Church of North America." But at the same time they secured internal control of their church through a constitution that gave them and their successors "the power of choosing our minister and assistant minister," provided that members were to be admitted only by the minister and church wardens, and specified that the officers of the church—the vestrymen and deacons—were to be chosen by ballot from among members of at least twelve months' standing. Finally, only "men of color, who were Africans, or the descendants of the African race," could elect or be elected to any church office except that of minister and assistant minister. Aided by Benjamin Rush, they had contrived a formula for maintaining black control of the church while allowing for the absence of trained blacks to fill the ministry. They had "declared a conformity to our Church in Doctrine, Discipline and Worship," wrote Bishop William White, but simultaneously they had gained a promise of ordination for their leader, Absalom Jones, and preserved the all-important right of self-government.[90]

Later in 1794 the African Church—renamed the African Episcopal Church of St. Thomas—formally requested Bishop White to qualify Absalom Jones "to act as our minister." The bishop gave permission for Jones to read services, and ten months later the Episcopal Convention of Pennsylvania approved Jones's appointment. It did so, however, only after arranging a *quid pro quo* whereby it waived the Greek and Latin requirement for the ministry in exchange for the stipulation that the African Church forgo the right to send a representative to the yearly convention where church policy was set.[91]

On July 17, 1794, the African Church of Philadelphia opened its doors for worship. The published account of the dedication ceremony indicates that most of the white ministerial opposition had melted. "The venerable Clergy of almost every domination," it was related, "and a number of other very respectable citizens were present." James Abercrombie, assistant minister of Christ Church, officiated; and Samuel Magaw, rector of St. Paul's Church, gave the sermon from the text "Ethopia shall soon stretch out her hands unto God." The discourse was from Isaiah: "The people that walked in darkness have seen a great light"—the same epigram that was etched in marble above the church doors.[92]

Magaw's sermon, a perfect display of white paternalism and Christian prejudice, stressed the need for gratitude and complaisance on the part of the blacks who crowded the church. They or their fathers, he preached, had come from the heathenish lands of Senegal, Gambia, Benin, Angola, and Congo. That burden of birth had been increased by the dismal effects of slavery, which "sinks the mind, no less than the body . . . destroys all principle; corrupts the feelings; prevents man from either discerning, or choosing aright in anything." Having providentially been brought from "a land of Pagan darkness, to a land of Gospel light," these former slaves must now maintain their gratitude to the white Christians who had freed them and donated or lent money to build the church. As for their brethren still in slavery, Philadelphia's free blacks should pray—but not take action. Magaw emphasized the need for black passivity and moderation in all things and warned his auditors to suppress the pride that was on the rise among them. Instead, they should cultivate "an obliging, friendly, meek conversation." Their church, Magaw counseled, owed its existence to the benevolent action of whites.[93] That the church had been founded amid discrimination and had arisen only when free blacks defied the opposition of white churchmen received no mention.

How did black Philadelphians receive Magaw's condescending message? No documents survive that speak explicitly to this point, but indirect evidence suggests that it confirmed among many of them the wisdom of forming a black church, not only to worship God in their own way but also as a means of proving themselves and thus achieving equality and true freedom. When set alongside Magaw's advice, the thoughts of Jones and Allen, published a few months before, make clear the social and psychological struggle in which free blacks were engaged. "You try what you can to prevent our rising from the state of barbarism you represent us to be in," wrote Jones and Allen in their reply to Mathew Carey, "but we can tell you from a degree of experience, that a black man, although reduced to the most abject state human nature is capable of, short of real madness, can think, reflect, and feel injuries, although it may not be with the same degree of keen resentment and revenge, that you who have been and are our great oppressors, would manifest if reduced to the pitiable condition of a slave." This indictment of white oppression and discrediting of blacks was followed by an insistence on the capabilities of Africans and their descendants, which echoed Benezet's teachings. "We believe, if you would try the experiment of taking a few black children, and cultivate their minds with the same care, and let them have the same prospect in view, as to living in the world, as you would wish for your own children, you would find upon the trial, they were not inferior in mental endowments."[94]

One month later, Absalom Jones enunciated the alternative black interpretation of the words from Isaiah—"the people that walked in darkness have seen a great light." The "darkness" through which they had walked was not the land of their birth but the experience of slavery. And the "great light" they had now seen was the light of freedom as well as the light of Christianity. In recording the "Causes and Motives" for establishing the African church, written just one month after the church opened, Jones again expressed the growing black determination to find strategies that would promote strength, security, and a decent existence. Black Philadelphians had learned, Jones wrote, "to arise out of the dust and shake ourselves, and throw off that servile fear, that the habit of oppression and bondage trained us up in."[95] In what seems to have been a direct reference to the charges of Bishop White about black "pride," Jones continued that they wished "to avoid all appearance of evil, by self-conceitedness, or any intent to promote or establish any new human device among us." Hence they had decided to "resign and conform ourselves" to the Protestant Episcopal Church of North America.[96] Nonetheless, this was to be a self-regulated black church, as their constitution spelled out.

While St. Thomas's African Episcopal Church was being completed and its affiliation with the Episcopal church formalized, Richard Allen continued to pursue his vision of black Methodism. He convened a group of ten black Methodists, including his brother John, on May 5, 1794, to devise a plan for finding a place of worship "separate from our white brethren." Allen proposed using his own money to purchase a blacksmith's shop and haul it to a site he had acquired at Sixth and Lombard streets, only a few blocks from St. Thomas's, in the southern part of the city. Renovated as a humble house of worship, it opened its doors seven weeks later. Bishop Francis Asbury officiated at the dedication service, and John Dickens, the white Methodist elder recently assigned to Philadelphia, prayed "that it might be a 'Bethel' to the gathering of thousands of souls."[97] This marked the birth of "Mother Bethel," the first congregation of what became in 1817 the independent African Methodist Episcopal Church.

Allen and his group waited only until November 1794 to promulgate publicly the rationale for a separate church. Since "inconveniences" had arisen when they worshiped with white Methodists, they chose to gather separately from their "white brethren." Hereafter no blacks would be warned away from Methodist worship by fear of degrading treatment, and black Methodists would be able to "build each other up." In deciding on matters of governance, Allen and his first circle of church leaders struck out boldly. As a licensed local preacher, Allen was permitted to preach at the church, but he was not an ordained minister entitled to administer sacraments or marry church members. In the articles and regulations printed in 1794 he vowed to abide by "the Methodist Episcopal Church for our Church government and discipline and with

Figure 10. Richard Allen's Bethel Church, shown here with the Walnut Street Jail in the background (c. 1794), began in a blacksmith's shop purchased by Allen and hauled in 1794 to a lot on Sixth Street in Cedar Ward, the heart of the emerging black community.

her creeds and articles for our faith." However, the adopted rules of internal church governance showed that the Bethelites were intent on autonomy within the walls of their church. Only "descendants of the African race" were to be accepted as members, though they welcomed white Methodists as visitors to their classes and love feasts. Equally important, they reserved to themselves the right to nominate as ministers, for ordination by the bishop or presiding elder, any "persons endowed with the gifts and graces to speak for God," thus signaling their goal of obtaining a fully ordained black ministry. They also asserted their right "to call any brother that appears to us adequate to the task to preach or exhort as a local preacher, without the interference of the Conference or any other person or persons whatsoever."[98] Like their black compatriots at St. Thomas's, the former slaves who followed Richard Allen were maintaining their membership in the ecclesiastic polity of a white church but at the same time ensured that they could worship as they chose and under whom they chose.

Three sources that measure the response of the mass of ordinary former slaves to the establishment of St. Thomas's and Bethel indicate the emergence of a black consciousness in Philadelphia. Fragmentary membership records for the black churches, baptism and burial records that appeared in annual bills of mortality, and records of white churches show an extraordinary response by free blacks to the establishment of separate churches where they might worship, organize themselves, and develop their own leadership apart from white supervision.

In 1794, the year they were founded, St. Thomas's and Bethel recorded 246 and 108 members respectively; one year later their members had increased to 427 and 121. In addition to these 548 registered members in the two churches, "a floating congregation of at least a hundred or more persons" attended St. Thomas's, according to the church's first historian, and numerous others must have done so at Bethel.[99] The proportion of black adults who joined the church reached nearly one-third of some eighteen hundred who lived in the city in 1795—a level of church participation at least equal to that among whites in general and higher than among laboring-class whites.[100] These figures are all the more impressive given the facts that about half of the city's free blacks were living in the households of whites, many as indentured servants, and therefore were not fully free to act autonomously; that hundreds of others were French-speaking blacks, recently manumitted by their Caribbean refugee masters, who worshiped at the city's Catholic churches; and that many others were newly arrived migrants, often destitute and old, from the South.

Marriage and baptismal records also indicate that Philadelphia's free blacks warmly embraced their separate churches. A few still married in white churches and brought their children there to be baptized.[101] But whereas 15 black marriages are recorded in white church records in 1792 and 21 in 1793, only 14 can be found in 1795 and 7 each in 1796 and 1797. The strong attraction of the black churches is also apparent in the number of baptisms: from 1795 to 1802 an average of 98 a year were performed at St. Thomas's and Bethel.[102]

The independent black church movement led by Absalom Jones and Richard Allen represented the growing self-confidence and determination of the free blacks of Philadelphia by the early 1790s. In turn, these two black churches became the most important instruments for furthering the social and psychological liberation of recently freed slaves. Bishop White had been correct, though in ways he knew not, when he reacted in anger in 1791 to word that free blacks were planning their own church, charging that their plan "originated in pride." The pride was really a growing feeling of strength and a conviction that black identity, self-sufficiency, self-determination, and the search for freedom and equality in a recalcitrant white world could best be nourished in the early years of the republic through independent black action.

5. A City of Refuge

In 1799 a slave named John Joyce escaped from his mistress at West River, Maryland, and made his way north to Boston. Only fifteen years old, he signed aboard the U.S. ship *Boston* and began seven years of naval service under some of the most notable American naval officers of this era—Commodores Preble, Chauncy, Cox, and Barron. In 1806 Joyce left the sea and went to Washington, where he found work in the household of Dr. John Bullas. Marrying a servant in the same household, he fathered two children. But family life was not for Joyce, and he soon shipped out again, this time with Captain Stephen Decatur. Shortly after a voyage in Decatur's *Congress,* Joyce abandoned his wife and made his way north to Philadelphia. He boarded with a black woman in Southwark for a week, then found work on the opposite side of the city with stablekeeper Adam Guyer. After two months Joyce found new employment as a servant for a doctor in Sansom Street; eight weeks later, he was hired as a coachman for a man who soon discharged him for stealing a watch. From there he found employment as a waiter in a tavern in Laetitia Court, near Market Street in the old part of the city. Soon after this, Joyce committed a murder for which he would sacrifice his life.[1]

Joyce was atypical of free blacks in committing a capital crime, but he shared with many black Philadelphians at the beginning of the nineteenth century a background in southern slavery, a flight north, and a search for subsistence in urban places that required the acquisition of varied skills and frequent changes of residence. Among the free blacks who flocked to the churches of Absalom Jones and Richard Allen after 1794, a majority were not native

Philadelphians but had migrated to the city. Slavery was breaking up in the northern states of the new nation and in a broad zone in the upper South stretching from Delaware to northern Virginia. Thousands of those who were freed in the upper Chesapeake area, lacking the capital required to take up independent farming, set out for the coastal cities, especially those in the middle states, in quest of economic survival and a chance to start life anew.[2] Thus even as it was coming into existence the black community in Philadelphia was being remade by successions of newly arrived migrants, as would happen again and again over the next century and a half.

This migration to the cities was especially heavy in the period from the end of the Revolution to about 1815. The origins of the already free, newly freed, and fugitive slaves who reached Philadelphia in this period cannot be traced precisely, but several sources reveal the main contours of this first great movement of Afro-Americans into the northern seaboard cities. The most important evidence comes from federal protection certificates, issued to merchant seamen beginning in 1796, and from the ships' crew lists that were regularly filed with customs officers by incoming sea captains. Both sources give the birthplaces of mariners sailing out of Philadelphia.[3] Even though work at sea by its nature involved a greater degree of transiency than work ashore, these maritime records provide a valuable source for measuring the gravitational pull of Philadelphia on the rapidly growing number of free blacks who lived within the broad trading network that connected Philadelphia to New England, New York and New Jersey, the southern states, and the West Indies.

The maritime records have a special relevance because the black migration into Philadelphia, especially the long-distance migration, was dominated by males. Historians have presumed otherwise because they have assumed that the 57-43 percent imbalance of females to males indicated in the 1820 census, the first to categorize blacks by sex and age, began much earlier and is explained by the multitude of opportunities for female domestic service in the cities and the relative scarcity of jobs for men.[4] The gender imbalance recorded in 1820, however, resulted partly because males had higher mortality rates and partly because the census takers undercounted two kinds of black males in the cities: mariners, who often were at sea when the census recorder made his rounds; and fugitive slaves, largely males, who took the precaution of concealing themselves from the eyes of federal officials.[5] How seriously the census takers undercounted black males becomes evident in a set of mortality lists published in annual almanacs in Philadelphia from 1787 to 1808 by Zachariah Poulson. If accurate, these mortality bills, which tabulated burials, demonstrate that male deaths exceeded female deaths by a sizable margin in the late eighteenth and early nineteenth centuries. Even if higher male mortality rates are discounted, the result of hazardous and debilitating labor, these data indicate that more men than women came to Philadelphia in the early years of freedom, in the classic pattern of rural migration to the city. By the early nineteenth century the sex ratio, according to the mortality statistics, had nearly evened out, eliminating any demographic barrier to normal family formation.

If those who pursued a maritime calling were roughly representative of Philadelphia's free black male population in this period, only about one-twelfth of the city's black residents had been born there (Table 3). Philadelphia, then, was a city of refuge, not the place of birth of most of its free black populace. Roughly two-

Table 3. Birthplaces of black Philadelphia mariners, 1803–1821

Birthplace	1803		1811		1821	
	No.	%	No.	%	No.	%
New England	9	5.5	13	7.1	18	6.3
New York and New Jersey	34	20.7	39	21.2	56	19.7
Philadelphia	14	8.5	9	4.9	24	8.5
Pennsylvania	19	11.6	33	17.9	55	19.4
Delaware and Maryland	43	26.2	64	34.8	87	30.6
Virginia and North Carolina	16	9.9	8	4.3	26	9.2
Lower South	6	3.6	14	8.5	17	6.0
West Indies	17	10.4	—	—	—	—
Africa	7	4.3	—	—	1	0.4
Other	1	0.6	3	1.7	—	—
Total	164		184		284	

Source: Ships' crew lists, Maritime Records of the Port of Philadelphia, 1798–1860, WPA transcriptions, Library of Congress.

thirds of them came from within one hundred miles of Philadelphia. Among the slaves freed in Pennsylvania's fertile wheat lands, so many headed for the capital city that the proportion of the state's black populace living there more than doubled from 1790 to 1800, while among white Pennsylvanians the proportion living in Philadelphia increased only slightly. By 1800, black Pennsylvanians were four times as likely to reside in the capital city as were white residents of the state (Table 4). Many others came from New York and New Jersey—about 20 percent of the city's residents if the mariners' records are a reliable guide. From farther north, where the black population had always been very small, came a trickle of migrants, about 5 to 7 percent of the growing black community (Table 3).

Migrants from the South augmented the incoming tide of blacks. In the half-century after independence, Delaware, Maryland, and Virginia masters manumitted thousands of slaves, many of whom headed northward. For the first time the North Star came to symbolize freedom, and it hovered, symbolically if not geographically, over Philadelphia, the city known to many of these people as a center of abolitionism and benevolence toward free blacks.[6] Adjoining three slave states, Pennsylvania became an asylum for southern blacks, particularly after Virginia, Maryland, and Delaware removed earlier restrictions on the private manumission of slaves.[7] In Delaware, for example, the declining viability of slavery, especially in corn-growing New Castle and Kent

Table 4. Black population of Philadelphia, 1790–1820

| | | | | | % of Pennsylvania population | |
| | | | | Decadal | --- | --- |
Year	Slave	Free	Total	increase (%)	Black	White
1790	273	1,805	2,078	—	20.3	9.5
1800	55	6,381	6,436	210	43.8	10.9
1810	3	9,653	9,656	50	41.7	10.6
1820	0	12,110	12,110	25	35.5	9.9

Source: Published federal censuses of 1790–1820. Included in the city are the adjacent urbanized areas of Northern Liberties, Southwark, Moyamensing, and, for 1820, Spring Garden and Kensington.

counties, together with strong Quaker and Methodist lobbying against slaveholding, reduced the slave population from 8,887 to 4,177 between 1790 and 1810. While freeing hundreds of slaves, Delaware masters often contracted indentures for them in Philadelphia. Many other slaves, once freed, independently made their way north to Pennsylvania's capital.[8]

A smaller flow of fugitive slaves traveled along the same sea-lanes and rough roads that carried free blacks searching for opportunity. Mobilized by revolutionary ferment and attracted to a region where slavery was being abolished, they sifted into Philadelphia throughout the Federalist era. Advertisements for runaway southern slaves in this era frequently mentioned an escaped bondsman "on his way to Pennsylvania" or headed for "the Philadelphia road."[9] In the first two decades of the nineteenth century, 35 to 40 percent of all Philadelphia mariners were men who had been born in the upper South but had made their way north, and another much smaller group came from the lower South (Table 3).

The odysseys of some of these southern refugees from bondage can be followed in the Vagrancy Docket kept by the Inspectors of the Walnut Street Prison, where slaves who could not conceal their identity often found themselves. In the seven months from August 1790 to February 1791, the dockets tell of Sall, who deserted her master in Kent County, Delaware; mulatto Tobey, who ran away from a master in York, Pennsylvania; Anthony, who fled by ship from his master in Bermuda; Robert Jackson, a runaway from outside the city; Simon, who belonged to George Hacker in Sussex County, New Jersey; Christian, who escaped from St. Croix; Jonas, belonging to William Frazer of New Castle County, Delaware; Sam, who arrived on a sloop from Bermuda; Jacob, the property of Thomas Priest of Maryland; and Sam, a mulatto slave of William Traverse of Northumberland County, Virginia.[10] From the summer of 1792 to the summer of 1794, sixty-eight such runaway slaves from outside the city are recorded in the Vagrancy Docket. All but five of them were male, and of the fifty-seven whose point of origin was specified, 60 percent had fled from Delaware, Maryland, and Virginia. Most of the others came from New Jersey and New York, from the Pennsylvania countryside, or from the British West Indies.[11] From the end of the Revolution to the Civil War, Philadelphia was the destination of an endless stream of such fugitives from slavery.

In addition to manumitted slaves and those who freed themselves through flight, other groups of blacks ended up in the city by arrangement, adding to the extraordinary mélange of skin tones, speech patterns, and work backgrounds that intermingled in the decades bracketing the turn of the century. Many were sent by Quakers in southern states or the West Indies who were convinced they must free their human property but could see only disastrous results if former chattels continued to live in slave territory. In 1791 Thomas Chamberlain, a Maryland Quaker, freed seventy-two slaves, and the Abolition Society assumed the task of indenturing twenty-five of them until they reached age twenty-one.[12] In 1795 David Barclay, a wealthy London Quaker who had received a 2,000-acre Jamaica cattle plantation in payment for a debt, sent twenty-eight manumitted slaves—eleven women, two girls, five men, and ten boys—to Philadelphia, entrusting them to the Abolition Society. Arranging with Absalom Jones to house them temporarily in the African Church (later called St. Thomas's), the PAS indentured them out, each bearing the surname Barclay. Some were assigned to domestic service in the city, some to country farmers, and some to urban artisans.[13] In 1796, North Carolina Quakers sent to the city sixteen slaves who were willing to leave family behind to "flee to a city of refuge."[14] Hardly a year passed in which the Abolition Society did not arrange the passage of some group of freed blacks from the South or the West Indies to Philadelphia. In most cases, PAS members secured a contract of indenture for each of the newcomers, believing that only with a period of supervised labor could former bondspersons successfully negotiate the social and psychological distance between southern slavery and a life of freedom in a northern city.

While many newly freed slaves reached Philadelphia by arrangement, others arrived fortuitously. In 1800, 134 Africans were brought to Philadelphia by a U.S. ship that had captured two illegal slave traders off the Delaware Cape and brought the vessels into Philadelphia for condemnation in the Admiralty Court.

Shocked to see the emaciated Africans in chains and completely naked, Philadelphians quickly provided clothing and sheltered them in tents on the banks of the Schuylkill River, a mile west of the city. In one poignant scene, two of the Africans, disembarking from different ships, recognized each other as man and wife. Commemorating the ship *Ganges* that made the capture, the Abolition Society officers gave each of the Africans the surname Ganges and then indentured them out to a variety of Chester and Bucks county farmers as well as to city artisans and merchants.[15]

The Africans aboard the *Ganges* who so unexpectedly found themselves delivered from slavery in Philadelphia were greatly outnumbered by another group of Africans who never dreamed that Philadelphia would be the city of their liberation—hundreds of French-speaking blacks who entered the city from 1792 to 1798 at the sides of masters and mistresses fleeing black rebellion in the French West Indies. The refugees from Santo Domingo (then known as Saint Domingue), mostly inhabitants of the capital town of Cap Français, brought with them not only some five hundred slaves but also tales of black insurgency that sent tremors of fear among whites up and down the American seaboard. It was widely believed that the black rebellion might spread to American slaves, and it is challenging to imagine the diversity of discussions that black Philadelphians had with these newcomers as they mastered the English language.[16]

Black revolution erupted on the lush green island of Santo Domingo in 1791 after nearly two centuries of killing plantation labor had swallowed up the lives of thousands of slaves, who produced nearly half of the world's sugar and coffee. In 1792 some 28,000 free persons of color, mostly mulattoes, were brutally suppressed after attempting to wrest from the white planter class the full political rights finally guaranteed them by the revolutionary National Assembly in Paris in that year. In the summer of 1792 a massive slave uprising engulfed large parts of the island. White planters, numbering only about 35,000 among half a million slaves, desperately attempted to enlist as allies the free blacks, who were their only hope of squelching the insurrection.

The bloody sequence of events was further complicated in 1793 by an impending British and Spanish invasion of the island. Most

large slaveowners welcomed the prospect, seeing British opposition to the French Revolution as their best hope of preserving their
own regime. The final crisis came in June 1793, when free black
forces, led by Jacobin commissioners from Paris, stormed the
planter class capital of Cap Français, which was defended by white
residents, the French governor-general, and sailors from the
French fleet. When the free black soldiery appeared to be near
defeat, the Jacobin commissioners summoned thousands of slaves
from the outlying sugar plantations, offering them freedom and
pillaging rights in return for their help. Cap Français was nearly
leveled in the ensuing battle. Some 5,000 lives were lost, and
several thousand terrified white survivors, along with a small
number of well-to-do free mulattoes, fled to the French fleet, most
of them carrying only their most mobile and liquid assets—
money and slaves.[17]

Philadelphians followed reports of the French fleet as it made its
way to the American mainland in June 1793. One hundred ninety
ships, with some 4,000 white refugees, 2,000 slaves, and several
hundred free mulattoes, headed for American ports from Charleston to Boston. Philadelphians watched a fleet of ships sail up the
Delaware River in July, and by early August a relief committee in
the city had gathered nearly $14,000 for the aid of about 750
distressed white immigrants.[18] The effort to relieve the suddenly
impoverished French colonials showcased the benevolence of
Philadelphians, who opened their pocketbooks despite the relief
committee's conviction that the refugees' "prejudice & aristocracy
of colour, [was] not less absurd and prejudicial to mankind than
the heretofore French nobles [and was] the principal cause of all
the evils which now assail them."[19]

The introduction into Philadelphia of some five hundred French
West Indian slaves had manifold effects. They immediately added
French to the language of the streets and in a single stroke created
biracial congregations at the city's three Catholic churches, especially St. Joseph's. Their presence also politicized Philadelphia's
resident free blacks, for they came bearing firsthand reports of the
most extensive black revolution in two centuries of slavery in the
Western Hemisphere.

The French influx also created important new work for the

Abolition Society. The immediate issue was the status of the arriving French slaves. The slaves themselves believed they were entitled to immediate freedom under the general emancipation decree issued by the Jacobin commissioners in Santo Domingo in August 1793, an edict that was extended by the National Convention in Paris when it outlawed slavery in all French colonies on February 4, 1794. Emigré slaveowners in Pennsylvania denied that these decrees extended to slaves brought to a neutral country, however, and it was even less certain whether they applied to those brought in before the decrees were issued, which was the case with most of the arriving slaves.[20] Not at issue, however, was the provision of the gradual abolition act of 1780 that any slave brought into the state was automatically free after six months. Even before the Cap Français bloodbath, French slaveowners who had already reached Philadelphia were petitioning the legislature for exemption from the law for "their domestic Negroes." The PAS lobbied with legislators to uphold the law, and their victory meant that many French-speaking black slaves began to walk the streets of Philadelphia as free persons by mid-1793.[21] The society's officers recorded 456 manumissions of French slaves from 1793 to 1796 as French colonials continued to arrive in the city.[22] As a result, names such as Félix, Félicité, Zaïre, Alcindor, Calypso, Zephir, Victoire, Laviolet, Figaro, and Jean Baptiste came to be commonly heard throughout the city.

Seeing black newcomers arrive from so many places, many white Philadelphians in the early nineteenth century believed the flood of migrants would overwhelm them. In the popular view, most of the newcomers, brought from Santo Domingo or fleeing the South either as fugitive slaves or recently manumitted persons, seemed unassimilable because of their lifeways and their lack of education and skills. Benjamin Rush, writing in 1810, spoke of "this late great increase" of southern blacks, and was certain that the census takers in that year, who recorded a black population of 9,656, had undercounted it by several thousand.[23] In 1812 prominent citizens who petitioned the legislature estimated wildly that 4,000 fugitive slaves had taken refuge in the city. In fact the black population had grown rapidly in the 1780s: the percentage of blacks in the city's population nearly doubled by the time of the first federal census in 1790. In the 1790s the black population more than tripled, growing from about 2,000 to more than 6,000 (Table 5). However, the rate of growth fell sharply in the early nineteenth century. Anxious white Philadelphians were witnessing a steady stream of southern black migrants into their city; but if we assume that the census takers' margin of error did not change markedly, the proportion of blacks in the total populace grew only slightly after about 1800 and declined after the War of 1812 in a demographic retreat that would continue for the rest of the century.

Much of the increased flow of black migrants into eastern Pennsylvania in the early nineteenth century stemmed directly from the actions of the states of the upper South in sealing their borders against migrating free blacks and then virtually driving from their midst slaves being freed by their masters. Fearing the effect of free blacks mingling with slaves, and frenzied by the black revolution in Santo Domingo beginning in 1791, white legislators throughout the upper South clamped down on the rights of free blacks. Gabriel Prosser's revolt near Richmond at the turn of the century heightened racial tensions in the region still further and increased the incentives for blacks to migrate northward. Then, in 1806, the Virginia legislature commanded all newly freed blacks to leave the state within twelve months—an expulsion that quickly convinced most of the Old Dominion's neighbors to deny entry to free

Table 5. Racial composition of Philadelphia's population, 1780–1830

		Black			Decadal increase (%)	
Year	White	No.	% of population	Total	White	Black
1780	30,900	1,100	3.6	32,000	—	—
1790	42,018	2,078	9.5	44,096	36	89
1800	63,242	6,436	9.2	69,678	51	210
1810	82,221	9,656	10.5	91,877	30	50
1820	100,662	12,110	10.7	112,772	22	25
1830	149,140	14,554	9.8	163,694	48	20

Sources: 1780: Gary B. Nash and Billy G. Smith, "The Population of Eighteenth-Century Philadelphia," *Pennsylvania Magazine of History and Biography*, 99 (1975), 366; and Constables' Returns, 1779–80, for black population. 1790–1830: published federal censuses.

blacks, lest they inherit those proscribed by Virginia. Thus were hundreds of manumitted blacks forced onto the waterways and roads that led north.[24] As one Philadelphia black leader explained: "Pennsylvania has always been a refuge from slavery, and to this state the Southern black, when freed, has flown for safety" because he "is obliged to flee, or remain and be again a slave."[25]

MIGRATING BLACKS who entered Philadelphia society from 1790 to 1815 faced an imposing number of obstacles. Many of them lacked urban skills or were in poor health, which made the adjustment to northern city life more difficult.[26] The extreme case, one almost of misplaced benevolence, was the Barclay group, who arrived in the summer of 1795. Although David Barclay published a rosy account of how his manumitted slaves fared in Philadelphia as an abolitionist argument against the idea that slaves could not be transformed into productive citizens, the physical and psychological adjustment of these Jamaica slaves proved to be very difficult. Of the eleven women who arrived, five died within three years. Nancy, age twenty-six, lived for only two months. Patience, thirty-two, described as of a "perverse disposition, very troublesome," was soon in the Pennsylvania Hospital and died in the almshouse three years after arriving. Phillis, twenty-two, also became sick and died in the almshouse in June 1798. Nanny, twenty-four when she arrived, died in the same year. Sabina and Clarissa, forty and thirty-five, were unable to maintain themselves by 1799. The other women did better, but chronic respiratory problems, which often afflicted blacks who moved from the West Indies to a northern climate, struck down many in the group. The Barclay men fared somewhat better; only one of the five died in the first few years. For the boys, the future seemed more promising: two were bound to a blacksmith in Southwark, two to hatters, one to a house carpenter, and another to a maker of Windsor chairs. But only one with the surname Barclay had become a successful artisan in the city by the early nineteenth century.[27]

Often disadvantaged by physical problems and their rural work backgrounds, black sojourners also faced worsening economic conditions in the early nineteenth century. Most black Philadelphians, along with arriving Irish, English, and German immigrants and city-born white laborers, suffered a punishing decrease in real wages and a substantial narrowing of employment opportunities after 1799. One reason for this was the decline in wages for maritime labor, a mainstay of black employment. Mariners' wages had nearly tripled between 1784 and 1793 and remained high through the 1790s during a period of war between England and France. In the first decade of the nineteenth century, however, the seaborne commerce on which Philadelphia's economy depended collapsed as Jefferson's Embargo of 1807 and the subsequent Nonintercourse Act took effect. The ensuing decline in wages for seamen did not reverse itself until about 1830, and this difficulty was compounded by a sharp increase in the cost of living that began in the 1790s and continued until 1814.[28]

While maritime work declined, industrial growth fostered by the stoppage of imported British manufactures afforded few new employment opportunities for the black working class. The first quarter of the nineteenth century wrought a major transformation on the city's economy, as the old commercial port, where commodity production for export had been very limited, gave way to increasing industrial output. However, the new industrial entrepreneurs, founders of textile mills, machine foundries, and boot and shoe manufactories, relied almost entirely on native-born and immigrant whites, freezing the city's free blacks out of the emerging industrial economy.

The greater economic difficulties that free blacks faced after 1800 are evident in the Abolition Society's reports. The PAS noted in 1800 that some homeowning blacks had been forced to sell their property in order to pay the groundrents.[29] Its Committee on Employment, which had observed that free blacks were "universally employed" in the 1790s, began to report black unemployment in 1801, when there were 88 black applicants for work but only 52 notices of white householders for servants. In 1802 the committee reported that it could procure places for only 20 of the 102 blacks who had applied to them for work.[30]

Largely excluded from the emerging industrial sector, black newcomers in the Federalist era had to find niches in the economy where their labor was desired. Most often they found employ-

ment at the bottom of the job hierarchy as common laborers—
loading ships, digging wells, graves, and house foundations, and
toiling as sawyers, sweepers, porters, ashmen, chimney sweeps,
and bootblacks. As in the postrevolutionary decades, maritime
labor also figured importantly, with probably one-fourth or more
of the city's young black males making their living at sea for at
least a few years. The ships' crew lists for 1803 contain the names
of 309 black mariners residing in Philadelphia, and this number
remained nearly constant for the next two decades.[31] Alternating
work along the docks with shipboard labor, these black sailors,
whose average age was between twenty-seven and twenty-eight
in 1803 and just over twenty-eight in 1811, composed about 20
percent of the city's large maritime labor force. Black women
found that washing the clothes of the city's prosperous whites
provided their surest source of income. "The women," reported
the Abolition Society in 1795, though with some oversimplifica-
tion, "both married and single, wash clothes for a living."[32]

White observers, upon whose testimony historians have usually
relied, tended to notice primarily unskilled black laborers, who
undoubtedly dominated the black workforce numerically. In
1794, for example, Benjamin Rush noted that migrants from the
rural South and from across the Delaware River in New Jersey,
who were inured to agricultural labor, "are chiefly employed as
servants and sailors."[33] In 1795 the PAS reported that "some of the
men follow mechanick trades and a number of them are mariners,
but the greatest part are employed as day labourers." Five years
later the society described black employment as "various," noting
that "some are mechanics, more are waiters, a still larger number
are day labourers. The [former] slaves are generally waiters."[34]

All these reports tend to understate the ability of a sizable fraction of free blacks to secure autonomous or semiautonomous positions for themselves in the urban economy. What is as noteworthy
as the large numbers who labored at the bottom of the occupational hierarchy, where immigrant groups have always toiled, is
the number of free blacks who took up skilled trades and the many
more who launched businesses of their own. City directories that
listed black households with their occupations and addresses indicate that a sizable black professional and entrepreneurial group

Figure 11. "Negroes in Front of the Bank of Pennsylvania, Philadelphia" (1814). Like many other black laborers, sawyers did their work in public spaces and were part of the daily cross-class mingling of white and black Philadelphians in the early republic.

was taking form by the early nineteenth century. This search for self-employment probably had its source in the same impulse that had led to the creation of independent black churches—the desire to live on one's own terms and to reduce, insofar as was possible, dependency on white Philadelphians. Significantly, many of the leaders of the independent black church movement were self-employed, including most of the trustees and elders of St. Thomas's and Bethel churches.[35] Self-employment seems to have been highly prized among the first generation of freed persons, for, as Emma Lapsansky has written, it allowed "the ambitious person to maximize his income," provided status within the black community, and "offered the greatest possible insulation against the perils of white hostility."[36]

At the top of the pyramid of independently employed free blacks stood a small but influential number of black doctors, ministers, teachers, and other professionals. The German traveler Johann David Schoepf noticed black doctors in Philadelphia as early as 1784, and at the turn of the century Samuel Wilson was so highly regarded for his skill in treating cancers that white Philadelphians readily went to him.[37] By 1810 at least a dozen black clergymen and teachers taught in the schools for free blacks associated with both white and black churches. The first black teacher in Philadelphia was Eleanor Harris, an African-born former slave described after her death in 1797 as a "woman of character" and a "well qualified tutoress of children."[38] In 1816 even a black accountant, a black fencing master, and a black "intelligence officer" had found employment in Philadelphia.

The main opportunities for self-employment, however, lay in the skilled crafts, in carting, in certain kinds of personal service such as hairdressing and barbering, and in shopkeeping and trading, especially in the clothing and food trades. In the skilled crafts free blacks found an important area of enterprise. Once the black community grew to several thousand, its residents could support black shoemakers, carpenters, tailors, bakers, and a variety of others who provided skilled services and crafted articles. Some artisans were so highly regarded for their craftsmanship that whites patronized them too. The most notable was James Forten, the black sailmaker who had worked for twelve years for the white sailmaker Robert Bridges, who had also employed Forten's father, and then took over his thriving business in 1798 when Bridges retired. Business hummed so briskly at Forten's sail loft on Front Street that by 1807 he was employing a racially mixed crew of thirty men. From his enterprise came the precisely fabricated sails for many of Philadelphia's largest merchant ships.[39] By 1795 other blacks were practicing as carpenters, shoemakers, bakers, brushmakers, confectioners, ropemakers, tailors, sievemakers, and tanners. The number of skilled occupations in which blacks found places grew steadily thereafter, with black craftsmen operating in thirty different trades by 1811. Most numerous among them in that year were shoemakers (12), carpenters (16), tailors (6), and painters (4). But there were also black paperhangers, brass founders, cabinetmakers, cigarmakers, coopers, gunsmiths, hatters, jewelers, silversmiths, mastmakers, plasterers, potters, shipwrights, and wheelwrights. In 1795 the city directory listed only twelve black artisans; but this number grew to 75 by 1811 and to 105 by 1816, when about 1 of every 15 of Philadelphia's black adult males engaged in a craft (Table 6).[40]

Carting became another occupation in which free blacks secured a proprietorial place for themselves. Driving one-horse, two-

Table 6. Occupations of black males in Philadelphia, 1795–1816

Occupation	1795		1811		1816	
	No.	%	No.	%	No.	%
Proprietorial	16	2.9	81	5.7	180	11.6
Professional	3	0.6	12	0.8	10	0.6
Minor officeholder	—	—	3	0.2	2	0.1
Artisan	12	2.2	75	13.0	105	6.8
Mariner	9	1.7	49	3.5	82	5.3
Personal service	23	4.2	137	9.7	130	8.4
Unskilled	21	3.9	171	12.1	327	21.1
Unknown	461	84.5	844	62.6	711	46.0
Total	544		1,412		1,547	
Percentage of adult males in city directory		15.3		37.4		54.0

Sources: City directories of 1795, 1811, and 1816. The total number of adult males has been estimated by extrapolation from federal census data.

wheeled carts, such early teamsters were critically important to the urban economy, for they were the principal means by which commodities moved within the city. Seen everywhere around the markets, docks, and streets, the carters had to know every byway, alley, and courtyard in the growing city. They were closely acquainted with merchants, ship captains, and shopkeepers, who provided them with much of their business. At least six black carters were operating in Philadelphia by 1795, and their number grew to twenty-three in 1811 and to thirty-five in 1816. In contrast to New York City, where blacks were excluded from the tight-knit fraternity of carters, Philadelphia's ex-slaves secured a valuable place in this often remunerative calling.[41]

Providing personal service for both whites and blacks, but particularly for the former, was another main area of employment—and one that frequently offered scope for at least semi-independent activity. Almost one-fourth of the blacks listed in the directories of 1795, 1811, and 1816 made their living as barbers, seamstresses, hairdressers, coachmen, nurses, gardeners, cooks, chimney sweeps, washerwomen, and waiters. Sometimes such pursuits involved a dependency relationship with whites, as in the case of cooks or coachmen who resided in the white household and hence lived in close and continuous contact with the master and mistress of the house; but in many more cases the washerwomen, cooks, and coachmen, as well as barbers, hairdressers, and waiters, maintained their own residences and contracted their labor on their own terms.

In another area of service activity, food catering, blacks were actually the pioneering entrepreneurs. Philadelphia's Robert Bogle, a former slave who began as a waiter, was the first to hatch the idea of contracting food services at funerals, weddings, and parties. Bogle's reputation grew to the extent that by 1829, when he operated as both undertaker and caterer, he was memorialized by Nicholas Biddle, the city's illustrious financier, in *Ode to Bogle*.[42] Other free blacks followed his lead, and by the 1820s the famous catering firm of Augustine and Baptiste, founded by two of the French slaves brought to Philadelphia during the St. Domingue rebellion, was serving foreign dignitaries and wealthy Philadelphians at many lavish balls and fêtes.

Also at such gala gatherings were black musicians. John Bernard, the famous English comedian who performed in Philadelphia from 1797 to 1803, described balls "of the first respectability" where "a crew of black fiddlers provided the music." A few years later, about 1809, there arrived in the city a seventeen-year-old French-speaking black from Martinique who would become Philadelphia's most famous musician of the antebellum period. Organizing a dance orchestra, Francis (Frank) Johnson by 1819 was in demand wherever the white Philadelphia aristocracy gathered for social events. Celebrated as a keyed-bugle, trumpet, and violin player and a prolific composer of dance and martial music, ballads, operatic arrangements, and ministrel songs, Johnson was described in 1819 as "leader of the band at all balls, public and private; sole director of all serenades . . . inventor-general of cotillions." He provided most of the music at the parades and parties honoring General Lafayette when the old Revolutionary War hero visited the city in 1824, and continued a brilliant career for another twenty years. Gathered around Johnson were numerous fellow black musicians and students who established careers as performers.[43]

In retailing food and clothing and in other proprietorial enterprises such as keeping stables and boardinghouses, free blacks established themselves in increasing numbers. This kind of independent activity seems to have grown steadily in the early nineteenth century, so that by 1816 about one of every nine adult males in the city operated some kind of small business (Table 6). In food retailing blacks had established themselves just after the Revolution. Jacob Mordecai recollected in 1836 that as a schoolboy he "oft purchased tarts & molasses buns" from "aged Africans" who maintained a shop near the State House Inn on Chestnut Street and described at another location, opposite the State House, "some humble wooden sheds" where he knew "a few orderly black women whose apple & cranberry tarts & beautiful pastry exceeds any thing now to be met with."[44] Other enterprising blacks moved into the oystering trade, both catching and retailing the delicacy. No black oystermen were listed in the city directory of 1795, the first to include black residents, but entries in the early nineteenth-century directories show that this area of retailing was quickly dominated by blacks. The 1811 directory listed sixteen black oystermen, and by 1816 the number had risen to forty-four. Blacks also retailed opossums, squirrels, and racoons at the public markets, as the English traveler Charles Janson noticed in 1806. On a larger scale, Robert Montier, probably one of the former St. Domingue slaves, became one of the city's most successful bottlers of beer by 1806.[45]

Black shopkeepers and proprietors of various kinds also became numerous. In 1795, when the number of adult free black males reached about 550, only 15 shopkeepers, dealers, hucksters, master chimney sweeps, and tavern, stable, and boardinghouse keepers were listed in the city directory. By 1811, with more than 1,400 black adult males living in the city, the directory included 81 men who ran their own businesses and hence operated in a way that, though never disconnecting them from the white community, allowed them a considerable degree of autonomy and independent decision making. By 1816, the number of male proprietors had more than doubled, to 180.

A small number of black women, many of them widows, also operated their own businesses, although the vast majority of women worked as domestic laborers, and many of these lived in white households. Only seven black female proprietors were listed in the 1795 directory, but this number increased to nine in 1811 and to sixteen in 1816. Among these sixteen were five boardinghouse keepers, who furnished rooms for scores of unmarried sailors and countless weary black migrants reaching Philadelphia. Though no sources remain to shed light on these women, there is little doubt that they helped to facilitate the adjustment of black sojourners to northern urban culture. Thus, while middle-class white women began to withdraw from proprietorial work roles amid the emerging industrial economy and its accompanying doctrine of domesticity and separate work spheres, and while lower-class white women began to provide factory labor, black women were everywhere to be seen working outside the home or as proprietors of various kinds.[46]

Artisan, service, and proprietorial work roles by no means guaranteed success, but enough blacks established themselves by the early nineteenth century to create the nucleus of a black middle class. Though many were frozen in unskilled jobs at the bottom of the urban workforce largely controlled by white Philadelphians, scores of free blacks created their own work roles and thus provided themselves with decent material rewards and, equally important, space to operate autonomously. In several areas, such as oystering, driving carriages, chimney sweeping, shoeblacking, catering, and hairdressing, they developed a near monopoly. To be sure, these were occupations that in the eyes of white Philadelphians held little glamor or prospect for accumulating a fortune. But most of these occupations required a notably public kind of work in which free blacks were continuously interacting with white city dwellers of all classes. Moreover, even the most mundane of occupations, such as master chimney sweep or oysterer, sometimes proved very profitable and usually involved organizing the work of others, buying and selling, and making economic decisions—forms of social intercourse that former bondsmen and bondswomen, a few years before, would have regarded as unlikely. Even the ragman made daily decisions with existential meaning that we can only guess at—which streets to walk, when to set out, when to quit work. Though he had to endure poverty, the ragman did not have to withstand the insulting comments of a boss, maintain a schedule set by somebody else, and face layoffs during an economic downturn.

The activities of Richard Allen, best known as a religious leader but also an entrepreneur from the day of his release from slavery, exemplify the striving for economic independence within the black community. Raised as a farm slave, Allen had acquired the skills of shoemaking and wagon driving as a young man, and he added to this repertoire after reaching Philadelphia. He purchased his first piece of property, a small lot, in 1792 and in the years that followed bought and sold real estate frequently. His household almost always included several indentured servants and apprentices.[47] In the city directories and other records he was identified variously as shoemaker, bleeder, dealer, master chimney sweep, and shoe store proprietor, and it is clear that he pursued several of these occupations simultaneously while also leading the black Methodist church. In 1794 he attempted to establish a nail factory with his friend Absalom Jones, and although the project never materialized, it betokened Allen's ambitious spirit, an outlook shared by many black Philadelphians in the first generation of freedom.[48]

The overall record of black Philadelphians in securing employment and launching independent businesses emerges more clearly when compared with the performance of other immigrant groups in the city in the early years after their arrival. No lists of immigrants or former indentured servants have survived that permit exact comparison, but some insights into the relative success of blacks can be gained from considering white and black Philadelphians whose names never appeared in city directories because they never achieved success in the urban North. The casualty rate among these sojourners in the city can be derived from contemporary almshouse and vagrancy records.

The almshouse records, which have survived almost intact from the 1790s on, detail dozens of cases of black men, women, and children who were sick, hungry, and homeless. Following the clerk's entries for a single month as the almshouse manager admitted the indigent conveys the perils of urban life. On New Year's Day in 1801, Joshua Mingo was the first person admitted in the Jeffersonian era. Born in the new president's home state, he had migrated to Salem, New Jersey, where he worked for five years for a tavernkeeper. Moving across the river to Philadelphia, he became so ill with pleurisy that he could not work. Also admitted on New Year's Day was Pompey Dorus, born in Delaware and for eight years a laborer in Philadelphia. A badly ulcerated leg had so crippled him that he could not work to support himself. Rose Stevens, venereal and very sick, accompanied him into the almshouse. Three days later the manager admitted the destitute French-speaking Joseph Tomlinson, a recent arrival from Cap Français. Priscilla, only eleven or twelve, became the next inmate on January 5. Arriving from Milford, Delaware, she had been sold as a servant to a Philadelphia ship captain, who apparently turned her out into the streets. On January 9 the seventeen-year-old John Lewis, born in St. Kitts and a resident in the city only since 1799, was admitted with consumption, of which he soon died. One day later came the abandoned children of Isaac Furman, a three-year-old boy and his older sister, who was promptly bound for fourteen years to a shoemaker.[49]

Before admitting the next inmates, the almshouse manager discharged Arthur Steward, who had arrived from Virginia two years before and could not support himself. Then he arranged for the burial of Caesar Hampton, who had come north from Charles City, Virginia, eight years before to work as a waiter "to different Gentlemen" but had been out of work and was admitted with frostbitten feet. On January 27 the manager admitted Richard Grace, twenty-eight years old and from Maryland's eastern shore. Released from slavery, Grace had come to Philadelphia in 1798 and worked as a laborer; but like so many blacks moving north, he developed rheumatic fever, of which he died in the almshouse five weeks later. The month of January ended with the admission of four other inmates—Perry Black, who had arrived from Chestertown, Maryland, after being manumitted in 1796 and was badly rheumatic; Mary Jackson, eighteen, whom the manager soon bound out to a ship captain; Jonathan Lewis, a one-legged rheumatic twenty-seven-year-old born in the city; and Jacob Johnson, a freeborn mulatto from Georgetown, Delaware, who had served for seven years in the revolutionary army and was consumptive and unable to find work.

The trail of sick, broken, orphaned, and indigent continued month after month. Most of those admitted had arrived in the city within the last few years, a great many of them debilitated or chronically ill. They came to the almshouse, especially in winter, seeking free medical treatment, food, and shelter. For different people, it provided a place to give birth, a shelter for the abandoned children of impoverished neighbors, or a place to die and be assured of a decent burial. By the early nineteenth century, when they composed one-tenth of Philadelphia's population, such blacks represented about 10 to 14 percent of those taken into the house, whereas in 1788 they had made up only about 5 percent of all those admitted.[50]

Despite this increase in the proportion of black inmates in the early nineteenth century, indigent blacks were still overshadowed, both in actual numbers and in terms of their share of the population, by Irish immigrants and possibly also by English and German newcomers to Philadelphia. The "daily occurrence dockets" kept by the almshouse manager, which recorded information on the race, sex, and place of origin of all admittees, allow for some direct comparisons of the urban experience of the different groups coming to the city. Among 384 persons admitted in two winter and three summer months of 1806, English- and Irish-born persons outnumbered free blacks 107 to 54, while 26 German immigrants were admitted. In all, blacks made up only 14 percent of those admitted. Thus, although free blacks were somewhat over-represented, other immigrant groups were even more so. No records exist for this period that would permit a calculation of the percentage of Philadelphia's population born in Ireland, England, and Germany; but it is safe to assume that it was much less than 42 percent of Philadelphia's population, which was the proportion of nonblack immigrants admitted in 1806 (Table 7).[51]

In 1810, when the managers made a census of the almshouse, they found a similar composition of inmates. Blacks made up one-tenth of the inmates, almost identical with their share of the population. Fifty-five blacks were sheltered there, almost the same number admitted in the sample months of 1806. Alongside them were 166 Irish, nearly twice as many as in the 1806 sample, and larger numbers of English and Germans than four years before (Table 7). The Irish composed nearly 30 percent, and English, German, and other European immigrants constituted another 19 percent. The immigrant adjustment to urban Philadelphia was difficult for all groups in these years; but it appears that the judgment of one Philadelphia newspaper in 1797, that "the most afflictive and accumulated distress" was to be found "amongst the Irish

Table 7. Ethnicity of Philadelphia almshouse inmates, 1806 and 1810

	1806		1810	
	No.	%	No.	%
Black	54	14.1	55	9.8
Irish	89	23.2	166	29.4
English	18	4.7	46	8.2
German	26	6.8	45	8.1
Other foreign	28	7.3	18	3.2
Native-born white	169	44.0	234	41.5

Source: Daily Occurrence Dockets, 1806, 1810, Archives of the City and County of Philadelphia, City Hall Annex, Philadelphia.

Emigrants and the French Negroes," continued to be true, at least for the Irish, into the early nineteenth century.[52]

Another indication of the ability of free blacks to adapt to urban life can be found in the vagrancy records. Of all migrant groups entering the city, blacks were the most vulnerable to arrest for vagrancy because Philadelphia was the destination of many runaway slaves, and dark skin gained one no favors in an era of increasing hostility toward blacks. However, among two samples of vagrants, 452 arrested from May 1790 to May 1791, and 81 apprehended in June and July 1804, 17.7 and 12.3 percent, respectively, were black.[53] If those arrested as suspected runaways are subtracted, blacks represented no more than their share of the population. Considering the truncated shape of the black social pyramid, with its relatively small upper and middle classes, merely to have the same proportion of vagrants as did the wealthier white community was noteworthy.

The crime rate of free blacks also provides a glimpse of the changing conditions of life in Philadelphia in the early nineteenth century. Even the most fervent white abolitionists thought that it would take years of moral tutelage and exceptional effort by former slaves to reform their morals and work habits so as to resist the temptations of crime. However, records of the Philadelphia courts show that in the 1790s, free blacks avoided crime to a greater extent than white immigrants and other Philadelphians of the same economic position. The census takers in 1790 found only 5 black inmates among 191 prisoners in the Walnut Street Prison, which more than confirmed the Abolition Society's view a few years later that "in point of morality" the free blacks of the city were "equal to those Whites who are similarly situated as to employment and means for improvement."[54] Among 675 prisoners presented for trial in Philadelphia from 1790 to 1792 and among 3,704 presented from 1798 to 1802, blacks represented only 7.6 percent and 3.5 percent of the cases, respectively.

Though low in the 1790s, the black crime rate began to soar in the early nineteenth century. In 1810 the census indicated that 45 percent of the 365 prisoners in the Walnut Street Prison were black, and six years later blacks represented 43 percent of convicted felons.[55] Especially when contrasted with the almshouse

admission data, this high percentage of blacks in the prison population is at first puzzling. An analysis of the crimes committed,
recorded in the Court Sentence Dockets, supplies at least a partial
answer. A large majority of the blacks sentenced to prison were
convicted of petty theft, usually clothing, food, and small salable
property—the kind of crime traditionally associated with poverty.
Twenty-two of twenty-eight sentences in 1805 were for larceny,
and two others were for burglary and robbery. A decade later the
court recorded fifty-six sentences of blacks, of which forty-eight
were for larceny, three for receiving stolen goods, and two for
burglary.[56] Black inmates, the newly formed Prison Society found
in 1816, were "seldom convicted of the higher order of crimes"
that led to the incarceration of whites—assault, homicide, and
burglary.[57] Moreover, most of the crimes were committed by
blacks who had migrated to the city—89 percent of blacks sentenced in 1805, and 87 percent in 1815.[58] It appears that many
destitute migrants and others sorely in need, especially during the
severe winter months, regarded petty theft as a better strategy for
survival than applying to the almshouse for relief. For those who
had fled slavery, of course, to apply for aid to public officials, who
might return them to bondage, was unthinkable, so petty theft
supplied a strategy for subsistence until employment could be
secured.

WHILE SECURING WORK and building careers, black Philadelphians continued the process of family formation that they had begun after the Revolution. In general, each new wave of ex-slaves
entering the city, and many persons in each new group of city-
born blacks coming of age, had to repeat the cycle of those who
had first been emancipated—initially indenturing themselves or
hiring out to white families if they could not maintain an independent existence; then extricating themselves from white households, often by stitching together composite households of relatives, friends, and boarders; and finally, as they were able,
establishing single-family households. Some families, the Abolition Society reported in 1801, "were found supporting their aged
parents and grandparents . . . and others providing for orphan and
destitute children."[59] Although systematic records are not avail-

able to reconstruct household composition, there is little reason to believe that such strategies, typical of the urban laboring class, did not continue.

As it had before 1790, the PAS facilitated the indenturing of a small number of black children of the "respectable poor" each year. Its Committee of Guardians, established in 1790, gained a reputation in the black community for finding advantageous places for black youngsters. Thus, Abraham Willing sought a place for his daughter Nancy, age six and a half, in January 1791. Chloe Sides asked for a "suitable place" for her son Thomas, whom the society placed with a Darby Township family a few miles from Philadelphia in the same year. In 1794 Lydia York wanted a place for her niece Hetty, the daughter of her sister who had died in Virginia, leaving Hetty to her care.[60] James Venables, sixteen, requested "a place to learn the smith's business" and was indentured to Conrad Keller for five years to learn tinplate working. John Williams gave power of attorney to the society to bind out his two children, ten-year-old Hannah and six-year-old Charles, in 1802.[61] By monitoring the conditions under which indentured children lived, the PAS established its credibility with black parents, who in small numbers brought their children to be bound out throughout the late eighteenth and early nineteenth centuries.[62]

The indenturing of children, often required by economic necessity, had its perils, and black parents frequently called on the Abolition Society for help in rescuing a child from harsh treatment or even the danger of being sold into slavery. Samuel Allen sought the society's aid in 1798 in obtaining the release of his son John, a lad of twelve. Allen had apprenticed the boy at an early age to one of the city's leading black citizens, Doras Jennings. But when the apprenticeship expired, the young Allen apparently set out from the city, only to be picked up at New Brunswick, New Jersey, sixty-five miles north of Philadelphia, on suspicion of being a runaway slave. Sold at public auction to a doctor, who in turn sold him to another physician, John Allen was in danger of losing his claim to freedom. The PAS worked for three and a half years to recover the boy and finally concluded that the only way to save him from slavery was to buy his indenture.[63]

In another case, Hagar Stevenson applied to the society's Com-

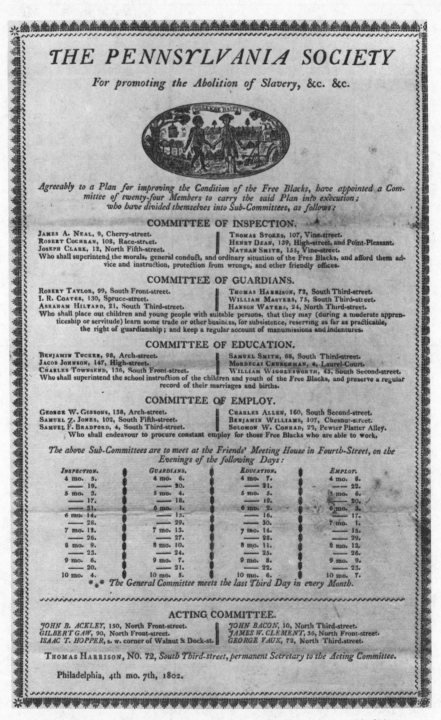

Figure 12. Broadside, July 4, 1802. For years the Pennsylvania Abolition Society distributed broadside advice throughout the black community. The inscription "Work & Be Happy" on the emblem typifies the middle-class moral exhortations of the PAS.

mittee of Guardians in 1799 on behalf of her two sons, whom she had indentured to William White and Caesar Wetherington, well-known figures in the black community. Instead of training the boys to a trade and giving them schooling, their mother complained, their masters had hired them out as chimney sweeps. With the society's intervention, a more suitable place was found for one of the boys and the other was promised training in domestic service by his black master.[64]

Though residence in a white household, often under an indenture lasting for years, provided the intermediate step between subservient and autonomous existence for many freed blacks, a growing proportion of them gradually worked their way free of such dependency. In 1790, half of the city's free blacks had lived in white households. Ten years later, census takers found 56 percent living in white households, an increase almost certainly caused by the indenturing of hundreds of French West Indian slaves after their release from bondage between 1792 and 1798. But by 1810, blacks living in white households had dropped sharply, to 39 percent of the entire black population, and in 1820 less than 27 percent of Philadelphia's blacks (and only 22 percent of males age fourteen and older) resided with a white family.[65]

In a culture that designated the family as the bastion of virtuous and orderly behavior, and as the social unit from which viable communities must be constructed, black Philadelphians again proved their mettle in making the transition from slavery to freedom. Not until 1820 did census takers enumerate black citizens by age and sex, thus permitting systematic analysis of black household composition and family formation. However, the enumerators did inscribe the name of each head of household as they made their way along the streets, and this information, along with the entries in the city directories, reveals that the male-headed household was the norm from the very beginning in Philadelphia's free black community. In 1790, 13.7 percent of black households for which the census takers recorded the name of the household head were directed by a woman, just a fraction more than the 13.3 percent of female-headed white households. By 1800 the proportion of black households headed by a woman had declined to 10 percent, almost one-third lower than the 14.4 percent recorded for whites. A decade later the percentage had risen to 12.1 percent but remained below the 15.5 percent of white households headed by a woman. Only in the second decade of the nineteenth century, when the proportion of female-headed households throughout society began a decades-long increase, did the proportion of black households directed by women outstrip the number of female-headed white households (Table 8). When one takes into account the lower-class position of most black males, whose work conditions caused higher mortality rates than for the white population in general, it appears that even as late as 1820 black families were more successful than white families in maintaining the traditional male head of household. In Cedar Ward and in Southwark, where the concentration of white and black laboring-class families allows a racial comparison among people of similar class status, female-headed families were consistently more common among white than among black households, although the gap between the two groups had almost closed by 1820.

In general, households headed by women were small, so it appears that the vast majority of black children in this era, possibly as many as 85 to 90 percent, grew up in male-headed, and in most cases two-parent, households.[66] Slavery had damaging effects on the black family, particularly when masters separated husband and wife or parent and child by selling one or more family members. But so far as the admittedly imperfect records will allow us to determine, black sojourners in Philadelphia constructed and reconstructed families very quickly and maintained them through the first quarter of the nineteenth century with at least as great success as white families of the working class.

Table 8. Percentage of female-headed households in Philadelphia, 1790–1830

Year	White	Black
1790	13.3	13.7
1800	14.4	10.0
1810	15.5	12.1
1820	18.1	20.5
1830	18.7	24.2

Source: Tom W. Smith, "The Dawn of the Urban-Industrial Age: The Social Structure of Philadelphia, 1790–1830" (Ph.D. diss., University of Chicago, 1980), p. 178, table 65.

Free black Philadelphians formed independent households only by cautious and sometimes painful steps. They married later than white Philadelphians, often because they were indentured until their middle to late twenties.[67] Frequently they joined together to form extended or augmented households, taking in relatives and friends who had arrived recently from the countryside and were emerging from slavery with few assets and little knowledge of urban life. Evidence of this doubling up survives in the city directories, which listed free blacks of different surnames living at the same address, and in the manuscript reports of a few census takers who made notes on the particular living arrangements along the streets they walked. In Gaskill Street, in the southern part of the city, for example, shoemaker Richard Bennett, mariner John Bahimy, and laborer Joseph Reed shared a house in 1811. Down the street washerwoman Phillis Exeter and porter Charles Brown lived in the same dwelling. The census taker in 1810, making his way through Mulberry Ward in the northern part of the city, found Amy Harrison with a family of five and James Limbo with a family of six sharing a house at 257 Race Street. The families of Robert Mount and Robert Lewis, thirteen people in all, doubled up in a house in Pennington Alley, and in Crown Alley, where black families predominated, Jacob Turner and William Rose's families divided space, as did the families of Tobias Clarkson and Robert Green next door.

Often the way to property ownership lay in acquiring a house, renting part of it to another family, and building small structures in the rear that could also be rented out. At 108 Cherry Street in 1810 fruit store owner Nathaniel Gray, with a family of five, shared a house with waiter Daniel Man and his wife. In the back house lived Elizabeth Griffith, a whitewasher, with her family of five, and Mary Galloway, a seamstress with a family of four. Nineteen people lived at one address in Webb's Alley, in the northern part of the city: mariner Raymond Andrew, with five in his family, shared the front house with James Robert, a coachman with a family of six. In the rear, Cato America and his family of eight occupied a small structure.[68]

As they worked themselves free of white households and established independent residences, black Philadelphians began to arrange themselves spatially in the city in new ways. In the days of slavery Afro-Americans lived with or were hired out to masters who lived in every part of the town. In the first decade of freedom this scattered residential pattern continued because nearly half of the locally manumitted or incoming former slaves took up employment or were indentured in white households spread throughout Philadelphia but concentrated especially in the commercial core of the city that stretched from Spruce to Vine streets along the Delaware River, extending west as far as Tenth Street (see Map 1). This dispersed pattern of black residence continued into the 1790s because free black families, such as Richard Allen and Absalom Jones, had purchased land and houses in the old commercial district of Philadelphia. Hence almost one-third of the 169 free black families in 1790 lived in the city's commercial core, where most of Philadelphia's merchants, insurance brokers, banks, and fashionable shops could be found.[69]

In the 1790s, as large numbers of blacks formed families and made independent decisions about where to locate, the old dispersed residential pattern began to change. Free black families now began clustering in two areas, one in a long-settled part of town and the other in a new, expanding part of the city. The old area, to the north of the commercial core, spread through North and South Mulberry wards, a relatively poor district with a concentration of cheaply built small houses occupied by a mélange of petty retailers, artisans, mariners, and laborers, many of them immigrants from Germany and Ireland. Located between Arch and Vine streets west of Fourth, these wards attracted about 30 of the city's 169 black households by 1790, while another 32 families lived in the Northern Liberties, just outside the city proper but contiguous to North Mulberry ward.

The other area into which free black families began to move was on the south and southwestern edge of the city. Comprising Cedar, New Market, and Locust wards and Southwark, a shipbuilding and river-oriented suburb, much of this area as late as 1785 had been open land. But within a few years developers began laying out new streets and erecting cheap housing to accommodate the city's booming population. By 1790 some fifty-six black households had established themselves in the area, the advance guard of what would soon become a huge movement of black

Philadelphians thither. A little less than one-third of black families were dispersed throughout the rest of the city.

In the three decades after 1790 several major shifts occurred in the residential patterns of the thousands of free blacks who formed families and made decisions about where to live in Philadelphia. The commercial core of the city became an area almost exclusively for white families, although, as befitted their higher economic and social status, their houses contained a disproportionate number of live-in free black servants. The number of independent black families in this central part of the city declined between 1790 and 1800 and grew only modestly thereafter, so that by 1810 only 64 black families lived among 3,745 white households in Walnut, Chestnut, High, Lower Delaware, Upper Delaware, North, Middle, South, and Dock wards. This area of Philadelphia quickly became a place for free blacks to work for whites but not to live autonomously among them (Map 1).

With the commercial core of the city becoming a white preserve, free black families moved to the periphery. This growing residential segregation was as much a matter of class as of race; laboring-class Philadelphians of all hues were being pushed outward as the city expanded in the nineteenth century.[70] The northern and southern edges proved equally attractive to free black families at first. This was apparent at the time of the devastating yellow fever epidemic in 1793, when a special committee made a house-by-house survey of every street, courtyard, and alley in the city and suburbs to determine the geographic pattern of mortality and to count how many white and black families had fled to the countryside or remained in the city. Along the narrow alleys and in the crowded courtyards where inferior housing had been constructed, blacks were almost equally divided between those living north of Market Street, the main east–west corridor dividing the city, and those living south of this busy thoroughfare. Nearly equal numbers of black families also dwelt on the city's northern and southern perimeters—258 in Southwark and 233 in the Northern Liberties.[71] Seven years later, at the time of the second federal census, 244 independent black families were found living in the northern sector of Philadelphia and 261 in the southern district.

In the first decade of the nineteenth century this roughly equal

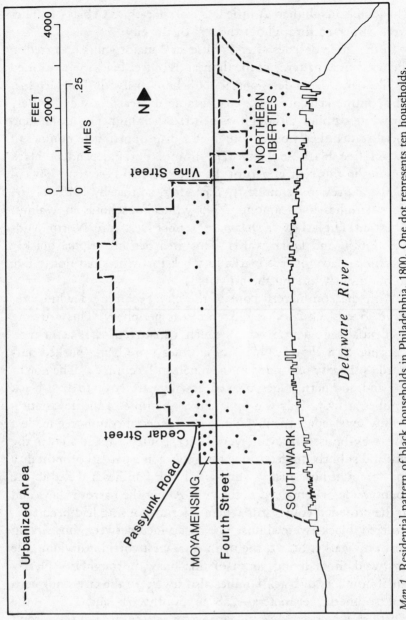

Map 1. Residential pattern of black households in Philadelphia, 1800. One dot represents ten households.

distribution underwent a dramatic change, with the southern part of the city exerting a magnetic pull on the hundreds of new families that were forming and looking for places to live. From 1800 to 1810, black households in North and South Mulberry wards and in the Northern Liberties increased from 244 to 316; but on the other side of the city the number of black families shot up from 261 to 714. Streaming into the area, often with the skimpiest resources, they took up residence in housing that was sometimes substantial but was usually, as one observer described it, no more than "cabins," "sheds," and "mean low box[es] of wood."[72] This "Cedar Street corridor" of black life, as Emma Lapsansky has called it, grew so rapidly in the early years of the nineteenth century that by 1810 it contained nearly two-thirds of all Philadelphia's black families, and by 1820 three-quarters (Table 9 and Map 2).[73]

Although it is difficult to weight precisely the factors involved in this sudden shift of residential patterns, it appears that economic and cultural forces were working in tandem. In part the movement of black families into the southern section was dictated by the decisions of Philadelphia's land developers, who engineered the construction of cheap tenements on both the northern and southern sides of the city but concentrated especially on Cedar and Locust wards and in West Southwark and Moyamensing. But also of great importance was the presence in this area of the independent black churches founded by Absalom Jones and Richard Allen. Finding land available at a price they could afford, both men had purchased property in the early 1790s within a few blocks of each other in the southern part of the city. St. Thomas's African Epis-

Table 9. Residential patterns of black households in Philadelphia, 1790–1820

Area	1790		1800		1810		1820	
	No.	%	No.	%	No.	%	No.	%
Northern sector	62	36.7	244	45.6	316	28.9	291	20.7
Southern sector	56	33.1	261	48.8	714	65.2	1,055	75.1
Commercial core	51	30.2	30	5.6	64	5.9	58	4.1
Total	169		535		1,094		1,404	

Source: Manuscript federal censuses of 1790, 1800, 1810, and 1820.

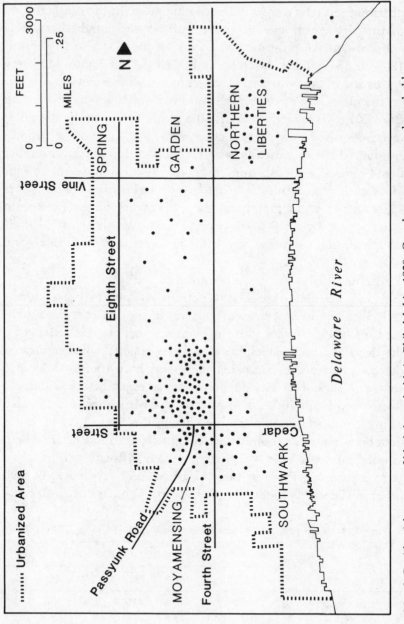

Map 2. Residential pattern of black households in Philadelphia, 1820. One dot represents ten households.

copal Church rose on the west side of Fifth Street, between Spruce
and Walnut, on the southern edge of Locust Ward. Allen located
his Bethel African Methodist Episcopal Church even closer to the
city's southwestern perimeter, on the east side of Sixth Street
between Pine and Lombard streets, in Cedar Ward. Once the two
black churches opened their doors in 1794, the area developed a
special attractiveness. As vital centers of black community life, the
churches formed the basis for neighborhoods. Once this formation of neighborhoods began, the area exerted a strong pull on
those who were working their way free of white households or
arriving in the city.

Although two broad areas attracted most black families, no
segregated black community emerged. Typically, substantial
houses lined the major thoroughfares while courtyards and alleys,
cutting between these streets, sheltered lower-class blacks and
whites in small, humble buildings. Neighborhoods remained
mixed by race and occupation. Yet the movement toward a racially and class segregated city had received a strong impetus as
builders constructed primarily cheap housing in new parts of the
city and black families sought the security and feeling of solidarity
that came with residential clustering.[74]

Some sense of these emerging neighborhoods, where free black
families mixed extensively with white artisans, laborers, aspiring
professionals, and sea captains, can be recaptured from the city
directories, which gave names, addresses, and occupations for a
large part of the city's householders. Gaskill Street, a narrow street
running only three blocks from Second to Fifth between Cedar
and Lombard, had only one black household indicated in the 1793
yellow fever survey, only two listed in the 1795 directory, and
only three recorded in the directory of 1811. But five years later
twenty-four black families were spread along Gaskill, twenty-two
of them in the block between Third and Fourth streets. All but
two of the families lived on the north side of the street, perhaps
because they found it possible to buy property there from one of
the developers building houses in this part of town.

The twenty-four black families on Gaskill Street in 1816 lived in
a neighborhood that formed a nearly perfect cross-section of Philadelphia's industrious middle and lower classes. On a daily basis,

Figure 13. "The Accident in Lombard Street" (1787). Lombard Street, depicted here with black chimney sweeps in the foreground, became a main artery of the Cedar Ward black community.

black families encountered white neighbors (who still outnumbered them by two to one), who were sawyers, carpenters, mariners and sea captains, coopers and cabinetmakers, riggers, glovers, accountants, news carriers, painters, mastmakers, teachers, turners, shoemakers, coachmakers, and two constables and a deputy turnkey. The black families on Gaskill Street earned their livelihood in humbler ways. Among them were four mariners, two sweepers, two porters, two sawyers, two shopkeepers, and one dealer, porter, sailmaker, harnessmaker, shoemaker, hatter, washer, waiter, and widow. Two of the houses on Gaskill Street contained both black and white residents, and at two other addresses white families lived in the front house with a black family occupying a small structure in the back. If black families doubled up, so too did white families. At 96 Gaskill Street the widow of Samuel Thompson shared the front house with Ruth Little, another widow, and the cabinetmaker Anthony Lemon. In the back, four white tradesmen—oak cooper Peter Connie, shoemaker John Hayes, mariner Anthony Marara, and rigger Daniel Marks—shared space with John Tusan, a black waiter.

Whereas Gaskill Street represented the racially mixed neighborhoods taking form on the northern and southern edges of the city, Middle Alley typified the creation of nearly all-black pockets sprinkled around Philadelphia. In 1811, fifteen families resided on Middle Alley, running east and west for a single block between Sixth and Seventh streets; in 1816 the number had increased to nineteen, but by then only three white families lived there. The occupations of the black residents indicate that Middle Alley housed families hovering much closer to the poverty line than those on Gaskill Street. Among the black residents were six laborers, two carters, two cooks, two washerwomen, a porter, a sawyer, a baker, a dealer, a painter, a farrier, and a waiter. Of the three white households on the alley, one was headed by a carter and the other two by women—one a widow and the other an Irish mantuamaker.

As Philadelphia grew rapidly in the early nineteenth century, becoming a city of 112,000 by 1820, the contours of the free black community took shape. The Delaware River port had served as a catchbasin for a broad region, reaching even to the West Indies. Arriving in Philadelphia from a multiplicity of regions, free black men and women with various backgrounds reshaped their working lives, formed families, created neighborhoods, and, through a thousand individual acts, become part of the fabrication of a community. As in all places where immigrants gathered, individual success came slowly even to the hardiest and most talented, and always it was tempered with numerous cases of misfortune and human failing. In addition, the fact that Philadelphia was continuously receiving new drafts of migrants made the formation of a black community difficult. Nonetheless, free blacks, whether older residents or newcomers, whether freeborn or former slaves, saw in Philadelphia a city of refuge; hence, despite the disabling effects of slavery and the many obstacles they faced, they applied themselves to establishing the social, religious, and political ligaments of community.

6. Establishing the Color Line

IN JUNE 1792, when the wife of the black fruitseller William Gray died suddenly, hundreds of Philadelphians of both races followed the funeral procession, led by two of the city's well-known Episcopalian clergymen, to the Potter's Field. Gray had played a leading role in organizing the African Church of Philadelphia in 1792, and in the next year he would gain wide respect for selflessly attending suffering whites during the dreadful yellow fever epidemic. Both the *Federal Gazette* and the *Independent Gazetteer* applauded the "pleasing indifference to complexion" demonstrated by the white neighbors and friends of the Grays, "notwithstanding all the persecution to which they [the blacks] have been exposed by the *less humane*." For some Philadelphians, the interracial concourse that paid homage to the much-esteemed Mrs. Gray represented "a happy presage of the time, fast approaching, when the important declaration in *holy writ* will be fully veryfyed that 'GOD hath made of one blood, all the nations of the Earth.' "[1] Benjamin Rush, also in attendance at the funeral, noted in his commonplace book that the sight of whites attending a black funeral "was a new one in Philadelphia" and one that augured well for the breaking down of "the partition wall which divided the Blacks from the Whites." Perhaps the dawn was breaking, mused Rush, on the day when whites and blacks would join in union "as brethren and members of one great family."[2]

The early years of the nineteenth century, a period of pell-mell growth in Philadelphia, shattered the hopes of those who had believed they were approaching a new era of racial unity. To their dismay, hostility against free blacks, always present in some quarters, began to grow in the center of American humanitarian reform. By the time Jefferson and Madison had completed their presidencies, Philadelphia had become a city of rising racial tension and sporadic violence rather than a locus of comparative interracial harmony. For their part, free blacks, living amid hardening white attitudes and worsening economic conditions, hurried the process of building a community, coping in their own ways and through their own institutions with their white neighbors, though sometimes divided among themselves.

RACIAL TENSION increased after 1800 in part because of the changing composition of the black populace. Although the proportion of blacks in Philadelphia rose only slightly in the early nineteenth century, white residents believed the city was being swamped by rebellion-prone and indigent dark-skinned newcomers. Lower-class white Philadelphians frequently found themselves mingling in densely settled neighborhoods with freshly arrived blacks who displayed southern speech patterns and southern ways. Usually lacking urban skills and formal education, these weary migrants often came bearing the marks of slavery—broken families, poor health, and psychological disorientation. Some were scooped up by the sheriffs for vagrancy, and it must have been clear to city officials that a new type of migrant was entering the city when they asked the names of blacks they apprehended and got such replies as "Come-today & Go-tomorrow" and "Nobody."[3]

If many white Philadelphians developed an image of a city swarming with dark-hued, impoverished, and criminal persons, it was partly because the number of black wanderers in the streets, paupers in the almshouse, and prisoners in the penitentiary did in fact rise sharply in the early nineteenth century. It mattered little that the immigrant Irish were the most destitute of Philadelphia's residents or that blacks were usually incarcerated only for petty theft. What mattered was that better-off white Philadelphians could visually discern a change in the makeup of the free black community, and white laboring-class Philadelphians felt themselves increasingly in competition for jobs with free blacks. Few were prepared to sympathize with former slaves driven northward by white racial hostility in the South or to identify with the struggles of these migrants who hoped Philadelphia would be a city of refuge. Surface impressions, not discussion of the eddies and crosscurrents of change, shaped public opinion; and the changing image of blacks also weakened confidence among upper-class white Philadelphians that in their city former slaves could become respectable citizens and thus dissolve white prejudice.

Adding to the negative image of free blacks that developed in Philadelphia was the widespread fear brought about by the black rebellion in Santo Domingo. Continuing reports of bloody insurgency on the island, along with the arrival in American ports of many slaves in the tow of their fleeing French masters, filled the minds of many whites with visions of black rebellion spreading all over America. With southern states barring the entry of free blacks from the West Indies and calling for the deportation of slaves previously brought in from the Caribbean, northern whites imagined their communities being invaded by unacculturated blacks bent on racial revenge.[4]

Although the issue of slave rebellion was largely irrelevant in Philadelphia, where by the late 1790s all but a handful of slaves had been freed and French émigrés were obliged by state law to free their slaves within six months of arrival, the issue of black resentment leading to violent behavior was highly pertinent. Beginning in 1793, when a slave set a fire in Albany, New York, that nearly leveled the town, many whites in northern cities began to fear that the contagion of liberty originating in Santo Domingo was converting all blacks, slave and free, into internal enemies. By 1796, when a black woman in Philadelphia was arrested for setting her master's house on fire in retaliation for brutal treatment, it seemed that conflagrations were breaking out everywhere along the seaboard.[5] Reflecting on the black arsonist in Philadelphia, Elizabeth Drinker connected her incendiarism to "repeated attempts . . . made by individuals to burn the town of Baltimore." Like many other white urban dwellers, she trembled at the report that a conversation had been overheard between two French and three American blacks about torching the urban centers of slaveholding America from north to south. An attempt to disprove the report by "A CITIZEN but no Alarmist," who complained that the story of the plot "has been servilely copied into every newspaper," had little effect.[6] Two months later, Drinker reacted to newspaper reports of fires in New Haven, Schenectady, Waterford, Boston, Hartford, New London, Norwich, Elizabethtown, Charlotte, Williamsburg, and Norfolk. "Never since the existence of the world," she exclaimed, "has any nation witnessed the devastations of fire in so striking a manner as we do at present."[7] Whether the primary suspects were white or black, rumors spread that the blazes were the vicious work of "some of those missionaries of hell who have long made the southern States the scene of their incendiary efforts."[8]

How touchy white Philadelphians had grown on the matter of black rebelliousness became apparent in the summer of 1798, eighteen months after the wave of arson had alarmed city dwellers from New England to Georgia. Following the British evacuation of Port-au-Prince, the last props of the French slave system in Santo Domingo fell, prompting several thousand French families, many with slaves, to leave the island. Two shiploads landed at Philadelphia in mid-June, and at the end of the month other vessels arrived at the Delaware Capes. Concerned about the role hundreds of French royalists might play if the threatened war between America and France materialized, and not eager to admit another wave of French-speaking blacks as in 1792-93, Governor Thomas Mifflin prohibited the landing of "any French negroes" and requested authority from President Adams both to stop the landing of the French blacks in adjacent states and to prevent their masters from entering Pennsylvania as well.[9] For the first time, Pennsylvania had attempted to erect a barrier on its borders against incoming blacks.

The governor's order was barely a day old when rumors swept Philadelphia that the royalist émigrés from Santo Domingo and hundreds of their slaves were breaking out of the quarantine imposed on ships entering Delaware Bay. The officer in charge of Fort Mifflin, downriver from Philadelphia, relayed the story that about 250 to 300 blacks, "well-armed, trained to war," and who "know no laws and count their lives for nothing," were about to pour ashore with their masters and march through New Jersey to

Philadelphia. The fear of marauding blacks quickly dissipated when it became clear from the French émigrés' letters to the Philadelphia press that only 55 slaves were aboard, that none of them were armed or had ever carried arms, and that their masters were no different from earlier slaveholders driven out of the French Caribbean islands by the intensity of black rebellion there.[10]

Although the momentary crisis over the landing of armed French blacks quickly disappeared, fear of black militancy re-emerged two years later when Gabriel Prosser, a slave in Richmond, Virginia, organized a full-fledged rebellion that he hoped would trigger slave revolts throughout the South. Although Richmond authorities stepped in to prevent the revolt, it was widely believed that the spirit of rebellion, born in Santo Domingo and nurtured by the Jacobin radicalism of the French Revolution, was still spreading and would leave untouched no part of the black population, enslaved or free.[11] In 1804 white Philadelphians saw concrete evidence that the virus of rebellion was spreading when several hundred young blacks commemorated the twenty-eighth anniversary of American independence in their own way. Assembling in Southwark on the evening of July 4, they formed themselves into military formations, elected officers, and then, armed with bludgeons and swords, marched through the streets. Whites who crossed their paths were subjected to rough treatment, and at least once they entered the house of a hostile white and pummeled him and his friends. On the evening of July 5, the militant young blacks gathered again, terrorizing those whom they encountered, "damning the whites and saying they would shew them St. Domingo."[12]

Amid growing white resentment and fear of blacks, the Abolition Society redoubled its efforts. Rather than attempting to convince white Philadelphians that the vast majority of the city's blacks were anything but angry arsonists, the all-white PAS exhorted free blacks to conduct themselves so impeccably as "to do credit to yourselves, and to justify the friends and advocates of your colour in the eyes of the world." In 1795 two members of the Abolition Society, working with black leaders, spoke to an assembly of some one thousand free blacks at the Quakers' Arch Street meetinghouse. The next year the PAS issued a broadside laying down nine rules of conduct that stressed churchgoing, educating the young, temperance, frugality, respectful behavior, and avoidance of "frolicking and amusements." The society also convened a large public meeting of free blacks, where the broadside was read aloud and blacks were besought "to reflect it is by your good conduct alone, that you can refute the objections which have been made against you as rational and moral creatures."[13] To reinforce such advice, members of the Abolition Society resumed the house calls that Quakers had initiated in the 1780s, going especially into the Southwark district, where free blacks were thickly settled, to warn against "disorderly meetings" and to give "friendly admonitions against such improprieties in their conduct." Hereafter the Abolition Society would issue moral guidelines annually to Philadelphia's free blacks and circulate broadsides throughout neighborhoods where blacks lived.[14]

Despite these efforts, the hostility of white Philadelphians toward their black neighbors grew in the early nineteenth century. The shifting attitudes became shockingly apparent on July 4, in about 1805, when Philadelphians commemorated their commitment to liberty and equality with an open display of racial antipathy. For many years it had been customary for city residents of all classes and colors to gather in the square facing Independence Hall between Fifth and Sixth streets, where the nation's birth certificate had been signed. Amid feasting and toasting, the city's leaders would harangue the crowd about the blessings of liberty and the prospects of national greatness. In 1805, however, the nation's prospects were prefigured not by oratorical fireworks but by the sullen resentment of dozens of white citizens who suddenly turned on the many free blacks assembled for the festivities and drove them from the square with a torrent of curses.[15] In the years that followed, as greater class separation brought the withdrawal of wealthier Philadelphians from public celebrations, July Fourth became a working-class festival, and black citizens could enter the socially redefined public space in front of Independence Hall only at their peril.[16]

Four weeks after this ugly incident a long pamphlet appeared in Philadelphia that not only embodied the change in racial attitudes but also probably stimulated further white fears and hostility to-

ward free blacks. It came from the pen of a tortured renegade
Catholic immigrant, Thomas Branagan, whose own career had
intersected with the racial upheavals of the hemisphere at the end
of the eighteenth century. Born into a middle-class Catholic family in Dublin on the eve of the American Revolution, Branagan
went to sea at thirteen, serving at one point on a ship carrying
slaves from West Africa to the West Indies. By 1793 he had signed
on a British privateer that preyed on the ships carrying French
planters and their slaves from Cap Français and Port-au-Prince to
American ports. Soon afterward he accepted a job overseeing a
sugar plantation in Antigua. After two years of this violent occupation, he returned to Dublin to settle his deceased father's estate.
Then in about 1798 he emigrated to Philadelphia.[17]

Shortly after his arrival, Branagan's heart was captured by
Methodism. His conversion from the life of slave overseer was so
complete that by 1801, he was roaming the city preaching the
gospel and taking special satisfaction in ministering "to the poor
and the needy, the halt, the maimed and the blind, in the Bet-
tering-house," where he "scarcely missed one Sabbath in about
two years."[18] Expiating his guilt through identification with those
he had formerly oppressed, in 1804 Branagan published a sen-
sationalist pamphlet dedicated to the Pennsylvania Abolition Society and the Society of Friends. In fiery prose meant to inspire
abolitionist sentiments, the *Preliminary Essay on the Oppression of
the Exiled Sons of Africa* related from firsthand experiences interwoven with various published accounts the most gruesome scenes
of cruelty perpetrated under slavery.

Although Methodism had convinced Branagan of the evils of
slaveholding, it had not cured him of deeply negative attitudes
toward its victims. How conflicted he was on the issue of race
might not have been apparent to readers of the *Preliminary Essay,*
and in fact the pamphlet was subsidized by Richard Allen.[19] Nor
would it have been evident in *Avenia,* the 308-page epic poem
modeled on the *Iliad* that he published in 1805 with the aid of
Allen, Absalom Jones, and James Forten. In *Avenia; or a Tragical
Poem,* Branagan tried to extirpate the haunting specter of his past
and, as David Essig has written, "to reaffirm the forgiveness of
God."[20] His ambivalence became transparent later that year, how-

ever, in his *Serious Remonstrances Addressed to the Citizens of the Northern States . . .* In more than eighty pages of lurid prose, Branagan described a city supposedly overrun by 15,000 to 20,000 blacks, many of them migrants from the South and many of them "starving with hunger and destitute of employ"—an ignorant, improvident, debauched population that crammed the almshouse and workhouse and lived more wretchedly in winter than West Indian slaves.[21] A colonizationist at heart, Branagan proposed to end "the contamination of the land which is sacred to liberty" by creating a black state in the newly acquired Louisiana Territory. To this remote region all the "poisonous fruit" of the tree of slavery might be shipped.[22]

Branagan's choicest comments were reserved for a discussion of racial intermingling in the city. In dripping language that reveals his obsession with miscegenation, he painted a picture of black males swarming over "white women of easy virtue," hell-bent on obtaining white wives, and producing "mungrels and mulattoes" so rapidly that "in the course of a few years . . . half the inhabitants of the city will be people of Colour."[23] In his antislavery pamphlet in 1804, Branagan had rejected arguments that Africans were an "inferior kind of men," defending them as "sensible, ingenious, hospitable, and generous as any people, placed in such circumstances, and laboring under such disadvantages."[24] But in *Serious Remonstrances* he characterized Philadelphia's black males as hopelessly degraded, burdensome to the city, and so sexually obsessed with white women that the fate of the white-dominated republic hung in the balance.

Interwoven with appeals to racial purity in *Serious Remonstrances* were gestures to working-class whites concerned about jobs. Blacks in the northern cities, charged Branagan, discouraged European immigration to the detriment of the republic. "How must it damp their spirits," he wrote, "when they come and have to associate with negroes, take them as companions, and, what is much worse, be thrown out of work and precluded from getting employ to keep vacancies for blacks."[25]

In a city in which the composition of the black community was changing, such antiblack literature seems to have heightened white anxieties at all levels of society, although the fears aroused had different sources at each social level. Upper-class whites were already displaying particular sensitivity to interracial contact. For example, Reverend Nicholas Collin, the rector of Gloria Dei Church, where many blacks had taken vows, had refused to marry a black man and the white widow of a sea captain who came to him in the winter of 1794. For the next few years Collin wrote disapprovingly in his marriage register of similar requests, remarking that he was "not willing to have blame from public opinion" for sanctioning mixed marriages. In 1800 Collin fretted that "a particoloured race will soon make a great portion of the population in Philadelphia," in spite of "public opinion disapproving such wedlocks."[26] Quakers' strong fear of interracial mingling burst into the open in 1795, when Hannah Burrows, a light-skinned woman who, as one Friend wrote, had "made her appearance frequently in our meetings as a preacher or teacher," tried to gain full admission to the Society of Friends in Philadelphia. The chief objection, revealed Joseph Drinker, a leading Quaker, was that if membership in the Society of Friends was granted, "the privilege of intermarriage with the whites could not be withheld," and "such mixtures are objectionable."[27]

Lower-class whites, sharing alleys, courtyards, and sometimes even houses with black Philadelphians, were generally much less tender on the matter of interracial sex and often consorted with blacks. But white laboring men were highly sensitive to economic competition with free blacks—the matter to which Branagan alluded in his *Serious Remonstrances*. In the first decade of the nineteenth century, immigrant laborers, especially the Irish, often experienced difficulty in obtaining subsistence and fared worse than black men. The almshouse records show that whereas males made up 48 percent of blacks admitted, 68 percent of the Irish admitted were males. Moreover, the proportion of those entering the almshouse because they could not find work was twice as high among the Irish as among blacks—29 to 15 percent.[28]

All of these fears, coming from different sectors of white society, converged by 1805 to produce a series of attempts to pass discriminatory legislation aimed at free blacks. Five times from 1805 to 1814 the legislature debated bills to seal the state off from incoming black migrants or to fasten a special tax on black householders for the support of indigents of their race. On three occasions these bills received approval in one legislative house, but none was finally approved. The first petitions for such bills came from Chester County, but by 1806 Philadelphia representatives in the Senate were also firmly backing a bill restricting black immigration.[29] The next year legislators introduced other bills, including ones requiring free blacks to carry freedom certificates when moving about. It must have heartened the black community—and also convinced it of the advantages of working collectively—that their petitions to the legislature, supported by remonstrances from the Abolition Society and the Society of Friends, helped to defeat the detested proposals.[30]

Although attempts to pass restrictive and discriminatory legislation failed in the first decade of the nineteenth century, racial prejudice continued to congeal. The exclusion of blacks from the July Fourth celebrations became customary, prompting one leading black citizen to remark bitterly in 1813, "Is it not wonderful, that the day set apart for the festival of liberty, should be abused by the advocates of freedom, in endeavoring to sully what they profess to adore?"[31] In 1809 a traveler from abroad noted that in the streets young white boys insulted blacks indiscriminately with their parents' approbation.[32] Many Philadelphians, wrote an anguished James Forten a few years later, considered black citizens "as a different species, and little above the brute creation . . . They are thought to be objects fit for nothing else than lordly men to vent the effervescence of their spleen upon, and to tyrannize over, like the bearded Mussulman over his horde of slaves. Nay, the Mussulman thinks more of his horse than the generality of people do of the despised black."[33] In 1813, writing in the Republican *Democratic Press,* "Volunteer" could describe Philadelphia's blacks only as "very numerous and useless," a group that might profitably be inducted en masse into the army so that the lives and fortunes of white men, with "useful vocations," could be spared in the second Anglo-American war.[34]

Attempts to revive the restrictive legislation first proposed in 1805-1807 were renewed during the War of 1812. Jacob Mitchell, a Republican merchant representing Philadelphia, championed the views of many of his constituents, who claimed that the city seethed with 4,000 runaway slaves who must be strictly controlled. In 1813 Mitchell proposed to prohibit blacks from entering the state, to require the registration of every black resident, and to punish black persons found without a certificate of registration by advertising them for six months so that any presumed owner could come forward to claim them as slaves, after which time they were to be sold for their labor or sentenced, without jury trial, to seven years' imprisonment. The bill also authorized the sale of any black convicted of a crime "for the purposes of compensating the persons they may have plundered" and taxed black householders for the support "of their own poor."[35] How widespread antiblack opinion had become is reflected in the fact that, unlike the bills introduced earlier, the proposed legislation in 1813 was supported by petitions from the mayor and aldermen of Philadelphia.[36]

The campaign against free blacks in 1813, meant to align Pennsylvania with the southern states in excluding former slaves from the state and placing those already there under a separate set of restrictive laws, brought passionate remonstrances from the free black community.[37] It also stimulated petitions from the Society of Friends and the Abolition Society. Just weeks before he died on April 18, 1813, Benjamin Rush, the steadfast friend of free blacks for twenty-five years and president of the PAS since 1803, signed a remonstrance that spelled out the flagrant inconsistency between a state constitution that declared "that all men are born equally free & independent" and therefore entitled to the same "inherent & indefeasible rights" and a law that designed a separate criminal code for one part of the population.[38]

The discriminatory legislation proposed in 1813 also evoked an angry denunciation from James Forten, one of Philadelphia's most prominent black citizens. The wealthy sailmaker had not been active in the Free African Society nor been counted among the early founders of the black Episcopal church to which he belonged. Circumspection and moderation were bywords with him. Now forty-six years old, Forten commanded nearly universal respect for his dignity and accomplishments. White Philadelphians had signified their acceptance of him after his wedding in about 1806, when a number of "the most respectable merchants in Philadelphia" crossed the racial boundary, calling on him "to congratulate him and drink punch with him."[39] Throughout the city, Forten was admired for his patriotism, benevolence, and civic spirit.

Appalled by the vicious laws proposed in January 1813, Forten penned *A Series of Letters by A Man of Color,* which were published in April as the legislature took up the proposed measures. Forten eloquently spelled out the malevolent nature of laws that proposed to sell into slavery any black found without a registration certificate, or, if no purchaser could be found, to commit him to seven years' hard labor. "Search the legends of tyranny and find no precedent," he thundered. "It has been left for Pennsylvania to raise her ponderous arm against the liberties of the black, whose greatest boast has been that he resided in a state where civil liberty and sacred justice were administered alike to all." Forten warned that the proposed legislation would convert the center of American benevolence into a center of repression and hence encourage the forces of slavery. "The story will fly from the north to the south, and the advocates of slavery, the traders in human blood, will smile contemptuously at the once boasted moderation and humanity of Pennsylvania!" As for the proposed sealing of Pennsylvania's borders against the emancipated southern black, Forten asked: "Where shall he go? Shut every state against him, and, like Pharaoh's kine, drive him into the sea.—Is there no spot on earth that will protect him? Against their inclination, his ancestors were forced from their homes by traders in human flesh, and even under such circumstances the wretched offspring are denied the protection you afford to brutes."[40]

PHILADELPHIA'S ESTABLISHED black citizens, living in an increasingly hostile environment, did not docilely turn their backs on those still in chains or on the impoverished and uneducated black migrants from the South who sought a new life in Philadelphia. In the years from 1800 to 1815 they strengthened their commitment to the cause of abolition and embarked upon an ambitious program of building institutions that would facilitate the transition of recently freed slaves to a life of freedom and equip a new generation with literacy, job skills, religion, and moral rectitude. At the same time, they rejected overwhelmingly all proposals to recolonize them, either somewhere in the trans-Appalachian West or in Africa. Although white Philadelphians increasingly spurned them, they fought doggedly to protect such rights as they had gained and to fortify themselves collectively.

The fear that white Americans would never accept their black brethren had led even such staunch friends of Afro-Americans as Anthony Benezet and Benjamin Rush to consider creating a colony beyond the Appalachians where free blacks might pursue their destiny untrammeled by white hostility and fears of racial mixture.[41] Philadelphia blacks, however, exhibited little interest in colonization. They had given no support to William Thornton's plan in 1787 for resettlement in Africa, although it aroused strong interest in black communities in Boston, Newport, and Providence. Nor had they responded positively in 1794, when the Providence black community revived the plan for repatriation to the west coast of Africa.[42]

By 1810, plans for an emigration of American blacks to Sierra Leone had gained new momentum, led by the efforts of Paul Cuffe, a black merchant and sea captain from New Bedford, Massachusetts. Well-known in mercantile circles, Cuffe was a Quaker convert who had been seized with visions of bringing Christianity to West Africa and repatriating American free blacks whose opportunities for a truly free and respectable life in New England seemed to be waning. A longtime correspondent of Quaker James Pemberton, president of the Pennsylvania Abolition Society from 1790 to 1803, Cuffe attracted the support of several Philadelphia Quaker merchants in planning a voyage to Africa after the expiration of the Nonintercourse Act in 1810.[43] Cuffe intended to reconnoiter the possibilities for northern free blacks to emigrate to Sierra Leone, and he also planned to investigate the prospect of African-American trade, a venture of some interest to his Quaker supporters. In 1810 he embarked from Philadelphia on his voyage to Africa. Passing through the city several times after his return in 1812, he tried to organize a Philadelphia branch of the Friendly Society of Sierra Leone, a proposed national organization of American blacks interested in emigration and missionary work in Africa.[44] It appears that James Forten was converted to the idea of colonization at this time, for he became president of the Philadelphia African Institution, a local adjunct of Cuffe's Friendly Society of Sierra Leone.[45]

The War of 1812 cut short Cuffe's plan. But three years later he resumed his colonization efforts. Forten and other black leaders endorsed a voyage intended to carry hundreds of northern urban blacks back to Africa. But in a city where by now about 12,000 blacks resided, only four people, the African-born Samuel Wilson and Antony Survance and their wives, could be found to sign up for the voyage.[46] Planning another voyage in 1816, Cuffe concentrated on recruiting in New York City and informed the London African Institution that its American branches "are not so living or so lively as I could wish."[47]

Black Philadelphians indicated their attachment to American soil by their overwhelming lack of interest in African repatriation; but they demonstrated it even more clearly by supporting the cause of abolition. Black rebellion in Santo Domingo, and echoes of it in the United States, dealt a severe blow to white abolitionism at the turn of the century. The long, bloody revolt of blacks in the French Caribbean had the opposite effect on American blacks, however, inspiring slave resistance in the South and fortifying free blacks in the North in their efforts to end the wretched system of bondage.

Unprecedented numbers of the city's free blacks mobilized at the turn of the century to bring pressure on both the state and national governments to end slavery and the slave trade. Since 1792, the Abolition Society and the Society of Friends had besought the Pennsylvania legislature to end slavery altogether in the state, and although both houses had carried over bills for this purpose from session to session, nothing had been done. In the winter of 1799 two groups of Philadelphia blacks petitioned the legislature to cleanse the state of the remnants of slavery and even offered to pay compensation to the remaining slaveowners through a special tax to be levied on free blacks.[48]

While sending petitions to the state legislature, the black community also pleaded its case to the national government. In 1794 Absalom Jones and Richard Allen had included in their defense of black behavior during the yellow fever epidemic the first explicit attack on slavery by black Americans after the ratification of the Constitution. Invoking history to prove how slavery debased both slave and master, the two black leaders pleaded, "if you love your children, if you love your country, if you love the God of love, clear your hands from slaves, burden not your children or country with them."[49]

Early in 1797, led by Jones, Allen, and James Forten, black Philadelphians for the first time petitioned the national government to end slavery and revoke the detested 1793 Fugitive Slave Act, which allowed claimants of fleeing slaves to seize their putative property without a warrant. On this occasion it was the plight of sixteen North Carolina blacks, recently arrived in the city, that galvanized the black community. Late in 1796 Jacob Nicholson, Jupiter Gibson, Job Albertson, and Thomas Pritchard sought out Absalom Jones. They told him of their fear that, having reached "a city of refuge," they would now be seized and sold back into slavery under the provisions of the 1793 fugitive slave law. Some years earlier, the four men had been manumitted along with others by Quaker masters in North Carolina. Most white North Carolinians regarded such acts of humanity as the work of "evil-minded persons intending to disturb the public peace"; consequently, during and after the Revolution the North Carolina legislature passed laws that permitted the reenslavement of blacks freed for reasons other than "meritorious service" in the war. These laws provided what amounted to hunting licenses for anyone with sufficient force at his disposal to seize the hundreds of manumitted slaves living in North Carolina and sell them back into bondage.[50]

Such laws shattered the hopes of recently freed slaves. Jupiter Gibson, working as a sailor after his release from slavery in the 1780s, had been pursued by armed men with dogs when he came ashore; he fled to Portsmouth, Virginia, and then to Philadelphia, leaving behind his father, mother, and brother, all of whom were seized and resold into bondage. Job Albertson recounted how he had been seized by Carolinians with clubs and mastiffs and taken to Hertford prison, where he sat for four weeks with little food before escaping. With his wife, he made his way north to Portsmouth, Virginia, where he worked for four years as a sawyer; then, seeking freer air, he trekked to Philadelphia and found employment as a dock worker and sawyer. Both his mother and sister, freed by Quaker masters, had been reenslaved in North Carolina.

Understanding that the Fugitive Slave Act was extending into the northern states the reign of terror they had experienced in North Carolina, the four North Carolina refugees had sought the aid of Absalom Jones. The law, as Jones wrote for the petitioners in January 1797, countenanced and conferred authority upon "men of cruel disposition . . . in violently seizing, imprisoning, and selling into slavery, such as had been so emancipated." Emboldened by the Fugitive Slave Act, kidnappers were already reaching northern port towns, spiriting away blacks who had been freed in southern states.[51]

With just a hint of irony Absalom Jones addressed the petition "To the President, Senate, and House of representatives of the— most free and enlightened nation in the world!!!"[52] In framing the appeal of the four men, Jones made clear that black Philadelphians regarded the abolition of slavery as no more than the restoration of the natural rights of Afro-Americans. He drove the point home by comparing the "unconstitutional bondage in which multitudes of our fellows in complexion are held" with the "deplorable . . . situation of citizens of the United States captured and enslaved . . . in Algiers." It was particularly grievous that men who had been emancipated and "tasted the sweets of liberty" should be "again reduced to slavery by kidnappers and man-stealers." Philadelphian William Lee published the petition in his *American Universal Magazine* only weeks after it was sent to Washington and asked "whether, instead of being the most free and enlightened nation in the world," the phrase Jones employed in the title of his address, "America is not rivalling Algiers in barbarity and oppression?"[53]

Confronted for the first time with a petition from Afro-Americans asking for a guarantee of their natural rights, Congress debated the issue only briefly. The majority, after listening to James Madison's argument that a petition from blacks "had no claim on their attention," dismissed the appeal, regarding any discussion of slavery at this time as inflammatory.[54]

Two years after the petition of the four black refugees from North Carolina, Richard Allen condemned slavery in an appendix to published articles of association for a mutual aid society formed at the Bethel African Methodist Episcopal Church.[55] In the same year the city's Afro-Americans again appealed to the president and Congress to revoke the Fugitive Slave Act of 1793. In a moving letter to Massachusetts representative George Thacher, who presented the petition to the House of Representatives, Forten wrote: "Though our faces are black, yet we are men, and . . . are as anxious to enjoy the birth-right of the human race as those who, from our ignorance, draw an argument against our petition, when the petition has in view the diffusion of knowledge amongst the African race, by unfettering their thoughts and giving full scope to the energy of their minds."[56] The petition itself, which carried the signatures or marks of seventy-three Philadelphia blacks, expressed gratitude for the release from "oppression and violence" that had been granted by those who recognized their "natural right to Liberty." But the free black community, "incited by a sense of Social duty" and mindful "of our afflicted Brethren" in the southern states, could not rest without reminding the president and Congress of the blatant contradiction between the principles enunciated in the Constitution's preamble and the continuation of the slave trade and the merciless operation of the Fugitive Slave Act. "In the Constitution, and in the Fugitive bill," Jones wrote, "no mention is made of Black people or Slaves—therefore if the Bill of Rights, or the declaration of Congress are of any validity, we beseech that as we are *men,* we may be admitted to partake of the Liberties and unalienable Rights therein held forth."[57]

A year later, shortly after Jefferson won the presidency, Absalom Jones carried another petition through the black community. While deploring slavery and implicitly calling for its abolition, the petition focused upon the renewal of the slave trade in Maryland. The black supplicants asked Jefferson to ponder whether "the efforts of Men driven almost to desperation by deprivation of a right implanted by the Author of their existence . . . is either more atrocious or unjust, than our Struggle with Great Britain for that National Independence to which we conceiv'd ourselves entitl'd."[58] America's revolutionary credo again became the standard against which black Philadelphians judged their present state as they protested a government that "unjustly detain'd" people of color "under the Galling Yoke of Slavery . . . contrary to the Declaration of Independence which expressly declares All Men to be Created equal." By this time it was necessary for the black petitioners to "totally disavow being concerned either directly or indirectly" with Gabriel's Rebellion in Richmond or with another insurrectionary outbreak at Patapsco, Maryland. Nonetheless, while white abolitionists were withdrawing to the shadows free blacks in Philadelphia continued their political campaign to abolish slavery at both the state and national levels, to revoke the Fugitive Slave Act, and to obtain legislation curbing the kidnapping of free blacks.[59]

Petitions were one way of raising political consciousness in the black community; sermons with political content were another. Beginning in 1808, when Congress finally prohibited the slave trade, Absalom Jones and other black preachers began delivering annual thanksgiving sermons on New Year's Day, the date the prohibition of trade took effect and also the date of Haitian independence in 1804. The appropriation of New Year's Day as the black Fourth of July seems to have started simultaneously in Jones's African Episcopal Church and in New York's African Zion Church. Jones, at the end of his sermon, called for January 1 to be "set apart in every year, as a day of publick thanksgiving."[60] It was a cutting reminder to whites that, since they would not extend the privileges that the Declaration of Independence had called inalienable for all human beings, black Americans must find a national day of thanksgiving and celebration that had relevance to their lives. For free blacks such freedom celebrations, which would spread throughout the country and be extended to other notable days, served to build and express a feeling of community and peoplehood.

The feeling of collectivity fostered by Absalom Jones in his sermon on January 1, 1808, "depended on an historical consciousness and the sense of belonging to a tradition," as one student of these freedom celebrations has written.[61] Jones drew a parallel between the deliverance of the people of Israel from Egyptian bondage and the odyssey of blacks in America. Just as the Passover liturgy kept alive for every Jew his or her links to the historic deliverance from slavery, so must black Americans "remember the rock whence we were hewn and the pit whence we were digg'd." "Let the history of the sufferings of our brethren," concluded Jones, "and of their deliverance, descend by this means [annual celebrations] to our children, to the remotest generations."[62]

In Philadelphia such New Year's Day orations took on a formulaic quality in the years after 1808. Always the addresses drew upon, as well as deepened, the collective consciousness of free blacks. They amply reflected the "double consciousness" of free blacks—of being black and of being American, of having both an African identity and an American identity. Black ministers recounted the horrors of the African diaspora and compared them with the sufferings of the Israelites during their captivity in Egypt; they thankfully recalled the partial dismantling of slavery in the North and commemorated the closing of the slave trade; they invoked the memory of early abolitionists such as Benezet, Sharp, Woolman, Rush, Wilberforce, and Clarkson; and they urged free blacks to remember their brothers and sisters still in bondage and cautioned them to lead peaceable, orderly lives that would help obliterate the stigma that whites attached to them as a people incapable of matching the achievements of persons of lighter skin.[63]

USING PETITIONS, sermons, and letters to the public, black leaders fought against the kidnapping of free blacks and the attempts of white legislators to pass restrictive and discriminatory laws. Sometimes several hundred black Philadelphians could be enlisted in these struggles; but in the main, these efforts had to be directed outside the immediate community where state and national political power were exercised. The multitude of ordinary black city dwellers could not be politically mobilized for such lobbying efforts because their energies were expended in the daily struggle for subsistence. In any event, free blacks in Philadelphia were excluded by custom from the formal political process, though the franchise would have profited them little because they were a small minority.[64] For these ordinary men and women, the building of local black institutions, especially churches, provided the key to their individual and collective security. It was there, in this private rather than public sector, that they concerted themselves, in a kind of subcommunity civic existence that operated outside the formal political life of the city. However, the fact that the black churches were far more political than white churches considerably narrowed the space that separated public and private spheres of life for black Philadelphians.

From the beginning, some black leaders had recognized the importance of autonomous black institutions; but the palpable racism that emerged in the early nineteenth century made more compelling the desire to build alternative organizations for the religious, moral, and educational benefit of their own progeny, as well as for the waves of black southern migrants reaching the city. The black church became the center of almost all these activities— not only religious but also educational, associational, and political. Religion for the black person, as C. Eric Lincoln has written, "was the organizing principle around which life was structured. His church was his school, his forum, his political arena, his social club, his art gallery, his conservatory of music. It was lyceum and gymnasium as well as *sanctum sanctorum*."[65] Beyond this, the black church was the primary instrument for the forging of black consciousness. Black churches, Will B. Gravely has pointed out, "enabled blacks to celebrate themselves as a collectivity and . . . provided the protective space whereby each could contend with the other about common concerns" while participating in "prayer, song, sermon, and sacrament in a distinctive Afro-American medium."[66]

After Bethel and St. Thomas's opened their doors in 1794, black Philadelphians gradually abandoned the white churches to which they had been going for years. A small number who lived as servants in the houses of Quakers continued attending the separate meetings that Quakers held for blacks. In 1796, after the Quaker Rebecca Griscomb published an essay chiding the Society of Friends for excluding blacks from their regular meetings, the Friends finally dropped the formal exclusion of blacks from their worship, but few blacks chose to commune with the Quakers.[67] A small number continued to worship at other white churches, but the registers of marriages and baptisms disclose a rapidly declining number of black parishioners.[68] In the late 1790s the French visitor La Rochefoucauld–Liancourt observed blacks still going to white churches "at their pleasure."[69] Many of the blacks from Santo Domingo who arrived from 1792 to 1795 at first worshiped and baptized their children at St. Joseph's Catholic Church, but by the turn of the century, as they integrated themselves within the black community, their number in the church had declined sharply.[70] White Methodists also had some success in attracting blacks to a new mission church named Zoar, built in 1796 at Fourth and Brown streets in Campertown in the Northern Liberties after Bishop Asbury had conferred with blacks in that area of the city.[71] However, the appeal of Absalom Jones and Richard Allen's black churches proved irresistible to most of the city's black Christians.

The success of Jones in drawing worshipers to the African Protestant Episcopal Church of St. Thomas was phenomenal in the first few years. From a founding congregation of 246 in 1794, his church swelled to 427 in one year. Thereafter the growth tapered off, with the church on Fifth Street counting about 500 members in 1803 and 560 in 1813.[72] In 1804 William White, the Episcopal bishop in Philadelphia, conferred full priestly orders upon Jones, although St. Thomas's was denied representation in the Episcopal Convention for many decades.[73] Jones had to endure a schism in the congregation that began in 1810 and continued until after his death in 1818, and there are hints that the disaffected members were intent on replacing Jones with a more evangelical minister.[74] The dissatisfaction with Jones notwithstanding, St. Thomas's continued to be a center of black activism, for its leader was a pillar of the black community who never shrank from involvement in the causes of free blacks.

Four blocks from Jones's African Episcopal Church, Richard Allen pursued his Methodist dream. In the first few years his flock grew slowly, never matching the size of Jones's congregation. But a religious revival that swept both white and black churches in the city early in 1798, perhaps inspired by another devastating yellow fever epidemic the previous fall, enlarged the membership at Bethel to nearly 200. This obliged Allen to enlarge the seating capacity in the converted blacksmith's shop, which held barely

150 worshipers.[75] In 1799 Bethel counted 211 members, and in the next five years the congregation soared to 457.[76] Baptisms at Bethel first outstripped those at St. Thomas's in 1802, and thereafter Allen's church was never second to Jones's in the breadth of its appeal to black Philadelphians.[77] A new brick church replaced the frame building in 1805, and by 1813 it was bursting with 1,272 members, now more than twice the membership at St. Thomas's.[78]

Allen's success at Bethel had much to do with the warmth, simplicity, and evangelical fervor of Methodism, which resonated with a special vibrancy among the manumitted and fugitive southern slaves reaching Philadelphia in this era. Black Methodism had several advantages over black Episcopalianism in a rapidly growing city where an underclass of Irish immigrants, ex-slaves from the French West Indies and southern states, and newcomers from the Pennsylvania, Delaware, and New Jersey hinterland jostled together in crowded lower-class neighborhoods. Methodists preached the gospel warmly and extemporaneously, eschewing finely crafted, highly rational sermons. Whereas the more formalized Protestant denominations shaped the religious experience around rites and dogmas, the Methodists instituted "class meetings" and "prayer bands"—cells of sinners meeting in homes on weekdays to search collectively for redemption. Whereas other denominations treasured ceremony, Methodists practiced simplicity and informality and sanctioned "love feasts" and funerals where emotions could be expressed openly and fully.[79] Finally, Methodists imposed upon their members a system of discipline that permeated their private lives more than that of any other religious group. Their intention, among both whites and blacks, was to reform and reorder people's lives, to convert poor sinners into honest, sober, industrious, God-fearing members of the community. To Allen and other black Methodist leaders it seemed a perfect system for lifting up an oppressed people and healing the suffering experienced under slavery. Methodism, writes Albert J. Raboteau, offered the people of bondage "a coherent pattern of values by which they could order their lives."[80]

The Methodism practiced at Allen's church was not, however, simply white Methodism in a black venue. Black Methodists put their own stamp on their forms of worship in ways that rendered their faith all the more appealing to themselves but at the same time offended white church leaders. In particular, the congregation involved itself deeply in the service with an emotionalism and expressiveness that horrified most white observers. The Russian artist Pavel Svinin described the tumult at a black Methodist church in Philadelphia, where the minister's fiery sermon about the hell that awaited sinners, delivered in the dim light of smoking torches, "loosed such a howl that the very foundations of the hall shook and the vaulted ceiling trembled." The penitent worshipers "leapt and swayed in every direction and dashed themselves to the ground, pounding with hands and feet, gnashing their teeth, all to show that the evil spirit was departing from them."[81] John F. Watson, a staunch white Methodist, complained of "the immoderate noise of the people" that punctuated the preacher's discourse as "a rising murmur" would periodically arise during the sermon

Figure 14. White visitors such as Russian watercolorist Pavel Svinin marveled at and shrank from the emotional intensity of black Methodist religious services, depicted here with some exaggeration in 1814 in Philadelphia.

and almost "drown his voice." Watson condemned the toleration of ministers who allowed "religion to run wild," but he was attacking precisely what made black Methodism so appealing to large numbers of the city's free blacks.[82]

Bethel's rise to the status of Philadelphia's largest black church was accomplished in the midst of a twenty-year struggle with white Methodist authority. Indeed, Bethel's growing popularity cannot be separated from the fact that its dogged contest over the right to control itself, within the general rules laid down by the Methodist General Conference, became virtually a part of the church's daily existence. In the first few years after opening Bethel's doors in 1794, Allen had no intention of denying the allegiance of his church to the Methodist General Conference, the higher organization that set policy and made clerical appointments for all Methodist churches. Nor was there ever a question of Allen's doctrinal loyalty. He remained intimately in touch with white Methodist leaders, and Bethel depended on white ministers supplied by the white elder assigned to St. George's to administer sacraments and perform marriages. Bishop Asbury frequently preached at Bethel, and so did other white stalwarts such as Ezekiel Cooper, Thomas Coke, and Joseph Pilmore.[83] The biracialism of the Methodists in the 1790s is reflected in the fact that at a time when the church still officially opposed slaveholding, eight white Methodist ministers, along with Benjamin Rush, ate at Allen's table in December 1797.[84] Asbury's decision to ordain Allen as the first black deacon in the Methodist church in June 1799 was another sign of the high regard that the Methodist bishop had for the Philadelphia leader whom Asbury had asked years before to accompany him on his journeys through the South.[85]

Despite his warm relations with leaders of the Methodist church, Allen was held in suspicion by white Methodists in his own city. One year after Bethel opened, John McClaskey, the elder in charge of St. George's, decided to restrain what he viewed as Allen's separatist tendencies and make him knuckle under to his authority. The Irish-born McClaskey had strenuously opposed the fund-raising project for the African Church of Philadelphia in 1792 and now had returned to Philadelphia after a two-year assignment in Baltimore. In what Allen and some white Methodists later charged was deliberate deception, McClaskey convinced Allen in 1795 that Bethel must be incorporated because unless it was a legal entity it could not receive legacies. McClaskey offered to save the cost of a lawyer by having Ezekiel Cooper, friendly to Allen and his black congregation and admired as an enemy of slavery, draw up the articles.[86] Allen agreed to this; but he also specified that the articles of incorporation should not infringe on Bethel's right to direct its own religious affairs. Allen had issued a public statement that amounted to "an assertion of black religious independence" in November 1794, only a few months after the opening of Bethel, and he reiterated to Asbury his determination to protect the autonomy of his congregation when the bishop was in Philadelphia in October 1795. The bishop worried that "the Africans of this town desire a church which, in temporals, shall be altogether under their direction, and ask greater privileges than the white stewards and trustees [of individual Methodist churches] ever had a right to claim," but he did not challenge Allen on this point.[87]

The articles of incorporation drawn up by Cooper in 1796 included acknowledgment of Bethel's denominational loyalty and specified the power of the elder of the Philadelphia Methodist Episcopal Church to nominate the preacher, to license lay exhorters, to administer baptism ordinances and communion at Bethel, and, with the advice of the trustees, to expel "disorderly walkers." However, the articles also required that Bethel's trustees must be "male coloured members" of the church and specified that only "Africans and descendants of the African race" were qualified for membership in the church. The goal of ordaining black deacons and ministers, and thus ending white supervision, expressed by Allen in 1794, was reiterated.

In a clause that would form the nexus of controversy between white and black Methodists, the articles of incorporation guaranteed control of the church property to the trustees "in trust for the religious use of the Ministers and Preachers of the Methodist Episcopal Church . . . and likewise for our African Brethren, and the descendants of the African race . . . and also for the Ministers and Teachers of our African Brethren duly licensed or ordained according to the form of discipline."[88] Allen later claimed that the Bethelites had not understood by this language that the white Methodist church of Philadelphia possessed legal title to church property. Lorenzo Dow, the eccentric early historian of the Methodist church, confirmed this, writing in 1815 that "there were three articles, that, when read in the abstract, would read very well—but when taken in a relative conjunction, implied what the coloured people never designed," a large degree of power by white Methodists over their church affairs and a legal title to their property. McClaskey and Cooper had not informed the Bethelites "whereby they could ken it," wrote Dow.[89] By 1815, when Dow wrote this, he was in disfavor among Methodist leaders for his picaresque appearance and unpredictable, frequently mystical behavior. But he was closely acquainted with black Methodists, having frequently attended the black Methodist church in New York City in 1813 and having spent many weeks in Philadelphia from 1813 to 1815.[90]

The Articles of Association of 1796 might have served usefully as an agreement designed for a biracial church with largely separate black and white congregations; and in fact they did so for almost a decade. In 1805, however, when racial tension in the city was beginning to rise, the Methodist General Conference assigned the Virginian James Smith to Philadelphia. Smith was among the southern Methodists who had reacted strongly to the unequivocal stance against slavery expressed by the Methodist Conference in 1800—a reaction that by 1804 had led to the wholesale watering down of the antislavery commitment.[91] By no means content with conceding to Bethel the degree of autonomy granted by the Articles of Association of 1796, Smith provoked a controversy that became, as Will B. Gravely writes, "a test of the viability of a biracial religious community."[92] Using a dispute over the expulsion of a disorderly woman by Bethel's black trustees as the occasion, Smith tried to put Bethel firmly under his heel. Smith "waked us up," Allen recollected, "by demanding the keys and books of the church, and forbid us holding any meetings except by orders from him." When Allen refused to comply, Smith threatened expulsion of the entire congregation from the Methodist General Conference. "We told him the house was ours," Allen replied, for "we had bought it, and paid for it." Smith retorted that "he would let us know it was not ours, it belonged to the Conference." When the shocked Allen carried the articles of incorporation to a lawyer, he was dismayed to find that Smith was right. Their beloved Bethel, Allen wrote, "belonged to the white Conference, and our property was gone."[93]

Believing they had been betrayed by McClaskey and Cooper nine years before, Allen and his trustees fought fire with fire by using a clause in the Articles of Association that provided for amendments by a two-thirds vote of the church membership. In what became known as "The African Supplement," a title signifying that this time those who were black would control the legal niceties, the Bethel members unanimously approved amendments that struck at the power of the white elder and greatly increased the autonomous status of their church. In the amendments, the trustees conferred upon themselves final control over church property. Furthermore, they invested themselves with the power to appoint black exhorters and preachers at Bethel, to authorize church meetings, to expel members for discipline, to refuse admission to those they regarded as unqualified, and to deny the pulpit to any preacher sent to Bethel by the white elder whom they did not approve.[94] Their purpose was not to separate themselves from the doctrine or discipline of the Methodist Episcopal Church, wrote Allen and the Bethel trustees. "Our only design is to secure . . . our rights and privileges to regulate our affairs temporal and spiritual, the same as if we were white people, and to guard against any oppression which might possibly arise from the improper prejudices or administration of any individual having the exercise of Discipline over us."[95] Allen had circumvented the lack of ordained black elders to supervise the congregational life of his church by denying the power of the white elder at St. George's and replacing his authority with that of Bethel's black trustees.

Bishop Asbury accepted the African Supplement in principle, or at least he did not countermand it. But this did not end the crisis of governance, for white Methodists in Philadelphia never acknowledged its legality.[96] The elders at St. George's and Bethel squabbled for several years, particularly about how much Bethel would pay for the services of white preachers who administered the sacraments there. In 1811 a new white elder, Stephen G. Roszel, renewed the offensive against Bethel's autonomy, repeating the demand that the Bethel trustees destroy the African Supplement. When the Bethelites refused, the Virginia-born Roszel was stymied, at least for the moment.[97] But white Methodists, who continued to treat Allen's black church as an adjunct of white St. George's, were determined to force a showdown. Black Methodists, by this time outnumbering white Methodists in the city by two to one, were equally determined to stand their ground. Fortifying their resolve was the knowledge that the Methodist Episcopal church was in full retreat from its earlier antislavery position, which made the authority of white elders stationed in Philadelphia, many of them southerners, all the more distasteful.[98]

While white Methodists battled with their black brethren over self-government at Bethel in 1807, white Presbyterians were demonstrating what interracial cooperation could accomplish toward spreading black Christianity in a city crowded with southern migrants. In the previous year Archibald Alexander, one of the leading Presbyterian ministers in the city, had founded the Presbyterian Evangelical Society to spread Presbyterianism among blacks and lower-class whites. A year later, Alexander's vision was rewarded by the arrival in Philadelphia of John Gloucester, a tall, muscular, thirty-one-year-old slave from Tennessee, who came with his master, the backwoods Presbyterian preacher Gideon Blackburn. Blackburn told Philadelphia Presbyterians of the extraordinary gifts possessed by Gloucester, who had preached in Tennessee with such ardor that many whites as well as blacks had become convinced of their sins. It would take more than two years for white Presbyterians to negotiate Gloucester's release from slavery, to license him, and to gather funds to build a church "to promote the present and future happiness of the Africans."[99]

Meanwhile Gloucester gathered nine women and thirteen men into the first black Presbyterian congregation in the United States. Meeting in a house in Gaskill Street, in the heart of the Cedar Ward district of the black community, his reputation began to spread. Soon the house overflowed and he moved outside, to an empty lot at the corner of Seventh and Shippen streets, where the African Presbyterian church was to be built. Gloucester would appear at six in the morning, when laboring-class blacks were trudging to work, singing hymns of praise in a deep voice that drew "a large concourse of people." "Such was the melody and rich tones of his voice," wrote William Catto, who interviewed early black Presbyterians in the 1850s for a history of Gloucester's church, "that whenever he sang, a volume of music would roll from his mouth, charming and enchaining, as by a spell, the listening audience." Ancient members of the church remembered years later that "in prayer he was mighty" and his energy was unflagging, for "to wear out was his motto, to rust out never."[100]

From 1807 to 1811 Gloucester preached intermittently in Philadelphia, while spending months of each year as an itinerant preacher, trying to gather donations to buy his wife and six children out of slavery. By the time the church was built and dedicated, in May 1811, he had recruited a congregation of 123.[101] The appeal of this "sweet singer" proved so great that black Methodists tried to draw him to their faith; but like Richard Allen, who remained faithful to the religious group through which he had gained his freedom, Gloucester held fast to the Presbyterianism that had been the instrument of his emancipation.[102]

Gloucester's powerful preaching drew important Philadelphia blacks to his congregation, including the oysterman James Prosser; the ragman Cato Freeman, who had been a founding member of the Free African Society; the sailmaker Jacob Craig; and Quommany Clarkson, a prominent black teacher. Samuel Cornish, who would become the coeditor of the first black newspaper in the United States and a leading black abolitionist, was one of his protégés; Benjamin Hughes, who would become a leading churchman and abolitionist in New York City, was another. Gloucester's three sons—James, Jeremiah, and Stephen—all followed their father into the ministry. By 1813 Gloucester's African Presbyterian Church boasted about 300 members, not to be compared with Allen's Bethel but nonetheless an impressive number for so new a congregation.

Gloucester's magnetism probably had little to do with the doctrinal aspects of Presbyterianism, for that denomination had attracted fewer black members in earlier decades than had any other church in Philadelphia. Rather, his ability to build a large congregation in the first few years stemmed from his extraordinary gifts of oral communication—in prayer, sermon, and song. His charisma also owed much to the authenticity of his experience as a southern slave recently released from bondage and still struggling to obtain the release of his family from slavery. When he first came to the city, white Philadelphians, learning of his plight, subscribed $500 for the purchase of Gloucester's family in Tennessee, but it took him until 1819, just three years before he died, to raise the remainder of the $1,500 demanded by their owner.[103] The pathos of his situation must have resonated deeply among the recent black migrants to Philadelphia who became part of his congregation.

John Gloucester was not the only former southern slave to found a black church in a northern city of refuge. In April 1809, the same year that Gloucester gathered the first African Presbyterian congregation, Henry Simmons, a former slave from Virginia, joined with twelve other blacks to found the African Baptist Church of Philadelphia. This gathering of black Baptists, like that of black Methodists, had secessionist overtones, for it came during the pastorates of southern-born whites at the Philadelphia Baptist church and at a time when that denomination, like the Methodist Episcopalians, was retreating from its earlier antislavery stance.[104] Simmons's odyssey resembled that of hundreds of southern migrants to the city. Purchasing his freedom sometime near the turn of the century, he had made his way north to Philadelphia, where he took up residence on the northern edge of the city. Working as a ragman, Simmons had slowly gathered the purchase price of a small piece of land for a church on Tenth Street between Race and Vine, in the fast-growing Spring Garden district. By 1813, when a small church was erected, the black Baptist flock had grown to sixty-one.[105]

Unlike the Methodist, Presbyterian, and Episcopalian entities, the Baptist Association of Philadelphia seated delegates from the African Baptist Church from the beginning. Within this biracial church organization, the African Baptist Church maintained a southern identity for many years. Henry Cunningham, a former slave from Savannah, Georgia, served from 1809 to 1811 as its first preacher, although he was not officially ordained. When he died,

Samuel Johnson, a lastmaker, assumed the position of lay preacher, while John King, a Virginia-born white minister, conducted services there intermittently. The church grew slowly, enduring a schism in 1816 and attaining a membership of eighty-four by 1818. Not until 1832, however, was a regular full-time minister found. Again it was a southerner, James Burrows, whose master in Northampton County, Virginia, had permitted him to go to Philadelphia to earn money to purchase his freedom in 1831, the same year that Nat Turner's insurrection broke out in the same county.[106]

In the decade following the racial incident on July 4, 1805, black Philadelphians, sometimes with the aid of whites and sometimes by themselves, organized four new churches that served the fast-growing black population and absorbed southern migrants into a religious and social community. In addition to the African Presbyterian and African Baptist churches, black Methodists in the northern part of the city organized Union Methodist Church in 1813, and just north of the city, in Frankford, another black Methodist congregation gathered in the same year.[107] In 1813 a Philadelphia magazine reported that almost 2,400 Philadelphians were members of the seven black congregations—nearly two of every five adults in the city.[108] Though all were still tied to biracial associations, synods, and presbyteries, these separate black congregations, worshiping in a distinctly Afro-Christian form, were tangible evidence of the strivings of the black community for control of its own religious life.

WHILE FORMING BLACK CONGREGATIONS that helped to heal the disabling scars of slavery and facilitated the adjustment of southern migrants to life as citizens in the urban North, black Philadelphians also made a concerted effort to provide schooling both for their youth and for illiterate adults. Both black and white leaders put great emphasis on education as a means of reclaiming those degraded under slavery and as the indispensable tool for preparing black children for useful lives. Religion could serve the spiritual needs of the black community, but only education would transform the children of slaves into accepted citizens in a society dominated by whites. The personal experience of men such as Richard Allen, James Forten, and Absalom Jones taught them that literacy had been a cardinal element in getting freedom and in getting ahead.

The black emphasis on education was an important correlative of the contemporary environmentalist view that if the circumstances of life could be changed for blacks, they would perform as capably as any other people. Anthony Benezet had argued this for years before his death in 1784, and it remained the belief of black leaders, who naturally rejected the opposing view that blacks were "men whose baseness is incurable," as Absalom Jones and Richard Allen had described the opinion of many whites in 1794. It was with the maturing generation, among the daughters and sons of former slaves, that leaders such as Jones and Allen placed their main faith, for they granted that the "vile habits often acquired in a state of servitude, are not easily thrown off." Too much should not be expected by way of reclaiming those ruined under slavery. "Why," they asked rhetorically, "will you look for grapes from thorns, or figs from thistles? It is in our posterity enjoying the same privileges with your own, that you ought to look for better things."[109]

More than any other urban Americans, white Philadelphians assumed responsibility for providing education for freed blacks, convinced that education was a vital instrument for uplifting the republic and was especially crucial for former slaves attempting to negotiate the perilous waters between bondage and freedom. The Society of Friends continued to play the leading role in the schooling of free blacks at the end of the century. They maintained their support of Benezet's old school in Willing's Alley, though the number of students enrolled was never large. In 1789, well-to-do young Quaker men and women established an Association for the Free Instruction of Adult Colored Persons that held separate classes for women and men in the evenings and on Sunday afternoons in three different locations. Enrolling upward of fifty adults in reading, writing, and arithmetic classes, they continued their work until about 1813.[110]

Abolition Society reformers, whose annual printed addresses to the free black community at first emphasized the necessity of schooling their young, also devoted themselves after 1790 to providing schools for free blacks. Buying a lot on Cherry Street, in the northern sector of the city, they moved a frame house there in 1793 and hired a black schoolmistress, the African-born Eleanor Harris, who taught there until her death four years later.[111] In 1799 the PAS provided Absalom Jones with funds to open a preschool for young children in his home.[112]

Despite these efforts, almost everyone associated with the black schools regarded the initial results as discouraging. The Abolition Society's first attempt to open a school in the Northern Liberties in 1797 lasted only a few months, although the school was reopened later. By 1799 the Cherry Street School had only twenty students, and a committee of the PAS lamented that "a large number of Children of Colour . . . are suffered to ramble the streets in a great measure unheeded and untaught." An inspecting committee that visited Absalom Jones's school in 1799 found him too lenient with the children and reached the same conclusion regarding the black teacher at the school in the Northern Liberties. Concluding that "it is not practicable at present to have the black children properly taught by a black person," the PAS decided to withdraw its support from the three schools with black teachers and opened a large, centrally located school at Sixth and Walnut streets with white teachers (Map 3).[113]

While Quakers and Abolition Society leaders launched white schools, blacks established schools of their own, usually in their churches or in their homes. Richard Allen had organized the first black Sunday school in America at Bethel in 1795, and he may have launched a night school there in the next year.[114] In 1800, when the Abolition Society withdrew its support from three PAS schools taught by blacks, the three teachers—Absalom Jones, Amos White, and Ann Williams—decided to continue teaching the children "on their own account." Three years later, in 1803, Cyrus Bustill, one of the oldest members of the free black community, opened a school in his home on Third Street in the northern part of the city.[115] Four years later, lamenting that many "free Africans" were "destitute of that education or information indispensible [*sic*] necessary to their being useful members of society," Allen organized a Society of Free People of Color for Promoting the Instruction and School Education of Children of African Descent—a group dedicated to raising money by subscription for a larger and revitalized school at Bethel. With a legacy from the Bray Associates in England, Absalom Jones reorganized and enlarged the school at St. Thomas's in 1804 and opened another school in the Northern Liberties.[116]

Despite such efforts, neither black nor white leaders could bring more than a fraction of the city's black youth into the schools. For lack of students, the Abolition Society reluctantly closed its reorganized boys' school in 1804 and shut the doors of the girls' school two years later.[117] If both black leaders and benevolent whites saw education as the key that would unlock the door of acceptance into the general society for a rising generation of free blacks, why did so few students avail themselves of the schools that had been created? The problem of educating black children, concluded the despairing PAS Committee on Education in 1800, lay primarily in black parents' need to indenture their children at an early age and the unwillingness of their white masters to release them from their work for school. Despite a rising tide of complaints about the illiterate and impoverished black migrants entering the city, white Philadelphians could not be convinced, as the frustrated Abolition Society leaders pointed out, that assistance to this "class of people . . . intimately concerns the whole community."[118] Sobered by the difficulties they had encountered, the reformers no longer stressed schooling for black children in their annual addresses to free black families. In 1804, for example, the PAS simply urged black parents to have their children "brought up to labor and taught to read and write and early place them as apprentices with suitable masters." A survey in 1805 showed that, of the city's several thousand school-age black children, the seven operating schools enrolled only 384 day students and another 172 evening students, some of them adults.[119] Eight years later, after a major effort by Quakers that led to the establishment of a Lancastrian school for poor black children in the northern part of the city and the opening of another school for black children by the white teacher Arthur Donaldson, the number of black students had actually decreased to 426. In a city with a burgeoning black population, the black school population slipped further to 414 by 1813.[120]

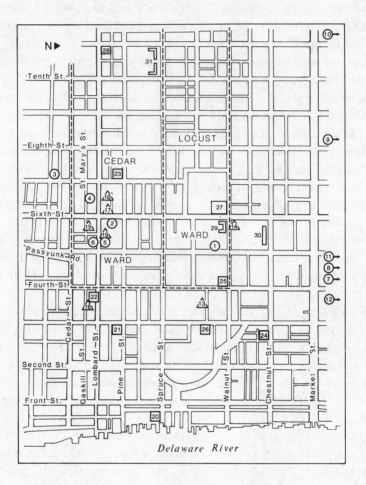

Map 3. Cedar Ward, center of black Philadelphia.

CHURCHES: ◯

1. St. Thomas African Episcopal
2. Bethel African Methodist Episcopal
3. First African Presbyterian
4. Second African Presbyterian
5. Wesley African Methodist Episcopal
6. Little Wesley African Methodist Episcopal
7. Union African Methodist Episcopal
8. Zoar African Methodist Episcopal
9. First African Baptist
10. Second African Baptist
11. Christ Church
12. St. George's Methodist

SCHOOLS: △

13. Benezet's (Quaker) African School
14. Penna. Abolition Society School
15. Black Public School (males), 1822–29
16. Black Public School (females), 1822–29
17. Augustine Hall
18. Lombard St. Black Public School
19. Bray Associates School

PRIVATE HOMES: ☐

20. Richard Allen
21. Absalom Jones
22. James Forten
23. John Gloucester
24. Anthony Benezet
25. Benjamin Rush
26. Thomas Harrison

OTHER INSTITUTIONS:

27. Strangers Burial Ground
28. African Masonic Lodge
29. Walnut St. Prison
30. State House
31. Almshouse

Legend to Map 3

The frustrations of black and white advocates of education always stemmed from the twin problems of paying for the education of black children in a society in which only the middle and upper classes could afford private schools or tutors, and releasing them from the work they did as indentured servants or apprentices, which was a condition of life for both white and black lower-class children. Reformers concentrated on solving the first problem but could do little about the second. Thus although the movement for public education, designed to subsidize the education of the children of the working poor, gathered momentum in the early nineteenth century, the matter of how laboring-class children would get released from work to attend those schools was left to chance.

Amid much rhetoric regarding the peril posed to the republic by an uneducated mass of Americans and, conversely, the increase in moral discipline that literacy would promote, reformers took up the notion of free public education, first proposed in 1787 by the old friend of free blacks, Benjamin Rush.[121] Convinced that "a republican nation can never be long free and happy" without schooling, Rush had called for a system of free city schools to be supported by a property tax.[122] Philadelphians proved unwilling to loosen their pocketbooks in the cause of republican virtue at this time; but fifteen years later, in 1802, the legislature authorized the Overseers of the Poor to levy taxes to pay for the education of poor children in private neighborhood schools. An amending law in 1809 called for compiling lists of children from age five to twelve whose parents could not pay for their education. In Philadelphia, however, no black children were subsidized, a fact that attracted the indignant notice of Arthur Donaldson, a white schoolteacher. And although further legislation in 1812 and 1818 established a system of public schools administered by popularly elected directors, the exclusion of black children continued.[123] White Philadelphians found no contradiction in excoriating what they described as a growing problem of black ignorance and immorality while denying publicly supported education to a new generation of black children—or at least those whose parents were able to keep them at home rather than binding them out at an early age.

Excluded from the benefits of the budding public system of education by both economic circumstances and racial prejudice, black Philadelphians had to continue relying on white charity schools and schools they organized themselves. When the Abolition Society opened a large new school in 1813, it attracted more students than had appeared early in the century. Daily attendance averaged about 60 and climbed to roughly 100 by 1816.[124] Most black youths, however, continued to obtain the rudiments of education only when the masters to whom they had been indentured or apprenticed provided it.

Black adults, whom many black and white leaders tried to attract to night school, also disappointed the reformers with their meager attendance, and adult illiteracy among former slaves remained high. From 1813 to 1815 only 28 percent of the Philadelphia black mariners who filed registration certificates could sign their names, in contrast to 80 percent of white mariners.[125] Even among better situated blacks, illiteracy was common. In 1807, for example, only 18 of the 49 male Bethel members who subscribed to the church's revised articles of incorporation could sign their names, although in 1822, 54 of 88 male members at more prosperous St. Thomas's could do so.[126]

Abolition Society leaders were discouraged by the fact that more adult blacks did not take advantage of the limited opportunities available to acquire the rudiments of education. However, to black migrants to Philadelphia, most of whom had grown up in an oral slave culture, the investment of time in an adult night school, at the end of a long day of physical labor, may have seemed like misplaced energy. After working ten or twelve hours, often washing clothes, cooking and cleaning, handling cargo on the docks, sawing wood, or hauling goods about the city, they had to choose between spending a few evening hours with family and at church or learning to read and write in a classroom. Moreover, in a city where the structural barriers to advancement were growing, many blacks may have questioned whether literacy would really gain them a better job, as advertised by whites.

The merits of schooling as the best means for inculcating moral values may also have seemed dubious to many free blacks. The enthusiastic attachment of black Philadelphians to their churches, which exceeded that of whites, is compelling evidence that they wished to dignify their status as free people through self-discipline and sober comportment. At church, as the surviving sermons of black preachers show, they imbibed the same moral calculus that white churchgoers did.[127] But it is notable that none of the sermons urged black parishioners to acquire the tools of literacy. This fact suggests that black preachers understood that, given the prevailing conditions, this would be an unrealistic demand and, moreover, that religion rather than literacy would provide the underpinning of self-improvement. In their lukewarm response to the charity night schools, black adults signaled their belief that in their churches, where communication was oral and the learning process communal, they could find the tools for fashioning an upstanding life. Some whites in the city believed they had accomplished this. Writing in 1816, one reported that "making due allowance for the oppression and wrong which this afflicted race have suffered from their more enlightened fellow men, they may, in point of moral honesty, stand on a footing of fair comparison . . . manifesting dispositions of forgiveness and moderation towards those who injure them, often to the admonition and instruction of their white neighbors."[128]

In one other way, through founding mutual benefit societies, Philadelphia's black citizens attempted to strengthen the bonds of their own community and overcome the effects of white prejudice. The Free African Society, established in 1786, was the first of these attempts. A decade later, in 1796, black congregants at Absalom Jones's St. Thomas's African Episcopal Church established the African Friendly Society of St. Thomas, and by 1801 two other societies had been formed. Then, between 1802 and 1812, as hundreds of southern migrants reached the city, black Philadelphians formed ten more societies, nine of them from 1810 to 1812.[129]

Many of the societies were associated with the black churches, and many of the names indicate the continuing identity of blacks with their African heritage—the Daughters of Ethiopia, Daughters of Samaria, Angola Society, Sons of Africa, and the several African Lodges of the Black Masons. Modeled after white mutual benefit societies, they collected modest dues and distributed money to needy members, especially widows and their families. Aside from this economic function, they provided vital networks for exchanging information about jobs, for mobilizing opinion on issues of importance to the black community, and for creating sociability among a populace in flux. "They have been the means," reported a white Philadelphian, "of turning the attention of this friendly people, in some measure, to a dependence on themselves and given them some juster notions of their own importance."[130]

While white Philadelphians were reshaping the old commerce-driven economy of the city and ushering in a contentiously participatory two-party system, they were also losing their concern for incorporating black city dwellers into their republican system. To many whites the black population, swollen with newcomers, seemed outside the realm of the new republic and only an impediment to accomplishing their goals. Black Philadelphians, confronted with this rising indifference and outright hostility, instinctively realized that they must move from a position of dependence upon white benevolence to one of self-reliance. This crucial step in the formation of the black community would become all the more important in the era of bad feelings that followed the War of 1812.

7. *The Bittersweet Cup of Freedom*

DURING THE SUMMER OF 1814, as a British flotilla entered Chesapeake Bay, city dwellers along the Atlantic seaboard scrambled to improve their defenses against the marauding English. On August 24, the day the British burned the national capital, nearly one thousand "of the hearty and patriotic sons of Africa" turned out to work on the fortifications on Brooklyn Heights guarding the approach to New York City. Philadelphians responded less quickly, but by early September calls went out for the city's free blacks, exempt from military service, to form brigades for improving the fortifications south of the city on the west bank of the Schuylkill River. A black Committee of Defence, led by James Forten, soon mobilized more than a thousand black Philadelphians, who marched out of town on September 21 and 22 along with brigades of Irish, Germans, and other white Philadelphians to strengthen the redoubt protecting the city. Philadelphia's blacks, while working alongside fairer-skinned city dwellers, must have considered themselves as part of the community of "Patriotic Diggers" memorialized in verse in New York:

> To protect our rights, 'gainst your flints and triggers,
> See on Brooklyn Heights, our patriotic Diggers.
> Men of every age, color, rank, profession,
> Ardently engage, labor in succession.[1]

In moments of crisis, white Philadelphians needed black Philadelphians, and the latter were eager to prove their patriotism and civic responsibility. But the interclass and interracial harmony that prevailed when black and white shovel brigades stood shoulder to shoulder in September 1814 did not last. Only a year later, white Philadelphians in the Northern Liberties, claiming to be bothered by the noise of emotional religious services in their neighborhood, destroyed a black house of worship.[2] This violent display of white hostility near the end of the War of 1812 prefigured race relations in the city before the Civil War and marked the beginning of generations of adversity for black Philadelphians. Within another two decades racial violence would fill the streets of American cities, and the vision of biracial equality and harmony held out by the center of American humanitarianism would be shattered. In a society where class differences were coming under increasing attack, the affirmation of racial distinctions assumed new importance among white Americans. Race, in effect, became a substitute form of hierarchy among white northerners drawn to the egalitarian ideal of an open, competitive society.

THE BLACK COMMUNITY in Philadelphia, as it had evolved by the 1820s, was far from an undifferentiated whole. The successive waves of migrants who made their way to the city and their continuous striving for place created a diverse and multileveled black society. But it was a society less divided internally than white society because, whatever their economic, religious, and ideological differences, these former slaves were bound together in the common plight of being black in an increasingly hostile society dominated by whites.

In sheer numbers, free blacks in Philadelphia increased from nearly 10,000 in 1810 to about 12,000 in 1820 and to 14,600 in 1830.[3] Since the white population was growing rapidly—the overall population of Philadelphia surpassed 100,000 for the first time about 1816 and by 1830 reached 164,000—the proportion of blacks in the city actually declined, dipping below 10 percent of the population for the first time in the late 1820s. As in the past, most of the numerical increase in the black population came from migrants. The settled black population was barely able to perpetuate its numbers because the high mortality rate, though much lower than that of black Americans in other seaboard cities, was roughly double that of the white population and therefore severely restricted natural increase. Also limiting the internal growth rate was fertility among black women, held down because so many of those who were indentured into their mid-twenties had to postpone marriage.[4] Thus the black community grew primarily because Philadelphia continued to function as a catchment for an area stretching from the West Indies to New England. New infusions of outsiders continued after the War of 1812 from the Pennsylvania hinterland; from New Jersey, New York, and New England; from the lower South; from the West Indies; and, most of all, from Delaware, Maryland, and Virginia.

By the third decade of the nineteenth century the economic circumstances of black Philadelphians had become far more differentiated than in the early days of freedom. Many suffered abject poverty after the War of 1812, when the most severe depression in Philadelphia's history threw as much as one-third of the labor force out of work.[5] The proportion of blacks in the almshouse outstripped their share of the population for the first time in about 1815 and continued to grow into the 1820s. An almshouse census in 1817 found that one-eighth of the 1,086 inhabitants were black; by 1826, blacks represented one-fifth of those admitted to the almshouse.[6] Poverty-related crimes against property, such as larceny and burglary, also increased in the second decade of the nineteenth century at rates that white leaders found alarming. By the end of the War of 1812, blacks made up 43 percent of the inmates of the penitentiary, and they continued to account for more than one-third of the prison population throughout the 1820s.[7]

At the opposite end of the economic spectrum stood many black families that had attained middle-class or even higher status in the early nineteenth century. The 1820 census revealed that among 1,970 black householders, 229 (11.6 percent) owned property with an aggregate value of $124,289, or more than $540 per home—a firm indication of middle-class position.[8] Although this was a lower percentage than for the city as a whole, it still proved that within a part of the population largely excluded from the usual wealth-producing occupations, a significant number of individuals had succeeded in material terms. Not only men such as

Figure 15. Black oystermen and clam sellers (1814). Black Philadelphians had a virtual monopoly on oyster and clam selling, an enterprise that flourished outdoors and in oyster cellars.

successful sailmaker James Forten or ministers such as Richard Allen, but also many others who made their livings as coachmen, barbers, carters, and craftsmen lived by this time in middle-class respectability.

While black Philadelphians continued to find a wide variety of crannies in the urban economy, those who were starting out faced more unfavorable odds of finding secure livelihoods than their predecessors in the early days of the free black community. The extended depression from 1816 to 1823 ravaged many parts of the Philadelphia economy and took an unusually heavy toll on the ranks of laboring people. In 1813 Philadelphia's first soup kitchens were established by the Society for Supplying the Poor with Soup, and the organization kept more than 3,400 people from starvation in 1817.[9] Surveying the city in 1818, John Melish estimated that 15,000 people were "either idle or occupied in unproductive labour."[10] In the next year a nationwide financial panic brought bankruptcies, foreclosures, and a further stagnation of the economy, driving unemployment in the city to "epidemic proportions."[11] Adding to the distress of laboring people, both black and white, were typhus and yellow fever epidemics in 1818 and 1820 and an unusually harsh winter in 1821. In the latter year an unprecedented 5,237 received poor relief, nearly twice the number of a decade before.[12]

Black Philadelphians were not the only disadvantaged, exploited, and disparaged residents of the city. In particular, the black experience was shared by the large numbers of Irish immigrants who were disembarking from ships along the Delaware wharves after the War of 1812. They too were trying to fit themselves into a society in which wealth was becoming much less evenly distributed, into an urban geography that was becoming more socially divided, and into an economy in which wage labor in larger and more highly capitalized enterprises was replacing small shop craft production.[13] In these changing cicumstances of urban life, laboring-class Irish and blacks lived in crowded alleys and courtyards in ramshackle housing that would have shocked an earlier generation, and more of them found themselves in the almshouse or prison. Both groups came to Philadelphia with all the liabilities of the migrating underclass—impoverishment, lack of education, physical debilitation, psychological disorientation, and the loss of familiar social networks. Both struggled for a foothold in the city and suffered discrimination, unemployment or underemployment, sickness, injury, disease, and poverty. Just as recently arrived free blacks struggled to find employment in the 1820s, Irish immigrants found, as one of their number wrote home in 1820, that "business of every kind is dull . . . and wages very low . . . and many from Ireland cannot get either."[14]

Unlike white immigrants pouring into the city in the 1820s, however, black Philadelphians were largely excluded from the industrializing textile, shoe, and metal sectors of the economy. Given the generally harsh circumstances of factory work and the inability of most immigrants to use it as a springboard to economic success, this exclusion may not have seemed a misfortune at the time. It may even have buffered them somewhat from the depression, when manufacturers laid off white workers en masse but retained the services of black cooks, coachmen, and washerwomen.[15] However, it began the process of separating white and black workers and initiated the general exclusion of blacks from industrial work that in the long run worked severely to their detriment.

The social elaboration of northern black society was evident not only in the black social hierarchy that took form but also in the different cultural styles developed in Philadelphia. On one side of this cultural divide stood the "respectable" black families, most of them tracing their Philadelphia residence back to the 1780s (and in some cases much earlier), who had achieved something close to a bourgeois style of life, even if their occupations did not connote middle-class status in the eyes of white neighbors. William Gray, the fruitseller; Cyrus Bustill, baker and schoolteacher; Richard Allen and Absalom Jones, businessmen and ministers; James Forten, sailmaker and rentier; Jonathan Trusty, mastersweep; Cyrus Porter, coachman; Quammony Clarkson, schoolteacher; Cato Collins, oysterman; and many others had acquired most of the accoutrements of respectability and displayed the cardinal virtues promoted by white society—industry, frugality, circumspection, sobriety, and religious commitment. They owned property, served as trustees and elders at their churches and as officers of black beneficial societies, schooled their children, dressed conservatively, and spoke proper English. Their self-conscious respectability was denoted in the adoption of middle names at least as early as the end of the eighteenth century. Their sense of continuity was denoted by the naming of sons after fathers, with "Junior" following the name, as was the white convention.[16]

The organization that best reflected this striving and accomplished part of the black community was the black Masonic lodge. Deciding to form a Masonic lodge in 1797, leading blacks, including Richard Allen, James Forten, and Absalom Jones, had applied for a license to the white Masonic lodge in the city, which included many of the city's leading citizens. When white Masons refused them permission to organize, the black leaders turned to Prince Hall, Boston founder of the first black Masonic lodge in America. Before the American Revolution, Hall had received a charter from England to establish a lodge, and after the war he remained a leader of Boston's free black community. Hall came to Philadelphia in 1797 to officiate over the installation of the first officers in Philadelphia's African Lodge of Pennsylvania.[17] Black masons had already been meeting for many months and in June 1797 had raised the eyebrows of one upper-class white Philadelphian by parading through the streets, led by lodge master Absalom Jones, on the same day that white Masons conducted their annual procession. "'Tis the first I have heard of negro Masons—a late thing, I guess," mused Elizabeth Drinker in her diary.[18]

Three years later, in 1800, Philadelphia's black Masons displayed their identification with respectable white society by walking in procession to commemorate the birthday of George Washington. Showing their regard for the sequence in which black institutions in the city developed, they invited the black "friendly society and the humain society" to march with them and decided it was proper that "the oldest society walk first, and the junior society next, and the Mason society last."[19]

Between 1810 and 1814 black Philadelphians founded three new Masonic lodges—Union, Laurel, and Phoenix. In 1815, declaring their independence from the Boston lodge, members of the three new lodges pooled their resources with the parent African Lodge of Pennsylvania and built the city's first black Masonic Hall. There the four lodges met, presided over by Grand Master Absalom Jones, as the First African Independent Grand Lodge.[20] By this time the black Masons' membership lists were virtually a roll call of Philadelphia's respectable and accomplished black residents. Their ranks included many members of Absalom Jones's increasingly middle-class African Episcopal Church of St. Thomas and many from Richard Allen's Bethel Church. It was such men who became the officers of the Society for the Suppression of Vice and Immorality, established in 1809; of the first black insurance company, founded the following year; of the Augustine Society, a literary club organized in 1817; and of many musical and literary societies founded in the 1820s and 1830s.

At an economic and cultural distance from the men who marched in procession as black Masons, schooled their children, attended discourses at the Augustine Society, and founded insurance companies were a mass of black city dwellers, many of them recent arrivals. Some of them spoke in southern dialect, drank and gambled, dressed flamboyantly, sometimes ran afoul of the law, and affected a body language—the sauntering gait, unrestrained singing and laughing, and exuberant dancing—that set them apart from "respectable" black society. Theirs was a precarious world, but they made the best of it in ways that whites and some well-to-do black leaders found offensive. We get occasional glimpses of this subculture through the often myopic descriptions of European travelers, who had little background for evaluating black culture, and from the attempts of Abolition Society and black church leaders to suppress it.

At the heart of this subculture was a penchant for conviviality, an unrestrained display of emotions, and a desire to present oneself as individualistically as possible, as if to obliterate the drudgery and submission required under slavery or, later, in the cities, the poverty and blasted ambitions of many free blacks. For these dispossessed urban refugees, "reputation" in the streets and privately created self-image figured more importantly than "respectability" in the community. The French aristocrat La Rochefoucald–Liancourt, who spent several months in Philadelphia in 1797, was amazed at the "love of finery" evident at frequently held balls, where a black domestic servant earning wages of one dollar a week would arrive in a coach wearing a dress "that costs sixty dollars."[21] The Frenchman may have exaggerated the price of the dress, and it is likely that the coaches were borrowed for an evening by black coachmen in the service of wealthy white Philadelphians, but he accurately captured the fondness of lower-class blacks for what would much later become known as "stylin' out."[22] The tireless diarist Elizabeth Drinker noted with some disapproval the way her servants Jacob Turner and Sarah Needham, soon to be married themselves, decked themselves out for the wedding of friends. "Jacob dressed in a light cloath coat, white cashmere vest and britches, white silk stockings, and new hat; Sarah, the bridesmaid, in white muslin dizen'd with white ribbons from head to foot, yellow morroco shoes with white bows." To top it off, the two servants arranged to be driven to the wedding in the coach of the merchant Benjamin Oliver, with his white coachman doing the driving.[23]

All such displays defied the restrained, provident, and self-denying ethos of the white middle class and hence unfailingly brought warnings to suppress such behavior. As early as 1796 the Abolition Society was warning blacks against boisterous gatherings where dancing and frolicking, no doubt accompanied by quaffing of spirituous liquors, occurred.[24] Thereafter the PAS and the American Convention of Antislavery Societies annually distributed advice sheets warning against drinking and frolicking. But no amount of lecturing by either black or white leaders could suppress the release that the black underclass found in wearing showy clothing to "frolicks" and balls, in drink, and in other forms of conviviality. In fact, as more emancipated or runaway blacks flocked into Philadelphia in the first quarter of the nineteenth century, the drinking, boisterous loitering, and propensity for fancy dress became an ever more distinctive style. The talented watercolorist Pavel Svinin, secretary to the Russian consul in Philadelphia, captured the fondness for display, and also the joyous release from day-to-day cares that came through emotional religious services, in a series of watercolors done in 1810. They show the wearing of colorful bandannas to have been widespread among women and top hats nearly universal among men, not only for ceremonial occasions but as a regular part of dress at work, even by sawyers and other laborers.[25]

In the eyes of white critics and some black ministers, such cultural expressions, which seemed to flaunt white standards of respectability and regard for one's proper place in society, became signs of degeneracy. Throughout the early nineteenth century both black and white leaders continued to lecture blacks against such gaiety, unseemly display, and raucous behavior, but there may have been subtle differences in their approaches. In its annual broadside advice sheets, which were distributed door to door and read aloud in churches and beneficial society meetings, the Abolition Society urged the practice of Christian virtues as the antidote to impiety and moral deficiencies allegedly acquired under slavery. Black leaders, subscribing to the gospel of moral improvement, added their voices. In 1808 Richard Allen used the public execution of the black migrant John Joyce as an opportunity to thunder at the "People of Colour" about the prevalence of drunkenness, stealing, and "midnight dances and frolics."[26] It was apparently this event, which involved the gruesome murder of a white woman by an intoxicated free black from Maryland who had recently arrived in the city, that led to the formation of the Society for the Suppression of Vice and Immorality in the following year by Allen, Absalom Jones, and James Forten. Such black leaders agreed with the white view that slavery had degraded Africans and left them with shrunken moral resources that could be restored only by the steadfast cultivation of Christian virtues. They were also painfully aware that strident behavior, flamboyant dress, intoxication, and all the other elements of "street culture" could be used by unfriendly whites to bolster their argument that African people were inherently immoral and hence unfit for freedom.

It became standard, in black sermons, in funeral eulogies, and in exhortatory addresses distributed by the annual intercity black conventions that began meeting in Philadelphia in 1830, to warn against such behavior.[27] None of those efforts, however, whether by black or by white reformers, reduced the fondness for making a stylishly individual statement through dress, and nothing could arrest intemperance among some of those caught in the trap of unemployment and despair. In 1822 an English traveler remarked on the "black dandys" and their extravagantly dressed female consorts.[28] In the same year another visitor found it only ridiculous to espy the "black face and great white eyes of a negress" under "a huge Leghorn bonnet and lace cap." This observer found proof that black women imitated the fashions of upper-class whites when he saw "several with their wool parted in front, drawn into a knot on the top of their heads, and ornamented with a large tortoise-shell comb."[29] This was probably a misreading of the cultural meaning of such hair styles. For slaves the shorn head carried the deep symbolic meaning of a person consigned to "social death," as Orlando Patterson has put it.[30] Conversely, to coiffure one's head elaborately was to display a powerful badge of independence and personal autonomy.

The lines that separated the cultural expressions of lower-class blacks and the black bourgeoisie, as these statements of self-presentation appeared in dress and forms of sociability, were never tightly drawn. As among whites, a reciprocal influence operated between high culture and popular culture. For example, the fondness for large convivial gatherings with animated behavior that took the form of street frolics among the underclass had its middle-class counterpart in elaborate balls supplied sumptuously by black caterers and enlivened by black musicians. Likewise, the black Masonic lodges, composed of the black elite, engaged in much "pomp and pageantry" in their annual processions.[31]

The intermingling of class-based cultural expressions was particularly prevalent in the black Methodist and Baptist churches. In a later period most of the black bourgeoisie would withdraw to the more sedate confines of St. Thomas's African Episcopal Church; but in this era many well-to-do and middling black families worshiped at the Baptist and Methodist churches. There they joined the humblest parishioners, including many from the South only recently released from slavery, in deeply emotional singing, chanting, and shouting. One white visitor described how "when the preacher ceased reading, all . . . fell on their knees, bowed their heads to the ground, and started howling and groaning with sad heart-rending voices." Later in the service the worshipers "began chanting psalms in chorus, the men and women alternating."[32] Reminiscent of the antiphonal tradition in African singing, these "short scraps of disjointed affirmations, pledges or prayers," as another white observer disparagingly termed them, were "lengthened out with long repetition choruses" and sung "in the merry chorus-manner of the Southern field harvest, or husk-ing-frolic method of black slaves." Accompanied by cadenced foot stomping and thigh slapping, the mode of "negro dancing in Virginia," such forms of emotion-engaging worship were re-garded by white churchmen as "gross perversions of true reli-gion" and as intolerable cacophonous interruptions of Sunday morning sleep by hard-drinking white workingmen recovering from Saturday night carousals.[33] Although black worshipers were condemned at all levels of white society, their emotional engage-ment within their own sanctuaries brought an intermixing of high and low culture, drawing together black Philadelphians who, in their economic standing and social aspirations, were becoming more distinct and class conscious.

WHETHER CONSIDERING the dress and behavior of the black lower class or of the black bourgeoisie, whether observing them in the street or at church, most white Philadelphians developed an increasingly negative view of black city dwellers. After the War of 1812 white Philadelphians at all levels of society threatened the personal freedom and opportunities for advancement of their black fellow citizens. This rising Negrophobia has often been in-terpreted as the product of increasing competition for jobs, hous-ing, and political voice at the lower levels of society as the north-ern cities entered a period of rapid growth and industrialization. The Irish, who lived and worked alongside black Philadelphians and who figured prominently in the racial violence that began in the late 1820s, have attracted special criticism from historians in this regard.[34] However, this intraclass hostility festered in a more general atmosphere of racial antipathy that was promoted by intel-lectual and political leaders in the city and by a growing middle-class resentment of blacks. Although some white reformers still befriended the black community, throughout the antebellum era a growing number of Philadelphia's white leaders began to league themselves against the former slaves who were attempting to achieve equality and respectability in the northern cities.

Providing the intellectual underpinnings for the rise of Negrophobia was a full-scale attack on the environmentalist theory that had dominated thinking about racial differences since the Revolution. Leading the onslaught was Charles Caldwell, who had received his medical education at the University of Pennsylvania under Benjamin Rush and became a member of the medical faculty there in 1810. In two long essays provoked by Samuel Stanhope Smith's reissued *Essay on the Causes of the Variety of Complexion and Figure in the Human Species,* Caldwell argued in 1811 and 1814 that differences between races were innate and thus completely resistant to environmental modification. Reflecting the "virtual collapse of [the] intellectual stance [of environmentalism] in America," Caldwell's assertions of the inherent inferiority of Africans and their descendants coincided with Rush's death in 1813, as if to punctuate the fact that one chapter of race relations in Philadelphia had ended and another begun.[35] Caldwell left Philadelphia for Kentucky in 1819, but he was succeeded by other racial theorists. Throughout the antebellum period phrenologists and anthropologists in the former center of environmentalist thought argued against innate human equality and ruminated gloomily about the social mixing of naturally superior whites and naturally inferior blacks.[36]

A few years after the defection of Rush's prize student, another dramatic reversal of support for the notion of black potentialities and interracial comity occurred in Philadelphia, further signaling a new climate of opinion among the city's intellectual leaders. A successful merchant and land speculator, a stellar political economist, an important officeholder and politician (first Federalist and then Republican), Tench Coxe was a man whose wealth and position linked him to a national as well as a local elite. From 1787 to 1789 he had been secretary of the Pennsylvania Abolition Society and a subscriber to the view that the degraded conditions under which Africans had lived in bondage explained any of their vicious habits; hence freedom and opportunity, if supported by attention to education and religion, would enable former slaves gradually to shed moral liabilities and advance to the status of whites.

By 1809, when he wrote a series of essays on the molding of a distinct American character, Coxe's earlier views on race were changing. Though still an abolitionist and expressing hope that "the humanity of white people" might elevate them "from their African condition," he claimed that blacks were inherently inferior.[37] In the next decade Coxe turned vehemently Negrophobic. In 1820, in *Considerations Respecting the Helots of the United States, African and Indian, Native and Alien, and Their Descendants of the Whole and Mixed Blood,* Coxe made a dramatic contribution to the growing doctrine of innate black inferiority. Mixing a hatred of slavery with a hatred of black people, he had become so convinced of black inferiority that, as his biographer has written, "he had only to contemplate fleetingly the notion of [racial] equality to be thrown into frenzied terror."[38] In a series of thirteen essays inspired by the renewal of the dispute over admitting Missouri to the Union, Coxe argued that blacks were innately inferior, were not to be considered a part of the social compact enunciated in the Declaration of Independence, and hence had never been citizens of Pennsylvania or the United States. Published in John Binns's anti-black *Democratic Press,* Philadelphia's most popular newspaper among Jeffersonian workingmen and shopkeepers, his diatribe amounted to a defense of slavery "that not even southern hard liners . . . could have bettered." Using language not heard in Philadelphia for decades, Coxe described blacks as "uncivilised or wild men, without our moral sense . . . [or] our notions of moral character," a people (along with American Indians) "not yet evinced, by the actual facts, to be capable of genuine modern civilization." To free more of them would mean "the prostration of everything from the cradle of the infant to the couch of age, the bed of virgin purity, and the half sacred connubial chamber."[39]

No direct line can be drawn between the changing theories of race differences promulgated by intellectual and political leaders and popular white opinion regarding black Philadelphians. Working-class whites would probably have been stirred to hostile attacks on the black community even without the published views of Charles Caldwell, Tench Coxe, and others, and indeed only the latter vented his repugnancy in the popular press. However, such upper-class writers influenced opinion at the middle and upper strata of society and hence legitimized behavior that earlier leaders would have condemned. When white prisoners refused to eat with black inmates in the penitentiary in 1818, they could, if it had been

necessary, have defended their position with the arguments provided by intellectual leaders. Likewise, in response to the demands
of white inmates, prison officials made their decision to institute a
segregated prison system in an atmosphere that stressed the unal-
terable inferiority of blacks.[40]

Such racial antipathy, festering in a new intellectual milieu and
intensified by the deep economic slump that began in 1816, became generalized throughout white society. White Philadelphians
turned their own suffering against their black neighbors by stig-
matizing the entire black community as a public burden that
soaked up poor taxes. "It is popular opinion," wrote the Pennsylvania Society for the Promotion of the Public Economy in 1817,
"that the greater part of the poor are descendants of Africa."
Although this was not "supported by the facts" derived from the
society's investigation of the almshouse admissions and its ques-
tionnaire to the directors of every benevolent society in Philadelphia, public opinion could not be moved by mere facts.[41] "There
exists a penal law," wrote an English visitor to Philadelphia in the
next year, "deeply written in the minds of the whole white population, which subjects their coloured fellow-citizens to uncondi-
tional contumely and never ceasing insult. No respectability," he
continued, "however unquestionable,—no property, however
large,—no character, however unblemished,—will gain a man,
whose body is (in American estimation) cursed with even a twentieth portion of the blood of his African ancestry, admission into
Society!!!"[42]

This characterization of the increasing racial antipathy in Philadelphia was vividly borne out in the same year these words were
published when a group of black men, including one of Richard
Allen's sons, announced plans to raise subscriptions for an African
Fire Association. White fire companies reacted with outrage. They
issued circulars and called for public meetings to halt what they
regarded as an invasion of a civic function that whites alone were
equipped to discharge. The primary centers of white working-
class democracy and sociability, the city's numerous fire companies announced defiantly that they would not brook such an
invasion of their fraternity by blacks, whom they saw attempting
to step out of subservient roles. Convinced that a fearsome white

backlash would be released, black leaders quickly convened and, under the chairmanship of James Forten, publicly asked the African Fire Association to disband.[43]

That white racial hostility was beginning to suffuse the community became tragically apparent in an incident at Richard Allen's church in November 1825. At a Sunday evening service, several white youths slipped into the back of the church and threw a heap of cayenne pepper and salt into the wood-burning stove. The church quickly filled with the fumes of the burning pepper, sending hundreds of worshipers into fits of coughing and choking. When the cry of fire was raised, hundreds rushed toward the doors, and in the melee two parishioners were trampled to death and others severely injured.[44] In the next decade black churches would become special targets of racist white attacks, especially resented, it seems, because they were centers of black strength and black pride.

White working-class hostility, fed by job competition during difficult times and by neighborhood rivalry, must have been deeply discouraging to black Philadelphians. But even more disheartening was the complicity of white officials and city leaders, who endorsed exclusionist policies and, through their actions and publicly stated views, created the milieu that encouraged those below them to vent their hostility toward black citizens. For example, white magistrates in the depression of 1816–1823 "encouraged suits [against free blacks] before them for trifling sums," according to a report of the Abolition Society, and frequently sent to prison free blacks "whose Cases are ignoramused by the Grand Juries"—a "most serious" oppression of the black community.[45]

TWO EVENTS occurring between January 1816 and January 1817 show how Philadelphians, white and black, dealt with the problem of deteriorating race relations in their city in the decade following the War of 1812. One event, the founding of the American Colonization Society, was controlled by whites; the other, the final breakaway of the Bethel African Methodist Episcopal Church from white authority, was directed by blacks. The former, organized and supported by some of the most important cultural and political leaders in America, intended to repatriate as many free black Americans as possible to Africa, and thus ease the growing racial tensions by sanitizing the country of former slaves. The latter, led by Richard Allen and other black religious leaders who rejected the idea of colonization, demonstrated the under-standing of black Philadelphians that any viable future in America depended on severing connections with white institutions and creating fully autonomous black centers of strength from which to carry on the struggle for freedom, dignity, and equality.

The attempts of white Methodists to rein in their nearly auton-omous coreligionists at Richard Allen's Bethel Church reached a climax in 1815–16 as Philadelphians began to suffer the effects of a postwar depression that would lengthen into the worst economic slump the city had ever known. The precipitating incident for Bethel's final secession occurred in July 1814, when John Emory, a future bishop of the Methodist Episcopal Church, issued a public letter disowning the entire membership of Bethel as Methodists. Emory was determined to force the trustees to abandon their au-thority over congregational life, which they had conferred upon themselves in the African Supplement of 1807 amending the church's articles of incorporation. When the Bethelites refused to back down, reasoning that their Methodist belief could not be erased by a white edict, Emory opened another meetinghouse virtually in Bethel's shadow and ordered Bethel's members to attend service there, "hoping thereby to split the congregation."[46] This too had little effect. Early in 1815, however, white Methodist authorities encouraged Robert Green, a former Bethel trustee who had been dismissed for a breach of conduct, to challenge in court the trustees' disciplinary authority. Supported by white Method-ists, Green took his case all the way to the Pennsylvania Supreme Court in July 1814. Six months later, the court ruled that pro-cedural defects by Bethel's trustees rendered Green's disciplinary trial illegal.[47]

Encouraged by the supreme court decision, Emory's successor in Philadelphia, Robert R. Roberts, decided to test again the will of the recalcitrant black Methodists at Bethel. Determined to es-tablish his authority, in the spring of 1815 he announced to several Bethel members that he intended to preach in the black church. A

Marylander by birth, and a man of stern visage, Roberts' announcement was an intentional challenge to the Bethelites' African Supplement, which gave the church's black trustees the right to approve anyone preaching in their church.[48] Arriving at Bethel on Sunday morning, Roberts found men of equally stern visage. Already in the pulpit stood Jacob Tapsico, a soapboiler by trade and an assistant minister at Bethel. As Roberts attempted to move down the aisle toward the pulpit, numerous black worshipers barred his way.[49] The symbolism of this collective gesture must not have been missed by those who had been pulled from their knees while in prayer at St. George's nearly a quarter century before. Thwarted like his predecessors, Roberts withdrew from the church.

Not to be defied, the white Methodist leadership concocted a final scheme in June 1815. Presiding elder Roberts, after obtaining the legal opinions of two eminent Philadelphia lawyers that the African Supplement was "not binding upon the Methodist Episcopal church," declared Allen's church the property of the white Methodist General Conference. Ordering the sheriff to sell it at auction, Roberts engaged the disaffected Bethelite Robert Green to bid for the property. Allen foiled this brazen tactic by outbidding Green at the auction, paying more than $10,000 for the deed.[50]

The frustrated Reverend Roberts soon had more on his mind than the determined Bethelites, for upon the death of Francis Asbury in March 1816, he was named bishop of the Methodist Episcopal church. His successor in Philadelphia, Robert Burch, a native of Ireland, repeated the exercise of trying to preach at Bethel as a way of discrediting the African Supplement. By now, however, Allen had armed himself with the counsel of nine lawyers who advised him "to fend off" any intruders who might attempt to officiate at Bethel. When Burch appeared on a Sunday morning, bearing an invitation to preach from Robert Green, the disaffected Bethelite, he found himself confronted with a large number of black parishioners armed not only with legal documents but also with "deadly weapons."[51]

Not easily dissuaded, Burch made one final attempt to carry his point by appealing to the Pennsylvania Supreme Court in December 1815 for authority to preach at Bethel. This too was unsuccessful.[52] Through the supreme court decision a few weeks later, on New Year's Day 1816, Bethel finally achieved legal recognition as an independent church, although this was only jurisprudential confirmation of what, in the hearts and actions of the Bethelites, had long been a reality. More than a hundred miles to the south, in a victory celebration that reflected the close communication developing between black communities in different cities, Daniel Coker preached to Baltimore's black Methodists on January 21, 1816. Seeking biblical sanction for the Bethelites' long struggle, he cited the Jewish escape from Babylonian captivity. "Those Jews," exhorted Coker, "had not equal privileges with the Babylonians, although they were governed by the same laws, and suffered the same penalties." Now the Philadelphia Bethelites, like their brothers and sisters in Baltimore who had waged a similar struggle and had finally seceded from the white Methodist church, were free "to sit down under our own vine to worship, and none shall make us afraid."[53]

Many years in the making, the final rupture of black and white Methodists in 1816 mirrored the maturation of the black community as well as the increasing racial tensions besetting the society at large. Six years before, in 1810, Daniel Coker had written of black churches and the black clergy as "a biblical embodiment of the cultural and religious transformation of enslaved Africans into free Afro-Americans." Coker had conveyed the growing sense among blacks that, far from an unregenerate and degraded people, they were the "chosen generation," a "holy nation," a "peculiar people" whom God had selected for special work. Already, Coker pointed out, fifteen congregations of separated black people worshiped under the care of thirteen ordained black clergy and eleven other licensed local preachers.[54] Coker's sense of black destiny was in fact predictive of what would happen at Bethel six years later.

The emergence of fully independent Afro-Christian churches, played out in Philadelphia in Bethel's historic separation from white Methodist authority, was part of a broader rise of black denominationalism in the first quarter of the nineteenth century. Coker himself had led a separatist movement of black Methodists in Baltimore that closely paralleled the Philadelphia experience. It had reached fruition just a few weeks before the January 1816 supreme court ruling in Pennsylvania. Even before that, in 1813, black Methodists in Wilmington, Delaware, led by Peter Spencer, had parted ways with white coreligionists and created an independent African Union Methodist church.[55] Six years after Bethel gained independence, free blacks in New York City forged a third African Methodist denomination—the African Methodist Zion Church.[56] Black Methodism could not be contained within the authority structure of the white church, particularly when that church reneged on earlier antislavery commitments, when it became instrumental in the colonization movement, and when it acted oppressively in the crucial areas of congregational life—in matters involving control of church property, congregational discipline, access to ordination, and representation in church-wide governing bodies. Black churchfolk, as William Gravely has stated, would not compromise their religious freedom. "They wanted to elect and be elected to church office, to ordain and be ordained, to discipline as well as be disciplined, to preach, exhort, pray, and administer sacraments—in sum, to have their gifts and graces acknowledged by the whole community."[57]

Just a few months after the Pennsylvania Supreme Court's momentous decision recognizing Bethel as a legally independent body, Richard Allen, who over the years had made his Philadelphia church the center of a regional network of black Methodists, convened a meeting of mid-Atlantic black Methodists in Philadelphia. Gathering on April 9, 1816, sixteen representatives of five black churches in Baltimore, Wilmington, eastern Pennsylvania, and Salem, New Jersey, agreed to confederate their congregations, all of which had experienced similar difficulties with white parent church bodies. Seventeen years of waiting to be appointed an elder in the Methodist church ended for Richard Allen, who now received sanction from his black coreligionists. The three-day meeting concluded with the delegates rising in Allen's Bethel Church to sing "Praise God from Whom All Blessings Flow."[58]

The assembled delegates, in breaking away from white denominational authority, had to install authorities of their own. The seventeen delegates first chose Daniel Coker as bishop, but, for reasons that have been disputed by church historians, he declined.

Born in slavery in Maryland to an English indentured servant woman and an African slave, Coker was very light-skinned. According to Daniel Payne, who in the 1850s gathered documents for the first history of the African Methodist Episcopal church and interviewed three members of the gathering in Philadelphia, the "pure blacks" objected to Coker's lightness, believing, as one member present at the convention later wrote, that "they could not have an African Connection with a man as light as Daniel Coker at its head."[59] Whatever the reasons for Coker's refusal of the position, Allen was then elected.

The final emancipation of the black Methodist church from white ecclesiastical jurisdiction was an event of extraordinary importance to the former slaves of northern cities such as Philadelphia and Baltimore. Just as their personal emancipations from slavery had involved a psychological rebirth, the collective emancipation of their church had enormously heartening effects on the black community. David Smith, the black Methodist preacher from Baltimore who was at the first annual conference, wrote that "no one can imagine with what enthusaism the colored people of these two great cities were filled, over these encouraging prospects."[60] But it was left to Benjamin T. Tanner, a distinguished Philadelphia black Methodist, to capture the full import of the declaration of independence. Taking his cue from the scriptural passage "Stand up, I myself am also a man" (Acts 10:26), Payne wrote, in the aftermath of the Civil War and the Emancipation Proclamation, that "the great offense," the "unpardonable crime," that Allen, Coker, and several thousand free blacks had committed in 1816 "was that they dared to organize a Church of men, men to think for themselves, men to talk for themselves, men to act for themselves." Black Methodists, while supported, supplied with preachers, and governed by the white Methodist church, could never develop a sense of their own strength or produce their own leaders. "When we were under the control of the [white] M. E. Church," wrote Payne, "they supplied our pulpits with preachers, deacons, and elders, and these in the vast majority of instances were white men. Hence, if the instructions given were of the right kind, the merit was the white man's and his alone. . . The colored man was a mere hearer . . . If the churches among the colored people were well governed, the merit was the white man's and his alone. The colored man was a mere subject." The point of this, Payne noted, was "to prove that the colored man was incapable of self-government and self-support and thereby confirm the oft-repeated assertions of his enemies, that he really is incapable of self-government and self-support." Looking back in the 1850s from a distance of a generation, Payne pointed with pride to the enormous growth of the African Methodist Episcopal church in the decades after 1816 as "a flat contradiction and triumphant refutation of this slander, so foul in itself and so degrading in its influence."[61]

In 1817, one year after the historic creation of the African Methodist Episcopal church, Allen, Coker, and James Champion (a master sweep who had become one of Allen's assistant ministers at Bethel) drew up bylaws by which the AME church would govern itself. In prefatory remarks, they expressed some of their anger at the "spiritual despotism which we have so recently experienced" and vowed to take a different course from that of white Methodists, "remembering, that we are not to Lord it over God's heritage, as greedy dogs, that can never have enough; but with long suffering, and bowels of compassion, to bear each other's burdens, and so fulfil the law of Christ."[62] The "discipline" that they constructed closely followed that of the white Methodists with two important exceptions: the office of presiding elder—the thorn in their sides for nearly two decades—was omitted, thus providing for more democratic church governance; and slaveholders were excluded from membership.

EARLY IN 1816, when Charles Fenton Mercer, a Federalist legislator in Virginia, launched a campaign to convince the federal government to colonize free blacks from America on the west coast of Africa, he unknowingly precipitated a crisis in Philadelphia's black community. Believing that hostility to free blacks would always block their efforts to rise in society, Mercer foresaw a growing class of frustrated, angry, and pauperized blacks who would threaten the harmony and stability of the republic. Before the year ended, Robert Finley, a Presbyterian clergyman who directed the Princeton Theological Seminary, had picked up Mercer's idea and transformed it into a plan for a national colonization society headquartered in Washington, where it could lobby Congress for funds to repatriate large numbers of free blacks on the west coast of Africa.[63] Like Mercer, Finley had come to believe that white prejudice and the disabilities supposedly acquired by blacks under slavery had doomed the best efforts of former slaves to rise to a position of equality in America. But if benevolent whites could help the nation's free black citizens remove to Africa, the latter would gain the opportunity to realize their potential and at the same time bring Christianity and civilization to a continent teeming with souls to be saved.

From Mercer's and Finley's efforts came the American Colonization Society, founded in the nation's capital in December 1816. At its first meeting, Elias Boudinot Caldwell, clerk of the Supreme Court and scion of a wealthy New Jersey family, argued that white prejudice would always block Afro-American accomplishment. If educated, blacks gained a "higher relish" for equality with whites—an equality that white northerners were proving every day they opposed. "The more you improve the condition of these people," argued Caldwell, "the more miserable you make them."[64] White racial prejudice was permanently relegating free blacks to a degraded position, which was a contradiction of the entire credo of the republican ideology emanating from the American Revolution. Caught in such an impasse, white reformers chose to remove the object of white racism rather than combat racism itself.

In the early months of its existence the American Colonization Society attracted support from various quarters, and it was this mixed character that makes its motives difficult to pin down and that at first blinded some black leaders to its essential thrust. Some of its support was drawn from the Protestant evangelical clergy, who were attempting to curb disorder, maintain the authority of religion, and regain social control in an era of rapid economic expansion and what they saw as moral backsliding. Free blacks, along with other lower-class groups, "constituted a threat to the order and decorum of society," and although other groups might be reformed, blacks must be removed. Advantages for blacks, it was thought, would attend this process.[65] Not only would Christianity and the civilizing commerce of America reach Africa, but the international slave trade might also be halted.

Such northern designs, initiated by Protestant evangelicals tinged with racism, were seized upon by southerners, who eagerly involved themselves in the Colonization Society and turned it into an organization for ridding the country of what they imagined were free black incendiaries who threatened the slave system and whose removal to Africa would secure the future of slavery. Robert Goodloe Harper, a Maryland political leader and avid colonizationist, labeled free blacks "a nuisance and burden" in 1817. Mercer, who played a leading role in the society in its early years, foresaw class warfare. For him, the growing number of free blacks in the upper South were a "banditti," composed of a "degraded, idle, and vicious population, who sally forth from their coverts . . . and plunder the rich proprietors of the valleys."[66] In the 1820s and 1830s this attitude would typify the society's southern members, whose support was vital to the colonization effort, even while some of them continued to believe that repatriating free blacks would serve the cause of abolition.

For Philadelphia's black leaders, the idea of colonization at first held considerable appeal. They knew that their attempts to end slaveholding in the republic had failed and that the vast new cottonlands opened to settlement following the Louisiana Purchase in 1803 were extending slavery westward. They recognized that white abolitionists had lost momentum, having falsely assumed that the end of the slave trade would deal a death blow to slavery. And they understood that in the North as well as the South prevailing opinion brazenly avowed the United States a white man's country where free blacks had no claim to equal rights and were, in reality, only half free.[67] Colonization challenged their national identity, encouraging them to think of themselves as Africans, not as Afro-Americans. Thus emigration was one way of solving what must sometimes have seemed an unbearable tension between being black and being American.

The idea of returning to Africa also had appeal because it had been the dream of Paul Cuffe, the black New England merchant-mariner with whom Philadelphia's black leaders and Quaker merchants had maintained a close friendship. They knew that Finley, in formulating his plans for a large colonization scheme, had corresponded with Cuffe, whose dreams for returning American blacks to their ancestral homelands had most recently resulted in carrying thirty-eight black settlers to Sierra Leone in 1815. Cuffe had been gratified to hear from Finley in December 1816 that "the great desire of those whose minds are impressed with this subject is to give an opportunity to the free people of color to rise to their proper level and at the same time to provide a powerful means of putting an end to the slave trade, and sending civilization and Christianity to Africa."[68] Cuffe had responded by recommending that Finley and his cohorts work with the African Institutions that he had founded in New York and Philadelphia to encourage emigration to Africa.

In the latter city it was James Forten who had taken the leading role. Forten had a number of reasons for supporting colonization, not the least of which was his discouragement at the rising tide of white hostility to free blacks in his city. In addition, his friendship with Cuffe was very close, and he shared the mixture of commercial enterprise and Christian commitment that Cuffe exuded. Moreover, Forten and other black leaders trusted Samuel Mills, Finley's associate, who was training black ministers to go out to Africa; and it was well known that John Gloucester, minister of the African Presbyterian Church, had sent his eldest son, Jeremiah, to Mills for training as a missionary.[69]

Philadelphia's black leaders must also have been impressed that some of Philadelphia's foremost white philanthropists and longstanding friends of the free black community were supporting colonization. At its first meeting after becoming incorporated on New Year's Day 1817, the Colonization Society had appointed Richard Rush, the son of Benjamin Rush, as an honorary vice-president, and another honorary vice-presidency went to Robert Ralston, a wealthy merchant who for twenty years had been a friend and benefactor of free blacks. The following year William White, bishop of the Episcopal church and longtime patron of Absalom Jones, became a vice-president, and Jacob Jones Janeway, the city's leading Presbyterian clergyman and a patron of John Gloucester, joined the cause.[70] Also supporting colonization were the two leading Quaker abolitionists and friends of free blacks in the city—Roberts Vaux, who had retired from business in 1814 to devote his life to benevolent causes, abolitionism foremost among them; and Samuel Emlen, Vaux's close friend, a man with close ties to English abolitionists, and a longtime friend of Paul Cuffe, James Forten, and other black leaders.[71] In his biography of Anthony Benezet, published in Philadelphia in 1817 as a spur to abolitionism, Vaux called for "fitting the younger generation of slaves for freedom and settlement, either on some section of country within the jurisdiction of the United States . . . or [by making] arrangements for conveying them to the land whence their fathers were treacherously and inhumanly estranged."[72]

With Paul Cuffe and so many seeming white friends of free blacks in the vanguard of the colonization movement, it is not surprising that Forten, Richard Allen, Absalom Jones, and other black leaders were attracted to the idea. Allen's bruising decade-long battle with white Methodists may also have led him to believe that the future for American blacks would become even bleaker. What these black leaders did not at first foresee was that from the moment of its founding the American Colonization Society would attract the enthusiastic support of southern politicians who viewed repatriation of free blacks as a way of preserving slavery. Henry Clay, a Kentucky slaveowner, chaired the first meeting of the society in December 1816, and when it was formally incorporated the next month, its officers and leading members were drawn primarily from among those representing the slaveholding interests. Whatever Finley's original purposes, the Colonization Society was soon firmly in the grasp of those resisting, not abetting, abolitionism, men whose thoughts on blacks, whether free or slave, easily turned to the topic of innate Negro inferiority and degradation.

If Philadelphia's black leaders could not perceive the uses to which the idea of colonization was quickly put, the mass of black Philadelphians understood almost instinctively. On January 15, 1817, when black leaders called a general meeting at Richard Allen's Bethel, nearly 3,000 black Philadelphians thronged the church on Sixth Street, jamming the main floor and packing the balcony that extended around the church. James Forten chaired the meeting, and Russell Parrott, the assistant pastor at Absalom Jones's African Episcopal Church, recorded minutes as secretary. Although no formal accounts of the meeting survive, it is apparent that Forten and the three most respected black ministers in Philadelphia—Jones, Allen, and John Gloucester—spoke of the advantages of colonization. But when Forten called for a vote on colonization, asking first for "ayes" from those who favored it, not a voice or hand was lifted. When Forten called for those who opposed colonization the response was one tremendous "no" that seemed, Forten wrote some years later, "as it would bring down the walls of the building."[73] Reporting to Paul Cuffe, Forten explained that "there was not a soul that was in favor of going to Africa" and that Philadelphia's blacks were "very much frightened . . . that all the free people would be compelled to go" in a massive deportation scheme. They uniformly disbelieved that whites wished to do "a great good" for a people they hated and were unanimous in the opinion that "the slaveholders want to get rid of them [free blacks] so as to make their property more secure."[74]

The emotional meeting at Bethel proved to be an extraordinarily annealing event in the black community, even though a sharp division had initially surfaced between the black leaders and the mass of ordinary people in attendance. From the meeting emerged a new commitment to abolitionism and a new feeling of unity among people of different condition, religion, and status. The unanimously adopted resolutions poignantly expressed the new unity: "whereas our ancestors (not of choice) were the first successful cultivators of the wilds of America, we their descendants feel ourselves entitled to participate in the blessings of her luxuriant soil, which their blood and sweat manured; and that any measure . . . having a tendency to banish us from her bosom, would not only be cruel, but in direct violation of those principles which have been the boast of the republic." Stung by the statement of Henry Clay at the first meeting of the Colonization Society that free blacks were "a dangerous and useless part of the community," Philadelphia's former slaves resolved that "we never will separate ourselves voluntarily from the slave population of this country," which was composed of "our brethren by the ties of consanguinity, or suffering, and of wrong."[75]

Challenged to rethink their position on colonization by people who for years had looked to them for advice, the city's black leaders met with Robert Finley, passing through Philadelphia on his way from Washington to New Jersey a few days after the mass meeting. Finley spent an hour with the eleven-man committee that had been appointed at the mass meeting, trying to convince them of the benevolent intent of the Colonization Society. Forten, Allen, Jones, and Gloucester were there and so were the other members of the committee—schoolteacher Quommany Clarkson, hairdresser Robert Douglass, fruiterer Robert Gordon, painter James Johnson, waiter Randall Shepherd, coachman Francis Perkins, and cigarmaker John Summerset, all men of importance in the black churches and organizations of the city.[76] All agreed that the situation for free blacks in the North was worsening and that something must be done. Finley recalled that Allen remained committed to the idea of African colonization and said that he himself would go if he were younger. Forten also continued to favor African colonization, remarking on "the peculiarly oppressive situation of his people" and arguing that "the more wealthy and the better informed any of them became, the more wretched they were made, for they felt their degradation more acutely."[77] In the privacy of his home, Forten wrote Cuffe a few days later that he still believed black people "will never become a people until they come out from amongst the white people." However, continued Forten, "as the majority is decidedly against me I am determined to remain silent, except as to my opinion, which I give freely when asked."[78]

Despite Finley's assurances of the good intentions of the Colonization Society, and despite the lingering support for the idea by some of the city's black leaders, almost all black Philadelphians remained opposed to an exodus from a land where most of them had been born—and where several million of their fellow blacks were still enslaved. Paul Cuffe also remained wedded to colonization, but in fact his health was failing rapidly and within eight months of the epic meeting at Bethel Church he would be dead.

In effect, those who had been led were doing the leading on the question of colonization. About a month before Cuffe died, Philadelphia's black citizens crowded into the black schoolhouse in Green's Court on a hot night in August 1817 for another mass

meeting on colonization. This time the black community was convened not to debate the advisability of returning to Africa but
to protest the formation of a Philadelphia branch of the American
Colonization Society. Forten, Allen, and Jones had apparently all
been convinced by now that the common people, some of them
recently freed or escaped from slavery, had judged correctly the
direction that the Colonization Society was taking. With James
Forten again in the chair and Russell Parrott again acting as secretary, the crowd thundered its support for an address to the
"humane and benevolent Inhabitants of the city and county of
Philadelphia" that renounced any connection with an organization
that was assisting the perpetuation of slavery and hence would
bring only "misery, sufferings, and perpetual slavery" to those
still in chains. Probably written by Forten, the remonstrance concluded: "Here, in the city of Philadelphia where the voice of the
suffering sons of Africa was first heard; where was first com-
menced the work of abolition . . . let not a purpose be assisted
which will stay the cause of the entire abolition of slavery in the
United States, and which may defeat it altogether."[79]

Many years later, when the abolitionist campaign had re-
gathered momentum, black Philadelphians would proudly recall
the "spirit of 1817" and contrast the advanced position they had
taken on colonization with the refusal of New York City's blacks to
speak out publicly against it.[80] By the time William Lloyd Garrison published his *Thoughts on African Colonization* in 1832, the idea
was firmly implanted that Philadelphia's black elite, with James
Forten in the vanguard, had unwaveringly opposed the American
Colonization Society. The reverse was closer to the truth—that
the elite had been the rearguard and the masses had assumed the
front rank. The social formation of the black community had
proceeded to the point where the intuitive understanding of the
unlettered black masses could reverse the thinking of the black
elite on the most weighty question of the day. In 1842, at James
Forten's funeral, Robert Purvis, the Philadelphia-based black
abolitionist, hinted at the reality of the matter in the winter of 1817
but at the same time held to the myth. "It was about this time that
this society of innate wickedness, mantled in the cloak of benevolence, came stalking over the land, so specious and whining in its
tone, so soft and insinuating in its low breathings, that many were

deceived." Forten, of course, was one of those who had been deceived. But Purvis then cast him heroically. "The clique of clerical wolves," he wrote, besieged Forten and promised that if he would abet the Colonization Society's efforts, he "would become the Lord Mansfield of their 'Heaven born republic' on the western coast of Africa." Forten responded by telling them "he would rather remain as James Forten, sailmaker, in Philadelphia, than enjoy the highest offices in the gift of their society."[81]

The two mass meetings in January and August 1817 did not end the efforts of the American Colonization Society to eliminate threats to the virtue of the white republic by removing blacks who had been freed from slavery. Most black Philadelphians, however, continued to regard the organization as a "deportation society" that symbolized white racial antipathy and oppression. The English abolitionist Thomas Clarkson held exactly the same view. He wrote Prince Saunders, a young black Haitian who was making a mark for himself in Philadelphia at this time, that "I should like to know what is the real motive of sending the free people of Colour out of the United States at all. Is it to get rid of them?"[82] Led by Forten and Allen, who had reversed their position on colonization, the city's blacks continued to remonstrate against expatriation in 1818 and 1819. But they spoke even more compellingly in their limited participation in the society's first expeditions to Africa. Of some 10,000 free blacks in Philadelphia, only 22 embarked on the first two ships sent to establish the colony of Liberia in 1819 and 1820. The Philadelphia group consisted of four families, one couple without children, and five single males, including the fifty-five-year-old hatter Terra Hall and twenty-nine-year-old carpenter Frederick James, who were elected to offices in the colony's first black government.[83]

In 1822 another twelve Philadelphians sailed for Liberia, and twenty others left in the following year. However, fewer were recruited in Philadelphia than in New York City, and far fewer than in Baltimore, whence more than five times as many free blacks embarked for Liberia.[84] In both New York and Baltimore slavery was dying much more slowly, and the free black communities were therefore more impelled to abandon their city for new opportunities, however perilous, elsewhere.

The issue of colonization not only united free blacks as never before, it also strengthened their sense of connectedness with southern slaves, for the decision to oppose colonization was partially inspired by the argument that if free blacks abandoned their fellow humans still in chains, slavery would be further strengthened. Resistance to colonization did not, however, produce abolitionist activism in every free black, and some who opposed African colonization would soon embrace colonization of a different kind. But the mass meetings and public debate about the motives of the American Colonization Society helped make northern blacks more aware that the heady early years of freedom were over and the time had come to gird for battle, just as the Bethelites had been obliged to do in the religious sphere.

Only a few years after Philadelphia's black community had resoundingly rejected the idea of African colonization its members had to rethink their position on securing their future in the American North. The hatred and violence of the early 1820s presented them with mounting evidence that the white republic intended no place of dignity and freedom for them. Moreover, they were dismayed by the Missouri Compromise, which extended the slaveholders' realm. Closer to home they faced the ever-present danger of kidnappers, who lurked in the northern cities in search of free blacks to sell into slavery in the South. On many occasions the Abolition Society had tried to strengthen the law passed in 1788 against kidnapping, which carried such light penalties as to make it nearly useless.[85] Nobody whose skin was dark could live without fear of the body snatchers, who preyed on free blacks under the license handed them by Congress in 1793. Even Richard Allen, known throughout the city, was seized about 1806 by a southerner armed with a sheriff's arrest warrant who claimed him as a fugitive slave. It did not take Allen long to reverse the tables on the predator, who was soon arrested for attempted kidnapping and lodged in the debtors' prison when he could not make bail. After three months Allen dropped charges against the man.[86] But the incident drove home the point that the freedom of even the most accomplished black persons, anywhere in the North, remained insecure so long as slavery and slave hunters still existed.[87]

After the War of 1812, when the demand for slaves soared in the South, kidnappers operated more brazenly, snatching up free blacks whom they claimed were escaped slaves and sometimes simply forcing them at gunpoint aboard small ships that then quietly slipped down the Delaware River and headed south for slave territory. Every kidnapping served as a wrenching reminder that the future of free blacks could not be separated from the future of slavery in the United States.[88] These reminders kept free blacks active in lobbying for legislation to strengthen the kidnapping law—a campaign that finally bore fruit in 1820, when the legislature increased the penalties for convicted kidnappers.[89]

The excitement in the Philadelphia community from 1824 to 1827 about emigrating to Haiti demonstrated that many free blacks were deeply discouraged and willing to quit the city if reasonable alternatives could be found, especially relatively nearby. Prince Saunders had presented the idea in 1818 at the American Convention for Promoting the Abolition of Slavery, which met annually in Philadelphia, but civil war on the island at that time made it impossible to do more than contemplate the idea.[90] Saunders had drawn on the support of Thomas Clarkson in England and other prominent abolitionists in Philadelphia.[91] However, it took concrete action by Haiti's president, Jean Pierre Boyer, to launch the movement. Boyer sent agents to the United States in 1824, with instructions to charter ships and recruit skilled free blacks who would help to stimulate the economy of the troubled island. Promising free passage and free land and provisions upon arrival, Boyer's agents met with considerable success in Philadelphia in the summer of 1824.

Richard Allen led the emigration efforts, convening a meeting of black community leaders at his house in late June 1824 and then calling a mass meeting at Bethel. As in 1817, black Philadelphians turned out in huge numbers to discuss colonization. But this time the mood was strikingly different, for the people who pressed into the church on July 4, while white Philadelphians celebrated independence at segregated ceremonies a few blocks away, came to debate a black-sponsored resettlement in the Caribbean rather than a white-sponsored repatriation to Africa. Allen chaired the meeting and spoke fervently in favor of emigrating to a land with which black Americans had identified since black revolution there a generation before had overthrown the slave regime. The crowd

warmed to Allen's words. Whereas they had unanimously opposed the African colonization scheme in 1817, they now overwhelmingly endorsed a plan that would help black Americans, as
it was phrased in a resolution placed before the assemblage, "leave
a country, where it is but too certain the coloured man can never
enjoy his rights." "Emigration to the Island of Hayti," it was
agreed, "will be more advantageous to us than the Colony in
Africa."[92]

Out of this meeting emerged the Haitian Emigration Society
of Philadelphia, organized by Richard Allen and James Forten.
Within six weeks, sixty Philadelphia blacks had gathered their
possessions, bade farewell to friends and relatives, and sailed from
the Delaware wharves aboard the *Charlotte Corday*.[93] A departure
song expressing the sense of thwarted hopes among the emigrants
soon rang out from the Caribbean-bound passengers:

> Brothers let us leave
> For Port-au-Prince in Hayti,
> There we'll be receive
> Grand as la Fayet-te
> No more tote the hod
> Nor with nail and stickee
> Nasty, dirty rag
> Out of gutter pickee.[94]

Hundreds more, encouraged by optimistic reports from the first
emigrants and by the enthusiasm of Richard Allen, emigrated later
in 1824. According to Allen, most of them were Methodists, some
of them probably inspired in part by their religious leader's
dreams of stretching the arms of the African Methodist Episcopal
Church to the Caribbean.[95] But more significant than their religious composition was the fact that this emigrating group was not
composed simply of those who despaired of finding a livelihood in
the Philadelphia community but included a number of the black
community's most respected members. Among them were John
Allen, Richard Allen's son; Belfast Burton, a stalwart at St.
Thomas's and later to become a national black leader; Benjamin F.
Hughes, an assistant minister at the African Presbyterian Church;
John Summerset, a founding member of the Augustine Society
and a leader at Bethel; and Robert Douglass, Jr., a founding mem-

ber of the African Presbyterian Church. Through the autumn and early winter of 1824, ships left Boston, New York, Philadelphia, and Baltimore carrying some 6,000–7,000 emigrants to the independent black nation.[96]

The hopes expressed by one of the Philadelphia emigrants upon reaching Haiti, that the arrival of free blacks from America in an anticipated land of true freedom and opportunity was "the precursor of African liberty in the United States," were dashed in the first year.[97] Many arrived with unrealistic expectations; others found the climate less congenial than they had hoped; and more found rural homesteading not to their liking.[98] By the fall of 1825 many of the emigrants, including most of the prominent black Philadelphians, had returned to the United States. The experience soured leaders such as Forten and Allen on any kind of colonization and led to their reappraisal of flight as an alternative to remaining in the northern cities to fight the rising tide of white hostility. By 1827 Allen was urging black Americans to remain in "this land which we have watered with our tears and our blood, [which] is now our mother country."[99]

Growing white racism in the northern cities made Haitian emigration a compelling experiment. Once it proved unsuccessful, Philadelphia blacks turned with renewed vigor to opposing the American Colonization Society. In 1826, when a group of free blacks in Baltimore endorsed the society's work, another mass meeting in Philadelphia, led by James Forten, John Bowers, and Jeremiah Gloucester, strenuously voiced its disapproval. A year later, writing as "A Man of Colour," Forten published an attack on the Society in *Freedom's Journal*, the black abolitionist newspaper published in New York by Samuel Cornish and John Russwurm. Forten argued that colonization, far from aiding the antislavery cause, would strip the country of free blacks who must stay to fight the slave interests.[100] The annual Negro conventions that began meeting in Philadelphia in 1830 staunchly opposed African colonization in their annual addresses while supporting colonization schemes in Canada.[101] Overwhelmingly, however, black Philadelphians had made their decision to remain in a city that had been their birthplace or adopted home and to struggle there against the rising tide of white hostility.

8. The Dream Deferred

"Sir," thundered South Carolina's Robert Y. Hayne in the memorable nullification debate in Congress in 1830, "there does not exist on the face of the earth, a population so poor, so wretched, so vile, so loathsome, so utterly destitute of all the comforts, conveniences, and decencies of life, as the unfortunate blacks of Philadelphia, New York, and Boston." Defending slavery in the face of mounting abolitionist pressure in the North, Hayne continued: "Liberty has been to them the greatest of calamities, the heaviest of curses."[1] The words were hurled at northern congressmen to silence their attacks on the extension of slavery into the western territories, and they were meant to shame the North for its treatment of emancipated slaves by comparing their condition unfavorably with that of Afro-Americans still held in bondage in the South.

It is true that the period from the end of the War of 1812 to the mid-1830s witnessed rising impoverishment and the decline of opportunity for free blacks in all the northern cities, although not one man or woman, as far as is known, voluntarily returned to slavery in order to escape the miseries of northern urban life. It is also true that in this era the conviction ebbed among most white Philadelphians that former slaves could be incorporated into the white republic. More and more they imbibed the thinking of the American Colonization Society, which in 1825 argued in its official journal, the *African Repository,* that free blacks were "notoriously ignorant, degraded and miserable, mentally diseased, brokenspirited, acted upon by no motive to honourable exertions, scarcely reached in their debasement by the heavenly light" and hence should gladly return to Africa.[2]

Black Philadelphians could have made sense of such descriptions only by concluding that their authors were blind or willfully malevolent; for, though they suffered much poverty, their community bore little resemblance to characterizations of this kind. Far from being an undifferentiated mass of impoverished, illiterate, unambitious, and irreligious people, black society had become nearly as stratified as white society, was full of accomplished and aspiring individuals, and had established a wide array of neighborhood institutions. And while more and more white Philadelphians came to perceive their dark-complexioned neighbors as an alien group, by the 1830s the black community in fact had deep roots in local soil. Though increasing mostly through in-migration, the city's black population contained the largest proportion of native-born Philadelphians yet, with nearly three of every five residents having been born in the state.[3] By the end of the decade the black population stood at about 18,000, an increase of nearly 4,000 since 1830. But the number of white Philadelphians had grown even faster, from 164,000 in 1830 to 204,000 in 1840. In the latter year black Philadelphians represented just over 8 percent of the city's population—the smallest proportion since the immediate post-revolutionary years.[4]

Although many descriptions of the black community, both by native Philadelphians and by visitors, read as if virtually all blacks were huddled in shanties and hovels, leading a life of misery and degradation, a process of social elaboration had been occurring steadily. By the second quarter of the nineteenth century a distinctly multitiered black society had emerged. White observers, because it suited their purposes, formed their opinions principally with reference to the poorest blacks in the city, particularly those crowding into new neighborhoods in Moyamensing and Cedar Ward, in the southern sector of the city. In their harsh characterizations of life among the poorest blacks they failed to understand that most of these people were still in possession of spiritual and physical resources and able to count on neighbors, friends, and relatives for at least occasional support, so that they were far from totally inadequate in the face of poverty and discrimination. Meanwhile, hostile white observers remained blind to the black bourgeoisie and elite that had come into being.

The existence of black middle and upper classes is evident from the house-to-house census conducted by the Abolition Society in 1837 as a part of its efforts to forestall attempts to disfranchise black Pennsylvanians through a constitutional revision.[5] Of the 3,652 households listed, dozens possessed wealth in excess of $3,000. Included in this economic elite were sailmaker James Forten, worth more than $40,000; Hagar Ballard, with real estate valued at $40,000 and a personal estate of $16,000; the widow Elizabeth Willson, with an estate of $50,000; clothes dealer Peter Augustus, with personal wealth of $10,000; and barber Robert Douglass, with an estate of $8,000. In all, 282 black Philadelphians owned real estate with an aggregate value of $322,532, an average of $1,143 apiece.[6] The rate of property ownership among black householders had declined since 1820 from 11.6 to 7.7 percent, which was about half the rate prevailing among white households, but the average property valuation had more than doubled in seventeen years.[7] These two statistics reflected the crystallizing of a black upper class and the increasing stratification within the black community.

At the other end of the social spectrum, a growing number of impoverished blacks lived in densely packed alleys and courtyards scattered throughout the city and adjoining districts but especially concentrated in the tenements and shanties of Moyamensing, Southwark, and Cedar Ward on the southern side of Philadelphia, where most of the increase in the black population since 1820 was concentrated (Map 4). With a mean family wealth of $165, Moyamensing and Southwark householders possessed barely half of what the average family in the city wards held ($321), although they were not nearly as poor as the 86 families in the rapidly industrializing district of Kensington, who held only $71 per family. The poverty of these black families in the districts adjoining the city proper was compounded by the peculiar magistrate system of justice in Philadelphia, which allowed magistrates to pocket fees from individuals committed to prison for trivial offenses such as fighting or swearing in the streets in exchange for

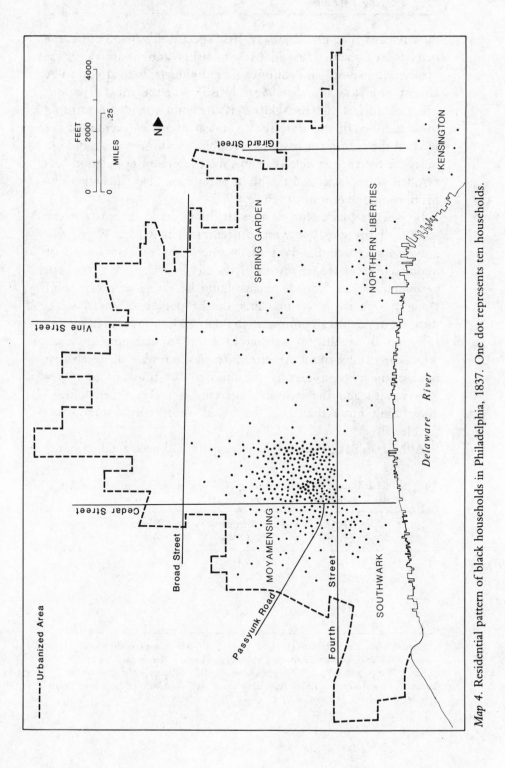

Map 4. Residential pattern of black households in Philadelphia, 1837. One dot represents ten households.

their release. The grand jury in 1837 specifically charged that the behavior of magistrates in Moyamensing and Southwark was "truly astonishing" in "committing individuals, who appear to be almost *pennyless* and *destitute* to prison, on the most frivolous grounds, (merely for the sake of private emolument)." According to a member of the state senate, racial prejudice accounted for most of the commitments, but often black transgressors could not raise the fee to gain release, and thus the prison population was swollen with blacks and the black population charged with a disproportionate amount of crime.[8]

Between a black elite, whose members lived in nearly every section of the city but were concentrated in Cedar Ward, and indigent souls confined in the penitentiary and almshouse or huddled in crowded tenements on the city's northern and southern perimeters, black Philadelphians could be found at every point along the social spectrum. Indeed, the degree of social stratification in the black community by the 1830s, as measured by distribution of wealth, was roughly equal to that among urban whites on the eve of the American Revolution, with the wealthiest tenth of the householders having amassed two-thirds of the aggregate wealth and the richest 5 percent—a truly affluent elite—controlling more than half the black community's total assets (Table 10).

Although black Philadelphians' wealth had become distributed

Table 10. Distribution of wealth among black and white Philadelphians, by decile group (in percentages)

Decile group	Whites 1774	Blacks 1837
0–30	1.1	2.1
31–60	4.0	5.7
61–90	22.6	24.7
91–95	16.8	13.0
96–100	55.5	54.7

Sources: White Philadelphians (1774): Gary B. Nash, *The Urban Crucible: Social Change, Political Consciousness, and the Origins of the American Revolution* (Cambridge, Mass., 1979), p. 395, table 3; black Philadelphians (1837): Papers of the Pennsylvania Society for the Abolition of Slavery, microfilm ed., reel 26, Historical Society of Pennsylvania (hereafter Census of 1837).

in a pattern common to all urban populations, their occupational composition, by the second quarter of the nineteenth century, differed radically from that of the white community in two respects. First, black society conspicuously lacked both a mercantile class and a professional corps of doctors and lawyers.[9] Second, artisans and industrial workers were becoming more and more underrepresented in the black work force. Like white city dwellers, black Philadelphians sorted themselves out by occupation and status, but they did so within a much narrower range of job roles. For black men, maritime work—on ships, along the docks, and in the warehouses that lined the Delaware River—continued to be a mainstay, although by the 1830s blacks were being muscled off the American ships plying the Atlantic sea-lanes and even off the docks. In 1837 the Abolition Society census counted 242 black porters who worked the docksides but only 122 black mariners, compared with the 220 listed on the ships' crew lists in 1821.[10]

Black artisans also decreased proportionately because more and more white craftsmen refused to accept black apprentices and tried to crowd journeymen out of the trades. Despite these obstacles, however, many black artisans continued to practice their skills, retaining a clientele not only among some whites but, more important, among the several thousand black families who sought their services. It was a sign of the determination of the black community to preserve its craft skills that in the rebuilding of the African Presbyterian Church in 1837, only black construction workers were employed.[11] Dozens of black bakers, tailors, shoemakers, carpenters, masons, and others in the construction and retail trades continued to follow their callings. In 1832 black leaders reported 400–500 black artisans at work in the city. Five years later, the Abolition Society census of black households counted only 306 male artisans, although 261 women worked in the needle trades.[12]

The striving for independent economic status that had begun years before, especially in retailing food and clothing, also continued. By 1837 black Philadelphians included 30 female shopkeepers, 13 boardinghouse keepers, and a scattering of female teachers, midwives, nurses, musicians, and artisans. One of every 9 male householders had found his way to a retail or proprietorial position; there were 9 restauranteurs, 14 grocers and oystermen, 55 clothes dealers, 65 hairdressers and barbers, 86 carters, and 55 hucksters. Catering and undertaking also proved attractive vocations, and a small number of black men could be found making a living as dentists, bleeders, shipping clerks, and firemen.

Another segment of the black community toiled at service jobs that carried little status in the eyes of whites but often provided comfortable livings. The 73 black coachmen, 105 cooks, 10 stewards, 13 musicians, and 236 waiters whose daily labor was directed at making life more comfortable for affluent whites counted for little in the genteel world of "proper" white Philadelphians. But in the black community such persons could often be found serving as elders and deacons of the black churches, as members of the black Masonic lodges, and as officers of black organizations. It was not unusual in the black community for people holding jobs of low status in the white hierarchy of occupations to amass considerable wealth. Among the largest 37 black property holders in 1837, all of whom owned $1,500 or more in real estate, were oystermen Cato Collins, James Wilson, and Samuel Turner with $3,400, $1,700, and $2,000 respectively; porters Samuel Tyne and Elymer Johnson, each with $1,500; laborer Samuel Watson with $3,000; and waiter George Johnson with $4,000.[13]

A large majority of black Philadelphians could not, of course, achieve artisanal or proprietorial status. As in previous decades, they labored alongside immigrant Irish and native-born whites, who likewise were struggling merely to subsist. In 1837, besides 122 mariners and 242 porters, 857 black males worked as laborers, several dozen as bootblacks and chimney sweeps, and scores of others as whitewashers, welldiggers, gravediggers, and sawyers. Black women, a large majority of whom worked, were overwhelmingly employed as washerwomen (1,071), as domestic servants (309), and in "day work" (581). Even in the service occupations, however, the Irish were competing for jobs that had been held predominantly by blacks in earlier decades.

Special notice must be given to widows, who appear to have been unusually numerous in the black community: no fewer than 597 are listed in the 1837 census. Composing nearly one-sixth of all women above the age of twenty-four, they accounted for 57 percent of the female-headed households.[14] The high incidence of black widowhood seems to have been one of the factors leading to the creation of so many female benevolent societies—at least 62 by 1837—for black women knew that most of them would outlive their husbands, and thus they needed to provide for their later years. "Reflecting on the vicissitudes of life to which the female part of the community are continually exposed," read the preamble to one female society, "and stimulated by the desire of improving our condition, [we] do conclude that the most efficient method of securing ourselves from the extreme exigencies to which we are liable to be reduced, is by uniting ourselves in a body for the purpose of raising a fund for the relief of its members."[15] Many of these widows lived in multiple households, often with other widows but sometimes with a brother, son or daughter, or other relation. Most of them worked as washerwomen and seamstresses, although a few, such as Sarah Allen, Richard Allen's widow, could afford not to work and were designated "ladies" after their husbands died.

Rising racial hostility, in an era of severe unemployment and growing immigration, added to the burdens of the black population and gradually began to alter its occupational structure. Resenting job competition from blacks, white workers did what they could to convince white employers not to hire them, as an official city report acknowledged in 1834.[16] Such pressure paid dividends for white working men by the early 1830s, when black leaders were vigorously complaining of "the difficulty of getting places for our sons as apprentices . . . owing to the prejudices with which we have to contend."[17] A few years later a black newspaper decried the growing displacement of black workers. "Within a few years," it maintained, blacks "have ceased to be hackney coachmen and draymen, and they are now almost displaced as stevedores. They are rapidly losing their places as barbers and servants. Ten families employ white servants now, where one did twenty years ago."[18]

IF ONE FORM of Negrophobia among white Philadelphians was to characterize the entire black community as indigent, intemperate, and degraded, another was to mock and attack those black city dwellers who behaved as if they were not. By the late 1820s the elegant dress and hair styles of middle-class blacks at fancy balls drew the fire of white Philadelphians, who resented the status inversion symbolized by the arrival of black couples in coaches with white drivers and footmen. In 1828 white ruffians gathered on South Street outside a dancing assembly hall, where a black subscription ball was being held, and assaulted women as they stepped from coaches, insulting them, tearing their gowns, and throwing some guests into the gutter. The *Pennsylvania Gazette* and the *Democratic Press,* without a word of criticism regarding the unprovoked violence of the whites, ridiculed the "sable divinities" dressed "in the most grotesque style" and huffed at the "white coachmen and *white footmen*" who attended the black couples. "If matters progress at this rate," the papers asked, "how long will it be before masters and servants change places?"[19] The *Philadelphia Monthly Magazine,* feeding the growing white prejudice, published a five-page satiric account of the dance. No person, the account read, "who could not trace his pedigree as far back as his mother, at the least," was admitted. The article concluded with a slap at sixty-eight-year-old Richard Allen, who, "contrary to reports," did not arrive "as Cardinal Wolsey."[20] *Freedom's Journal,* a black newspaper published in New York City but widely read in Philadelphia, responded angrily. While stating its opposition to "the mania which many have for dancing," it condemned the behavior of white bullies and accused white Philadelphia editors of calculated racism in describing the black partygoers as dressed as "Grandees, Princesses, Shepherdesses, and so on."[21]

The lampooning of middle- and upper-class black Philadelphians became so popular in the 1820s that it led to a new commercial art form—graphic racial caricatures produced to adorn the walls of the city's genteel white citizens. David Claypool Johnston, a descendant of one of the first Quaker families in Philadelphia, may have originated the genre in about 1819 with his "Splendid Procession of [Black] Free Masons" and his "Meeting of the Free & Independent Wood Sawyers, Boot Cleaners, Chimney Sweepers, Porters, of Phila." (Figures 16 and 17). In Johnston's depiction the black woodcutters complain that they cannot

Figure 16. "A splendid procession of free masons." The annual processions of black Masons, which began in the 1790s, became the subject of white ridicule by 1819, when Philadelphia artist David Claypool Johnston created this racist caricature in which black Masons are animalistic and cannot spell the simplest words.

walk the streets "widout bein sulted" by whites. One member of the association suggests sending all whites back to Africa "where dey come from," but a committee appointed to study the problem "tink de best way to git clar on em is to send em to de norf pole."[22] William Thackera, a noted artist and engraver in the city, contributed a series of prints poking fun at black dandies who aped the extravagant dress of their white employers as well as their "cant terms." The drawings sold "tolerably well," the artist noted in about 1820, well enough apparently for Edward Clay, soon to become the premier cartoonist of the Jacksonian era, to execute a series of fourteen colored prints entitled "Life in Philadelphia" in the late 1820s.[23]

Clay's caricatures, ten of them depicting the emerging black middle class, were more vicious than Thackera's. They showed black Philadelphians as stupidly pretentious, always reaching be-

Figure 17. "A Meeting of the Free & Independent Wood Sawyers, Boot Cleaners, Chimney Sweepers, Porters, of Phila." (1819), another of David Claypool Johnston's lithographs produced for the amusement of white middle-class families, reflected the growing white sentiment that black Philadelphians, by refusing to stay in subservient roles, were a social menace.

yond their abilities, and incurably given to malapropisms.[24] In one print (Figure 18), an overweight black man dressed in a cloak covered with Masonic symbols exclaims to a friend, "what 'fect you tink Morgan's deduction [the abduction of William Morgan, who had written an exposé of Masons in New York] gwang to hab on our siety [society] of free masons?" "For honour," answers

Figure 18. Edward Clay's lithograph series *Life in Philadelphia,* lampooned the social pretensions of both whites and blacks, but his racist caricatures such as "Morgan's Deduction" (1829) had the most lasting effects.

another black mason in wing collar, cutaway, and top hat, "I tink he look rader black, 'fraid we lose da 'lection in New York." In another print (Figure 19), a black dandy, meeting a lady friend in the street, inquires: "How you find youself dis hot weader Miss Chloe?" Miss Chloe, dressed in a stupendously hooped, long-sleeved dress with billowing shoulders and a gigantic hat piled with artificial fruit and flowers, answers: "Pretty well I tank you Mr. Cesar only I aspire too much!"

Figure 19. "Miss Chloe" (1829), another in Edward Clay's *Life in Philadelphia* series, sneered at blacks' dialect and supposed lack of education.

Clay's sneering depictions of black middle-class life, etched from 1828 to 1830, were part of a nationwide movement to create a comic black character type for the amusement of white Americans. His prints reached the Philadelphia public at exactly the time when T. D. Rice first performed the Jim Crow song and dance that originated black minstrelsy, soon to become white America's favorite form of entertainment.[25] Clay's racist caricatures crossed the Atlantic and were reproduced in London in 1830 with an unconnected story in *The New Comic Annual,* then recrossed the ocean two years later to be published serially in Philadelphia's new *Saturday Evening Post.* Thus Clay tapped a market for racist art that flourished from the 1820s to the Civil War and beyond—a form of communication suffused with the message that it was futile to extend freedom to blacks in the United States. Consistent with popular politics in the Jacksonian democracy, vernacular art contributed to the ideology of white supremacy. For Philadelphia's black citizens, the popularity of the prints among whites could only have been interpreted as another sign of what they were up against—condemned in general terms as a degraded and vicious class of people and ridiculed and resented when they rose above lower-class status.

THE REACTION of the black community to racial hostility and oppression was not despairing passivity, though disillusionment and a sense of futility must have overcome nearly everyone at many moments. One alternative had been to seek refuge from white American hostility in Haiti. But when that limited experiment failed in the late 1820s, the main response of Philadelphia's black citizens was to continue strengthening community institutions and thus to create an Afro-American society within American society. Consequently, the quarter-century after 1815 became an era of unprecedented institution building that demonstrated the resilience of those regarded increasingly by whites as incapable pariahs. In the formation of churches and benevolent societies and in the education of black children, this was an era of intense creativity and accomplishment. Black Philadelphians could not hold back the storm of racial hatred, but they could try to weather it by strengthening their own neighborhoods and community.

At the beginning of this era Philadelphia's free blacks had already founded Episcopal, Methodist, Presbyterian, and Baptist churches, and the Zoar Methodist Church had a mixed but primarily black congregation. Some 2,366 black congregants, composing nearly half of all adults in the city, belonged to these five churches in 1813. In the next decade black Philadelphians built five more churches, three of them Methodist, one Presbyterian, and one Baptist. By this time, baptisms at the black Methodist churches outnumbered those at all other churches combined, with nearly three-quarters of the 236 baptisms recorded in 1822 being performed at Methodist churches.[26] Then, from 1825 to 1837, black Philadelphians formed yet another five congregations, two of them Methodist, two Baptist, and one Lutheran. In this era of church building, black Methodists and Baptists, particularly the former, led the way. Representing about three-fifths of the city's church members in 1813, the two evangelical denominations embraced nearly 90 percent of about 4,000 black church members by 1837, with black Methodists alone boasting almost three-quarters of all church members (Table 11).

The burgeoning attraction of the African Baptist and especially the African Methodist churches for black Philadelphians can be accounted for in part by the great growth in popularity of the evangelical faiths among all poorer and less hierarchically inclined people during the Second Great Awakening.[27] Black Methodism continued to be particularly magnetic because it provided a personal and emotionally engaging religious experience, nurtured

Table 11. Black church membership in Philadelphia, 1813 and 1837 (number of churches in parentheses)

Year	Methodist	Episcopalian	Presbyterian	Baptist	Lutheran	Total
1813	1,426 (2)	560 (1)	300 (1)	89 (1)	—	2,375 (5)
1837	2,860 (8)	250 (1)	325 (2)	700 (4)	10 (1)	4,145 (16)

Sources: 1813: Donaldson's *Juvenile Magazine*, no. 3 (1813); 1837: *Present State and Condition of the Free People of Color . . .*, p. 32. The number of members at St. Thomas's has been corrected on the basis of the Census of 1837.

through class meetings, love feasts, and participatory church services. The black evangelical denominations in the 1820s also
derived some of their strength in the northern cities from the
political content of their millennial message. Black Christians in
the Baptist and Methodist churches heard the message over and
over again that, contrary to white belief, God had not made them
inferior to whites; indeed, they were superior to white Christians,
who were mired in the sins of slaveholding and racism. It must
have been an elevating thought that God's wrath would descend
on the land unless the sin of slavery was removed and that it was
black Christians, God's chosen people, who would have to re-
deem white America from un-Christian behavior and thus prepare
the nation for the coming millennium.[28]

But the powerful appeal of their religious doctrine and practice
and of the political message embedded in their millennial stance
does not completely explain the overwhelming magnetism of
the evangelical churches, and particularly the black Methodist
churches, in the northern cities. The black Episcopal church had
been enormously popular into the second decade of the nineteenth
century, and black Presbyterianism had also attracted many worshipers. The other factor affecting the growth or decline of particular black churches was the emergence of charismatic black leaders, women as well as men. This, in turn, depended on the degree
of autonomy that particular black churches enjoyed in their relationship with white parent institutions. In the churches that received or wrested this autonomy from parent institutions, new
leaders quickly emerged—men and women who, if imperfectly
educated for the ministry by white standards, were richly endowed, by black standards, with the gift of inspiring religious
devotion.

The best example of the problems engendered by lack of autonomy was Philadelphia's oldest black congregation, St. Thomas's
African Episcopal Church. When Absalom Jones died in 1818, the
congregation was still numerous, although it had been troubled by
a schism during the last years of his life. The search for a successor
to Jones proved difficult, for candidates educated sufficiently to
satisfy white Episcopal church officers, who had the power to
ordain or withhold ordination, could not be found. For a time it

was hoped that Jacob Oson, a self-educated black teacher and lay preacher in New Haven, Connecticut, might fill the position. Oson came to Philadelphia in October 1821 to explore the possibility and won the support of the vestrymen. But despite many letters of recommendation and petitions from St. Thomas's male members warning of their church's decline since Jones's death, white Episcopal authorities could not be moved to overlook what they regarded as Oson's inadequate education.[29]

Ministered to by white clergymen, St. Thomas's congregation began to drift away. In 1822 Russell Parrott, a protégé of Absalom Jones, became a candidate to fill the place of the venerated founding minister. A brilliant young man, Parrott had published an oration at St. Thomas's in 1812, at age twenty-one, commemorating the abolition of the slave trade. Thereafter he quickly emerged as one of the leaders of the second generation of free blacks. A printer by trade, Parrott also authored many addresses to the city's black residents, was a founding member of the Augustine Society, and became a leader in the anticolonization protests.[30] The white bishop of Philadelphia licensed Parrott as lay reader in 1822, and shortly thereafter the church's black vestrymen nominated him as Jones's successor. However, he was dropped by the vestry after many in the congregation voiced objections to him. Less than two years later he died of tuberculosis. St. Thomas's limped along with the white clergy in the city supplying the pulpit while experienced black vestrymen, such as the venerable Cato Collins, served as lay leaders. But the congregation dwindled, shrinking to about 200 by 1837, about one-third of its former size.[31]

White control over ministerial appointments also hobbled black Presbyterians in replacing a founder and longtime leader. John Gloucester's death in 1822 brought division in the African Presbyterian Church over whether his successor should be his protégé Samuel Cornish or his son Jeremiah, both of whom had been licensed by white church officials. Two years later, those who favored Jeremiah Gloucester founded their own church, the Second African Presbyterian Church, erecting a building on St. Mary's Street between Sixth and Seventh streets. Unable to secure the services of Samuel Cornish, who by now had fully embraced the struggle for abolition and moved to New York City to found the first black newspaper, *Freedom's Journal,* with John B. Russwurm, the parent church languished for a number of years before it could find a new leader. By 1837, black Presbyterians, served mostly by visiting white ministers, numbered only a few dozen more than they had under John Gloucester in the first few years of his ministry (Table 11).[32]

While black Episcopal and Presbyterian congregations stagnated or declined, black Baptist and Methodist churches thrived. Black Baptists remained under the authority of the white-directed Philadelphia Baptist Association, but they were very loosely controlled. In 1816 seceding members of the African Baptist Church founded the Second African Baptist Church on Thirteenth Street between Race and Vine, on the northwest perimeter of the city. Black Baptists founded two other churches, Blockley African Baptist Church and Union African Church, in 1827 and 1832, respectively. By 1837 black Baptist congregations included 700 parishioners, making the denomination the second largest in the city (Table 11).[33]

Although the black Baptists registered the most rapid rate of growth of any black denomination in this period, it was the black Methodists who became overwhelmingly dominant in Philadelphia. In 1813, before the final split with white Methodists, the Bethelites had established the Union African Methodist Church. Erected on Coates Street between Fourth and Fifth, near the Old York Road in the northern part of the city, the church served many of the black families in the Northern Liberties, Kensington, and the new district of Spring Garden. In 1817 it had a congregation of nearly 100, and by 1837 the number had nearly doubled.[34]

Black Methodists formed two other congregations in the early 1820s. The first, Wesley African Methodist Episcopal Zion Church, emerged from a denominational dispute at Bethel in 1819. Acquiring property only ninety feet from Bethel, the dissidents erected a church in 1820 and affiliated with the AME Zion Church of New York City. Claiming 300 members in 1821, AME Zion jousted for many years with the New York group, as well as with neighboring Bethel, but maintained their independence. The other black Methodist congregation began meeting in the same neighborhood, in Gill's Alley between Fifth and Sixth streets on Lombard, in the early 1820s.[35]

A crucial element in the rise of the black Methodist church was its freedom from white ecclesiastical control, which left black Methodists free to ordain lay preachers and regular ministers as they saw fit. When Bethel gained its independence in 1816, black Methodists in Philadelphia already had four preachers ordained by Bishop Asbury—Allen, James Champion, Jacob Tapsico, and Jeffrey Buelah.[36] Once Bethel made the final break from the white Methodist church, other men rose from obscurity to assume leadership responsibilities. At the 1816 AME convention, two additional Philadelphia ministers were licensed—Clayton Durham, a sawyer, and Thomas Webster, a laborer. In the next few years other men, such as William Cousins and Jacob Mathews, were authorized to preach, and thereafter dozens were licensed in the Philadelphia area.[37] This ability to recruit for leadership roles ordinary people drawn from the neighborhoods and workplaces of hundreds of black Philadelphians, not only enhanced the appeal of black Methodism but also ensured that when a founder died, as Richard Allen did in 1831, his place could be quickly filled. So great was this reliance on an untrained ministry, recalled a later AME bishop of the 1830s, that many ministers would introduce their sermons "by declaring that they had 'not rubbed their heads against college-walls,' at which the people would cry, 'Amen!' they had 'never studied Latin or Greek,' at which the people would exclaim, 'Glory to God!' they had 'never studied Hebrew,' at which all would 'shout.' "[38]

A final element in the powerful appeal of the African Methodist church was the role it provided women. All black churches, like white churches, depended heavily on women, as teachers in church schools, as moral persuaders of wayward husbands, as leaders of prayer meetings, and as organizers of auxiliaries that supported church programs. But only the black Methodist church recognized the spiritual contributions of women sufficiently to allow nonordained females to preach from the pulpit. The privilege of preaching was not granted to women without a struggle; black Methodists followed the white Methodist discipline, which made no provision for women preachers. But the inspired Jarena Lee, a Philadelphia Bethelite who in 1807, at age twenty-four, felt the call to preach, broke the barrier. At first Richard Allen would not permit her to preach. But in about 1817, pressed again on the matter by Lee, he relented after hearing her deliver an inspired, spontaneous exhortation. Thereafter Lee preached occasionally at Bethel and also at annual conferences while pursuing a career as an itinerant minister known for her charismatic spiritual gifts.[39] In the late 1830s, after Allen's death, the male ministry sharply restricted Lee's access to the pulpit in Philadelphia, but for many years the recognition of her talents, even if given grudgingly, must have made the black Methodist church especially attractive to the many women who believed that not only males were divinely commissioned to preach.[40]

As black churches proliferated in the second quarter of the nineteenth century, the character of each denomination, and of particular churches in each denomination, began to form along lines defined by wealth and status as well as by ideological predilection. There were no distinctly upper-, middle-, or lower-class black churches in Philadelphia, but the social profiles of the various black congregations that can be constructed from the Abolition Society's household census of 1837 do show some differentiation.

Paralleling almost exactly the social differentiation among white denominations, black congregations in Philadelphia ranged in wealth from the more sedate Episcopal church at the top to the evangelical Baptist and Methodist churches at the bottom, with the Presbyterians occupying the middle. With a mean wealth of $1,255, black Episcopalians in Philadelphia in 1837 possessed more than twice as much as black Presbyterians, three times as much as black Baptists, and more than six times as much as black Methodists (Table 12). But even at St. Thomas's the congregation was drawn from all ranks of black society. In a few more decades the church would be known as the temple of Philadelphia's black bourgeoisie, but in the 1830s about half the congregation was composed of men with estates of less than $250. Into the pews on Sunday mornings filed many congregants with wealth of $50 or less, including many men and women who made their living as laborers, mariners, cooks, washerwomen, and even bootblacks and chimney sweeps. Even though the congregation included an unusual number of artisans and small business owners of various kinds, three of the six most prevalent occupations among its

Table 12. Church membership and wealth of black Philadelphians by denomination, 1837

Denomination	No. of members	Total wealth ($)	Mean wealth ($)
Episcopalian	195	244,776	1,255
Presbyterian	203	103,171	508
Baptist	261	107,955	414
Catholic	89	28,390	319
Methodist	1,970	388,278	197

Source: Census of 1837.

members were porter, laborer, and washerwoman. If one mark of bourgeois status was the exemption of wives from labor outside the home, then most of St. Thomas's congregation remained beyond the pale, for two-thirds of the female members continued to supplement the family income through outside work while managing their own households.

At the other extreme stood the African Methodist churches. Bethel, by far the largest, had a much larger proportion of members with less than $100 than did St. Thomas's. But Bethel was not simply a church of the dispossessed. Nearly one-fifth of its congregants boasted personal wealth in excess of $250, not to be compared with more than half of St. Thomas's members in that category but still a substantial fraction (Table 13). Attending Bethel on Sunday morning were houseowning artisans, black dentists and physicians, proprietors of clothes stores and eating houses, and men and women who had accumulated substantial

Table 13. Distribution of wealth among Bethel and St. Thomas's members, 1837

Wealth ($)	Bethel		St. Thomas	
	No.	%	No.	%
0–20	174	14.8	7	3.8
21–50	350	29.8	24	13.0
51–100	251	21.4	25	13.6
101–250	189	16.1	30	16.3
251–1,000	173	14.7	65	35.3
1,000 +	37	3.2	33	17.9
Total	1174		174	

Source: Census of 1837.

wealth. The black community's third wealthiest individual, the glass- and papermaker James Dawson, was a Bethelite, as were the wealthy barber Abner Rolley, oysterman Samuel Turner, and clothes dealer Samuel Flutchins. Of Bethel's female members, 84 percent worked outside the home—an even higher percentage than at St. Thomas's.

To some extent, black Philadelphians chose their church not only for its doctrinal appeal, which was linked to their class standing, but also for its location. All the Philadelphia black churches were neighborhood churches in the sense that they drew most of their members from a four-to-five-block radius. But some churches were more completely identified with their immediate neighborhood than others. St. Thomas's was the only African Episcopal church in Philadelphia in this era, so those who had been charter members in the mid-1790s often maintained their allegiance even if they moved to other parts of the city. Bethel, too, drew from outside its immediate area, for the sway of Richard Allen was great throughout the city. Smaller Methodist and Baptist churches, however, were more local in their appeal, catering to neighborhoods on the north side of the city, as did Zoar Methodist Church and First African Baptist Church, or to the fast-growing black neighborhoods in Moyamensing, as did Wesley African Methodist Episcopal Zion Church (Map 5).

The era of church building and the powerful appeal of black churches that had achieved full independence reflected the fact that black Philadelphia was an intensely religious community and a community that fortified itself from within its religious sanctuaries. By the mid-1830s, with nearly 4,000 church members in fourteen churches, and with the influence of the members extending "to non-professing friends and acquaintances in their immediate vicinity," black Philadelphians could justifiably be amazed, as was the Abolition Society in its 1838 report, that the immorality of a small portion of the black community should lead to "such a mass of opprobrious slander [as] has been so lavishly bestowed upon the whole [black] people."[41]

ALTHOUGH black Philadelphians could construct churches, and could build their lives around the church, it was far more difficult

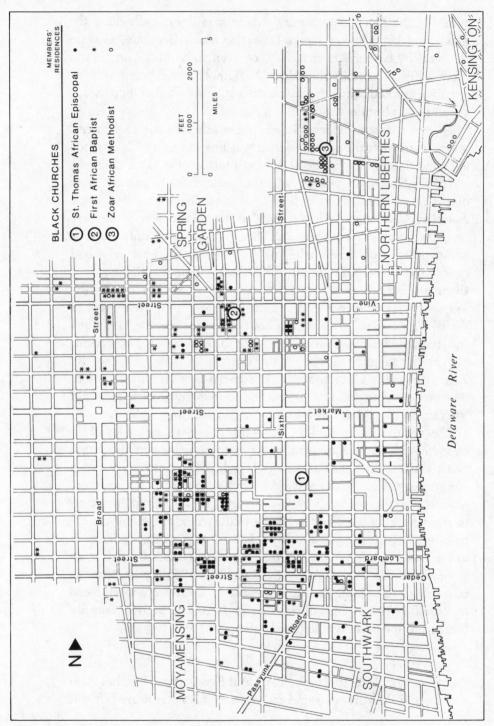

Map 5. Residential distribution of three black Philadelphia congregations, 1837.

to create schools for educating their children. The churches always contributed to training black youth, through Sunday schools and weekday church schools, usually directed by the minister or his assistants as time allowed. Black Sunday school teachers instructed three-quarters of all school-age children in the city and 55 percent of those in the adjoining districts, according to the 1837 census. But all black ministers had many demands on their time, not the least of which was supplementing their small salaries by practicing a second vocation. Nonetheless, the 1820s and 1830s brought a dramatic increase in the schooling of black children.

In theory, the problem of educating black children was solved in 1818 when the legislature, recognizing the failure of earlier attempts to establish free public schools, passed a comprehensive law establishing a Lancasterian system to educate the children of the poor at public expense in the city and county of Philadelphia.[42] All boys from ages six to fourteen and all girls from ages five to thirteen were to be provided with an education, supervised by elected commissioners in specified districts of the city and suburbs. But democratic school governance, in an era when American institutions were being democratized, meant racist governance, which specifically translated into separate and unequal schools for black youths. The elected commissioners decided at the outset that black and white children should not attend school together. Then, while building neighborhood schools for white children in various parts of the city, the commissioners rented rooms in St. Mary's Street and Gaskill Street, where black boys and girls were to be taught. By 1827, 326 black children traveled from all over the city and adjacent suburbs to these cramped rented quarters, but this was only a fraction of the eligible black school population.[43]

Black leaders did what they could to supply what white elected officials would not. Six months after the legislature passed the comprehensive public education law, they founded the Augustine Society of Pennsylvania "for the establishment and maintenance of a Seminary, in which children of colour shall be taught all the useful and scientific branches of education, as far as may be found practicable." Absalom Jones, Richard Allen, James Forten, John Gloucester, Quommany Clarkson, Russell Parrott, Samuel Cornish, and Robert Douglass, representing all the black denominations in the city, were included among the founding members. In a stirring preamble to the society's regulations the black leaders expressed their indignation at the racial barriers erected to contain them. Most whites regarded them as "contemptible and degraded" because they lacked education and were congregated at the bottom of society. At the same time, white prejudices, "powerful as they are unjust," had erected "formidable barriers rendering it almost impossible to obtain for our offspring such instruction as we deem essentially necessary to qualify them for the useful walks of society."[44] The fact that the city's black leaders organized the Augustine Society so soon after passage of the public education law is an indication that they already knew by the fall of 1818 how little elected commissioners were prepared to do toward including black children in the school system being erected.

By 1822 the Augustine Society seminary was one of ten black schools taught by black teachers in the city. In addition white teachers taught black children at the Abolition Society's Clarkson schools and at the Society of Friends' schools in Willing's Alley and in the Northern Liberties. In all, 603 children were receiving education—a substantial increase from the years before the War of 1812. Only 44 of these 603 students were servants or under indenture, an indication that privately operated schools had made substantial progress in educating the children of black families that could spare their children from indentured labor.[45]

In the decade after 1828 the schooling of black children continued to improve, partly through the efforts of black and white leaders who provided private education and even more through the building of the first public black schools—on Lombard Street in 1829 and in the Northern Liberties in 1832. The annual reports of the school controllers show that when free public schools were available for black children, their parents would send them there as readily—in fact more frequently—than white parents. Public school enrollment rose dramatically, from 268 in 1828 to 606 in 1833, and the two biggest jumps in enrollment occurred just after new public schools were opened in 1829 and 1832.

Private schools enrolled hundreds of other black children. By 1837 these included not only the old schools run by the Quakers, the Episcopalians, and the Pennsylvania Abolition Society but also thirteen schools that charged tuition, ten of them taught by black teachers. Whereas education for black children had been largely unavailable a generation before, 65 percent of the 2,018 school-age black children in the city and Northern Liberties, where schools were readily accessible, were attending either public or private schools in 1837. In Moyamensing, Southwark, and Kensington— the districts from which children had to travel some distance to reach schools—only 40 percent of school-age children were enrolled.[46] But even more important than the accessibility of schools was the economic status of the parents. When black families were not obliged by economic necessity to set their children to work at an early age, they proved eager to enroll them in schools (Table 14).

Although Americans in general placed faith in education as the means to combat vice and create responsible citizens, the spread of education in the black community did little to temper white racial prejudice. In 1828 the public school directors had noted their satisfaction with "the improved manners and morals, and proficiency in elementary branches [of education] of the negro scholars," which, they argued, offered "incontestable evidence" of the learning abilities of those who were "by some denied the possession of any attribute of humanity."[47] Nonetheless, racial antipathy grew among the general populace. The era in which church membership and education among blacks grew impressively, and in which black Philadelphians founded three female and two male libraries

Table 14. Family wealth and school attendance of black Philadelphians, 1837

District	Mean family wealth ($)	% of school-age children in common schools
City	321	66.4
Northern Liberties	298	53.4
Spring Garden	202	51.9
Southwark	165	48.7
Moyamensing	165	41.2
Kensington	71	21.4

Source: Census of 1837.

and literary societies, was also the era in which race relations reached new lows, as if every black accomplishment only intensified white resentment and hostility.[48]

One of the most frequent accusations against black Philadelphians in this period was that they had flooded into the city as impoverished migrants and consequently drove up the poor-tax rates by filling the almshouses and jails. During the depression of 1817–1823 the publicly elected Overseers of the Poor, reflecting the growing antiblack sentiment of their constituents and hard pressed to relieve widespread suffering, had adopted a flagrantly racist policy by largely excluding black families from outrelief, which was financed by the taxes of black as well as white property owners. Even after economic conditions improved, the overseers continued their discriminatory policy. An official committee appointed to study pauperism in 1827, noting that only 41 of 1,036 (3.7 percent) pensioners given outrelief in the previous year were black, scoffed, "If the same indifference manifested towards the [black] applicants for relief [was practiced] among the whites, how small would be the number of those whose actual wants require such assistance."[49]

By the 1830s affluent Philadelphians were losing patience with all indigents, regardless of color. Mathew Carey, shocked at the extent of suffering in the city, traced the rise of harsh new attitudes toward the poor and measured the emergence of a new hardheartedness, in a city known for benevolence, by the sharp decline in charitable donations. Carey identified most of the poor as widows with children and men whose seasonal unemployment left them destitute in winter. But a "sore evil" had arisen in Philadelphia, he charged, "a false view of the situation and claims of the poor, by the most wealthy of our citizens." In particular, the upper class had withdrawn its support from the city's much-venerated charitable institutions, leaving the Philadelphia Dispensary, the Female Hospital Society, the Orphan's Society, the Widow's Society, and the Provident Society with only about one-third as many subscribers as a decade before.[50]

Facing such discrimination in the distribution of public relief funds and a general decline in the support of private philanthropic societies, black Philadelphians worked together to solve their problems from within their own neighborhoods. An intense effort to increase the number of black mutual aid societies began during the depression of 1817–1823. Like the white beneficial societies on which they were modeled, the black organizations served men or women united by religious affiliation, trade association, neighborhood, or simply friendship. In 1813, when a list of such societies was compiled, some 514 black Philadelphians, 10 percent of the adult population, belonged to eleven societies. By 1831 the number of societies had risen to forty-four.[51]

Even the efforts of black Philadelphians to lessen their reliance on public poor relief—in effect, to become independent of the white community in yet another way—met with criticism from some white residents, who saw black mutual aid societies only as an "incentive to extravagance and dissipation, and formed merely to gratify . . . ostentatious desire." In defense, black leaders published articles pointing out that in 1831 nearly $6,000 had been disbursed by some 44 societies. By the early 1830s the societies were virtually operating as a privately supported substitute for the public poor relief system in the city. Only 4 percent of those receiving outrelief or admitted to the almshouse in 1832 were black, whereas a decade before the proportion had been one-fifth or more.[52]

The black benevolent societies grew at an increasing rate in the 1830s. They exceeded fifty in 1832 and then, in a spectacular burst of organizing, reached nearly one hundred by 1837. Operating in every neighborhood of the city, they enrolled about 80 percent of the city's black adults, compared with only 10 percent a generation before. Collectively, these societies by 1837 were gathering annually nearly $18,000 in dues and distributing $14,000, twice as much as in 1831.[53] Far from living off the tax dollars of their white neighbors, black Philadelphians appear to have been among the most provident and self-reliant of city dwellers.

ON A SUMMER EVENING IN 1834, a violent attack on black Philadelphians dropped a blood-drenched curtain on a drama begun two generations before in William Penn's "green country town." On August 12 an ugly fight broke out between whites and blacks in South Street at a place where Philadelphians came to ride the Flying Horses, an early carousel. Before the constables could restore order, the white mob had demolished the Flying Horses and was roaming nearby streets, attacking black residents and stoning their houses. The next evening a crowd of whites began a two-day assault on black Philadelphians. Breaking into houses on Shippen, Bedford, Small, and Seventh streets and in adjacent alleys and courtyards in Cedar Ward and adjoining Southwark, the white marauders destroyed furniture, dragged black residents from their beds and beat them, smashed windows, completely destroyed the black Methodist church on Wharton Street, and severely damaged the African Presbyterian Church. Stephen James, described in a report on the riot as "an honest, industrious colored man, a kind husband and a good father," was beaten to death. Especially singled out in the rampage were prosperous blacks, including the son of James Forten.[54]

By the time of the riot in 1834, almost all the characters in the biracial drama that had begun in Philadelphia after the American Revolution—Absalom Jones, Benjamin Rush, Richard Allen, Thomas Harrison, John Gloucester, Robert Ralston, William Gray, and a host of others—were dead. Only a few, such as James Forten and Cato Collins, still remained to remember the initial optimism that had filled many black and white Philadelphians and the atmosphere of relative racial harmony that had briefly prevailed. In the intervening years a deadly contest between black aspirations and white fears had developed. Convinced that they would be truly free only when they were no longer dependent on whites, however benevolently inclined, and possessed by the "double consciousness" of being both black and American, black Philadelphians had formed independent families, carved out their own vocations, built their own businesses, organized separate churches, founded black schools, and formed beneficial, literary, and Masonic societies. All of these strands of community life had become woven together as slaves crossed the crucial threshold to freedom and struggled to achieve the social dignity, economic security, and personal equality that would give full meaning to legal freedom.

This maturing of the black community received little recognition from most white Philadelphians, who formed their mental picture of black society from observing its least successful segment, composed of a relatively small number of the destitute, criminal, intemperate, and immoral.[55] The disparity between the white image and the reality of black society displayed the inability of whites to conceive of black Americans as something more than dependent, slavelike people, even a generation after slavery. This mental limitation was formed by the compulsion of a sprawling, democratizing society to reinstitute order and hierarchy through racial stratification and by the economic advantages white Philadelphians derived from keeping black Americans in a servile position. Thus disposed, upper-class white Philadelphians such as the annalist John Fanning Watson could interpret black accomplishment only as inappropriate striving. "Their aspirings and little vanities," sneered Watson in 1830, "have been rapidly growing since they got those separate churches . . . Thirty to forty years ago, they were much humbler, more esteemed in their places, and more useful to themselves and others."[56] Those situated lower on the social ladder than Watson, following such cues, could dismiss all of black society as worthless and, with that justification, use the democratized political process as fully as possible to limit the rights of black citizens to compete equally in society. The city's first major race riot occurred in Cedar Ward in November 1829, when "a furious battle" between whites and blacks broke out following a loud and emotional black church service. A local newspaper commented that "on Sundays, especially, [blacks] seem to think themselves above all restraint, and their insolence is intolerable."[57]

By the 1830s, as the national abolitionist movement entered its militant phase, the fissures that scarred Philadelphia ran both horizontally, by class, and vertically, by race. In 1831, reacting to widespread white fear caused by Nat Turner's bloody insurrection in Virginia, the Pennsylvania legislature once more debated a bill to seal the state off from incoming blacks, as well as a bill to repeal the fugitive slave laws of 1820 and 1826, which had provided free blacks with some relief from kidnappers who would sell them into slavery in the South. Once again James Forten led an assemblage of free black citizens protesting the discriminatory legislation.

"Why," they remonstrated, "are [Pennsylvania's] borders to be surrounded by a wall of iron, against freemen whose complexions fall below the wavering and uncertain shades of white? . . . It is not to be asked [of the incoming migrant], is he brave—is he honest—is he just—is he free from the stain of crime—but is he black—is he brown—is he yellow—is he other than white?"[58] When colonizationists renewed their arguments that the city's blacks should return to Africa, Forten countered: "Here I have dwelt until I am nearly sixty years of age, and have brought up and educated a family . . . Yet some ingenious gentlemen have recently discovered that I am still an African; that a continent three thousand miles, and more, from the place where I was born, is my native country. And I am advised to go home. Well, it may be so. Perhaps," the old sailmaker concluded sardonically, "if I should only be set on the shore of that distant land, I should recognize all I might see there, and run at once to the old hut where my forefathers lived a hundred years ago."[59]

By 1835, a year after the assault on the black community, Philadelphia was riven with strife. A violent election riot in Moyamensing, occurring just two months after the attack on the black community, left dozens injured and many houses in smoldering ashes. A series of strikes and tumultuous labor protests, reminiscent of those first witnessed by Philadelphians in the late 1820s, punctuated the next two years, and Irish Catholic immigrants began to feel the rising wrath of nativism among Protestant, American-born workers.[60] The old commercial port town on the Delaware now stood squarely at the brink of the new industrial age. Although black Philadelphians were only marginally involved in this momentous transformation, they were directly affected by the frustrated hopes and blocked opportunities experienced by many white Philadelphians occupying the lower layers of society with them.

The new era of radical abolitionism, coinciding with the emergence of industrial conflict, brought Philadelphia's free blacks to the vortex where the swirling waters of race and class commingled. Seeing their gains from over two generations of struggle threatened, they embraced the abolitionist cause with new vigor, understanding that their own continued freedom was inextricably involved with the fate of the two million slaves residing in the American South. David Walker's fiery *Appeal*, emanating from Boston in 1829, followed two years later by the appearance of William Lloyd Garrison's *Liberator*, "has roused up a spirit in our young people," James Forten confided to Garrison, "that has been slumbering for years."[61]

At the same time, increasing white hostility, met by blacks with renewed determination, had put Philadelphians of different complexions on a deadly course. The founding of the American Anti-Slavery Society at a meeting in Philadelphia in December 1833 gave new encouragement to those in the Pennsylvania Abolition Society, now led by Roberts Vaux, Thomas Shipley, and Edwin Atlee, who had struggled through lean years. But each step taken forward by abolitionists encountered an equivalent reaction on the other side. One of the delegates to the first meeting of the American Anti-Slavery Society described how, when the delegates passed along the streets on their way to the convening session, they "were repeatedly assailed with most insulting words" and found police officers guarding the entrance to the building where the convention met. "These incidents," wrote Samuel May, "helped us realize how we and the cause we had espoused, were regarded in that City of Brotherly Love and Quakers."[62] In 1835 an angry white crowd hurled boxes of abolitionist literature into the Delaware River with the city's mayor standing by. James Forten worried about the militant demands of white Philadelphians that black and white abolitionists "put down all discussion of the [antislavery] question."[63] In May 1838 a taunting white crowd, several thousand strong, attacked the newly opened Pennsylvania Hall, built by abolitionist supporters at Sixth Street near Franklin Square as a rallying place and symbol of the new abolitionist determination. Sarah and Angelina Grimké, Benjamin Lundy, William Lloyd Garrison, and other national abolitionist leaders, who had come to the city to mobilize support for the abolition of slavery, all watched as the crowd threw abolitionist literature into the streets, burned the building to the ground, and then, while city officials stood by, stormed the Society of Friends' Shelter for Colored Orphans and a black church in the northern part of the city.[64]

Figure 20. "Destruction by Fire of Pennsylvania Hall, on the Night of the 17th of May." The deliberate burning in 1838 of the newly opened Pennsylvania Hall, a symbol of the emergence of radical abolitionism, was followed by many other violent attacks on the black community in Philadelphia in the antebellum period.

A few months after the burning of Pennsylvania Hall, as the legislature debated formal disfranchisement of Pennsylvania's free blacks, articles flooding the Philadelphia press marked how widespread Negrophobia had become. Urging disfranchisement of black Pennsylvanians, the *Spirit of the Times* charged that blacks had usurped privileges belonging only to those whose skin was white, assumed an air of superiority, and were inveterately lazy. "Who, in fine, is the most *protected,* the most *insolent,* the most *assuming,* the most *depraved,* the most *dangerous* of our population? We answer the *Negro;* THE NEGRO; THE NEGRO!—the Thick-Lipped, Wooley-Headed, Skunk-Smelling, combination of the MONKEY AND THE DEVIL."[65] In such a direction had the racial attitudes of most white Philadelphians traveled since the Revolution, when the preamble to the 1780 abolition act, as black leaders reminded their white Philadelphia neighbors, had averred: "It is not for us to enquire, why, in the creation of mankind, the inhabitants of the several parts of the earth were distinguished by a difference in feature or complexion—it is sufficient for us to know that all are the work of an Almighty hand."[66]

During the remainder of the antebellum era, marked by intensification of the sectional crisis, attacks on Philadelphia's black community became common. Through it all, black Philadelphians not only endured but also continued to build the independent institutions that were vital in the continual reception of large numbers of new members. Thus by the time William E. Burhardt Du Bois wrote his classic study of the Philadelphia black community in 1899, its residents had organized fifty-five black churches and several hundred mutual aid societies. Not until the second quarter of the twentieth century would black Philadelphians witness the beginning of a reversal of the segregationist and exclusionary forces set in motion in the early nineteenth. Even today they have not completely regained the ground that allowed their predecessors in the postrevolutionary era to imagine and work optimistically toward a multiracial and equal society.

Abbreviations

CICFB	Committee for Improving the Condition of Free Blacks, Pennsylvania Society for the Abolition of Slavery
HSP	Historical Society of Pennsylvania, Philadelphia
LCP	Library Company of Philadelphia
PAS	Pennsylvania Society for the Abolition of Slavery
PAS Minute Book	General Meeting Minute Book, vol. I (1775–1787, 1787–1800), microfilm edition, reel 1, HSP
PCA	Archives of the City and County of Philadelphia, City Hall Annex, Philadelphia
PGS	Pennsylvania Genealogical Society, Philadelphia
PMHB	*Pennsylvania Magazine of History and Biography*
PPAS	Papers of the Pennsylvania Society for the Abolition of Slavery, microfilm edition, HSP
RPRG	Records of Pennsylvania's Revolutionary Governments, 1775–1790, Pennsylvania State Archives, Harrisburg
SPG	Society for the Propagation of the Gospel, microfilm edition, Van Pelt Library, University of Pennsylvania

Notes

Introduction

1. Benjamin Rush to Julia Rush, Aug. 22, 1793, in L. H. Butterfield, ed., *The Letters of Benjamin Rush,* 2 vols. (Princeton, N.J., 1951), II, 639.

2. The incident is recounted in Peter Kent Opper, "North Carolina Quakers: Reluctant Slaveholders," *North Carolina Historical Review,* 52 (1975), 56–57.

3. Francis N. Thorpe, comp. and ed., *Federal and State Constitutions, Colonial Charters, and Other Organic Laws . . . ,* 5 vols. (Washington, D.C., 1909), V, 3082.

4. Rush to Nathanael Greene, Sept. 16, 1782, in Butterfield, *Letters of Benjamin Rush,* I, 286.

5. Rush to Richard Price, Oct. 15, 1785, ibid., p. 371.

6. PAS to London Society for the Abolition of Slavery, Nov. 20, 1787, in PAS Minute Book, 1775–1787, p. 17.

7. Michael Kraus, *The Atlantic Civilization: Eighteenth-Century Origins* (Ithaca, N.Y., 1949), p. 125.

8. "Address of the American Convention of Antislavery Societies to the Free Africans and Descendants of Africans in the United States," 1798, PPAS, reel 25.

9. Reinhold Niebuhr, *Moral Man and Immoral Society: A Study in Ethics and Politics* (New York, 1932), p. ix.

10. Frederick Douglass, quoted in *National Anti-Slavery Standard,* Oct. 19, 1848.

11. For an incisive discussion of the historiography of urban black studies see Kenneth L. Kusmer, "The Black Urban Experience in American History," in Darlene Clark Hine, ed., *The State of Afro-American History* (Baton Rouge, 1986), pp. 91–122.

1. Slavery and Antislavery in the Capital of Conscience

1. Nicholas More to William Penn, Dec. 1, 1684, in Richard S. Dunn and Mary Maples Dunn, eds., *The Papers of William Penn*, vol. II: *1680–1684* (Philadelphia, 1982), p. 608.

2. Ibid.

3. Darold D. Wax, "Quaker Merchants and the Slave Trade in Colonial Pennsylvania," *PMHB*, 86 (1962), 143–159; Wax, "Negro Imports into Pennsylvania, 1720-1766," *Pennsylvania History*, 32 (1965), 254-287.

4. I have traced twelve merchants who emigrated from the West Indies to Philadelphia between 1682 and 1710 in "The Early Merchants of Philadelphia: The Formation and Disintegration of a Founding Elite," in Richard S. Dunn and Mary Maples Dunn, eds., *The World of William Penn* (Philadelphia, 1986), pp. 339–340, 355–358.

5. Calculated from data in Jean R. Soderlund, *Quakers and Slavery: A Divided Spirit* (Princeton, N.J., 1985), p. 64, table 3.1. Soderlund's data do not include slaveowners in Southwark and the Northern Liberties. For the percentage of male laborers, see Gary B. Nash, *The Urban Crucible: Social Change, Political Consciousness, and the Origins of the American Revolution* (Cambridge, Mass., 1979), pp. 109–110; for the decline of unfree labor after the Seven Years' War see Sharon V. Salinger, "Colonial Labor in Transition: The Decline of Indentured Servitude in Late Eighteenth-Century Philadelphia," *Labor History*, 22 (1981), 165–191.

6. Ralph Sandiford, *The Mystery of Iniquity; In a Brief Examination of the Times . . .*, 2d ed. (Philadelphia, 1730), p. 5.

7. Gary B. Nash, "Slaves and Slaveowners in Colonial Philadelphia," *William and Mary Quarterly*, 3d ser., 30 (1973), 227–231; Thomas Willing to Coddrington Carrington, Sept. 3, 1756, quoted in Darold D. Wax, "The Negro Slave Trade in Colonial Pennsylvania" (Ph.D. diss., University of Washington, 1962), p. 32.

8. Wax, "Negro Slave Trade," pp. 47–48.

9. Nash, "Slaves and Slaveowners," pp. 234–237.

10. Ibid., pp. 236–237; Benezet to Granville Sharp, Feb. 18, 1773, Sharp Letterbook, LCP. Philadelphia merchants were exporting slaves to Charleston, South Carolina, in the summer of 1773. See Thomas Mason and [?] Patton to Shirley and Price, July 24, 1773, Etting Papers, Miscellaneous MSS, II, 64, HSP.

11. An advertisement in the *Pennsylvania Journal*, May 27, 1762, described Gambian slaves as "much more robust and tractable than any other slaves from the Coast of Guinea and more Capable of undergoing the Severity of the Winter Seasons in the North-American colonies, which occasions their being Vastly more esteemed and coveted in this Province and those to the Northward, than any other Slaves whatsoever." The estimate of 1,000

slaves imported directly from Africa is drawn from data assembled in Wax, "Negro Imports into Pennsylvania," pp. 282–287; also see Wax, "Africans on the Delaware: The Pennsylvania Slave Trade, 1759–1765," *Pennsylvania History,* 50 (1983), 38–49.

12. Emma Lapsansky, "Since They Got Those Separate Churches: Afroamericans and Racism in Jacksonian Philadelphia," *American Quarterly,* 22 (1980), 57–58.

13. Of 521 slaveowners on the 1767 tax list, the earliest extant list detailing slave property, 57 percent owned only a single slave between 12 and 50 years old (the taxable limits); another 26 percent owned only two; Nash, "Slaves and Slaveowners," p. 244. Slave importer Jonathan Dickinson, who brought slaves with him to Philadelphia from Jamaica, wrote in 1715 that slaves were hired out at 18*d.* to 2*s.* 6*d.* per day; Dickinson to Charles Hill, July 14, 1715, Dickinson Letter Book, 1715–1721, HSP. On Dickinson's thirty-two slaves see Edward R. Turner, *The Negro in Pennsylvania: Slavery—Servitude—Freedom, 1639–1861* (Washington, D.C., 1911), p. 13 n. Jonathan Mifflin owned nine slaves, five of whom were hired out. The inventory of his estate is in *PMHB,* 14 (1890), 104. William Masters owned thirty-three slaves at his death in 1757. They are listed in his will, in Philadelphia Will Book M, no. 27, Office of the Recorder of Wills, City Hall Annex, Philadelphia.

14. Nash, "Slaves and Slaveowners," p. 249; Jean R. Soderlund, "Black Women in Colonial Pennsylvania," *PMHB,* 107 (1983), 60.

15. Whitfield J. Bell, ed., "Addenda to Watson's *Annals of Philadelphia:* Notes by Jacob Mordecai, 1836," *PMHB,* 98 (1974), 139. Two of Coates's slaves are listed in the Constables' Returns to the Assessors, 1775, PCA. The silversmith Philip Syng also kept his slave Cato in leg and neck irons, according to a runaway advertisement in the *Pennsylvania Gazette,* May 5, 1748.

16. John Smith Diaries, 1748–1752, June 22, 1748, Smith Manuscript Collection, LCP; Elizabeth Drinker Journal, Sept. 19, 1759, HSP; Merle G. Brouwer, "The Negro as a Slave and as a Free Black in Colonial Pennsylvania" (Ph.D. diss., Wayne State University, 1973), pp. 332–333.

17. Brouwer, "The Negro in Pennsylvania," p. 313.

18. *Pennsylvania Gazette,* Aug. 25–Sept. 1, 1737, cited in Brouwer, p. 186. Brouwer's treatment of slave life in Pennsylvania is the best available. See especially chap. 11, "Black Resistance to Slavery."

19. *Minutes of the Provincial Council of Pennsylvania,* 16 vols. (Philadelphia and Harrisburg, 1852–53), V, 102–103; Elizabeth Drinker Journal, Nov. 17, 1762, HSP. Again in 1773 two blacks were sentenced to hang for burglary; Records of the Proprietary Government, 1682–1776, Record Group 21, Pennsylvania State Archives, Harrisburg.

20. John F. Watson, *Annals of Philadelphia, and Pennsylvania, in the Olden Times . . . ,* 3 vols. (Philadelphia, 1830; reprint, 1900), II, 265. For one

recollection of a slave, "Daddy Ceasar," in whose dialect "there was as much African as English" and who entertained his master's family with "his African songs," see Mrs. F. B. Hoskins, "Fanny Saltar's Reminiscences of Colonial Days in Philadelphia," *PMHB,* 40 (1916), 189. A majority of Philadelphia slaves before the 1770s were probably African-born. In one small sample, a listing of slaves belonging to members of the Moravian Church in 1766, six of nine were born in Africa; William Henry Egle, ed., *Notes and Queries, Historical, Biographical, and Genealogical Relating Chiefly to the Interior of Pennsylvania, Annual Volume, 1896* (Harrisburg, 1897; reprint, Baltimore, 1970), p. 215. For similar burial-place practices in the South see Elizabeth A. Fenn, "Honoring the Ancestors: Kongo-American Graves in the American South," *Southern Exposure,* 8 (1985), 42–47.

21. Hoskins, "Fanny Saltar's Reminiscences," p. 187.

22. In most Chesapeake counties by the mid-eighteenth century, from half to three-quarters of all slaves inhabited plantation living units of twenty or less; Allan Kulikoff, *Tobacco and Slaves: The Development of Southern Cultures in the Chesapeake, 1680–1800* (Chapel Hill, N.C., 1986), p. 338, table 37.

23. *Minutes of the Provincial Council,* I, 380–381; Ancient Records of Philadelphia, p. 11, HSP; Watson, *Annals of Philadelphia,* I, 62; Brouwer, "The Negro in Pennsylvania," pp. 178–179.

24. Register Books of Christ Church: Marriages, Christenings, and Burials, HSP; and Records of St. Paul's Church and St. Michael's Church, PGS, provide the most data on black marriages and births but reveal only a fraction of the complete record.

25. Philadelphia was probably no different from New York City, where in 1746, 1756, and 1771 the ratio of children (under age sixteen) to adults was about the same in the black and white populations; Evarts B. Greene and Virginia D. Harrington, *American Population before the Federal Census of 1790* (New York, 1932), pp. 99, 101–102. For the slave family in New York City before the Revolution see Vivienne L. Kruger, "Born to Run: The Slave Family in Early New York, 1626 to 1827" (Ph.D. diss., Columbia University, 1985), chap. 4. Billy G. Smith has found that lower-class white families in the late eighteenth century had an average of two children, and the Anglican baptism records show that this average was nearly the same for black families. See idem, "Struggles of the 'Lower Sort': The Lives of Philadelphia's Laboring People, 1750 to 1800" (Ph.D. diss., University of California, Los Angeles, 1981), pp. 301–302.

26. For the frequency of slave sales see Nash, "Slaves and Slaveowners," p. 243.

27. For example, of the thirty-three slaves owned by William Masters in 1761, ten were hired out to masters as far away as Wilmington, Delaware; Inventory of William Masters estate, 1761, Office of the Recorder of Wills,

City Hall Annex, Philadelphia. For similar findings regarding slave family life in New York City, see Kruger, "Born to Run."

28. Runaway advertisements in Philadelphia papers describe separated husbands and wives trying to reconnect severed marriages. See, for example, *Pennsylvania Gazette,* Oct. 26, 1758, for the flight of Anne, slave of Philadelphian Robert Wakelu, and her husband, Frank, slave of Alexander Collay, who lived in Whitemarsh, outside the city.

29. Burton Alva Konkle, *Benjamin Chew, 1722–1810* (Philadelphia, 1932), p. 64; *The Life Experience and Gospel Labors of the Rt. Rev. Richard Allen, To Which Is Annexed The Rise and Progress of the African Methodist Episcopal Church in the United States of America* (Nashville, 1960), pp. 15–16.

30. Documents in Benjamin Chew Papers, Box GRL B-4 and Receipt Book, 1770–1810, HSP.

31. *Pennsylvania Gazette,* Sept. 23 and Aug. 26, 1762.

32. *The Journals of Henry Melchior Muhlenburg,* trans. Theodore G. Tappert and John W. Doberstein, 3 vols. (Philadelphia, 1942), I, 721.

33. Soderlund, *Quakers and Slavery,* table 6.2. By the 1760s, Quakers owned only about one-sixth of the city's slaves.

34. George Ross to David Humphreys, March 1, 1728, and Sept. 1, 1726, quoted in Frank J. Klingberg, "The African Immigrant in Colonial Pennsylvania and Delaware," *Historical Magazine of the Protestant Episcopal Church,* 11 (1942), 131–132. For the dilemma of "how to preach a Gospel premised on individual autonomy within the framework of slavery" see Milton C. Sernett, *Black Religion and American Evangelicalism: White Protestants, Plantation Missions, and the Flowering of Negro Christianity, 1787–1865* (Meteuchen, N.J., 1975), chap. 3; and James D. Essig, *The Bonds of Wickedness: American Evangelicals against Slavery* (Philadelphia, 1982), chap. 1.

35. Register Books of Christ Church: Marriages, Christenings, and Burials, I (1709–1750); II (1750–1762); III (1762–1810), HSP.

36. Charles H. Maxson, *The Great Awakening in the Middle Colonies* (Chicago, 1920), p. 62; *Pennsylvania Gazette,* Nov. 8, 1740.

37. Albert J. Raboteau, *Slave Religion: The "Invisible Institution" in the Antebellum South* (New York, 1978), pp. 126–130.

38. For Whitefield's 1739 and first 1740 appearance in Philadelphia see Maxson, *Great Awakening,* pp. 47–53; Whitefield's comments on Philadelphia blacks are in *George Whitefield's Journals* (London, 1960), pp. 411, 422. His lecture to southern slaveowners, *A Letter to the Inhabitants of Maryland, Virginia, and North and South Carolina Concerning Their Negroes,* was published by Franklin in *Three Letters from the Reverend George Whitefield* (Philadelphia, 1740).

39. On Whitefield's defense of slavery and ambiguous attitudes toward blacks see Stephen J. Stein, "George Whitefield on Slavery: Some New Evidence," *Church History,* 42 (1973), 243–256. A much earlier attempt to

educate urban slaves had occurred in New York City, where the Anglican missionary Elie Neau had opened a school in 1704.

40. Stephen Bloore, "Samuel Keimer: A Footnote to the Life of Franklin," *PMHB*, 54 (1930), 265–266.

41. For Bolton's closing of the dancing school and concert room see Leonard Labaree and William Wilcox, eds., *The Papers of Benjamin Franklin*, 25 vols. to date (New Haven, 1959–), II, 257–258. The school probably opened in early May 1740 because Whitefield noted in his journal on May 11 that "many of the [Philadelphia blacks] have begun to learn to read"; *Whitefield's Journals*, p. 422. A notice of the school and the attempts to close it was given in the *Boston News-Letter*, Aug. 21, 1740.

42. Maxson, *Great Awakening*, p. 67.

43. Ibid., pp. 60–63.

44. Aeneas Ross to Secretary of SPG, March 15, 1742, in William S. Perry, ed., *Papers Relating to the History of the Church in Pennsylvania* (n.p., 1871), p. 230. Whitefield noted in his journal that Cummings had denied him access to Christ Church on April 15, 1740; *Whitefield's Journals*, pp. 406–407.

45. Robert Jenney to Secretary of SPG, Jan. 26, 1744, in Perry, *History of the Church*, pp. 235–36.

46. Jenney to Secretary of SPG, Nov. 14, 1745, ibid., pp. 236–237; also see Richard I. Snelling, "William Sturgeon, Catechist to the Negroes of Philadelphia," *Historical Magazine of the Protestant Episcopal Church*, 8 (1939), 388–401.

47. Whitefield's preaching was remarked on in the *Pennsylvania Gazette*, Sept. 25, 1745; for the prayer society "of Negro Women and Children" see *The Works of the Reverend George Whitefield . . .*, 6 vols. (London, 1771–72), I, 176.

48. Tennent's connection with black Philadelphians is obscure, but his evangelical preaching seems to have made him an attractive figure, at least at first, to the slaves awakened by Whitefield.

49. For the "Ethiopian's Conversion" see Arnold Dallimore, *George Whitefield: The Life and Times of the Great Evangelist of the 18th Century Revival*, 2 vols. (London, 1970–79), I, 500; William Sewall, one of Whitefield's traveling companions, described his invitation to blacks in *Journal of a Voyage from Savannah to Philadelphia* (London, 1740), pp. 6–7.

50. *Pennsylvania Gazette*, Aug. 22, 1745; Sept. 4, 1746. I am indebted to Billy G. Smith of Montana State University for this reference.

51. Jenney to Secretary of SPG, Nov. 14, 1745, in Perry, *History of the Church*, p. 237.

52. Snelling, "William Sturgeon," p. 391; Edgar L. Pennington, "The Work of the Bray Associates in Pennsylvania," *PMHB*, 58 (1934), 4–5.

53. Between Sturgeon's arrival in 1747 and 1758, 142 blacks were baptized at Christ Church, compared with only 3 at Tennent's Second Presbyte-

rian Church; Second Presbyterian Church, Register of Baptisms and Marriages, 1744–1833, Presbyterian Historical Society, Philadelphia. For Whitefield's 1746 visits, when he drew huge crowds again, see *Pennsylvania Gazette,* May 22 and Aug. 21, 1746. Sturgeon's reports to his superiors in London are published in John C. Van Horne, ed., *Religious Philanthropy and Colonial Slavery: The American Correspondence of the Associates of Dr. Bray, 1717–1777* (Urbana, Ill., 1985).

54. Benjamin Franklin to John Waring, Jan. 3, 1758, in Labaree and Wilcox, *Papers of Benjamin Franklin,* VII, 356.

55. Pennington, "The Work of the Bray Associates," pp. 6–13; Richard I. Snelling, "Benjamin Franklin and the Dr. Bray Associates," *PMHB,* 63 (1939), 285–286.

56. Sturgeon to Secretary of SPG, Aug. 21, 1761, in Perry, *History of the Church,* p. 332. In 1764 Franklin visited the school and found only fifteen students; Franklin to Rev. John Waring, June 25, 1764, in Van Horne, *Religious Philanthropy,* p. 214.

57. Norris S. Barratt, *Outline of the History of Old St. Paul's Church, Philadelphia, 1760–1899* ([Lancaster, Pa.], 1917), pp. 64–65; Deborah Gough, "Pluralism, Politics, and Power Struggles: The Church of England in Colonial Pennsylvania, 1685–1789" (Ph.D. diss., University of Pennsylvania, 1978), pp. 307–311.

58. Registers of Christ Church, HSP; only two marriages were performed before 1745–in 1728 and 1737; both involved free black couples.

59. For twenty-one baptisms at St. Mary's and St. Joseph's from 1765 to 1775 see *Records of the American Catholic Historical Society of Philadelphia,* I (Philadelphia, 1887), 246–350; twenty-one marriages at St. Michael's and Zion (German) Lutheran churches from 1756 to 1776 are recorded in *Pennsylvania Archives,* 2d ser., IX (Harrisburg, 1880), 287–440; nine marriages and eleven baptisms from 1759 to 1776 at Gloria Dei Swedish Lutheran Church, are listed in Baptisms and Marriages, 1750–1789, PGS; a small number of black marriages were recorded in the First Presbyterian Church, Register of Marriages and Baptisms, 1701–1746, 1760–1806; Second Presbyterian Church, Register of Baptisms and Marriages, 1744–1833, Presbyterian Historical Society; and First Moravian Church, Baptisms and Marriages, 1743–1821, PGS microfilm.

60. Sydney James, *A People among People: Quaker Benevolence in Eighteenth-Century America* (Cambridge, Mass., 1963), pp. 104–105.

61. David B. Davis, *The Problem of Slavery in Western Culture* (Ithaca, N.Y., 1966), p. 222.

62. Thomas E. Drake, *Quakers and Slavery in America* (New Haven, 1950), pp. 40–45; Samuel M. Janney, *History of the Religious Society of Friends, from Its Rise to the Year 1828,* 3 vols. (Philadelphia, 1867), II, 245–246; and Davis, *Problem of Slavery,* pp. 323–324, for Lay incidents. In 1737, when the

Philadelphia Yearly Meeting would not approve his militant antislavery tract *All Slavekeepers That Keep the Innocent in Bondage, Apostates Pretending to Lay Claim to the Pure & Holy Christian Religion,* Lay prevailed upon Benjamin Franklin to print it. Prominent Friends denounced the pamphlet in an advertisement in the *American Weekly Mercury,* Franklin's rival newspaper.

63. James, *People among People,* pp. 123–30.

64. Jack D. Marietta, *The Reformation of American Quakerism, 1748–1783* (Philadelphia, 1984), pp. 113–114.

65. James, *People among People,* pp. 130–140; Drake, *Quakers and Slavery,* pp. 48–72.

66. James *People among People,* pp. 316–319.

67. Soderlund, *Quakers and Slavery,* chap. 3; J. William Frost, "The Origins of the Quaker Crusade against Slavery: A Review of Recent Literature," *Quaker History,* 67 (1978), 56–58.

68. James, *People among People,* pp. 111–114.

69. Philadelphia Quarterly Meeting, Minutes, June 4, 1766; Aug. 3, 1767; Aug. 6, 1770; May 2, 1774, Friends Historical Collection, Swarthmore College. I am grateful to Jean Soderlund for providing extracts from these minutes.

70. Ibid., pp. 233–234; Henry Cadbury, "Negro Membership in the Society of Friends," *Journal of Negro History,* 21 (1936), 167–169. The only black marriage in a Philadelphia Quaker meetinghouse that I could find was in 1774. See Turner, *Negro in Pennsylvania,* p. 46 n.

71. Roberts Vaux, *Memoirs of the Life of Anthony Benezet* (Philadelphia, 1817), pp. 120–121, 138–140; George Brookes, *Friend Anthony Benezet* (Philadelphia, 1937), chaps. 3 and 4. The fullest study of Benezet is Nancy Slocum Hornick, "Anthony Benezet: Eighteenth-Century Social Critic, Educator, and Abolitionist" (Ph.D. diss., University of Maryland, 1974).

72. Vaux, *Memoirs of Benezet,* p. 29.

73. Benezet, *A Caution and Warning to Great Britain . . .* (Philadelphia, 1766), pp. 11–12; Roger Bruns, "Anthony Benezet's Assertion of Negro Equality," *Journal of Negro History,* 56 (1971), 230–238; Nancy Slocum Hornick, "Anthony Benezet and the Africans' School: Toward a Theory of Full Equality," *PMHB,* 99 (1975), 399–421. Five years earlier, in *A Short Account of Africa* [Philadelphia, 1762], Benezet had written that "Negroes are generally sensible and humane and sociable, and . . . their Capacity is as good, and as capable of improvement as that of white people"; quoted in Hornick, "Benezet and the Africans' School," p. 417.

74. Franklin to John Waring, Dec. 17, 1763, in Labaree and Wilcox, *Papers of Benjamin Franklin,* X, 395–396.

75. Vaux, *Memoirs of Benezet,* p. 29.

76. James, *People among People,* pp. 235–236; Hornick, "Benezet and the Africans' School," pp. 404–412.

77. See especially Soderlund, *Quakers and Slavery,* and Marietta, *Reformation of American Quakerism.*

78. Soderlund, *Quakers and Slavery,* chap. 6.

79. Ibid.

80. Rush to Granville Sharp, Oct. 20, 1773, and Nov. 1, 1774, in John A. Woods., ed., "The Correspondence of Benjamin Rush and Granville Sharpe, 1773–1809," *Journal of American Studies,* 1 (1967), 3 and 13.

81. For the population of Philadelphia (including Southwark but not the Northern Liberties), see Gary B. Nash and Billy G. Smith, "The Population of Philadelphia," *PMHB,* 99 (1975), 366; the number of slaves and slaveowners has been derived from the 1767 tax lists and 1775 Constables' Returns. To include Southwark I have added 10 percent (see "Slaves and Slaveowners," p. 237, table IV).

82. Nash, "Slaves and Slaveowners, p. 238, n. 33; manumissions by will are compiled in Soderlund, *Quakers and Slavery,* p. 103, table 4.3; the number given here is calculated from a master list of manumissions in Philadelphia that Jean Soderlund and I have compiled for a forthcoming book tentatively titled *Freedom by Degrees: The Death of Slavery in Pennsylvania.*

83. Benezet to Sharp, May 20, 1773, Granville Sharp Letter Book, LCP; quoted in Brouwer, "The Negro as a Slave and as a Free Black," p. 132. Franklin, in 1751, and Edward Wigglesworth of Boston, in 1775, reached the same conclusion. See Nash, "Slaves and Slaveowners," p. 239.

84. The bills of mortality are available in Charles Evans, comp., *American Bibligraphy: A Chronological Dictionary of all Books, Pamphlets, and Periodical Publications Printed in the United States . . . 1639 . . . 1820* (Chicago and Worcester, Mass.), 1903–59.

85. Nash, "Slaves and Slaveowners," p. 241; Billy G. Smith, "Death and Life in a Colonial Immigrant City: A Demographic Analysis of Philadelphia," *Journal of Economic History,* 37 (1977), 871.

86. Constables' Returns to the Assessors, 1775, PCA. The Constables' Returns give ages for 89 percent of the city's slaves. For further data on the relative infertility of black women see Nash, "Slaves and Slaveowners," pp. 239–240, and Herbert S. Klein and Stanley L. Engerman, "Fertility Differential between Slaves in the United States and the British West Indies: A Note on Lactation Practices and Their Possible Implications," *William and Mary Quarterly,* 3d ser., 35 (1978), 357–374.

87. Nash, "Slaves and Slaveowners," p. 237, table IV. The percentage of blacks in the city's population dropped from about 9 percent in 1767 to 3.4 percent in 1775.

88. James T. Mitchell and Henry Flanders, comps., *The Statutes at Large of Pennsylvania from 1682 to 1801,* IV (Harrisburg, 1899), 59–64; the following paragraph is derived from the law of 1726. For discussions of the law see Turner, *Negro in Pennsylvania,* pp. 111–114; and A. Leon Higginbotham, Jr.,

In the Matter of Color: Race and the American Legal Process; The Colonial Period (New York, 1978), pp. 285–288.

89. *Pennsylvania Gazette,* March 5, 1750/51.

91. Nash, "Slaves and Slaveowners," pp. 240–241.

2. The Black Revolution in Philadelphia

1. The only general treatment of blacks in the American Revolution is Benjamin Quarles, *The Negro in the American Revolution* (Chapel Hill, N.C., 1961). Blacks who joined the British have been admirably investigated by James W. St. G. Walker, *The Black Loyalists: The Search for the Promised Land in Nova Scotia and Sierra Leone, 1783–1870* (New York, 1976); and Ellen Gibson Wilson, *The Loyal Blacks* (New York, 1976). The only searching colonial studies are Jeffrey J. Crow, *The Black Experience in Revolutionary North Carolina* (Raleigh, 1977); and Peter H. Wood, " 'Taking Care of Business' in Revolutionary South Carolina: Republicanism and the Slave Society," in Jeffrey J. Crow and Larry E. Tise, eds., *The Southern Experience in the American Revolution* (Chapel Hill, N.C., 1978). The profound importance of the American Revolution as a war of black liberation is touched upon in some of the essays in Ira Berlin and Ronald Hoffman, eds., *Slavery and Freedom in the Age of the American Revolution* (Charlottesville, Va., 1983), and is directly confronted in Peter H. Wood, " 'Impatient of Oppression': Black Freedom Struggles on the Eve of White Independence," *Southern Exposure,* 12, no. 6 (1984), 10–16.

2. John Hughes to John Swift et al., Nov. 5, 1765, Miscellaneous MSS Collection, box 1, LCP.

3. See Bernard Bailyn, *Pamphlets of the American Revolution, 1750–1776,* I (Cambridge, Mass., 1965), 140–150; Winthrop D. Jordan, *White over Black: American Attitudes toward the Negro, 1550–1812* (Chapel Hill, N.C., 1968), part 3; Duncan J. MacLeod, *Slavery, Race and the American Revolution* (Cambridge, 1974), chap. 1; David Brion Davis, *The Problem of Slavery in the Age of Revolution, 1770–1823* (Ithaca, N.Y., 1975), chap. 6; F. Nwabueze Okoye, "Chattel Slavery as the Nightmare of the American Revolutionaries," *William and Mary Quarterly,* 3d ser., 37 (1980), 3–28.

4. Quoted in Wood, " 'Impatient of Oppression,' " p. 10.

5. A general treatment of the antislavery activity of the Society of Friends in the revolutionary period is provided by Thomas E. Drake, *Quakers and Slavery in America* (New Haven, 1950), chap. 5. A more exacting analysis of the Quaker antislavery movement is Jean R. Soderlund, *Quakers and Slavery: A Divided Spirit* (Princeton, N.J., 1985).

6. David Freeman Hawke, *Benjamin Rush: Revolutionary Gadfly* (Indianapolis, 1971), pp. 12–19; Davies' statement is quoted in Jordan, *White over Black,* p. 188.

7. Hawke, *Benjamin Rush,* pp. 104–106.

8. "African Slavery in America," in Philip Foner, ed., *The Complete Writings of Thomas Paine,* 2 vols. (New York, 1945), II, 15–19; Paine published a second antislavery essay, "A Serious Thought," in the *Pennsylvania Journal* on Oct. 18, 1775.

9. Quoted in Arthur Zilversmit, *The First Emancipation: The Abolition of Negro Slavery in the North* (Chicago, 1967), p. 97. Lord Mansfield's decision was in fact more limited; he ruled that no law permitted a slaveowner to hold a slave by force in England or to carry him or her out of the country.

10. The early membership was disproportionately Quaker, with seven of the original ten members and seventeen of the twenty-four who participated in the four meetings belonging to the Society of Friends.

11. Edward R. Turner, "The First Abolition Society in the United States," *PMHB,* 36 (1912), 92–109; Edward Needles, *An Historical Memoir of the Pennsylvania Society for Promoting the Abolition of Slavery* . . . (Philadelphia, 1848), pp. 17–18. The four cases are detailed in PAS Minute Book.

12. Needles, *Historical Memoir,* p. 19.

13. James Madison to William Bradford, Nov. 26, 1774; Bradford to Madison, Jan. 4, 1775, in William T. Hutchinson and William M. E. Rachel, eds., *The Papers of James Madison,* I (Chicago, 1962), 129–130, 132.

14. The data are drawn from Jean R. Soderlund's compilation of all manumissions recorded in wills for Philadelphia (including Southwark and the Northern Liberties) and from my compilation of manumissions recorded in the Philadelphia Court of Quarter Sessions, PCA; in the Manumission Books of the PPAS, reels 23–25; and in the record of manumissions compiled by the three Philadelphia Monthly Meetings (Quaker Collection, Haverford College Library).

15. Rush to Granville Sharp, May 1, 1773, in L. H. Butterfield, ed., *The Letters of Benjamin Rush,* 2 vols. (Princeton, N.J., 1951), I, 81.

16. *Pennsylvania Evening Post,* Dec. 5, 12, 1775; for Dunmore's proclamation and the black response in Virginia, see Quarles, *Negro in the American Revolution,* chap. 2.

17. *Pennsylvania Evening Post,* Dec. 14, 1775.

18. Francis Pingeon, "Slavery in New Jersey on the Eve of the American Revolution," in *New Jersey in the American Revolution* (Trenton, 1976), pp. 134–140; Graham Hodges, "Colonel Tye: Escaped Slave and Freedom Fighter of the American Revolution," a chapter of a work in progress.

19. John Leacock, *The Fall of British Tyranny* (Philadelphia, 1776), pp. 44, 47–48; for a discussion of Leacock's play see Kenneth Silverman, *A Cultural History of the American Revolution* (New York, 1976), pp. 310–311.

20. Robert Morris to Commissioners in France, Dec. 21, 1776, in Peter Force, comp., *American Archives* . . ., 5th ser., 3 vols. (Washington, D.C., 1848–53), III, 334; quoted by Harry M. Tinkcom, "The Revolutionary City,

1765–1783," in Russell F. Weigley, ed., *Philadelphia: A 300-Year History* (New York, 1982), p. 129.

21. Nicholas B. Wainwright, "A Diary of Trifling Occurrences: Philadelphia, 1776–1778" (diary of Sarah Logan Fisher), *PMHB,* 82 (1958), 448.

22. The fullest account of the occupation is Joseph Jackson, *With the British Army in Philadelphia, 1777–1778* (San Rafael, Calif., 1979).

23. *The Journals of Henry Melchior Muhlenberg,* trans. Theodore G. Tappert and John W. Doberstein, 3 vols. (Philadelphia, 1942–58), III, 78 (Sept. 20, 1777). In some cases fleeing Philadelphians took with them slaves purchased just after the Council of Safety, the revolutionary government of the state, ordered them confiscated from Loyalists. For example, just north of the city, ten slaves were confiscated from Edward Stiles and sold in October 1777. Petitions from Stiles to recover his property from 1777 to 1788, and associated documents, are in RPRG.

24. *Pennsylvania Evening Post,* Sept. 18, 1777.

25. Thomas Willing to Robert Morris, April 27, 1778, in Thomas W. Balch, ed., *Willing Letters and Papers* (Philadelphia, 1922), unpaginated. For a similar case concerning Dick, slave of Robert Turner, who hid in the city when his master fled at the approach of the British, see *Pennsylvania Evening Post,* July 14, 1778, and *Pennsylvania Packet,* Aug. 6, 1778. For Peter, who similarly fled his master John McCalla one day before the British occupied the city, see *Pennsylvania Gazette,* June 2, 1779.

26. *Pennsylvania Packet,* Jan. 1, 1780.

27. Petition of Jedidiah Snowden to the Supreme Executive Council, Sept. 27, 1779, RPRG, reel 15, frames 1306–07 (hereafter frs.).

28. *Journals of Muhlenberg,* III, 78 (Sept. 20, 1777).

29. Copies of letters from Daniel Wier, Commissary to the Army in America, to John Robinson, Secretary to the Lords Commissioners of the Treasury, 1777, Dreer Collection, HSP.

30. *Journals of Muhlenberg,* III, 105 (Nov. 13, 1777).

31. *Pennsylvania Ledger,* Feb. 11 and 21, 1778.

32. Ibid., Jan. 6 and April 18, 1778; Dec. 24, 1777. For other runaways, see the advertisements for thirteen-year-old Jack, slave of Richard Footman (Dec. 10, 1777); Jack, alias John Morris, twenty-year-old slave of Francis Harris (Jan. 17, 1778); and Caesar, slave of Alexander Wilcox (Jan. 14, 1778).

33. Ibid., May 6, 1778.

34. PAS Minute Book, May 29, 1775, and Feb. 23, 1784; Petition of Harry to Supreme Executive Council, Aug. 16, 1777, RPRG, reel 2, frs. 754–755, 798–799.

35. Data compiled as indicated in note 14, above. These are minimum figures, since some manumissions were not recorded.

36. Mary Cadwalader Dickinson to John Dickinson, July 6, 1778; Philemon Dickinson to John Dickinson, June 18, 1778, Dickinson Papers, LCP.

37. Deborah Logan to Jamor Garden, Sept. 20, 1822, Smith Manuscript Collection, box 6, folder 32, LCP. Although historical accounts usually describe Dinah as a slave, she had been freed by William and Hannah Logan in the spring of 1776. See Jean R. Soderlund, "Black Women in Colonial Pennsylvania," *PMHB*, 106 (1983), 49–50.

38. John W. Jackson, *The Pennsylvania Navy, 1775–1781: The Defense of the Delaware* (New Brunswick, N.J., 1974), p. 416 n. 50; "List of Officers & Men on Ship Jay," Aug. 2, 1779, and Blair McClenachan in Account with Matthew Clarkson, 1779–1781, Court of Admiralty Papers, 1766–1789, HSP. When the state ship *General Greene* was launched in 1779, its officers could not compete with privateers in attracting a crew and finally resorted to impressing prisoners in the city jail. Caught in their net was one runaway slave; M. V. Brewington, "The State Ship *General Greene*," *PMHB*, 60 (1936), 233.

39. The details of Forten's early life are recounted in two funeral discourses delivered in 1842: Stephen Gloucester, *A Discourse Delivered on the Occasion of the Death of Mr. James Forten, Sr., in the Second Presbyterian Church of Colour of the City of Philadelphia . . .* (Philadelphia, 1842); and Robert Purvis, *Remarks on the Life and Character of James Forten . . .* (Philadelphia, 1842). In both accounts Forten is said to have shipped out with the *Royal Louis* in 1780, at age fourteen, but the privateer was not issued letters of marque and reprisal until July 1781. The letters are in Papers of the Continental Congress, 1774–1789, microfilm ed., M247, roll 204, item 196, National Archives. In 1833 Forten told Samuel Breck, a prominent Philadelphian, that he had shipped on the *Hyder Ally;* Nicholas B. Wainwright, ed., "The Diary of Samuel Breck," *PMHB*, 103 (1979), 249–250.

40. William C. Nell's florid account of Forten's navy experience was published thirteen years after his death; *Colored Patriots of the American Revolution* (Boston, 1855), pp. 167–170.

41. George H. Moore, *Historical Notes on the Employment of Negroes in the American Army of the Revolution* (New York, 1862), p. 16.

42. "Return of Negroes in the Continental Army," *Pennsylvania Archives*, 5th ser., II (Harrisburg, 1906), 705; John B. Trussell, *The Pennsylvania Line: Regimental Organization and Operations, 1776–1783* (Harrisburg, 1977), p. 248. In his exhaustive study of the Philadelphia militia during the Revolution Steven Rosswurm found only a single free black, who presumably enlisted voluntarily. "Antibiastes," in *Observations on the Slaves and Indentured Servants, inlisted in the Army, and in the Navy of the United States* (Philadelphia, 1777), states that "an amazing number" of slaves joined the continental forces. But then, since they were not offered freedom but only the chance to buy their way out of bondage with their meager wages, most of them deserted to the British "as soon as they could." The anonymous author, who was probably a member of the Continental Congress, did not specify where

the "amazing number" of slaves were from, but I have found no indication that they were from Philadelphia.

43. Records of the Supreme Executive Council, RPRG, reel 37, frs. 160–161.

44. Nell, *Colored Patriots of the Revolution,* quoted in James W. St. G. Walker, "Blacks as American Loyalists: The Slaves' War for Independence," *Historical Reflections/Réflexions Historiques,* 2 (1975), 52.

45. Ibid., pp. 54–57.

46. "State of the Facts Respecting Emmanuel Carpenter," PPAS, reel 23.

47. Quarles, *Negro in the American Revolution,* Chaps. 7 and 8; Sylvia R. Frey, "The British and the Black: A New Perspective," *The Historian,* 38 (1975–76), 225–238. A description of the "Tartar horde" of blacks who fled to the British and the problems it caused the British command is in Johann von Ewald, *Diary of the American War: A Hessian Journal* (New Haven, 1979), pp. 305–306. For the belief of blacks that abolition was a British war policy, see Walker, "Blacks as American Loyalists," pp. 54–57.

48. Detailed accounts of the *meschianza* were published in the Loyalist Philadelphia newspaper *Royal Pennsylvania Gazette,* May 26, 1778, and in London's *Gentlemen's Magazine,* August 1778. For historical accounts see J. Thomas Scharf and Thompson Westcott, *A History of Philadelphia, 1609–1884,* 3 vols. (Philadelphia, 1884), I, 378; Ellis P. Oberholtzer, *Philadelphia: A History of the City and Its People,* 4 vols. (Philadelphia, 1912), I, 274–276.

49. "Letters of Major Baurmeister during the Philadelphia Campaign, 1777–1778," *PMHB,* 60 (1936), 179–180.

50. *Pennsylvania Packet,* Dec. 12, 1779.

51. "List of Negroes belonging to Citizens of Pennsylvania carried away by the British," Aug. 9, 1786, Records of the Supreme Executive Council, RPRG, reel 27, frs. 17–24. This list is an extract from the 1783 "Inspection Roll of Negroes, Taken on Board Sundry Vessels at Staten Island and Bound for Nova Scotia," Papers of the Continental Congress, roll 9, National Archives. For the case of one escaped slave from Philadelphia, Edward Green, who left with the British but returned to the city a few years later, see Lewis Nicola to Supreme Executive Council, April 26, 1780, RPRG, reel 15, frs. 1268, 1270.

52. Based on an analysis of the evacuation lists; also see Debra L. Newman, "They Left with the British: Black Women in the Evacuation of Philadelphia, 1778," *Pennsylvania Heritage,* 4 (1977), 20–23. One intrepid nineteen-year-old named Dinah escaped with the British "near the time of her lying in." Her case is detailed in a runaway advertisement in *Pennsylvania Packet,* July 16, 1778.

53. Constables' Returns for the City of Philadelphia, Nov. 1779–Jan. 1780, PCA. The altered age structure of slaves between 1775 and late 1779, as revealed in the Constables' Returns, seems to reflect the age-selective flight

of slaves. In 1775, 15 percent of the slaves whose ages were given (89 percent of all those listed) were under twelve, and 8 percent were fifty or older. In late 1779, when 72 percent of the ages can be determined, 21 percent were under twelve and 10 percent were fifty or older.

54. The slaves of Christopher Elliot of Kingsessing, on the southern border of the city, provide a confirming case. Of Elliot's fifteen slaves, ten were children (nine of them eight years or younger), two were young women (probably the mothers of most of these children), and three were adult males aged eighteen, twenty-three, and twenty-eight. All three males "ran & left him," Elliot reported when he registered his slaves in 1780; the others remained. Elliot's registration of slaves is in PAS Papers, reel 23.

55. Robert Morris to John Brown, June 26, 1778, Dreer Collection, HSP.

56. For the Quaker experience in Philadelphia during the war see Jack D. Marietta, *The Reformation of American Quakerism, 1748–1783* (Philadelphia, 1984), chap. 11; and Arthur J. Mekeel, *The Relation of the Quakers to the American Revolution* (Washington, D.C., 1979).

57. Many of these documents are published in Roger Bruns, ed., *Am I Not a Man and a Brother: The Antislavery Crusade of Revolutionary America, 1688–1788* (New York, 1977).

58. Zilversmit, *First Emancipation*, pp. 126–127; the council's message to the assembly is in *Pennsylvania Archives*, 1st ser., VII (Philadelphia, 1853), 79.

59. Zilversmit, *First Emancipation*, pp. 126–127; the bill was published in the *Pennsylvania Packet*, March 4, 1779.

60. The fullest account of the seething tension that culminated in the Fort Wilson riot is Steven Rosswurm, *Arms, Country, and Class: The Philadelphia Militia and "Lower Sort" during the American Revolution, 1775–1783* (New Brunswick, N.J., 1987), chaps. 5 and 6.

61. *Journals of the House of Representatives of the Commonwealth of Pennsylvania . . .* (1776–81) (Philadelphia, 1782), pp. 398–399. For Bryan's plebeian orientation see Alexander Graydon, *Memoirs of a Life, Chiefly Passed in Pennsylvania . . .* (London, 1822), pp. 287–288.

62. On the British army in Philadelphia see Jackson, *British Army in Philadelphia*, pp. 266–267. Philip Foner attributes the preamble of the abolition bill to Thomas Paine, who was appointed clerk of the Assembly on the day the bill was introduced, but there is no definite evidence of this; Foner, *Complete Writings of Paine*, II, 21. For Bryan's authorship see Edward R. Turner, *The Negro in Pennsylvania: Slavery—Servitude—Freedom, 1639–1861* (Washington, D.C., 1911), p. 79, and Bryan's obituary in *Pennsylvania Gazette*, Feb. 2, 1791.

63. The bill was printed in *Pennsylvania Packet*, Dec. 23, 1779; it is reprinted in Bruns, *Am I Not a Man and a Brother*, pp. 446–449.

64. Sharon V. Salinger, "Artisans, Journeymen, and the Transformation

of Labor in Late Eighteenth-Century Philadelphia," *William and Mary Quarterly*, 3d ser., 40 (1983), 63–84.

65. For the essay by "A Citizen" see *Pennsylvania Packet,* March 13, 1779. Attempting to rally public opinion for the bill, Bryan candidly stated that the age of twenty-eight was agreed upon "to recompence the charge of nurture"; ibid., Jan. 1, 1780. Bryan's only biographer, the filiopietistic Burton A. Konkle, identifies Bryan as the author of this appeal; *George Bryan and the Constitution of Pennsylvania, 1731–1791* (Philadelphia, 1922), pp. 189–198.

66. Robert William Fogel and Stanley L. Engerman, "Philanthropy at Bargain Prices: Notes on the Economics of Gradual Emancipation," *Journal of Legal Studies,* 3 (1974), 377–401.

67. *Pennsylvania Gazette,* Feb. 2, 1780. The author appears to have been Anthony Benezet. Across the river, in New Jersey, John Cooper also deplored gradual abolition in "To the Publick," *The New Jersey Journal,* Sept. 20, 1780; quoted in Bruns, *Am I Not a Man and a Brother,* pp. 456–459.

68. Needles, *Historical Memoir,* p. 23.

69. For a comparison of the five state gradual abolition acts see Fogel and Engerman, "Philanthropy at Bargain Prices," pp. 380–381.

70. The petition is in *Freedom's Journal,* Sept. 21, 1781; also see Turner, *Negro in Pennsylvania,* p. 78 n. Benjamin Rush claimed in 1785 that "many hundreds" of slaves received their freedom in this way; *Considerations upon the Present Test-law of Pennsylvania,* 2d ed. (Philadelphia, 1785), p. 7 n. A number of Philadelphians petitioned the legislature for restoration of their slaves whom the courts ordered freed for their masters' failure to register them by the Nov. 1, 1780, deadline; *Journals of the House,* pp. 576 (widows Sarah Clinton, Mary Bogart, and Anne Rose), 573 (Thomas Kittery), 591 (widow Martha Wall), and 595 (John and Richard Tittermary).

71. *Journals of the House,* pp. 605, 607.

72. *Freedom's Journal,* Sept. 19 and 21, 1781.

73. Ibid., Sept. 19, 1781.

74. Ibid., Sept. 21, 1781.

75. *Journals of the House,* pp. 690, 693, 696.

76. Data from master list of manumissions cited in note 14, above.

3. Becoming Free

1. Of the 318 slaves for whom ages were given in the Constables' Returns to the Assessors, 1779–80, PCA, only 23 had been born in 1775–1780 and 43 in 1770–1775—a clear indication of the disruption of family life during the war years. A slave population of 900 on the eve of the Revolution had produced only 4 or 5 offspring a year who were still alive and in the city by 1780.

This distorted demographic structure is all the more apparent when compared with that of outlying Bucks County, where a much larger proportion of slaves were children. Of 473 slaves in Bucks County in 1780, 175 were ten years old and younger. Thus, 7.2 percent of Philadelphia's slave population was ten years old and younger in 1780, compared with 37 percent in Bucks County. The Bucks County Register is in Pennsylvania State Archives, Harrisburg.

2. Certificate of freedom and testimonial of Thomas Attmore for Moses Johnson, PPAS, reel 23; Minutes of the Acting Committee, 1784–1788, PPAS, reel 4, pp. 6–8; Letter of Marque for the Ship *Revolution,* Papers of the Continental Congress, 1774–1789, microfilm ed., roll 204, item 196, National Archives.

3. Benjamin Wynkoop was the second son of Abraham and Mary Wynkoop, a wealthy Sussex County planter-merchant who died in 1753. He left Benjamin a 1,000-acre plantation in Cedar Creek Hundred, £400 in cash, and, apparently, the slave family into which Absalom was born in 1746; Will of Abraham Wynkoop, Sussex County, Delaware, Probates, vol. A109, pp. 125–126, Delaware Archives, Hall of Records, Dover; "Sketch of Rev. Absalom Jones," in William Douglass, *Annals of the First African Church in the United States of America, now styled The African Episcopal Church of St. Thomas* (Philadelphia, 1862), pp. 119–120.

4. "Sketch of Jones," in Douglass, *Annals,* pp. 119–120.

5. Ibid., pp. 119-121; the wartime purchase of the house and lot from Edward Shippen and John Brickell, on Jan. 25, 1779, is noted in a later deed for the property in Deed Book D20, pp. 565–566, PCA.

6. "Sketch of Jones," in Douglass, *Annals,* p. 121.

7. On postwar conditions in Philadelphia see George W. Geib, "A History of Philadelphia, 1776–1789" (Ph.D. diss., University of Wisconsin, 1969), chap 9; Robert L. Brunhouse, *The Counter-Revolution in Pennsylvania, 1776–1790* (Harrisburg, 1971), chaps. 5 and 6.

8. Benjamin Rush to Granville Sharp, Nov. 28, 1783, in John A. Woods, ed., "The Correspondence of Benjamin Rush and Granville Sharp, 1773–1809," *Journal of American Studies,* 1 (1967), 20.

9. The first federal census in 1790 reported 1,805 blacks in Philadelphia (including Southwark and Northern Liberties), but it is almost certain that the census takers undercounted free blacks by a least 10 percent. For a report that poorer families underreported their numbers because they believed they were "to be taxed according to their number," see *The General Advertiser,* Nov. 19, 1790. The manumissions are tabulated from a master list I compiled with Jean R. Soderlund, of Swarthmore College. Another 75 slaves who were freed in these years in nearby areas such as New Jersey, Delaware, and southeastern Pennsylvania had their manumissions recorded in the PAS manumission books.

10. Gary B. Nash, "Forging Freedom: The Emancipation Experience in

the Northern Seaport Towns, 1775–1820," in Ira Berlin and Ronald Hoffman, eds., *Slavery and Freedom in the Age of the American Revolution* (Charlottesville, Va., 1983), pp. 4–8.

11. *The Autobiography of Benjamin Rush,* ed. George W. Corner (Princeton, N.J., 1948), p. 160; "Letters of Phineas Bond, British Consul at Philadelphia . . .," *Annual Report of the American Historical Association for the Year 1896,* 2 vols. (Washington, D.C., 1897), I, 568. For the difficulties of laboring families in this period see "A Poor Tradesman," *Pennsylvania Packet,* Oct. 20, 1784; *Pennsylvania Gazette,* June 12, 1791.

12. CICFB Minute Book, 1790–1803, pp. 23 (March 25, 1791), 40 (March 2, 1792), 42 (March 6 and 9, 1792), PPAS, reel 6; Rush to Granville Sharp, August 1791, in L. H. Butterfield, ed., *The Letters of Benjamin Rush,* 2 vols. (Princeton, N.J., 1951), I, 608.

13. W. E. B. Du Bois, *The Philadelphia Negro: A Social Study* (1899; reprint, New York, 1967), pp. 141–142; Leon F. Litwack, *North of Slavery: The Negro in the Free States, 1790–1860* Chicago, 1961), pp. 153–186.

14. Edmund Hogan, *The Prospect of Philadelphia and Check on the Next Directory . . .* (Philadelphia, 1795). The directory does not include Southwark or the Northern Liberties, where many blacks resided.

15. The marriages are recorded in *Pennsylvania Archives,* 2d ser., VIII–IX (Harrisburg, 1880); marriages at the Moravian church have been traced in First Moravian Church, Baptisms and Marriages, 1743–1821, PGS; and for the Catholic churches in *Records of the American Catholic Historical Society of Philadelphia,* I, II, and IV (Philadelphia, 1887–93).

16. Committee to Inquire into the Condition of Freed Slaves, Minute Book, 1781–1785, Jan. 1 and Aug. 4, 1783; Jan. 31 and May 1, 1784, HSP.

17. *Heads of Families at the First Census of the United States Taken in the Year 1790: Pennsylvania* (Washington, D.C., 1908); 13.7 percent of black households were headed by females, compared with 13.3 percent of white households. White households contained an average of 6.06 persons; Tom W. Smith, "The Dawn of the Urban-Industrial Era: The Social Structure of Philadelphia, 1790–1830" (Ph.D. diss., University of Chicago, 1980), p. 178, tables 64 and 65.

18. Minutes of the Committee of 24, p. 26, PPAS, reel 6.

19. The indenture books of the Philadelphia House of Employment and the Pennsylvania Abolition Society recorded 237 black indentures, mostly of children, from 1778 to 1790; of these, only a few persons were indentured to farmers or craftsmen outside the city; PPAS, reel 23.

20. *The Statutes at Large of Pennsylvania from 1682 to 1801,* VIII (Harrisburg, 1902); reprinted in *A Compilation of the Poor Laws of the State of Pennsylvania from the Year 1700 to 1788* (New York, 1971), p. 59. The lengths of the indentures, however, were influenced by traditions established in the slavery period. The basic black code laid down in 1726 in Pennsylvania required all children of free Negroes to be bound out to white families until age twenty-

four if male and twenty-one if female and all free mulatto children to be bound out until age thirty-one; Edward R. Turner, *The Negro in Pennsylvania: Slavery–Servitude–Freedom, 1639–1861* (Washington, D.C., 1911), p. 92. It appears that this law was not rigorously enforced if the parents were known to live respectably and were self-sufficient.

21. *Pennsylvania Packet*, Jan. 1, 1780.

22. Philadelphia House of Employment Indenture Papers, 1757–1798, PPAS, reel 23; Indenture Book C, ibid.

23. Jane H. Pease and William H. Pease, *They Who Would Be Free: Blacks' Search for Freedom, 1830–1861* (New York, 1974), pp. 3–5.

24. Turner, *Negro in Pennsylvania*, pp. 89–90.

25. Not until the 1820 census were the age and gender of blacks living in white households indicated, but it seems probable that from the earliest days of freedom female domestic servants, ranging from teenage girls to old women, were the most numerous among free blacks who hired out to live and work in white households.

26. M. Meyers Fortes, "Names among the Tallensi of the Gold Coast," *Afrikanische Studien*, 26 (1955), 349; quoted in Richard Price and Sally Price, "Saramaka Onomastics: An Afro-American Naming System," *Ethnology*, 11 (1972), 342–367. On the importance of naming as a reflection of consciousness I have been guided by Niles Newbell Puckett's pioneering "Names of American Negro Slaves," in George P. Murdock, ed., *Studies in the Science of Society* (New Haven, 1937), pp. 471–494; and Wilbur Zelinsky, "Cultural Variation in Personal Name Patterns in the Eastern United States," *Annals of the Association of American Geographers*, 60 (1970), 743–769. Several historians of the slave experience have investigated what the Prices call the "art of naming," but most of their work concerns the plantation South, where very different naming patterns, reflecting a different consciousness, prevailed. See Ira Berlin, *Slaves without Masters: The Free Negro in the Antebellum South* (New York, 1974), pp. 51–52; Eugene D. Genovese, *Roll, Jordon, Roll: The World the Slaves Made* (New York, 1974), pp. 443–450; Peter H. Wood, *Black Majority: Negroes in Colonial South Carolina from 1670 to the Stono Rebellion* (New York, 1974), pp. 181–185; and, for the most elaborate discussion of southern naming practices, Herbert G. Gutman, *The Black Family in Slavery and Freedom, 1750–1925* (New York, 1976), pp. 185–256.

27. W. E. Burghardt Du Bois, *The Souls of Black Folk* (New York, 1970), p. 3.

28. Puckett, "Names of American Negro Slaves," p. 471.

29. Berlin, *Slaves without Masters*, pp. 51–52.

30. In categorizing forenames I have relied on Alfred J. Kolatch, *Complete Dictionary of English and Hebrew First Names* (New York, 1984).

31. For slave names from Philadelphia wills I am indebted to Jean Soderlund. Those from the church records, recorded in marriage and baptism registers, have been gathered from PGS transcripts.

32. Runaway advertisements in *Pennsylvania Gazette,* Feb. 13, 1750; April 6, 1758; for another case see ibid., Dec. 21, 1758. I am indebted to Billy G. Smith and Richard Wejpowicz, Montana State University, for these advertisements.

33. Census takers probably failed to record some black surnames, recording blacks only by the forenames familiar to them. Many families listed in the first federal census were listed simply as "blacks."

34. Oronoko Dexter: Manumission Book A, p. 35, PPAS, reel 20; in 1794 John Pemberton willed £20 per year to James Oronoke Dexter; Will Book X, no. 178, ibid. Samuel Stephens: Writs of Habeas Corpus, Negro Slaves, 1786–87, Records of the Pennsylvania Supreme Court, Pennsylvania State Archives, Harrisburg.

35. These cases of self-naming are recorded in Inspectors of the Walnut Street Jail, Vagrancy Dockets, I (1790–1797), 159, 137, 125, 396, PCA. In some cases, particularly in the South, masters assigned surnames to slaves they were manumitting. For example, the PAS recorded the manumission of the slaves of John Teake of Accomack County, Virginia, in 1789, transcribing Teake's will, which specified that "for as much as the introduction of the above mentioned negroes into society makes a second name necessary, for the better ascertaining their identity from other negroes, which may be or have been manumitted, I do hereby annex the name of Planter as a second name to each of their respective first names"; Manumission Book D, pp. 406–407, PPAS, reel 23.

36. For the black Paul Jones see Almshouse Census for 1810, Surgical Ward, Records of the Guardians of the Poor, PCA. The historical figure known as John Paul Jones was actually named John Paul but had taken the name Paul Jones when, in great difficulties, he fled from England to America just before the Revolution.

37. Collective analysis of surnames of former slaves indicates that only four of eighty-eight manumitted slaves whose last names are recorded in manumission documents had the same surnames as their masters, and the incidence of taking the master's surname among the much larger number who bore only a slave name on the manumission document was even lower.

38. These names have been checked against the 1785 city tax list, which is much more comprehensive than the first city directory in that year. Some of the surnames are drawn from the lists of black church members recorded in Douglass, *Annals,* pp. 471–486.

39. See the analyses in Berlin, *Slaves without Masters;* Genovese, *Roll, Jordan, Roll;* Gutman, *Black Family.*

40. Likewise, the names Chester, Bristol, and Gloucester, borne by the three male slaves of merchant Luke Morris, who freed them in 1776, never appear in the records of Philadelphia blacks during the next decade.

41. Jack D. Marietta, *The Reformation of American Quakerism, 1748–1783* (Philadelphia, 1984), chap. 12.

42. Philadelphia Yearly Meeting, Minutes, Sept. 26–Oct. 5, 1778, Friends Historical Library, Swarthmore College.

43. Quoted in Marietta, *Reformation of American Quakerism,* p. 275.

44. Philadelphia Quarterly Meeting, Minutes, Nov. 1, 1779, Aug. 6, 1781, Friends Historical Library, Swarthmore College. I am indebted to Jean Soderlund for providing excerpts from these records.

45. Committee to Inquire into the Condition of Freed Slaves, Minute Book, 1781–1785, HSP; Minutes of the Philadelphia Yearly Meeting, 1776, Friends Historical Library, Swarthmore College; quoted in Sydney V. James, *A People among People: Quaker Benevolence in Eighteenth-Century America* (Cambridge, Mass., 1963), p. 227.

46. Committee to Inquire into the Condition of Freed Slaves, Minute Book, 1781–1785, July 30, 1785, HSP.

47. Thomas E. Drake, *Quakers and Slavery in America* (New Haven, 1950), pp. 75–76; Warner Mifflin, *The Defense of Warner Mifflin* (Philadelphia, 1796), pp. 9–10.

48. James *People among People,* pp. 231–34.

49. Philadelphia Quarterly Meeting, Minutes, Aug. 2, 1779, Friends Historical Library, Swarthmore College.

50. Marietta, *Reformation of American Quakerism,* pp. 243–248; for Benezet's attempts to revive the PAS see Benezet to John Pemberton, Oct. 10, 1783, in George S. Brookes, *Friend Anthony Benezet* (Philadelphia, 1937), pp. 395–399.

51. James, *People among People,* pp. 235–236; Nancy Slocum Hornick, "Anthony Benezet and the Africans' School: Toward a Theory of Full Equality," *PMHB,* 99 (1975), 399–421.

52. *Pennsylvania Evening Post,* June 17, 1782; *Pennsylvania Packet,* Aug. 3, 1782.

53. Papers of the Continental Congress, 1774–1789, microfilm ed., roll 57, item 43 (Oct. 4, 1783). Each member of Congress was provided with a copy of *The Case of our Fellow-Creatures, the Oppressed Africans, the appeal of London Quakers to Parliament.* Philadelphia Quakers sent additional petitions to the Continental Congress in 1785 and 1786; see Drake, *Quakers and Slavery,* pp. 94–95.

54. Madison to James Madison, Sr., Sept. 8, 1783, in William T. Hutchinson and William M. E. Rachel, eds., *The Papers of James Madison,* VII (Chicago, 1971), 304. The fate of Billey is not disclosed in the Madison Papers, but no freedom papers for him are recorded in the PAS manumission books.

55. Anthony Benezet to John Pemberton, Aug. 10, 1783, in Brookes, *Benezet,* pp. 397–398.

56. The preamble of the PAS constitution, adopted in 1787, gives a realistic sense of what the members hoped to accomplish. Regarding "all the children of men . . . as members of the same family, however diversified

they may be, by colour, situation, religion, or different states of society," the society regarded it as its duty "to extend the blessings of freedom to every part of the human race" and hoped in particular to obtain freedom for those "entitled to freedom by the laws and constitutions of any of the United States" but "detained in bondage, by fraud or violence." The constitution is reprinted in Roger Bruns, ed., *Am I Not a Man and a Brother: The Antislavery Crusade of Revolutionary America, 1688–1788* (New York, 1977), pp. 512–515.

57. Members of the Abolition Society have been gleaned from the PAS Minute Book for the General Meetings from 1775 through 1787, at which new members were nominated and elected. The religion of the members has been traced in the marriage records of the Philadelphia churches, transcribed by the Pennsylvania Genealogical Society, and in the records of the Society of Friends, Friends Historical Library, Swarthmore College.

58. The Elliot case is detailed in PAS Minute Book, p. 21; Acting Committee Minute Book, 1784–1788, pp. 12 (May 27, 1784), 17 (June 24, 1784), 23 (Aug. 20, 1784), 49 (June 20, 1785), 53 (Aug. 31, 1785), 63 (Nov. 4, 1785), PPAS, reel 4; and Indenture Book C, reel 24.

59. A sketch of Harrison, who has been ignored by historians, is in L. Maria Child, *Life of Isaac T. Hopper* (Boston, 1853), pp. 122–123.

60. Acting Committee Minute Book, 1784–1788, pp. 7 (April 24, 1784), 28 (Nov. 27, 1784), 42–43 (April 23 and May 20, 1785), PPAS, reel 4.

61. Tench Coxe to David Barclay, Mar. 6, 1787, in Bruns, *Am I Not a Man and a Brother,* pp. 510–512.

62. Records of the Supreme Executive Council, 1775–1790, RPRG, reel 19, fr. 634.

63. Dexter would soon change his first name to James Saviel, and Gray, within a few years, would be among the small number of black shopkeepers; Saviel was identified on the 1790 census as a limeseller, and Gray was identified in 1786 as a "free Negro who sells limes"; Testimony of Amis Johnston, Sept. 1788, Records of the Supreme Executive Council, RPRG, reel 24, fr. 357.

64. Roberts Vaux, *Memoirs of the Life of Anthony Benezet* (Philadelphia, 1817), pp. 150–152; Brookes, *Benezet,* pp. 458–461; Benjamin Rush to Granville Sharp, April 27, 1784, in Butterfield, *Letters of Benjamin Rush,* I, 331.

65. Carol V. R. George, *Segregated Sabbaths: Richard Allen and the Rise of Independent Black Churches, 1760–1840* (New York, 1973), p. 25; Barbara Clark Smith, *After the Revolution: The Smithsonian History of Everyday Life in the Eighteenth Century* (New York, 1985), pp. 157–162; Rhys Isaac, "Preachers and Patriots: Popular Culture and the Revolution in Virginia," in Alfred F. Young, ed., *The American Revolution: Essays in the History of American Radicalism* (De Kalb, Ill., 1976), pp. 137–140.

66. On Benjamin Chew see Burton A. Konkle, *Benjamin Chew, 1722–*

1810 (Philadelphia, 1932); and *The Life Experience and Gospel Labors of the Rt. Rev. Richard Allen, To Which Is Annexed The Rise and Progress of the African Methodist Episcopal Church in the United States of America* (Nashville, 1960), p. 17. Allen's master, thought by historians to be a Mr. Stokely, since that was the name Allen gave in his autobiography, was actually Stokely Sturgis, as is recorded in Allen's manumission papers, PPAS, box 29. In the PAS manumission book where the freedom papers were recorded Allen's name is listed only as Richard. The original papers also show that Allen had only the name Richard when he was manumitted by Sturgis on Jan. 25, 1780.

67. Lorenzo Dow, *History of the Cosmopolite; or the Four Volumes of Lorenzo's Journal . . .*, 3d ed. (Philadelphia, 1816), p. 559.

68. *Life Experience of Allen,* pp. 18–23.

69. Ibid., pp. 23–24. An early black historian, George F. Bragg, says that Jones and Allen met first in Delaware, but this seems unlikely in view of the fact that Allen, born in Philadelphia in 1760 and sold to Sturgis in Delaware later in that decade, was only two years old when Jones was brought to Philadelphia in 1762; Bragg, *Richard Allen and Absalom Jones* (Baltimore, 1915), unpaginated. Lorenzo Dow claimed in 1816 that when Allen arrived in Philadelphia only five blacks were worshiping at St. George's Methodist Church; *Cosmopolite,* p. 559.

70. Preamble of the articles of incorporation of the Free African Society of Philadelphia, in Douglass, *Annals,* p. 15.

71. Du Bois, *Philadelphia Negro,* p. 19. The Free African Union Society of Providence, Rhode Island, may have preceded the founding of the Free African Society of Philadelphia, but the founding date of the former, often cited as 1780, is unclear. See William H. Robinson, ed., *The Proceedings of the Free African Union Society and the African Benevolent Society, Newport, Rhode Island, 1780–1824* (Providence, 1976).

72. Minutes of the Free African Society, April–Dec. 1787, in Douglass, *Annals,* pp. 17–19. Douglass reprinted extracts from the minutes, to which he had access, but they have apparently not survived.

4. *"To Arise Out of the Dust"*

1. William Douglass, *Annals of the First African Church in the United States of America, now styled The African Episcopal Church of St. Thomas* (Philadelphia, 1862), pp. 17–18, 23; for Dougherty see Sydney V. James, *A People among People: Quaker Benevolence in Eighteenth-Century America* (Cambridge, Mass., 1963), p. 236.

2. Gaillard Hunt, "William Thornton and Negro Colonization," *American Antiquarian Society Proceedings,* n.s., 30 (1920), 32–61; Floyd J. Miller, *The Search for a Black Nationality: Black Colonization and Emigration, 1787–1863* (Urbana, Ill., 1975), pp. 9–15.

3. Brissot de Warville, *New Travels in the United States of America, 1788,* trans. Mara Soceanu Vanos and Durand Echeverria (Cambridge, Mass., 1964), p. 149.

4. "Negro Petitions for Freedom," *Collections of the Massachusetts Historical Society,* 5th ser., III (Boston, 1877), 436–437; quoted in Miller, *Search for Black Nationality,* p. 5.

5. Thornton to de Warville, Nov. 29, 1788, William Thornton Papers, Library of Congress.

6. Winthrop D. Jordan, *White over Black: American Attitudes toward the Negro, 1550–1812* (Chapel Hill, N.C., 1968), pp. 542–569; Henry N. Sherwood, "Early Negro Deportation Projects," *Mississippi Valley Historical Review,* 2 (1916), 495.

7. "To the Black Inhabitants of Pennsylvania Assembled at one of their State Meetings in Philadelphia," William Thornton Papers, Library of Congress.

8. "General Outline," ibid.

9. Free African Union Society of Newport to Free African Society of Philadelphia, Sept. 1, 1789, in Douglass, *Annals,* pp. 25–26.

10. Ibid., pp. 31–32.

11. Ibid., pp. 28–29.

12. Wayne J. Eberly, "The Pennsylvania Abolition Society, 1775–1830" (Ph.D. diss., Pennsylvania State University, 1973), chaps. 1–4 passim.

13. Rush had apparently purchased William Grubber in 1776; he first refers to him in a letter to his wife on July 23, 1776, in L. H. Butterfield, ed., *The Letters of Benjamin Rush,* 2 vols. (Princeton, N.J., 1951), I, 106. In his autobiography Rush noted Grubber's death in 1799 and recorded that he had freed him after ten years of service (although in fact Rush promised Grubber freedom in 1788); *The Autobiography of Benjamin Rush,* ed. George W. Corner (Princeton, N.J., 1948), p. 246.

14. Roberts Vaux, *Memoirs of the Life of Anthony Benezet* (Philadelphia, 1817), p. 35; on Clarkson's influence on Rush see David Freeman Hawke, *Benjamin Rush: Revolutionary Gadfly* (Indianapolis and New York, 1971), pp. 360–361, although Hawke does not specify, as Rush did, that it was his reading of Clarkson's pamphlet that converted him to the abolitionist cause.

15. Benjamin Rush, "Paradise of Negro Slaves," in *Essays, Literary, Moral, and Philosophical* (Philadelphia, 1798), pp. 315–320; Clarkson's *An Essay on the Slavery and Commerce of the Human Species* was published in London in 1786 and reached Rush the next year. Rush wrote that "Mr. Clarkson's ingenious and pathetic essay" made "so deep an impression upon my mind, that it followed me in my sleep, and produced a dream of so extraordinary a nature, that I have communicated it to the public"; *Essays,* p. 305.

16. Grubber did not get his freedom until 1794; see Hawke, *Rush,* pp. 361–362.

17. Rush to Jeremy Belknap, Aug. 18, 1788, in Butterfield, *Letters of Benjamin Rush,* I, 482.

18. Hawke, *Rush,* p. 106.

19. Butterfield, *Letters of Benjamin Rush,* I, lxix.

20. A list of members in 1789 was included in the Act of Incorporation of the Society, *The Statutes at Large of Pennsylvania from 1682 to 1801,* XIII (Harrisburg, 1908), 424–432. The new recruits included 33 merchants, 4 shopkeepers, 6 officials, 22 professionals, 19 artisans, 5 printers, and 8 men whose occupations have not been identified.

21. "To the honorable the Convention of the United States now assembled in the city of Philadelphia," June 2, 1787, PPAS, microfilm ed., reel 25.

22. PAS Minute Book, p. 30 (April 19, 1787); for public sale of slaves see *American Museum,* 1 (May 1787), 471.

23. See, for example, *American Museum,* 1 (1787), nos. 1–4; 4 (1788), nos. 1–6; 5 (1789), nos. 1, 2, 5, 6; *Pennsylvania Gazette,* Dec. 3, 1788; Dec. 2, 1789.

24. For the "outburst of discussion about the Negro" in the late 1780s, which he sees as part of the need to define a national identity at this time, see Jordan, *White over Black,* pp. 482–497, and Jordan's introduction to the much-expanded 1810 edition of Smith's essay (Cambridge, Mass., 1965), pp. vii–xxxii.

25. Charles E. Wynes, "Dr. James Durham, Mysterious Eighteenth-Century Black Physician: Man or Myth?" *PMHB,* 103 (1979), 325–333; Jordan, *White over Black,* pp. 448–449; Rush's account of Durham is in Butterfield, *Letters of Benjamin Rush,* I, 498.

26. For Fuller see Jordan, *White over Black,* p. 449; and (Philadelphia) *General Advertiser,* Dec. 28, 1790. A month after the notice on Fuller, Benjamin Franklin Bache's *General Advertiser* (Jan. 28, 1791) took notice of "Mr. Listel," a free black elected to the Royal Academy of Sciences in Paris, whose brilliant meteorological observations further helped to break down "the strong and long established line of distinction between colours." On Nov. 24, 1791, the *Advertiser* printed James McHenry's essay on the almanac of the black mathematician Benjamin Banneker, making the point that Banneker was "fresh proof that the powers of the mind are disconnected with the colour of the skin, or, in other words, a striking contradiction to Mr. Hume's doctrine that the Negroes are naturally inferior to the whites, and unsusceptible of attainments in arts and sciences."

27. Arthur Zilversmit, *The First Emancipation: The Abolition of Slavery in the North* (Chicago, 1967), pp. 157–158; Eberly, "Pennsylvania Abolition Society," p. 59.

28. Paul Finkelman, *An Imperfect Union: Slavery, Federalism, and Comity* (Chapel Hill, N.C., 1981), pp. 46–65; Stanley I. Kutler, "Pennsylvania

Courts, the Abolition Act, and Negro Rights," *Pennsylvania History,* 30 (1963), 14–27.

29. PAS Minute Book, 1787–1800, Oct. 19, 1789.

30. Douglass, *Annals,* pp. 39–40.

31. Ibid., pp. 34–42.

32. Ibid., pp. 22–23.

33. Carol V. R. George, *Segregated Sabbaths: Richard Allen and the Rise of Independent Black Churches, 1760–1845* (New York, 1973), p. 57.

34. Douglass, *Annals,* p. 9; for the attraction of the impoverished to Methodism, see William H. Williams, *The Garden of Methodism: The Delmarva Peninsula, 1769–1820* (Wilmington, Del., 1984), pp. 105–107.

35. Doris Elisabett Andrews, "Popular Religion and the Revolution in the Middle Atlantic Ports: The Rise of the Methodists, 1770–1800" (Ph.D. diss., University of Pennsylvania, 1986), chaps. 1–3.

36. Donald G. Mathews, *Slavery and Methodism: A Chapter in American Morality, 1780–1845* (Princeton, N.J., 1965), chap. 1; George, *Segregated Sabbaths,* p. 43.

37. Douglass, *Annals,* p. 24.

38. Rush to Julia Rush, July 16, 1791, in Butterfield, *Letters of Benjamin Rush,* I, 600.

39. *Extract of a Letter from Dr. Benjamin Rush, of Philadelphia, to Granville Sharp* (London, 1792), pp. 6–7. Rush's letter in its full, original form is in Butterfield, *Letters of Benjamin Rush,* I, 608–609. The quoted phrases are from the "Address of the Representatives of the African Church," the printed appeal for subscriptions. No copy of this document, published in Philadelphia in 1791, is extant, but Sharp appended it to the *Extract of a Letter from Rush,* and it was published in the *General Advertiser* on Feb. 20, 1792. Rush noted in his journal that "many hundred [of free blacks] . . . now spend that day [Sunday] in idleness," although the Pennsylvania Abolition Society reported that "all these poor People profess some system of Religion" and noted that "many frequent some place of public worship"; *Autobiography of Rush,* p. 202; CICFB Minute Book, 1790–1803, pp. 26–29 (April 1, 1791), PPAS, reel 6.

40. *Extract of a Letter from Rush,* p. 4. Rush reported in August 1791 that the city's blacks were disheartened "from their being deprived of the means of regular education and religious instruction"; Rush to Granville Sharp, in Butterfield, *Letters of Benjamin Rush,* I, 608.

41. Gayraud S. Wilmore, *Black Religion and Black Radicalism: An Interpretation of the Religious History of the Afro-American People* (Garden City, N.Y., 1972), p. 114. For an illuminating analysis of the union church movement and other independent black churches see Will B. Gravely, "The Rise of African Churches in America (1786–1822): Re-examining the Contexts," *Journal of Religious Thought,* 14 (1984), 58–73.

42. *Extract of a Letter from Rush*, p. 4; Douglass, *Annals*, pp. 45–46.

43. Frederick E. Maser and Howard T. Maag, eds., *The Journal of Joseph Pilmore, Methodist Itinerant* (Philadelphia, 1969), pp. 235–247; Norris S. Barratt, *Outline of the History of Old St. Paul's Church, Philadelphia, 1760–1899* [Lancaster, Pa.], 1917), pp. 113–124. Pilmore's register of marriages is in *Pennsylvania Archives*, 2d ser., IX (Harrisburg, 1880), 462–492. Few black marriages were performed at St. Paul's before Pilmore's arrival—none before 1786, and only six from January 1786 to May 1789.

44. *Extract of a Letter from Rush*, p. 4. Rush and Jones presented the plan to "a dozen free Blacks," undoubtedly the deacons and elders, on July 25, 1791. Three days later it was adopted, perhaps with some alterations. William Gray thanked Rush the following summer for "the great pains and trouble you have taken in prescribing the rules and regulations which ought to be observed in the Africans Church." Two days later Gray asked Rush to draw up "a form of the credentials or whatever is necessary for the Elders and Deacons to have after their Ordination in Order to Authorize them to sit in their respective stations"; Gray to Rush, Oct. 24 and 26, 1792, Correspondence of Rush, XXIV, 116–117, LCP.

45. Wiltshire: Acting Committee Minute Book, 1784–1788, p. 74 (May 22, 1786), PPAS, reel 4. Collins: Henry Cadbury, "Negro Membership in the Society of Friends," *Journal of Negro History*, 21 (1936), 159; and Collins to John Blakey, Aug. 7, 1796, Cox-Parrish-Wharton Collection, XVIII, 40, HSP. Stewart: Douglass, *Annals*, p. 25–32.

46. "Address of the Representatives of the African Church," in *Extract of a Letter from Rush*, pp. 6–7.

47. Gravely, "Rise of African Churches," p. 59.

48. "Address of the Representatives of the African Church," in *Extract of a Letter from Rush*, pp. 6–7.

49. Wilmore, *Black Religion and Black Radicalism*, p. 106; see also George Levesque, "Interpreting Early Black Ideology: A Reappraisal of Historical Consensus," *Journal of the Early Republic*, 1 (1981), 281.

50. Douglass, *Annals*, pp. 3, 11. Benjamin Quarles writes that "racial pride was . . . a central motif in antebellum black history. Like other Americans of their day, blacks were engaged in the quest for self-identity. Because blacks bore heavy burdens, however, black self-identity more readily flowed into group identity, with history a connecting link, in effect becoming history-as-identity"; "Black History's Antebellum Origins," *American Antiquarian Society Proceedings*, n.s., 89 (1980), 94.

51. A copy of the broadside is in General Meeting, Loose Minutes, 1789, PPAS, reel 9.

52. Rush to Julia Rush, July 16, 1791, in *Letters of Rush*, I, 599–600.

53. J. B. to Benjamin Rush, July 24, 1791, Correspondence of Rush, LCP.

54. Rush to Julia Rush, July 16, 1791, in Butterfield, *Letters of Benjamin Rush,* I, 599–600; *Autobiography of Rush,* p. 202.

55. *Autobiography of Rush,* p. 202; *The Life Experience and Gospel Labors of Rt. Rev. Richard Allen, To Which Is Annexed The Rise and Progress of the African Methodist Episcopal Church in the United States of America* (Nashville, 1960), pp. 26–27. For a more positive view of White's role see Ann C. Lammers, "The Rev. Absalom Jones and the Episcopal Church: Christian Theology and Black Consciousness in a New Alliance," *Historical Magazine of the Protestant Episcopal Church,* 51 (1982), 159–184.

56. Benjamin T. Tanner, *An Apology for African Methodism* (Baltimore, 1867), p. 16.

57. Rush to Granville Sharp, [August 1791], in Butterfield, *Letters of Benjamin Rush,* I, 602, 608–609; Sharp to Rush, [September 1792], Correspondence of Rush, XXVIII, 106, LCP; receipt for £25 from Rush, Benjamin Rush Papers, box 9, HSP; for the Newport contribution see Gravely, "Rise of African Churches," p. 64.

58. *Life Experience of Allen,* pp. 27–28; the decision of the Free African Society to draw up subscription papers in March 1792 is recorded in its minutes; Douglass, *Annals,* p. 44. The purchase of lots, which caused some controversy, was noted in the minutes of Feb. 17, 1792, ibid., p. 43.

59. Douglass, *Annals,* pp. 47–48. Of the ten, only William Wiltshire joined the church after it opened two years later.

60. Rush to Jeremy Belknap, June 21, 1792, in Butterfield, *Letters of Benjamin Rush,* I, 620.

61. *Life Experience of Allen,* p. 25.

62. The misdating of the incident at St. George's seems to have originated in Richard Allen and Jacob Tapsico's introduction to the *Doctrines and Discipline of the African Methodist Episcopal Church,* published in 1817, after Allen had made final his split with the Methodists. The introduction—a "brief statement of our rise and progress"—dates the incident around November 1787. Many early Methodist historians and almost all historians writing since have accepted this date. Milton C. Sernett, however, has provided convincing evidence that Allen, writing a quarter of a century after the fact, telescoped the events of 1787–1792. In his autobiography Allen related that the incident occurred after the galleries and new flooring had been installed; but, using the building records in the vault of St. George's Church, Sernett shows that the galleries were not finished until May 1792. Moreover, the initials of the elders and pastors that Allen recounted as connected with the incident cannot be associated with any St. George's officials in 1787 but correspond to those serving in 1791–92; Sernett, *Black Religion and American Evangelicalism: White Protestants, Plantation Missions, and the Flowering of Negro Christianity, 1787–1865* (Metuchen, N.J., 1975), pp. 117–118, 219–220.

63. Richard Allen and Jacob Tapsico, *Doctrines and Discipline of the African*

Methodist Episcopal Church (Philadelphia, [1817]), in Bishop R. R. Wright, *The Bishops of the African Methodist Episcopal Church* (Nashville, 1963), p. 60; *Life Experience of Allen,* p. 26.

64. Rush to John Nicholson, Nov. 28, 1792, in Butterfield, *Letters of Benjamin Rush,* I, 624. On Nicholson see Robert D. Arbuckle, *Pennsylvania Speculator and Patriot: The Entrepreneurial John Nicholson, 1757–1800* (University Park, Pa., 1975).

65. Absalom Jones and William Gray to John Nicholson, Dec. 3, 1792, and Feb. 7 and 9, 1793, John Nicholson Papers, General Correspondence, 1772–1819, Pennsylvania State Archives, Harrisburg, microfilm ed. at HSP, reel 10, frs. 1300–01, 1303, 1305 (hereafter Nicholson Correspondence). Also see Jones and Gray to John Nicholson, May 11, 1793, ibid., fr. 1307; and Jones, Gray, and William Wiltshire to John Nicholson, Nov. 28, 1792, Correspondence of Rush, XXIV, 118, LCP.

66. *Life Experience of Allen,* p. 28. Details on the building contracts and donations of building materials by white Philadelphians are recorded in the minutes of the Free African Society; Douglass, *Annals,* pp. 50–57.

67. For the cost of building, Douglass, *Annals,* p. 50; for seating capacity, William Catto, *A Semi-Centenary Discourse . . . in the First African Presbyterian Church . . .* (Philadelphia, 1857), p. 105. For white Philadelphians reneging and Gray's trip to Baltimore see Jones to John Nicholson, Aug. 2, 1793, and Gray to Nicholson, Aug. 13, 1793, Nicholson Correspondence, reel 10, frs. 1308–09, 1311–12; and Joseph G. Bend to Rush, Aug. 12, 1793, Correspondence of Rush, XXII, 82, LCP.

68. Nicholson to Absalom Jones and William Gray, Aug. 8, 1793, Correspondence of Rush, XII, 16, LCP; Gray to John Nicholson, Aug. 13, 1793, Nicholson Correspondence, reel 10, frs. 1311–12; Rush to John Nicholson, Aug. 12, 1793, in Butterfield, *Letters of Benjamin Rush,* II, 636. On the raising of money for the refugees from Santo Domingo, see Mathew Carey, *A Short Account of the Malignant Fever Lately Prevalent in Philadelphia . . .* (Philadelphia, 1793), p. 13.

69. Rush to Julia Rush, Aug. 2, 1793, in Butterfield, *Letters of Benjamin Rush,* II, 639.

70. J. H. Powell, *Bring Out Your Dead: The Great Plague of Yellow Fever in Philadelphia in 1793* (Philadelphia, 1949), pp. 8–63.

71. Ibid., pp. 64–89. The quotations are from Carey's *Short Account of the Malignant Fever,* 4th ed. (Philadelphia, 1794), p. 23.

72. Powell, *Bring Out Your Dead,* pp. 90–113.

73. Rush to Richard Allen, [Sept. 1793], Correspondence of Rush, XXXVIII, 32, LCP. For a discussion of the partial resistance of blacks to the yellow fever see Kenneth F. Kiple and Virginia Himmelsteib King, *Another Dimension to the Black Diaspora; Diet, Disease, and Racism* (Cambridge, 1981), chap. 2.

74. A[bsalom] J[ones] and R[ichard] A[llen], *A Narrative of the Proceedings of the Black People, During the Late Awful Calamity in Philadelphia, in the year 1793 . . .* (Philadelphia, 1794), pp. 24–25.

75. Powell, *Bring Out Your Dead,* pp. 96–98; Rush to _____, Sept. 7, 1793, in Butterfield, *Letters of Benjamin Rush,* II, 654.

76. Rush to Julia Rush, Sept. 10, 1793, in Butterfield, *Letters of Benjamin Rush,* II, 658.

77. Rush to Julia Rush, Sept. 13 and 25, 1793, ibid., 663, 683–684.

78. Jones and Allen, *Narrative of the Black People,* pp. 15–16; *Minutes of the Proceedings of the Committee . . . to Attend to and Alleviate the Sufferings of the Afflicted . . .* (Philadelphia, 1794), p. 204. According to the house census recorded in these minutes, only 209 blacks left the city.

79. Martin S. Pernick, "Politics, Parties, and Pestilence: Epidemic Yellow Fever in Philadelphia and the Rise of the First Party System," *William and Mary Quarterly,* 3d ser., 29 (1972), 559–586.

80. Jones and Allen, *Narrative of the Black People.* The pamphlet was published on Jan. 24, 1794.

81. Ibid., pp. 7–12.

82. Ibid., pp. 15–16. Carey had distorted the evidence despite Benjamin Rush's description of the heroic work of many blacks; Rush to Mathew Carey, Oct. 29, 1793, in Butterfield, *Letters of Benjamin Rush,* II, 731–732. The PAS investigated the matter at the request of Jones and Allen and concluded in June 1794, after examining the evidence, that the black leaders had actually suffered financially from their services; CICFB Minute Book, 1790–1803, pp. 83–84 (June 24, 1794), PPAS, reel 6.

83. For the Irish see Edward Carter II, "A 'Wild Irishman' under Every Federalist's Bed: Naturalization in Philadelphia, 1789–1806," *PMHB,* 94 (1970), 331–346.

84. Jones and Gray to John Nicholson, Dec. 20 and 27, 1793, Nicholson Correspondence, reel 10, frs. 1313–15.

85. *Life Experience of Allen,* pp. 28–29. The first election of deacons and elders in 1792 is recorded in Douglass, *Annals,* p. 49.

86. *Life Experience of Allen,* pp. 28–29.

87. For a history of the heterogeneous and generally "low church" character of the Anglican churches in Philadelphia see Deborah Gough, "Pluralism, Politics, and Power Struggles: The Church of England in Colonial Philadelphia, 1685–1789," (Ph.D. diss., University of Pennsylvania, 1978).

88. *Life Experience of Allen,* pp. 29–30.

89. George F. Bragg, *Richard Allen and Absalom Jones* (Baltimore, 1915), unpaginated.

90. The constitution is in Douglass, *Annals,* pp. 96–99. White's statement is quoted in Edgar L. Pennington, "The Work of the Bray Associates in Pennsylvania," *PMHB,* 58 (1934), 2.

91. Douglass, *Annals,* pp. 100–102. St. Thomas's leaders understood the *quid pro quo* to be temporary, but their successors found that when their black ministers were able to satisfy the Latin and Greek requirements the diocese still denied them representation in the Convention. Not until after the Civil War would the Convention accede to St. Thomas's claim. Douglass chronicled the long struggle for recognition in ibid., pp. 139–171. For further discussion see Lammers, "Jones and the Episcopal Church," pp. 178–179, 183–184. Bishop William White ordained Jones as deacon on Aug. 23, 1795, and nine years later as priest. An invitation to the ordination ceremony to John Nicholson, Aug. 22, 1795, is in Nicholson Correspondence, reel 10, fr. 1318.

92. *A Discourse Delivered July 17th, 1794, in the African Church of the City of Philadelphia, on the occasion of opening the said Church, and holding public worship in it the first time* [Philadelphia, 1794], reprinted in Douglass, *Annals,* pp. 58–85; quoted passages on pp. 58–59, 64.

93. Ibid., pp. 64–85; quoted passages on pp. 66, 76, 80–81.

94. Jones and Allen, *Narrative of the Black People,* pp. 23–24.

95. "The Causes and Motives for Establishing St. Thomas's African Church of Philadelphia," in Douglass, *Annals,* pp. 93–95. It may be significant that Jones left the word *Episcopal* out of the title. The quotation is on p. 94.

96. Ibid., p. 95.

97. *Life Experience of Allen,* p. 31; for the May 5 meeting see Charles H. Wesley, *Richard Allen: Apostle of Freedom* (Washington, D.C., [1935]), pp. 77–78.

98. Benjamin Tucker Tanner, *An Outline of Our History and Government for African Methodist Churchmen Ministerial and Lay* (Philadelphia, 1884), pp. 142–148. For an excellent treatment of this see Will B. Gravely, "African Methodisms and the Rise of Black Denominationalism," in Russell E. Richey and Kenneth E. Rowe, eds., *Rethinking Methodist History: A Bicentennial Consultation* (Nashville, 1985), pp. 111–124.

99. A list of St. Thomas's members in 1794 is given in Douglass, *Annals,* pp. 107–110. Douglass's membership figure for 1795 and his comment on the floating congregation are on p. 110. Bethel's membership is taken from *Minutes Taken at . . . Conferences of the Methodist Episcopal Church in America for the Year 1795* (Philadelphia, 1795). Tanner reported a membership list for Bethel dated Nov. 3, 1794, with 108 names, but I have been unable to locate it; Tanner, *Outline of Our History and Government,* p. 19.

100. Based on an extrapolation from the 1790 and 1800 federal census data of free blacks in Philadelphia. Many other former slaves lived in Southwark and the Northern Liberties, on the fringes of the city, and some of them probably gravitated to the city's churches. In a 1795 household census the PAS counted 381 independent black families in the city; CICFB Minute

Book, 1790–1803, p. 112 (Nov. 30, 1795), PPAS, reel 6. Ira Berlin suggests similarly that a higher proportion of free blacks than whites belonged to churches in the South in the antebellum period; *Slaves without Masters: The Free Negro in the Antebellum South* (New York, 1974), pp. 287–303.

101. François A. La Rochefoucauld–Liancourt noted in 1798 that black Philadelphians, despite having "the African church," went "to the other churches at their pleasure"; *Travels through the United States . . . 1795–97*, 2 vols. (London, 1799), II, 387.

102. Calculated from the transcribed church records at the Pennsylvania Genealogical Society and from the baptismal statistics listed for St. Thomas's and Bethel in the anual bills of mortality published by Christ Church and in Zachariah Poulson's almanacs. By the late 1790s only an occasional black baptism occurred in the white churches. Douglass used a "Baptismal Record" and interment book to give the total number of baptisms and burials at St. Thomas's from 1796 to 1818, but I can find no trace of these records. See Douglass, *Annals*, p. 123.

5. A City of Refuge

1. *Confessions of John Joyce, alias Davis, Who was Executed on Monday, the 14th of March, 1808 . . . With an Address to the Public and People of Colour By Richard Allen . . .* (Philadelphia, 1808), reprinted in Dorothy Porter, ed., *Early Negro Writing, 1760–1837* (Boston, 1971), pp. 421–422.

2. W. E. B. Du Bois first noted this movement to the cities in his classic study, *The Philadelphia Negro: A Social Study* (1899; reprint, New York, 1967), p. 17. Ira Berlin also draws attention to this migration in "The Structure of the Free Negro Caste in the Antebellum United States," *Journal of Social History*, 9 (1976), 300. For further insights on changes in the South see Richard S. Dunn, "Black Society in the Chesapeake, 1776–1810," in Ira Berlin and Ronald Hoffman, eds., *Slavery and Freedom in the Age of the American Revolution* (Charlottesville, Va., 1983), pp. 49–82; and Allan Kulikoff, "Uprooted Peoples: Black Migrants in the Age of the American Revolution, 1790–1820," in ibid., pp. 143–171.

3. Seamen's Protective Certificate Applications to the Collector of Customs for the Port of Philadelphia, Records of the Bureau of Customs, National Archives; the ships' crew lists are in Maritime Records of the Port of Philadelphia, 1798–1860, WPA transcriptions, Library of Congress. The origin of the certificates and information contained in them is detailed by Ira Dye, "Early American Merchant Seafarers," *Proceedings of the American Philosophical Society*, 120 (1976), 331–334.

4. Du Bois, *Philadelphia Negro*, p. 55; Theodore Hershberg, "Free Blacks in Antebellum Philadelphia," *Journal of Social History*, 5 (1971–72), 190; Robert W. Fogel and Stanley L. Engerman, "Philanthropy at Bargain

Prices: Notes on the Economics of Gradual Emancipation," *Journal of Legal Studies,* 3 (1974), 393. I made the same error in "Forging Freedom: The Emancipation Experience in the Northern Seaport Cities, 1775–1820," in Berlin and Hoffman, *Slavery and Freedom,* pp. 11–15.

5. The census takers in 1810, for example, recorded only 25 black mariners. The crew lists for 1811 list 220 black mariners who maintained residence in Philadelphia; but many of these were not heads of household and therefore would not have appeared on the census schedules.

6. Ira Berlin, *Slaves without Masters: The Free Negro in the Antebellum South* (New York, 1974), pp. 29–35; Dunn, "Black Society in the Chesapeake"; Kulikoff, "Uprooted Peoples."

7. Berlin, *Slaves without Masters,* pp. 25–35. Virginia repealed the prohibition on private manumissions in 1782, and Delaware followed suit in 1787; three years later Maryland allowed manumission by will for the first time. For the liberalization of the manumission laws in Delaware, where former slaves had the easiest access to Philadelphia, see Patience Essah, "Slavery and Freedom in the First State: The History of Blacks in Delaware from the Colonial Period to 1865" (Ph.D. diss., University of California, Los Angeles, 1985), chap. 3.

8. Essah, "Slavery and Freedom in the First State," app. 1, p. 228; the manumissions and indentures are recorded in Manumission Books A–F and Indenture Books C and D, PPAS, reels 20–22.

9. Berlin, *Slaves without Masters,* pp. 37–41; Carl Oblinger found 450 advertisements for runaway slaves in southeastern Pennsylvania from 1781 to 1802; "Alms for Oblivion: The Making of a Black Underclass in Southeastern Pennsylvania, 1780–1869," in John E. Bodnar, ed., *The Ethnic Experience in Pennsylvania* (Lewisburg, Pa., 1973), p. 114 n.

10. Inspectors of the Walnut Street Prison, Vagrancy Dockets, I (1790–1797), PCA.

11. Ibid.

12. CICFB Minute Book, 1790–1803, pp. 37–43 (Sept. 20, 1791; Feb. 28, 1792), PPAS, reel 6.

13. David Barclay, *An Account of the Emancipation of the Slaves of Unity Valley Pen, in Jamaica* (London, 1801); CICFB Minute Book, 1790–1803, pp. 99–107, 121–123, 145, PPAS, reel 6; the manumission and indenture documents for the Barclay group are in Manumissions, Indentures, and Other Legal Papers, PPAS, reel 22. The Abolition Society manumission books show that from 1788 to 1816 twenty-three other British West Indies slaveowners manumitted thirty-six slaves and sent them to Philadelphia.

14. Cox-Parrish-Wharton Collection, XIV, 54, HSP.

15. Elizabeth Drinker Journal, August 5, 1800, HSP; *Claypoole's Daily Advertiser,* Aug. 5, 1800; General Meeting Minute Book, 1800–1824, pp. 2–3 (Aug. 7, 1800); Eliza Cope Harrison, ed., *Philadelphia Merchant: The Diary of*

Thomas P. Cope, 1800–1851 (South Bend, Ind., 1978), p. 9; the indentures for the Ganges group are in Manumissions, Indentures, and Other Legal Papers, PPAS, reel 22. The Africans were apparently given a choice of forenames with which to begin life in Philadelphia. Many were listed in the manumission books with conventional English names such as Mary, Charles, Sarah, and Thomas; but nearly half of them retained African names such as Abia, Seza, Juba, Nandusa, Setafa, Messu, Kea, Abanna, and Yelle. Four-year indentures were contracted for the adults.

16. Winthrop D. Jordan, *White over Black: American Attitudes toward the Negro, 1550–1812* (Chapel Hill, N.C., 1968), pp. 375–386.

17. For the black revolution in Santo Domingo see T. Lothrop Stoddard, *The French Revolution in Santo Domingo* (Boston, 1914); C. L. R. James, *The Black Jacobins,* 2d ed. (New York, 1963); and David Patrick Geggus, *Slavery, War, and Revolution: The British Occupation of Saint Domingue, 1793–1798* (Oxford, 1982).

18. *Federal Gazette,* July 9, Aug. 5, and Aug. 9, 1793; Mathew Carey, *A Short Account of the Malignant Fever, Lately Prevalent in Philadelphia . . .* (Philadelphia, 1793), p. 13. The *Federal Gazette* listed ships arriving from the French West Indies throughout the summer of 1793. For signed passenger agreements from the French West Indies to Philadelphia see Dutilh and Wachsmuth Papers, Library of Congress.

19. *Federal Gazette,* July 12, 1793.

20. Lawrence Embree to James Pemberton, Jan. 24, 1795, Cox-Parrish-Wharton Collection, XI, 102, HSP.

21. PAS Minute Book, 1787–1800, pp. 180–181 (Jan. 7, 1793).

22. Many of the released French slaves, especially if they were children or adolescents, immediately signed indentures to their masters. The PAS may have recommended this policy, although I have found no specific reference to it. Hundreds of such indentures are recorded in Indenture Books C (1758–1785) and D (1795–1835), PPAS, reel 22. When he lived in Philadelphia for four months in 1797, François La Rochefoucauld–Liancourt described this process: "Having conducted them before magistrates, they [refugee planters] engage them [released slaves] till the time when they shall attain the age of twenty one, or twenty-eight; but the consent of the negro to this effect is necessary, without which they are declared free"; *Travels through the United States . . . 1795–97,* 2 vols. (London, 1799), II, 335. A second but much smaller wave of French slaves entered the city in 1798, when the British evacuation of Santo Domingo convinced hundreds of planters to flee the island with their chattels. See (Newark) *Centinel of Freedom,* July 3, 1798.

23. Benjamin Rush to Richard Rush, Oct. 19, 1810; Rush to Samuel Bayard, Oct. 23, 1810, Correspondence of Rush, LCP; *Journal of the 23rd House of Representatives of the Commonwealth of Pennsylvania* (Harrisburg, 1813), p. 417.

24. Berlin, *Slaves without Masters,* pp. 92–99.

25. [James Forten], *A Series of Letters by A Man of Color* (Philadelphia, 1813); reprinted in Herbert Aptheker, ed., *A Documentary History of the Negro People in the United States* (New York, 1951), pp. 59–66; the quote is on p. 66.

26. In 1794 the CICFB, considering the arrival in the city of many aged and infirm former slaves, asked the Overseers of the Poor for help; CICFB Minute Book, 1790–1803, p. 87, PPAS, reel 6. From 1787 to 1801, males accounted for about 55 percent of deaths among blacks. Since males had higher death rates than females (because of weaker immune systems as infants and greater occupational hazards as adults), the excess of adult males was probably not as great as the burial statistics suggest. The winter months, when respiratory diseases struck, were particularly perilous for blacks, whereas whites were most afflicted by the summer and autumn yellow fever epidemics that were prevalent in the 1790s and early 1800s. Susan Klepp, of Rider College, has generously provided the following data on black burials in Philadelphia, from 1787 to 1800, compiled from mortality lists published in Richard Poulson's almanacs: for 1787–1791, 153 males and 121 females (55.8 percent males); for 1792–1795, 284 males and 213 females (57.1 percent males); and for 1796–1800, 531 males and 476 females (52.7 percent males).

27. Barclay, *Account of the Emancipation of the Slaves,* passim; Tobias Barclay became a successful hatter and is listed in the 1816 Philadelphia directory. James Barclay, a laborer, is the only other person of this surname listed in either the 1811 or 1816 directory.

28. For the doubling and tripling of house rents in the 1790s, see Carey, *A Short Account of the Malignant Fever,* p. 13. Billy G. Smith charts real wages for laborers, mariners, and lower artisans in "Material Lives of Laboring Philadelphians," *William and Mary Quarterly,* 3d ser., 38 (1981), 181–200. For early nineteenth-century economic conditions and wages, see Diane Lindstrom, *Economic Development in the Philadelphia Region, 1810–1850* (New York, 1978); and Donald R. Adams, Jr., "Wage Rates in the Early National Period: Philadelphia, 1785–1830," *Journal of Economic History,* 28 (1968), 404–426.

29. PAS Minute Book, 1787–1800, p. 353 (April 7, 1800).

30. CICFB Minute Book, 1790–1803, pp. 23, 36, 40, 42, 212, 250, 256, PPAS, reel 6.

31. Ships' Crew Lists, Maritime Records of the Port of Philadelphia. The 1811 lists include 220 mariners who resided in Philadelphia; in 1816 the number was 295.

32. Quoted in Leon F. Litwack, *North of Slavery: The Negro in the Free States, 1790–1860* (Chicago, 1961), p. 154.

33. Rush to Sharp, August 1791; Rush to President of the Pennsylvania Abolition Society, [1794], in L. H. Butterfield, ed., *The Letters of Benjamin Rush,* 2 vols. (Princeton, N.J., 1951) I, 608; II, 754–756.

34. CICFB Minute Book, 1790–1803, p. 112, PPAS, reel 6.

35. I have traced in the city directories and other sources the occupation of twelve of the nineteen men who served as trustees of Bethel and the African Church of Philadelphia between 1794 and 1796. Nine of these twelve had created independent economic roles, two as master sweeps and one each as grocer, trader, dealer, oysterman, ragman, teacher-minister, and sawyer. Of the other three, two were waiters and one a coachman.

36. Emma Jones Lapsansky, "Friends, Wives, and Strivings: Networks and Community Values among Nineteenth-Century Philadelphia Afro-American Elites," *PMHB*, 108 (1984), 12.

37. Schoepf, *Travels in the Confederacy,* ed. and trans. Alfred J. Morrison (Philadelphia, 1911), I, 76; Elizabeth Drinker Journal, May 1, 1804, HSP.

38. *American Mercury,* March 6, 1797; I am indebted to Shane White, of the University of Sydney, for this reference.

39. Nicholas Wainwright, ed., "The Diary of Samuel Breck," *PMHB,* 103 (1979), 250; Robert Purvis, *Remarks on the Life and Character of James Forten* (Philadelphia, 1842), pp. 9–10.

40. Although the city directories are usually believed to have excluded most of the lowest rank of unskilled workers, they often included a very high percentage of those listed on the decennial censuses. Some Philadelphia directories, particularly those published in the year following the federal census, appear to have been constructed from the manuscript census takers' schedules. See Claudia Golden, "The Economic Status of Women in the Early Republic: Quantitative Evidence," *Journal of Interdisciplinary History,* 16 (1986), 381–385. Not too much should be made of the changes in occupational distribution between 1795 and 1811, because the 1811 directory, which appears to have been derived from the census of the preceding year, included a substantially greater proportion of households than did the 1795 directory.

41. Graham Russell Hodges, *New York City Cartmen, 1667–1850* (New York, 1986), pp. 25, 31, 35, 103, 152, 158–159.

42. Nicholas Biddle, *Ode to Bogle* (Philadelphia, 1829).

43. Bernard, *Retrospections of America, 1797–1811* (New York, 1887), pp. 189–190; Eileen Southern, *Biographical Dictionary of Afro-American and African Musicians* (Westport, Conn., 1982), pp. 205–207. The description of Johnson in 1819 is from Peter Atall (Robert Waln), *The Hermit in America on a Visit to Philadelphia* (Philadelphia, 1819), pp. 152–153.

44. Whitfield J. Bell, ed., "Addenda to Watson's Annals of Philadelphia: Notes by Jacob Mordecai, 1836," *PMHB,* 98 (1974), 149, 158.

45. Claudia Goldin's analysis of census schedules and city directories considerably modifies the conventional "golden age" thesis that the advance of a market economy rapidly pushed women out of proprietary roles they had enjoyed in the colonial era, but the argument still retains some validity. See Goldin, "The Economic Status of Women," pp. 375–404. The experi-

ence of black and white lower-class women began to diverge more sharply when laboring white women were drawn into factory work in the Philadelphia region, a topic discussed in Cynthia J. Shelton, *The Mills of Manayunk: Industrialization and Social Conflict in the Philadelphia Region, 1787–1837* (Baltimore, 1986).

46. Janson, *The Stranger in America: Observations Made During a Long Residence in that Country . . .* (London, 1807), pp. 179–180; for Montier, see Susanna Emlen to William Dillwyn, Dec. 8, 1809, Dillwyn Letters, LCP.

47. Charles H. Wesley, *Richard Allen: Apostle of Freedom* (Washington, D.C., 1935), pp. 76–77; for Allen's indentured servants see Indenture Book C, pp. 21, 25, 35, 60, 66; Book D, pp. 99, 109, PPAS, reel 22; two of Allen's runaway servants are recorded in Inspectors of the Walnut Street Jail, Vagrancy Dockets, I (1790–1797), 72, 240; for property acquisition see Deed Books, D20, p. 565; D70, pp. 306–308; EF2, p. 563; IC21, p. 708, PCA.

48. For a general analysis of black occupations in the antebellum cities see Leonard P. Curry, *The Free Black in Urban America, 1800–1850: The Shadow of the Dream* (Chicago, 1981), chap. 2.

49. Philadelphia Guardians of the Poor, Daily Occurrence Dockets, II (1795–1802), PCA. Many examples of this kind of destitution are surveyed in Billy G. Smith and Cynthia J. Shelton, "The Daily Occurrence Docket of the Philadelphia Almshouse, 1800," *Pennsylvania History,* 52 (1985), 86–116.

50. Of 1,400 persons admitted to the almshouse from 1797 to 1803, 159 (11.4 percent) were black. In a census conducted in 1810, 10 percent of the inmates were black. I am indebted to Billy G. Smith, of Montana State University, for these data. For similar findings for New York City see Robert E. Cray, Jr., "White Welfare and Black Strategies: The Dynamics of Race and Poor Relief in Early New York, 1700–1825," *Slavery and Abolition,* 7 (1986), 273–289.

51. It is impossible to calculate the number of Irish-born residents of Philadelphia in this period, but according to historians of the Irish diaspora the level of immigration was moderate during these years. See Maldwyn A. Jones, "Ulster Emigration, 1783–1815," in E. R. R. Green, ed., *Essays in Scotch-Irish History* (New York, 1969); William F. Adams, *Ireland and Irish Emigration to the New World from 1815 to the Famine* (New Haven, 1932); and Kerby A. Miller, *Emigrants and Exiles: Ireland and the Irish Exodus to North America* (New York, 1985), pp. 193–197.

52. *Gale's Independent Gazetteer,* Jan. 3, 1797, quoted in John K. Alexander, *Render Them Submissive: Responses to Poverty in Philadelphia, 1760–1800* (Amherst, Mass., 1980), p. 78.

53. Inspectors of the Walnut Street Jail, Vagrancy Dockets, I (1790–1797) and II (1804–1809), PCA.

54. *Heads of Families at the First Census of the United States Taken in the Year 1790: Pennsylvania* (Washington, D.C., 1908), p. 244; the black incarceration

rate was about half that of whites; the Abolition Society comment is in PAS Minute Book, 1787–1800.

55. Manuscript census of 1810; *A Statistical View of the Operation of the Penal Code of Pennsylvania* . . . (Philadelphia, 1817), p. 14.

56. Court Sentence Dockets, 1804–1810 and 1810–1815, PCA; the samples taken were from Jan. 1, 1805, to March 26, 1806; and from November 15, 1814, to June 15, 1815.

57. Benjamin Johnson to Stephen Grellet, May 25, 1816, Grellet Papers, I, 217, LCP at HSP. The Prison Society's investigation in 1816 demonstrated the low level of violent crime in the city; *A Statistical View*, pp. 12–13.

58. Court Sentence Dockets, 1804–1810 and 1810–1815, PCA.

59. Report of PAS to American Convention of Abolitionist Societies, June 3, 1801, PPAS, reel 28.

60. Committee of Guardians Minute Book, 1797–1802, pp. 23 (Jan. 21, 1791), 32–33 (Sept. 20, 1791), 72–73 (May 23, 1794), PPAS, reel 6.

61. Ibid., p. 12 (June 9, 1790); letters of attorney from numerous blacks to the society are in PPAS, reel 24.

62. For the operations of the committee in indenturing black youth, see Committee of Guardians Minute Book, 1797–1802, pp. 103 (Jan. 2, 1795) and 120 (Feb. 23, 1795), PPAS, reel 6. Scores of cases are recorded in Indenture Books C and D, PPAS, reel 22.

63. Committee of Guardians Minute Book, 1797–1802, pp. 58 (May 24, 1798), 62–63 (June 5, 1798), 65 (July 10, 1798), 73 (Jan. 1, 1799), 101 (Nov. 19, 1799), 125 (July 1, 1800), 157 (June 2, 1801), 159 (June 16, 1801), 164–165 (July 20, 1801), 179 (Dec. 15, 1801), 182 (Jan. 12, 1802), 196–197 (June 29, 1802), PPAS, reel 6.

64. Ibid., pp. 81–82 (March 26, 1799), 86 (April 9, 1799), 102 (Nov. 19, 1799), 105 (Dec. 17, 1799).

65. Derived from analysis of manuscript censuses for 1800, 1810, and 1820, microfilm ed., National Archives.

66. For a discussion of the "problem of the black family" and an argument that urban poverty, not the residual effects of a "defective" slave family experience, led to the decline of the male-headed nuclear household in the period 1850–1880, see Frank F. Furstenberg, Jr., Theodore Hershberg, and John Modell, "The Origins of the Female-Headed Black Family: The Impact of the Urban Experience," *Journal of Interdisciplinary History*, 6 (1975), 211–233. The effect of slavery on household structure can be seen, however, in the substantially higher proportion of free black households headed by a woman in New York City, where slavery still flourished, in these years: 17.2 percent in 1790, 18.8 percent in 1800, and 17.4 percent in 1810. These data are taken from Shane White, " 'We Dwell in Safety and Pursue Our Honest Callings': Free Blacks in New York City, 1783–1810," *Journal of American History* (forthcoming).

67. Among forty-three blacks married at Gloria Dei Swedish Lutheran Church in the years 1793–1805, the median age for black males and females was 27.5 and 26.0, respectively; among fifty-seven whites married, the median age was 23.5 and 20.0, respectively. I am indebted to Susan Klepp for these data.

68. City directory of 1811; manuscript census of 1810.

69. The black residential pattern has been plotted from the listings of black households in *Heads of Families . . . Pennsylvania* and in the manuscript census for 1800, 1810, and 1820.

70. Norman J. Johnston, "The Caste and Class of the Urban Form of Historic Philadelphia," *Journal of the American Institute of Planners,* 32 (1966), 334–349; for the increasingly class-divided social geography of New York City in this period see Betsy Blackmar, "Rewalking the 'Walking City': Property Relations in New York City, 1780–1840," *Radical History Review,* no. 21 (1980), 131–148.

71. *Minutes of the Proceedings of the Committee . . . to Attend to and Alleviate the Sufferings of the Afflicted . . .* (Philadelphia, 1794), appendix, unpaginated; in the alleys and courtyards, 115 lived south of Market Street and 112 north of Market in 1793. Along the main numbered streets and the principal east–west streets such as Chestnut, Vine, and Arch, blacks living south of Market outnumbered those living north of it by two to one, but most of these were residents in white homes.

72. The descriptions of housing, taken from contemporary newspaper accounts, are quoted in Alexander, *Render Them Submissive,* pp. 21–22.

73. The development of the southwestern sector of the city is detailed in Lapsansky, "South Street Philadelphia," pp. 119–140.

74. For similar housing patterns in other cities in the early nineteenth century see Curry, *Free Black in Urban America,* chap. 4.

6. Establishing the Color Line

1. *Federal Gazette,* June 19, 1792; *Independent Gazetteer,* June 23, 1792.

2. *The Autobiography of Benjamin Rush,* ed. George W. Corner (Princeton, N.J., 1948), p. 221.

3. Inspectors of the Walnut Street Jail, Vagrancy Dockets, II (1809–1817), 44, 293, PCA. Theodore Hershberg's argument that ex-slaves in Philadelphia outperformed freeborn blacks is not supported by the evidence and will be taken up in Chapter 8. See Hershberg, "Free Blacks in Antebellum Philadelphia: A Study of Ex-Slaves, Freeborn, and Socioeconomic Decline," *Journal of Social History,* 5 (1971–72), 183–209.

4. Winthrop D. Jordan, *White over Black: American Attitudes Toward the Negro, 1550–1812* (Chapel Hill, N.C., 1968), pp. 375–384.

5. *The Minerva, and Mercantile Evening Advertiser,* Dec. 22, 1796.

6. Elizabeth Drinker Journal, Dec. 31, 1796, HSP; *The Minerva,* Dec. 19, 1796.

7. Elizabeth Drinker Journal, Feb. 25, 1797, HSP.

8. *American Mercury,* March 6, 1797.

9. Governor Mifflin to President John Adams, June 27, 1798, in *Claypoole's American Daily Advertiser,* June 28, 1798.

10. Ibid., June 28, June 29, and July 2, 1798; *Brown's Gazette,* June 28, 1798.

11. Jordan, *White over Black,* pp. 393–402.

12. *New York Evening Post,* July 10 and 12, 1804, copied from (Philadelphia) *Freeman's Journal.* I am indebted to Shane White, University of Sydney, for this reference. Two blacks, Benjamin Lewis and Simon Fox, were arrested but later released; Prisoners for Trial Docket, 1802–1805, PCA.

13. Samuel Emlen, Jr., to Samuel Emlen, Oct. 5, 1795, Dillwyn Letters, LCP; *To the Free Africans and Other Free People of Colour* (Philadelphia, 1796). The broadside is reprinted in Sheldon H. Harris, *Paul Cuffe: Black America and the African Return* (New York, 1972), pp. 272–274.

14. Committee of Guardians Minute Book, 1797–1802, pp. 42–47 (March 27, 1798), PPAS, reel 6; for the distribution of 1,000 copies of the "Address" to free blacks in 1806, see Acting Committee Minute Book, 1803–1810, March 14, 1806, PPAS, reel 5.

15. [James Forten], *A Series of Letters by A Man of Color* (Philadelphia, 1813); reprinted in Herbert Aptheker, ed., *A Documentary History of the Negro People in the United States* (New York, 1951), p. 64. Forten did not mention the year of the July 4 incident, but I am guessing that it was 1805.

16. Susan G. Davis, *Parades and Power: Street Theatre in Nineteenth-Century Philadelphia* (Philadelphia, 1986), pp. 38–48.

17. Branagan related this part of his career in *The Penitential Tyrant* (New York, 1807).

18. Branagan, "A Beam of Celestial Light," in *The Charms of Benevolence* (Philadelphia, 1812), p. 296.

19. James D. Essig, *The Bonds of Wickedness: American Evangelicals against Slavery, 1770–1808* (Philadelphia, 1982), p. 199, n. 72.

20. Ibid., p. 153.

21. Branagan, *Serious Remonstrances* (Philadelphia, 1805), pp. 37, 68–70, 76. The only appreciation of Branagan's literary contributions is by Lewis Leary, "Thomas Branagan: Republican Rhetoric and Romanticism in America," *PMHB,* 77 (1953), 332–352. Leary omits mention of *Serious Remonstrances* and casts Branagan as a consistent friend of abolitionism.

22. Branagan, *Serious Remonstrances,* pp. 36–37; Essig, *Bonds of Wickedness,* pp. 155–156.

23. Branagan, *Serious Remonstrances,* pp. 65–73, 80.

24. Branagan, *Preliminary Essay on the Oppression of the Exiled Sons of Africa,* p. 101.

25. Branagan, *Serious Remonstrances,* p. 79.

26. Susan E. Klepp and Billy G. Smith, "The Records of Gloria Dei Church: Marriages and 'Remarkable Occurrences,' 1794–1806," *Pennsylvania History,* 53 (1986), 129, 136, 137.

27. Elizabeth Drinker Journal, March 11, 1795; Jan. 21, 1796; Jeremiah Warder, Jr., to John Warder, [1795], Cox-Parrish-Wharton Collection, V, 111, HSP; see also Thomas E. Drake, "Joseph Drinker's Plea for Admission of Colored People to the Society of Friends, 1795," *Journal of Negro History,* 32 (1947), 11–12.

28. Philadelphia Guardians of the Poor, Daily Occurrence Dockets, 1800–1810, PCA; these figures are based on an analysis of all admissions in Jan.–Feb. and July–Sept. 1801 and 1806.

29. *Journal of the Fifteenth House of Representatives of the Commonwealth of Pennsylvania* (1804–05) (Lancaster, 1805), pp. 114–115 (hereafter *House Journal*); *Journal of the Senate of the Commonwealth of Pennsylvania* (1804–05) (Lancaster, 1805), 256, 278, 320 (hereafter *Senate Journal*); *Senate Journal* (1805–06), pp. 90, 151.

30. *Senate Journal* (1806–07), pp. 239, 271, 296, 300; for petitions from free blacks and Society of Friends see *Senate Journal* (1806–07), p. 331; *House Journal* (1806–07), pp. 591, 652.

31. [Forten], *A Series of Letters,* p. 64.

32. "A Stranger in the United States," *Philadelphia Gazette,* Nov. 24, 1809.

33. [Forten], *A Series of Letters,* p. 64.

34. *Democratic Press,* Jan. 13, 1813. I am indebted to Ronald Schultz, University of Wyoming, for this reference.

35. *House Journal* (1812–13), pp. 216, 417, 432, 588–589.

36. Ibid., p. 481.

37. Ibid., p. 588.

38. Memorial of PAS to the Pennsylvania Senate and House of Representatives, March 13, 1813, PPAS, reel 25.

39. Susanna Emlen to William Dillwyn, Dec. 8, 1809, Dillwyn Letters, LCP.

40. [Forten], *A Series of Letters,* p. 66.

41. Henry N. Sherwood, "Early Negro Deportation Projects," *Mississippi Valley Historical Review,* 2 (1916), 484–508; Jordan, *White over Black,* pp. 546–569.

42. Floyd J. Miller, *The Search for a Black Nationality: Black Colonization and Emigration, 1787–1863* (Urbana, Ill., 1975), pp. 15–21.

43. William Dillwyn to Samuel Emlen, Aug. 24, 1809; Jan. 28, 1811, Dillwyn Letters, LCP; Miller, *Search for a Black Nationality,* pp. 21–26.

44. Miller, *Search for a Black Nationality,* pp. 26–34.

45. Julie Winch, *Philadelphia's Black Elite: Activism, Accommodation, and the Struggle for Autonomy, 1787–1848* (Philadelphia, 1988), pp. 32–34.

46. Miller, *Search for a Black Nationality*, pp. 40–42; Harris, *Paul Cuffe*, pp. 185–192; Lamont D. Thomas, *Rise to Be a People: A Biography of Paul Cuffe* (Urbana, Ill., 1986), pp. 93–98.

47. Miller, *Search for a Black Nationality*, pp. 42–43; Harris, *Paul Cuffe*, p. 228.

48. Arthur Zilversmit, *The First Emancipation: The Abolition of Slavery in the North* (Chicago, 1967), pp. 203–204.

49. A[bsalom] J[ones] and R[ichard] A[llen], *A Narrative of the Proceedings of the Black People during the late awful calamity in Philadelphia, in the year 1793* . . . (Philadelphia, 1794). The quoted passage is in Aptheker, *Documentary History*, p. 37.

50. "To the President, Senate, and House of Representatives," January 1797, in Aptheker, *Documentary History*, 40–44; Peter Kent Opper, "North Carolina Quakers: Reluctant Slaveholders," *North Carolina Historical Review*, 52 (1975), 37–39; John Hope Franklin, *The Free Negro in North Carolina, 1790–1860* (Chapel Hill, N.C., 1943), pp. 19–25. The sixteen North Carolina refugees are listed in a document in the Cox-Parrish-Wharton Collection, XIV, 54, HSP.

51. Edward R. Turner, *The Negro in Pennsylvania: Slavery—Servitude—Freedom, 1639–1861* (Washington, D.C., 1911), pp. 115–117. For contemporary reports on kidnapping incidents in Philadelphia, see (Newark) *Centinel of Freedom*, Sept. 15, 1801; *Pennsylvania Gazette*, Nov. 25, 1801; Elizabeth Drinker Journal, Jan. 21, 1804, HSP; and especially [Edward Darlington], *Reflections on Slavery* . . . (Philadelphia, 1803), pp. 18–32.

52. Sidney Kaplan attributes the language of the petition to Jones but offers no supporting evidence; *The Black Presence in the Era of the American Revolution, 1770–1800* (Greenwich, Conn., 1973), p. 231. In 1810 Daniel Coker, who knew the black leaders in Philadelphia well, identified Absalom Jones and James Forten as authors of a petition to Congress when it was sitting in Philadelphia, but this could have been the petition of 1799; Coker, *A Dialogue between a Virginian and an African Minister* (Baltimore, 1810), p. 14.

53. *American Universal Magazine*, 1 (1797), 182–186.

54. Donald Robinson, *Slavery in the Structure of American Politics, 1765–1820* (New York, 1971), pp. 287–290.

55. *Articles of Association of the Bethel Society* (Philadelphia, 1799).

56. Forten to Thacher, January, 1800, Cox-Parrish-Wharton Collection, XIV, 65, HSP; printed in John Parrish, *Remarks on the Slavery of the Black People* . . . (Philadelphia, 1806), pp. 51–52.

57. Petition of the free blacks of Philadelphia to the President and Congress of the United States, Dec. 31, 1799, National Archives; excerpted in Kaplan, *Black Presence*, pp. 237–239.

58. Cox-Parrish-Wharton Collection, II, 3, HSP; Winch says that Jones carried it through the streets; *Philadelphia's Black Elite*, p. 73.

59. Zilversmit, *First Emancipation,* pp. 204–206, discusses the flagging of Quaker efforts to obtain state legislation for the total abolition of slavery in Pennsylvania; however, John Parrish, a leading Philadelphia Quaker, renewed the campaign with his *Remarks on the Slavery of the Black People* in 1806; and in 1812 Pennsylvania's Republican governor, Simon Snyder, called on the legislature to complete the abolition of slavery and noted the "inconsistency of suffering the free air of Pennsylvania to be tainted by the breath of slaves"; Russell Parrott, *An Oration on the Abolition of the Slave Trade* (Philadelphia, 1814), reprinted in Dorothy Porter, ed., *Early Negro Writing, 1760–1837* (Boston, 1971), pp. 383–390.

60. Absalom Jones, *A Thanksgiving Sermon Preached January 1, 1808 . . . on Account of the Abolition of the African Slave Trade . . .* (Philadelphia, 1808); Will B. Gravely, "The Dialectic of Double Consciousness in Black American Freedom Celebrations, 1808–1863," *Journal of Negro History,* 67 (1982), 303.

61. Gravely, "Dialectic of Double Consciousness," p. 307.

62. Jones, *A Thanksgiving Sermon,* pp. 17, 19.

63. See, for example, Russell Parrott's *An Oration on the Abolition of the Slave Trade* (Philadelphia, 1812), *An Oration on the Abolition of the Slave Trade* (Philadelphia, 1814), and *An Address . . .* (Philadelphia, 1816); and Jeremiah Gloucester, *An Oration . . .* (Philadelphia, 1823).

64. In 1822 Samuel Breck, a gentleman reformer and politician in Philadelphia, wrote that "notwithstanding the laws of Pennsylvania do not forbid it, no blacks vote at elections, at least in the eastern part of the state . . . Owing to custom, prejudice or design, they never presume to approach the hustings, neither are they taxed or summoned upon juries or at militia musters"; Nicholas B. Wainwright, ed., "The Diary of Samuel Breck, 1814–1822," *PMHB,* 102 (1978), 505. Breck was mistaken in believing that free blacks did not pay taxes.

65. C. Eric Lincoln, Foreword to Leonard E. Barrett, *Soul-Force: African Heritage in Afro-American Religion* (Garden City, N.Y., 1974), p. viii.

66. Will B. Gravely, "The Rise of African Churches in America (1786–1822): Re-examining the Contexts," *Journal of Religious Thought,* 41 (1984), 65.

67. For black servants of the wealthy Drinker family attending special meetings for blacks, see Elizabeth Drinker Journal, Aug. 4, 1795; Aug. 1, 1796; April 2 and May 8, 1798, HSP. In November 1796 the Philadelphia Yearly Meeting accepted a committee report recommending that "receiving Persons into membership is not limited with respect to Nation or Colour"; Pemberton Papers, LV, 43, HSP.

68. Based on examination of all extant marriage and baptism registers for Philadelphia churches.

69. François A. La Rochefoucauld–Liancourt, *Travels through the United States . . ., 1795–97,* 2 vols. (London, 1799), II, 387.

70. "Sacramental Registers of St. Joseph's Church," *Records of the American Catholic Historical Society of Philadelphia*, XV–XX (Philadelphia, 1904–09), passim.

71. Charles H. Wesley, *Richard Allen: Apostle of Freedom* (Washington, D.C., [1935]), p. 83; Elmer T. Clark, J. Manning Potts, and Jacob S. Payton, eds., *The Journal and Letters of Francis Asbury*, 3 vols. (London and Nashville, 1958), II, 92, 102.

72. The membership in 1795 is given in William Douglass, *Annals of the First African Church in the United States of America, now styled The African Episcopal Church of St. Thomas* (Philadelphia, 1862), p. 123; for 1803, Absalom Jones to Dorothy Ripley, June 3, 1803, in *Journal of Negro History*, 1 (1916), 440–441; for 1813, *Juvenile Magazine*, no. 3 (1813).

73. Douglass, *Annals*, p. 105. St. Thomas's did not gain representation in the Episcopal Convention of Pennsylvania until 1862.

74. Ibid., pp. 115–116, where William Douglass refers to "the noise of an angry tumult" that began in 1810 and lasted "for many years" after Jones's death. Little is known of this schism, but one faction in the church invited Alexander Summers, from Jamaica, to minister to them. Little is known about Summers, who is listed in the 1811 city directory as a schoolteacher but is not in the city directory in 1816 or in the 1820 census.

75. Richard Allen and Jupiter Gibson to Bishop Asbury, Feb. 22, 1798, in Wesley, *Richard Allen*, pp. 89–90.

76. Allen to Dorothy Ripley, June 24, 1803, *Journal of Negro History*, 1 (1916), 441. Until 1816 the membership figures were reported in the *Minutes of the Annual Methodist Conference*, published annually in Philadelphia.

77. Black baptisms were recorded in bills of mortality published by the Anglican (Episcopal) church and in Zachariah Poulson's yearly almanacs. See Susan E. Klepp, "The Demographic Characteristics of Philadelphia, 1788–1801: Zachariah Poulson's Bills of Mortality," *Pennsylvania History*, 53 (1986), 201–221.

78. *Juvenile Magazine*, no. 3 (1813), 21–22.

79. The Quaker diarist Elizabeth Drinker described a black Methodist funeral procession that passed her door: "Six men went before the Coffin, one with a book in his hand; they sang aloud, songs I suppose, in a very loud and discordant voice; a large concourse follow'd"; Elizabeth Drinker Journal, June 10, 1798, HSP.

80. Albert J. Raboteau, "Richard Allen and the African Church Movement," in Leon Litwack and August Meier, eds., *Black Leaders in the Nineteenth Century* (Urbana, Ill., forthcoming).

81. Avrahm Yarmolinsky, *Picturesque United States of America, 1811, 1812, 1813, Being a Memoir on Paul Svinin, Russian Diplomatic Officer, Artist, and Author* . . . (New York, 1930), p. 20.

82. John F. Watson, *Methodist Error, or Friendly Christian Advice to those*

Methodists who Indulge in Extravagant Emotions and Bodily Exercises . . . (Cincinnati, 1819), pp. 13–14, 16.

83. *Autobiography of Rush,* pp. 239, 250; Clark, Potts, and Payton, *Journal of Asbury,* II, 64, 235, 432; George A. Phoebus, comp., *Beams of Light on Early American Methodism* (New York, 1887), pp. 217, 219, 222, 286.

84. *Autobiography of Rush,* p. 239.

85. Clark, Potts, and Payton, *Journal of Asbury,* III, 366.

86. Lorenzo Dow, *History of the Cosmopolite; or the Four Volumes of Lorenzo's Journal . . ., 3d ed.* (Philadelphia, 1816) pp. 560–561; Richard Allen and Jacob Tapsico, *Doctrines and Disciplines of the African Methodist Episcopal Church* (Philadelphia, 1817); reprinted in Richard R. Wright, *The Bishops of the African Methodist Episcopal Church* (Nashville, 1963), p. 61.

87. Will B. Gravely, "African Methodisms and the Rise of Black Denominationalism," in Russell E. Richey and Kenneth E. Rowe, eds., *Rethinking Methodist History: A Bicentennial Historical Consultation* (Nashville, 1985), p. 113; Wesley, *Richard Allen,* p. 87. The November 1794 declaration of the Bethelites is reprinted in Benjamin Tucker Tanner, *An Outline of Our History and Government for African Methodist Churchmen, Ministerial and Lay* (Philadelphia, 1884), pp. 142–148.

88. The articles of incorporation are reprinted in Richard R. Wright, ed., *Encyclopedia of African Methodism* (Philadelphia, 1947), pp. 330–332.

89. Allen and Tapsico, *Doctrines and Discipline,* p. 61; Dow, *Cosmopolite,* p. 561.

90. Lorenzo Dow, *The Dealings of God, Man, and the Devil; as Exemplified in the Life, Experience, and Travels of Lorenzo Dow,* 4th ed. (Norwich, Vt., 1833), pp. 203, 272, 278–279, 310.

91. William B. Gravely, "Early Methodism and Slavery: The Roots of a Tradition," *Drew Gateway,* 34 (1964), 154–156; Donald R. Mathews, *Slavery and Methodism: A Chapter in American Morality, 1780–1845* (Princeton, N.J., 1965), pp. 21–26.

92. Gravely, "African Methodisms," pp. 114–115; idem, "The Rise of African Churches in America," pp. 58–73.

93. Allen, *The Life Experience and Gospel Labors of the Rt. Rev. Richard Allen,* 2d ed. (New York, 1960), p. 32; Dow, *Cosmopolite,* p. 561, identifies the triggering incident as Elder Smith's giving a ticket to a love feast at Bethel to a woman whom the black trustees had expelled for disorderly walking. When the Bethelites would not admit the woman to the love feast, Smith took it as "disregarding his POWER and AUTHORITY." Also see accounts of the incident in Carol V. R. George, *Segregated Sabbaths: Richard Allen and the Rise of Independent Black Churches, 1760–1845* (New York, 1973), pp. 66–68; and Wesley, *Richard Allen,* pp. 134–136.

94. "The African Supplement" is reprinted in Wright, *Encyclopedia of African Methodism,* pp. 332–333.

95. Memorial of the Trustees of the African Methodist Episcopal Church, called Bethel, to the Philadelphia Conference of the Methodist Episcopal Ministers assembled, April 8, 1807, Methodist Historical Society, Philadelphia; quoted in George, *Segregated Sabbaths,* pp. 74–75.

96. Asbury acknowledged the African Supplement in his letter to the Trustees of the African Methodist Episcopal Church called Bethel, April 9, 1807, Methodist Historical Society, Philadelphia.

97. George, *Segregated Sabbaths,* p. 81; Gravely, "African Methodisms," pp. 114–115.

98. For the retreat of the white Methodists on the issue of slavery, see Mathews, *Slavery and Methodism,* pp. 3–29; and H. Shelton Smith, *In His Image, But . . .: Racism in Southern Religion, 1780–1910* (Durham, N.C., 1972), chap. 1.

99. The quotation is from the Philadelphia Evangelical Society's subscription paper for the African Presbyterian Church, "Appeal for funds to erect a church for negroes" (Philadelphia, 1809). On Gloucester see William T. Catto, *A Semi-Centenary Discourse, Delivered in the First African Presbyterian Church, Philadelphia, May, 1857* (Philadelphia, 1857), pp. 26–31; Emma Jones Lapsansky, "South Street, Philadelphia, 1762–1854: 'A Haven for Those Low in the World' " (Ph.D. diss., University of Pennsylvania, 1975), pp. 193–197.

100. "Appeal for funds," pp. 26, 31, 38; Benjamin Rush to Samuel Bayard, Oct. 10 and 23, 1810, Correspondence of Rush, LCP.

101. John Gloucester to Benjamin Rush, Jan. 11, 1812, Correspondence of Rush, LCP; Catto, *Semi-Centenary Discourse,* p. 65; Robert Jones, another black Presbyterian minister, wrote later that Gloucester had traveled to England at this time to raise money for the purchase of his family; *Fifty Years in the Lombard St. Central Presbyterian Church* (Philadelphia, 1894), pp. 8, 141.

102. Catto, *Semi-Centenary Discourse,* pp. 29, 48.

103. Benjamin Rush to Samuel Bayard, Oct. 23, 1810, Dreer Collection, HSP; Gloucester to Rush, Jan. 11, 1812, Correspondence of Rush, LCP.

104. Carter L. Woodson, *History of the Negro Church* (Washington, D.C., [1921]), p. 74.

105. Donald Scott, "Unearthing the Bones of Her Ancestors," *Philadelphia Inquirer,* June 10, 1984; Mechal Sobel, *Trabelin' On: The Slavery Journey to an Afro-Baptist Faith* (Westport, Conn., 1979), pp. 197, 271–272.

106. Charles H. Brooks, *Official History of the First African Baptist Church, Philadelphia, Pa.* (Philadelphia, 1922), pp. 9, 16; membership figures were reported annually in the *Minutes of the Philadelphia Baptist Association . . .* Samuel Johnson is identified as the minister of the church in *Census Directory for 1811 . . .* (Philadelphia, 1811), p. 463. The 1816 directory lists Johnson, living on North Eighth Street near the church, as a lastmaker. The 1816 schism is detailed in *Minutes of the Philadelphia Baptist Association* (Philadelphia, 1816), pp. 6–8.

107. Benjamin Rush reported the organizing of several of the new churches in a letter to James Rush, Oct. 19, 1810, Correspondence of Rush, LCP; Donaldson's *Juvenile Magazine,* no. 3 (1813) gave a list of the black churches, with their founding dates and current membership.

108. *Juvenile Magazine,* no. 3 (1813), pp. 21–22.

109. Jones and Allen, *Narrative of the Proceedings of the Black People . . . ,* in Aptheker, *Documentary History,* pp. 36, 37.

110. *History of the Association of Friends for the Free Instruction of Adult Colored Persons in Philadelphia* (Philadelphia, 1890); Sydney V. James, *A People among People: Quaker Benevolence in Eighteenth-Century America* (Cambridge, Mass., 1963), pp. 291–292. Susanna Emlen described the initiators of this project as "generally young men and women of leisure" in a letter to her father, William Dillwyn, Feb. 28, 1790, Dillwyn Letters, LCP.

111. CICFB Minute Book, 1790–1803, pp. 53, 56, 61–62, 71, 90, 97, 103, 131, 135–136, 146, 148, PPAS, reel 6; PAS Minute Book, 1787–1800, pp. 182–183, 229–230; Eleanor Harris's death was noted in *The Minerva,* June 3, 1797.

112. CICFB Minute Book, 1790–1803, p. 177, PPAS, reel 6.

113. Ibid., pp. 163–164, 191, 100–104, 210–211; Board of Education Minutes, I (1797–1803), 65, 76, 84–87, PPAS, reel 7.

114. Wesley, *Richard Allen,* p. 90; Charles S. Smith, *A History of the AME Church* (Philadelphia, 1922), p. 52.

115. List of black schools in 1805, prepared by Joseph Clark, Cox-Parrish-Wharton Collection, IV, 70, HSP.

116. (Philadelphia) *Aurora,* July 24, 1804; Douglass, *Annals,* pp. 110–111.

117. Board of Education Minutes, II (1803–1819), 16, 35–36, PPAS, reel 7. The schools did not reopen until 1813; ibid., pp. 50–58.

118. CICFB Minute Book, 1790–1803, pp. 219–220, PPAS, reel 6.

119. Address of PAS to American Convention, 1804, PPAS, reel 29.

120. *A Sketch of the Origin and Progress of the Adelphi School in the Northern Liberties . . . for the Instruction of Poor Children* (Philadelphia, 1810); "An Account of the school for the people of colour established by Arthur Donaldson," *Juvenile Magazine,* no. 3 (1813), 22–23, which also lists all schools teaching blacks in the city and their enrollments.

121. Rush Welter, *Popular Education and Democratic Thought in America* (New York, 1962), pp. 25–28.

122. Benjamin Rush, "A Plan for Free Schools," March 28, 1787, in *Letters of Rush,* I, 412–415.

123. Harry L. Silcox, "Delay and Neglect: Negro Public Education in Antebellum Philadelphia, 1800–1860," *PMHB,* 97 (1973), 44–45.

124. Attendance data are scattered through the Board of Education Minutes, II (1803–1819), PPAS, reel 7.

125. Seamen's Protective Certificate Applications to the Collector of Customs for the Port of Philadelphia, Records of the Bureau of Customs, Na-

tional Archives. Among Philadelphia-born mariners, 43 percent could sign their names, compared with only 24 percent among those born in the southern states, including Delaware.

126. The Bethelites' signatures are reproduced in Wright, *Encyclopedia of African Methodism*, p. 334; .he St. Thomas's signatures are on a petition in Archives of the Episcopal Church, RG50-5, Austin, Texas.

127. Cyrus Bustill's "An Addrass to the Blacks in Philadelfiea" in 1787 is the first of a number of exhortations on the necessity of "peace and love, kindness, respect, regard, gratitude, sobriety, meekness . . . a frugal, steady industry." The address is reprinted in Melvin H. Buxbaum, "Cyrus Bustill Addresses the Blacks of Philadelphia," *William and Mary Quarterly*, 3d ser., 29 (1972), 102–108. See also Monroe Fordham, *Major Themes in Northern Black Religious Thought, 1800–1860* (Hicksville, N.Y., 1975), chap. 2.

128. Benjamin Johnson to Stephen Grellet, May 25, 1816, Grellet Papers, I, 217, LCP at HSP.

129. Report of PAS to American Convention, June 3, 1801, PPAS, reel 25; a list of black mutual benefit societies appeared in *Juvenile Magazine*, no. 3 (1813), 22–23.

130. Benjamin Johnson to Stephen Grellet, May 25, 1816, Grellet Papers, I, 217, LCP at HSP.

7. The Bittersweet Cup of Freedom

1. *Poulson's Daily American Advertiser*, Oct. 5, 1814; for other information on the mobilization of black Philadelphians see ibid., Aug. 25 and Sept. 3, 7, 19, 20, 1814; William Nell, *Colored Patriots of the American Revolution* (Boston, 1855; reprint, New York, 1968), p. 176; Martin Robinson Delany, *The Condition, Elevation, Emigration, and Destiny of the Colored People of the United States, Politically Considered* (Philadelphia, 1852; reprint, New York, 1968), pp. 74–75; and *Minutes of the Committee of Defence of Philadelphia, 1814–1815,* in *Memoirs of the Historical Society of Pennsylvania*, VIII (Philadelphia, 1867), p. 47.

2. "Report of the Committee Appointed at a Town Meeting of the Citizens of the City and County of Philadelphia," Sept. 3, 1834, in *Hazard's Register of Pennsylvania* . . . , 14 (1834), 201.

3. The data are derived from the published decadal censuses.

4. I am indebted for these data to Susan Klepp of Rider College. Tom W. Smith discusses differential mortality and fertility rates by race in "The Dawn of the Urban-Industrial Age: The Social Structure of Philadelphia, 1790–1830" (Ph.D. diss., University of Chicago, 1980), chap. 3. Comparative urban statistics on black mortality in the early 1820s are given in Nathaniel Niles, Jr., and John D. Russ, *Medical Statistics or a Comparative View of the Mortality in New York, Philadelphia, Baltimore, and Boston* . . .

(New York, 1827). The mortality rate declined rapidly in the 1830s for both black and white Philadelphians. George Emerson, the main student of the subject at the time, found "a remarkable diminution in the mortality of the colored population" by the mid-1830s, at which time the death rate of lower-class whites, he concluded, "falls little short of the proportion in the colored population"; *The Present State and Condition of the Free People of Color, of the City of Philadelphia and Adjoining Districts . . .* (Philadelphia, 1838), pp. 34–35.

5. Priscilla Ferguson Clement, "The Philadelphia Welfare Crisis of the 1820s," *PMHB,* 105 (1981), 150–153; William A. Sullivan, *The Industrial Worker in Pennsylvania, 1800–1840* (Harrisburg, Pa., 1955), p. 51.

6. *Report of the Pennsylvania Society for the Promotion of the Public Economy* (Philadelphia, 1817); the data for 1826 are derived from an analysis of the Philadelphia Guardians of the Poor, Daily Occurrence Dockets, PCA.

7. For annual statistics on crime from 1794 to 1815, see *A Statistical View of the Operation of the Penal Code of Pennsylvania* (Philadelphia, 1817), p. 13. For the 1820s, see Visiting Committee to the Acting Committee of the Pennsylvania Prison Society, Jan. 8, 1821, Pennsylvania Prison Society Papers, II, pt. A, HSP. Edward R. Turner, *The Negro in Pennsylvania: Slavery—Servitude—Freedom, 1639–1861* (Washington, D.C., 1911), p. 156, gives statistics from the *Philadelphia Gazette,* March 5, 1828, that show blacks committing about 40 percent of the crimes from 1823 to 1826, but this proportion began to drop by the early 1830s (*Present State and Condition,* p. 17).

8. *Philadelphia in 1824 . . .* (Philadelphia, 1824), p. 46.

9. Pennsylvania Society for the Promotion of the Public Economy, *Report of the Library Committee* (Philadelphia, 1817).

10. John Melish, *The Necessity of Protecting and Encouraging the Manufactures of the United States* (Philadelphia, 1818), p. 9.

11. Sullivan, *Industrial Worker,* p. 51.

12. Clement, "The Philadelphia Welfare Crisis," pp. 151–153.

13. From 1815 to 1819, as the city's economy foundered, sixty-two shiploads of immigrants from Ireland reached Philadelphia. After a lull in the early 1820s, the heavy influx from Ireland resumed, reaching unprecedented heights in the mid-1830s. For the Irish immigration see Cynthia J. Shelton, *The Mills of Manayunk: Industrialization and Social Conflict in the Philadelphia Region, 1787–1837* (Baltimore, 1986), pp. 59–60, 95–98; Maldwyn A. Jones, "Ulster Emigration, 1783–1815," in E. R. R. Green, ed., *Essays in Scotch-Irish History* (New York, 1969); William F. Adams, *Ireland and Irish Emigration to the New World from 1815 to the Famine* (New Haven, 1932); and Kerby A. Miller, *Emigrants and Exiles: Ireland and the Irish Exodus to North America* (New York, 1985), pp. 193–197. The best treatment of changing conditions of labor in this era is Bruce Laurie, *Working People of Philadelphia, 1800–1840* (Philadelphia, 1980).

14. Quoted in Miller, *Emigrants and Exiles,* p. 195.

15. For example, a survey of thirty branches of industry, in which blacks were rarely employed, showed a precipitous decline in employment, from 9,425 in 1816 to 2,137 in 1819; *Niles' Weekly Register,* 17 (Oct. 23, 1819). David Lehman kindly supplied this reference.

16. See, for example, the names William F. Bush and Thomas Crawford Jones, members of the black Masonic lodge in Philadelphia, in Charles H. Wesley, *Prince Hall: Life and Legacy* (Philadelphia, 1977), p. 218; and the name William Harding, Jun. on the black Masons' list of 1800, ibid. The manuscript censuses of 1800–1830 show an increasing use of middle initials by black males. For a more general treatment of the quest for respectability see Monroe Fordham, *Major Themes in Northern Black Religious Thought, 1800–1860* (Hicksville, N.Y., 1975), chap. 2.

17. Harry E. Davis, *A History of Freemasonry among Negroes in America* (Cleveland, 1946), pp. 73–76.

18. Elizabeth Drinker Journal, June 24, 1797, HSP.

19. Minutes of the African Lodge of Philadelphia, in Wesley, *Prince Hall,* p. 218.

20. Davis, *Freemasonry among Negroes,* pp. 79–81; Wesley, *Prince Hall,* p. 94.

21. François A. La Rochefoucauld–Liancourt, *Travels through the United States . . . 1795–97,* 2 vols. (London, 1799), II, 386.

22. Thomas Kochman, *Rappin' and Stylin' Out: Communication in Urban Black America* (Urbana, Ill., 1972).

23. Elizabeth Drinker Journal, January 3, 1799, HSP.

24. Address to the Free Blacks of Philadelphia, 1796, PPAS, reel 25; CICFB Minute Book, 1790–1803, p. 154 (Aug. 10, 1797), PPAS, reel 6.

25. Svinin's watercolors and sketches are reproduced, with an account of his career in the United States, in Avrahm Yarmolinsky, *Picturesque United States of America, 1811, 1812, 1813, Being a Memoir on Pavel Svinin . . .* (New York, 1930).

26. *Confession of John Joyce . . . with an Address to the Public, and People of Colour By Richard Allen . . .* (Philadelphia, 1808), reprinted in Dorothy Porter, ed., *Early Negro Writing, 1760–1837* (Boston, 1971), pp. 414–426.

27. See, for example, the addresses of the Annual Negro Convention, beginning in 1830, to "The Free Colored Inhabitants of these United States," in Herbert Aptheker, ed., *A Documentary History of the Negro People in the United States* (New York, 1951), pp. 133–137, 142–146; Fordham, *Black Religious Thought,* chap. 2.

28. Quoted in Turner, *Negro in Pennsylvania,* p. 141 n.

29. *An Excursion through the United States and Canada during the Years 1822–23, by an English Gentleman,* quoted in ibid., p. 141 n.

30. Orlando Patterson, *Slavery and Social Death: A Comparative Study* (Cambridge, Mass., 1982), pp. 60–62.

31. John F. Watson, *Annals of Philadelphia, and Pennsylvania, in the Olden Times . . .*, 3 vols. (Philadelphia, 1830; reprint, 1900), II, 261. On reciprocal influences between high and popular culture see David D. Hall, "Introduction," in Steven L. Kaplan, ed., *Understanding Popular Culture: Europe from the Middle Ages to the Nineteenth Century* (Berlin, 1984), pp. 5–18.

32. Yarmolinsky, *Picturesque United States*, p. 20.

33. John F. Watson, *Methodist Error, or Friendly Christian Advice to those Methodists who Indulge in Extravagant Emotions and Bodily Exercises . . .* (Cincinnati, 1819), p. 16; the African origins of these musical forms are discussed in Eileen Southern, *The Music of Black Americans: A History* (New York, 1971), pp. 91–92. For another account of a black church service, in which the sermon was followed by an hour of singing, "in full thundering chorus . . . while all the time they were clapping hands, shouting, and jumping," see William Faux, *Memorable Days in America . . .* (London, 1823), in Reuben G. Twaites, ed., *Early Western Travels, 1748–1846,* 16 vols. (Cleveland, 1904), XII, 84–85.

34. Leon F. Litwack, *North of Slavery: The Negro in the Free States, 1790–1860* (Chicago, 1961), pp. 160–166; Leonard P. Curry, *The Free Black in Urban America, 1800–1850: The Shadow of the Dream* (Chicago, 1981), passim.

35. [Charles Caldwell], "An Essay on the Causes of the Variety of Complexion and Figure in the Human Species . . . ," *American Review of History and Politics*, 2 (1811), 128–166; C[aldwell], "An Essay on the Causes of the Variety of Complexion and Figure in the Human Species . . . ," *Port Folio*, 4th ser., 4 (1814), 8–33, 148–163, 252–271, 362–382, 447–457; for a further discussion of Caldwell, see Jordan, *White over Black*, pp. 530–538.

36. William R. Stanton, *The Leopard's Spots: Scientific Attitudes toward Race in America, 1815–1859* (Chicago, 1960), pp. 24–44.

37. Coxe, "New World," in *Democratic Press*, Oct. 10–Nov. 16, 1809; quoted in Jacob E. Cooke, *Tench Coxe and the Early Republic* (Chapel Hill, N.C., 1978), p. 507.

38. Cooke, *Coxe and the Early Republic*, p. 513.

39. Cooke, *Coxe and the Early Republic*, p. 513, quoting from Coxe, *Considerations Respecting the Helots of the United States . . .* , published in the *Democratic Press* between Nov. 25, 1820, and Feb. 5, 1821.

40. Turner, *Negro in Pennsylvania*, p. 146.

41. Pennsylvania Society for the Promotion of the Public Economy, *Report of the Library Committee*, pp. 16–17.

42. Henry Bradshaw Fearon, *Sketches of America: A Narrative of a Journey of Five Thousand Miles through the Eastern and Western States of the United States* (London, 1819), p. 167–168.

43. J. Thomas Scharf and Thompson Westcott, *History of Philadelphia, 1609–1884,* 3 vols. (Philadelphia, 1884), III, 1906–07.

44. *United States Gazette,* Nov. 22, 1825.

45. Report of PAS to Commissioners on Pauperism, July 19, 1821, CICFB Loose Minutes, PPAS, reel 9.

46. Lorenzo Dow, *History of the Cosmopolite; or the Four Volumes of Lorenzo's Journal . . . ,* 3d ed. (Philadelphia, 1816), p. 562; *The Life Experience and Gospel Labors of the Rt. Rev. Richard Allen . . .* (Nashville, 1960), p. 34.

47. Legal notes on *Green* vs. *Trustees of Bethel Church,* Yeates Papers, HSP; Will B. Gravely, "African Methodisms and the Rise of Black Denominationalism," in Russell E. Richey and Kenneth E. Rowe, eds., *Rethinking Methodist History: A Bicentennial Historical Consultation* (Nashville, 1985), pp. 115–116.

48. On Roberts's background and character see Charles Elliott, *The Life of the Rev. Robert B. Roberts* (Cincinnati, 1844), pp. 13–32.

49. The incident is well recounted in Carol V. R. George, *Segregated Sabbaths: Richard Allen and the Rise of Independent Black Churches, 1760–1840* (New York, 1973), p. 83; for a contemporary account see *Biography of Rev. David Smith of the A. M. E. Church . . .* (Xenia, Ohio, 1881; reprint, Freeport, N.Y., 1971), pp. 29–30.

50. George, *Segregated Sabbaths,* pp. 83–84; John Emory to Samuel Shoemaker, April 6, 1815; opinions of Shoemaker and Joseph Hopkinson; and handbill of sheriff's sale, June 12, 1815, all in Edward Carey Gardiner Collection, HSP.

51. Statement of Robert Burch, Dec. 16, 1815, Edward C. Gardiner Collection, HSP; Richard Allen to Daniel Coker, Dec. 18, 1816, in Benjamin Tucker Tanner, *An Outline of Our History and Government for African Methodist Churchmen, Ministerial and Lay* (Philadelphia, 1884), pp. 152–155; *Life Experience of Allen,* pp. 34–35.

52. Statement of Burch, Dec. 16, 1815; George, *Segregated Sabbaths,* p. 84.

53. Daniel Coker, *A Sermon, delivered extempore in the African Methodist Episcopal Church in the city of Baltimore . . .* [Baltimore, 1816]; excerpted in Aptheker, *Documentary History,* pp. 68–69.

54. Daniel Coker, *A Dialogue between a Virginian and an African Minister* (Baltimore, 1810); reprinted in Dorothy Porter, ed., *Negro Protest Pamphlets* (New York, 1969); Will B. Gravely, "The Rise of African Churches in America (1786–1822): Re-examining the Contexts," *Journal of Religious Thought,* 41 (1984), 49–50.

55. The best treatment of Spencer and his movement is Lewis V. Baldwin, *"Invisible" Strands in African Methodism: A History of the African Union Methodist Protestant and Union American Methodist Episcopal Churches, 1805–1980* (Meteuchen, N.J., 1980). Seceding from the white Methodist conference in 1813, Spencer's church in Wilmington incorporated itself as the Union Church of African Members and quickly established connections

with five other black congregations in Delaware, Pennsylvania, and New York.

56. See Gravely, "African Methodisms," pp. 119–120.

57. Gravely, "The Rise of African Churches in America," p. 62.

58. George, *Segregated Sabbaths,* pp. 87–89; Charles H. Wesley, *Richard Allen: Apostle of Freedom* (Washington, D.C., [1935]), pp. 150–157, 165; Benjamin T. Tanner, *An Apology for African Methodism* (Baltimore, 1867), p. 66.

59. Payne did not include this information in his official history of the AME church, which was not published until 1891, but he related it in his memoirs; working from early documents, Payne wrote that Allen tried to conciliate the light- and dark-skinned blacks who had contended at the first conference of the AME church in 1816 by appointing as bishops both Edward Waters, "a dark man," and Morris Brown, "who was not a black man"; *Recollections of Seventy Years* (Nashville, 1883), pp. 100–101. On Payne's career, see Josephus R. Coan, *Daniel Alexander Payne: Christian Educator* (Philadelphia, 1935).

60. *Biography of David Smith,* p. 32.

61. Tanner, *Apology for African Methodism,* p. 16; Daniel Payne, *History of the African Methodist Episcopal Church* (1891; reprint, New York, 1969), pp. 9–10.

62. The AME Discipline is in Richard Allen, Daniel Coker, and James Champion, *The Doctrines and Discipline of the African Methodist Episcopal Church* (Philadelphia, 1817), p. 9.

63. Douglas R. Egerton, " 'Its Origin Is Not a Little Curious': A New Look at the American Colonization Society," *Journal of the Early Republic,* 5 (1985), 463–480.

64. Quoted in P. J. Staudenraus, *The African Colonization Movement, 1816–1865* (New York, 1961), p. 29.

65. George M. Frederickson, *The Black Image in the White Mind: The Debate on Afro-American Character and Destiny* (New York, 1971), pp. 6–8; Staudenraus, *African Colonization Movement* (New York, 1961), chaps. 1–2.

66. Robert G. Harper, *A Letter from General Harper of Maryland to Elias Caldwell . . .* (Baltimore, 1818), pp. 9–11, quoted in Frederickson, *The Black Image,* p. 8; David B. Davis, *The Problem of Slavery in the Age of Revolution* (Ithaca, N.Y., 1975), pp. 199–200. Mercer's characterization of free blacks is quoted in Egerton, " 'Its Origin Is Not a Little Curious,' " pp. 479–480.

67. James D. Essig, *The Bonds of Wickedness: American Evangelicals against Slavery, 1770–1808* (Philadelphia, 1982), traces the disillusionment of the early abolitionists.

68. Finley to Cuffe, Dec. 5, 1816, quoted in Floyd J. Miller, *The Search for a Black Nationality: Black Colonization and Emigration, 1787–1863* (Urbana, Ill., 1975), p. 45.

69. Julie Winch, *Philadelphia's Black Elite: Activism, Accommodation, and the Struggle for Autonomy, 1787–1848* (Philadelphia, 1988), p. 34.

70. Staudenraus, *American Colonization Movement*, p. 39.

71. For Vaux see Alan Zachary, "Social Thought in the Philadelphia Leadership Community, 1800–1840" (Ph.D. diss., Northwestern University, 1974), pp. 8, 38; Samuel Emlen to Roberts Vaux, Sept. 19, 1817, Vaux Papers, 1683–1893, Correspondence, HSP.

72. Roberts Vaux, *Memoirs of the Life of Anthony Benezet* (Philadelphia, 1817), p. 71.

73. Benjamin F. Quarles, *The Black Abolitionists* (New York, 1969), pp. 3–4, quoting James Forten's account in *The Emancipator*, June 30, 1835.

74. Forten to Cuffe, Jan. 25, 1817, in Sheldon Harris, *Paul Cuffe: Black America and the African Return* (New York, 1972), p. 244.

75. "The Protest and Remonstrance of the People of Colour in the City and County of Philadelphia . . . ," reprinted in Aptheker, *Documentary History*, pp. 71–72.

76. The committee members appointed at the meeting are listed at the end of the resolutions passed, which are printed in William Lloyd Garrison, *Thoughts on African Colonization* . . . (Boston, 1832), pt. II, pp. 9–10.

77. Isaac Van Arsdale Brown, *Biography of the Rev. Robert Finley* (Philadelphia, 1857), p. 123, where "J. F." is called John Foster, but this was undoubtedly James Forten.

78. Forten to Cuffe, Jan. 25, 1817, quoted in Harris, *Paul Cuffe*, p. 244.

79. Garrison, *Thoughts on African Colonization*, pt. II, pp. 10–13.

80. Winch, *Philadelphia's Black Elite*, pp. 37–39.

81. Robert Purvis, *Remarks on the Life of James Forten* . . . (Philadelphia, 1842), p. 14.

82. Miller, *Search for a Black Nationality*, p. 54; Thomas Clarkson to Prince Sanders, Dec. 3, 1819, Miscellaneous MSS, Henry Huntington Library, San Marino, Calif.

83. Miller, *Search for a Black Nationality*, pp. 54–62; "Roll of Emigrants That Have Been Sent to the Colony of Liberia, Western African, by the American Colonization Society . . . ," *Senate Documents*, 28th Cong., 2d sess., 1844, IX, 152–154. None of the 1820 emigrants are listed in the Philadelphia city directory for 1817; this fact suggests that most of them had arrived recently in the city.

84. The emigration lists, cited in n83, show 78 passengers departing from Philadelphia between 1820 and 1843 and 414 from Baltimore.

85. Turner, *Negro in Pennsylvania*, pp. 115–117.

86. The incident is recounted in L. Maria Child, *The Life of Isaac T. Hopper* (Philadelphia, 1852), pp. 208–209.

87. For reports of kidnapping, often by rings of men operating in the city, see (Newark) *Centinel of Freedom*, Sept. 15, 1801; *Pennsylvania Gazette,*

Nov. 15, 1801; [Edward Darlington], *Reflections on Slavery . . .* (Philadelphia, 1803), pp. 15–32; and Elizabeth Drinker Journal, Jan. 21, 1804, HSP.

88. For a particularly vicious case see *Philadelphia Gazette,* July 25, 1818.

89. Turner, *Negro in Pennsylvania,* p. 117.

90. Prince Saunders, *Memoir Presented to the American Convention . . .* (Philadelphia, 1818); reprinted in Porter, *Early Negro Writing,* pp. 269–278. For an account of Saunders' efforts and letters relative to it see Earl Leslie Griggs and Clifford H. Prator, *Henry Christophe & Thomas Clarkson: A Correspondence* (Berkeley and Los Angeles, 1952).

91. The letters from Thomas Clarkson to Roberts Vaux, March 8, 1819, and Jan. 31, 1820, and from Vaux to Clarkson, May 1, 1820, detail the involvement of Philadelphia abolitionists in the Haitian emigration movement; Vaux Papers, 1686–1893, Correspondence, HSP.

92. *Poulson's American Daily Advertiser,* July 5, 1824; *U.S. Gazette,* July 5, 8, and 26, 1824.

93. Allen's endorsement of emigration to Haiti is in the *U.S. Gazette,* Jan. 11, 1825; for letters to him from Haitian officials and Philadelphia leaders who went there see ibid., Dec. 4, 1824; Jan. 11, 1825; Feb. 22, 1825. The emigration is covered in detail in James O. Jackson III, "The Origins of Pan-African Nationalism: Afro-American and Haytien Relations, 1800–1863" (Ph.D. diss., Northwestern University, 1976), and in Miller, *Search for a Black Nationality,* chap. 3.

94. B. S. Hunt, *Remarks on Hayti as a Place of Settlement for Afric-Americans and on the Mulatto as a Race for the Tropics* (Philadelphia, 1860), p. 11. According to Hunt, who lived periodically in Haiti in the 1840s and 1850s, the chief sailmakers at Port-au-Prince and Cap Haitien were former apprentices of James Forten, and the Methodist church was under the care of a former Philadelphian; ibid., pp. 6, 16.

95. George, *Segregated Sabbaths,* pp. 119–121. A report of the PAS's Committee on Emigration to Haiti, Aug. 27, 1824, states that 60 had left and "upwards of 500 others have engaged to go"; CICFB Loose Minutes, PPAS, reel 9.

96. Miller, *Search for a Black Nationality,* pp. 78–82; *Philadelphia Gazette,* Sept. 4, 6, and 11; Oct. 15, 16, and 17; Nov. 17, 1824.

97. Hunt, *Remarks on Hayti,* pp. 11–12.

98. Letters reporting the discouragement of Philadelphia emigrants were published in the *U.S. Gazette* and other Philadelphia newspapers. See, for example, *U.S. Gazette,* April 18 and June 14, 1825.

99. Quoted in *Freedom's Journal,* Nov. 2, 1827.

100. Ibid., May 18, 1827; Quarles, *Black Abolitionists,* p. 7; Miller, *Search for a Black Nationality,* pp. 82–83. For the career of Samuel Cornish, one of the hundreds of Delaware-born free blacks who migrated to Philadelphia, see Jane H. Pease and William H. Pease, *Bound with Them in Chains: A*

Biographical History of the Antislavery Movement (Westport, Conn., 1972), pp. 140–161; and David E. Swift, "Black Presbyterian Attacks on Racism: Samuel Cornish, Theodore Wright, and Their Contemporaries," in David W. Wills and Richard Newman, eds., *Black Apostles at Home and Abroad: Afro-Americans and the Christian Mission from the Revolution to Reconstruction* (Boston, 1982), pp. 43–84.

101. For addresses at annual conventions and a general treatment of the black convention movement see Howard H. Bell, *A Survey of the Negro Convention Movement, 1830–1861* (New York, 1969).

8. The Dream Deferred

1. Quoted in Leon F. Litwack, *North of Slavery: The Negro in the Free States, 1790–1860* (Chicago, 1961), p. 39. It is one of the ironies of this period that southern defenders of slavery, advocates of colonization in Africa, and northern white friends of free blacks tended to describe, each for their own purposes, the plight of urban Afro-Americans in much the same way.

2. *African Repository,* 1 (1825), 68.

3. The household census commissioned by the Pennsylvania Abolition Society in 1837 noted whether householders were born in or outside of Pennsylvania. The PAS employed agents "to visit every colored family in the city and suburbs [of Philadelphia]" and relied heavily on Charles W. Gardner, a black Methodist minister. The results of the census, which was far more detailed than federal censuses of this era, were summarized in *The Present State and Condition of the Free People of Color, of the City of Philadelphia and Adjoining Districts* . . . (Philadelphia, 1838). The manuscript census, cited hereafter as Census of 1837, is in PPAS, reel 26.

4. *Sixth Census or Enumeration of the Inhabitants of the United States* . . . (Washington, 1841).

5. For the antiblack sentiment and restrictive measures that emerged at the 1837–38 convention to amend the Pennsylvania constitution see *Pennsylvania Constitutional Debates of 1837–1838* . . . , 9 vols. (Philadelphia, 1839), IX, passim.

6. Census of 1837; the census data on real and personal property are summarized in *Present State and Condition,* pp. 6–8. For the crystallizing of the black elite after 1840, see Emma Jones Lapsansky, "Friends, Wives, and Strivings: Networks and Community Values among Nineteenth-Century Afroamerican Elites," *PMHB,* 108 (1984), 3–24. Theodore Hershberg's argument that slave-born Philadelphia blacks did better than their freeborn neighbors, as measured by property ownership, personal wealth, church membership rate, and beneficial society membership, is based on a faulty interpretation of data in the Census of 1837. In only about one-fourth of the households indicated as containing former slaves is it possible to determine

whether the household head was slave-born or freeborn (and inference is required in many of these cases); it is not possible, as Hershberg claims, to identify 314 households headed by ex-slaves or to determine in more than a small number of cases whether such household heads were manumitted or had bought their freedom; "Free Blacks in Antebellum Philadelphia: A Study of Ex-Slaves, Freeborn, and Socioeconomic Decline," *Journal of Social History*, 5 (1971–72), 183–209; reprinted in Theodore Hershberg, *Philadelphia: Work, Space, Family, and Group Experience in the Nineteenth Century* (New York, 1981). Nor, contrary to Hershberg's assertion, is it possible to discern whether households included one or two parents. An additional difficulty with such a purely quantitative aggregate analysis is that it obscures the great variety of life within the black community and ignores the resilience of most of the city's black residents, and the accomplishments of large numbers of them, in spite of worsening conditions.

7. Using samples from tax lists, Tom W. Smith reports property ownership rates among white households in 1820 and 1830 of 20.9 and 15.7 percent, respectively; "The Dawn of the Urban-Industrial Age: The Social Structure of Philadelphia, 1790–1830" (Ph.D. diss., University of Chicago, 1980), p. 151, table 60.

8. *Present State and Condition*, pp. 16–17, 23.

9. The Census of 1837 reported two black physicians, three midwives, one "botanic physician," two dentists, four bleeders, one cupper, and two "Indian doctors" (herbal physicians).

10. Census of 1837; Maritime Records of the Port of Philadelphia, 1798–1860, WPA transcriptions, Library of Congress.

11. *The Colored American*, Oct. 22, 1837.

12. "Memorial of the People of Color of the City of Philadelphia and Its Vicinity to the Honorable the Senate and House of Representatives of the Commonwealth of Pennsylvania," January 1832, in Herbert Aptheker, ed., *A Documentary History of the Negro People in the United States* (New York, 1951), p. 132; Census of 1837.

13. Census of 1837.

14. The proportion of widows has been extrapolated from the number of women age twenty-four and older as enumerated in the federal censuses of 1830 and 1840.

15. Quoted in *Present State and Condition*, p. 24.

16. *Hazard's Register of Pennsylvania*, 14 (1834), 201.

17. "Memorial of the People of Color," p. 132; for similar trends in other cities in this era see Leonard P. Curry, *The Free Black in Urban America, 1800–1850: The Shadow of the Dream* (Chicago, 1981), chap. 2.

18. *Colored American*, July 28, 1838, quoted in Litwack, *North of Slavery*, p. 166.

19. *Pennsylvania Gazette* and *Democratic Press*, Feb. 29, 1828.

20. *Philadelphia Monthly Magazine,* 2 (1828), 53–57.

21. *Freedom's Journal,* March 14, 1828, which reproduced the article from the *Pennsylvania Gazette.* In 1830, in the first full-scale history of Philadelphia, John Fanning Watson disparaged "dressy blacks and dandy coloured beaux and belles, as we now see them issuing from their proper churches" and found equally distasteful the "overwhelming fondness for display and vainglory in [black] processions"; *Annals of Philadelphia, and Pennsylvania, in the Olden Times . . . ,* 3 vols. (Philadelphia, 1830; reprint, 1900), I, 479. See also Emma Jones Lapsansky, " 'Since They Got Those Separate Churches': Afro-Americans and Racism in Jacksonian Philadelphia," *American Quarterly,* 32 (1980), 54–78.

22. For Johnston, see *David Claypool Johnston: American Graphic Humorist, 1798–1865: An Exhibition held by the American Antiquarian Society* (Worcester, Mass., 1970).

23. Thackera Family Papers, Notebooks, HSP. Philip Lapsansky of the Library Company of Philadelphia has generously provided this information.

24. Several sets of the prints are at the Library Company of Philadelphia. A few are reproduced in Lapsansky, " 'Since They Got Those Separate Churches.' " On Clay, see Nancy Reynolds Davison, "E. W. Clay: American Political Caricaturist of the Jacksonian Era" (Ph.D. diss., University of Michigan, 1980).

25. *Saturday Evening Post,* Jan. 7–April 7, 1832. Clay's renderings were tame compared with the vicious caricatures, published as broadsides, of black freedom celebrations in Boston—"Bobalition of Slavery" (1819) and "Reply to Bobalition of Slavery" (1821), Rare Books Department, Boston Public Library.

26. These data, generously provided by Susan Klepp of Rider College, are drawn from Zachariah Poulson's annual bills of mortality, published in his almanacs.

27. The growth of "popular religion" in Philadelphia in the first half of the nineteenth century awaits full historical analysis, but efforts in this direction can be found in Bruce Laurie, *Working People of Philadelphia, 1800–1850* (Philadelphia, 1980), and Doris Elisabett Andrews, "Popular Religion and the Revolution in the Middle Atlantic Ports: The Rise of the Methodists, 1770–1800" (Ph.D. diss., University of Pennsylvania, 1986).

28. Albert J. Raboteau, "The Black Experience in American Evangelicalism: The Meaning of Slavery," in Leonard I. Sweet, ed., *The Evangelical Tradition in America* (Macon, Ga., 1984), pp. 181–197.

29. I am indebted to Randall K. Burkett, at the W. E. B. Du Bois Institute, Harvard University, for information on Oson and for allowing me to read his unpublished paper, "The Reverend Harry Crosswell and Black Episcopalians in New Haven, 1820–1860," on which this paragraph is based. The petition of the St. Thomas's members is in Archives of the Episcopal Church, Record Group 50-5, Austin, Texas.

30. Little has been written about Parrott, although he was one of the most prolific black Philadelphia writers of the early nineteenth century. See his orations on the abolition of the slave trade in 1812, 1814, and 1816; his appeal for blacks to work on fortifications in 1814; his address with Forten and Cuffe on African colonization in 1815; and his address with Forten in 1817—"Address to the Humane and Benevolent Inhabitants of the City and County of Philadelphia"—all cited in William Douglass, *Annals of the First African Church in the United States of America, now styled The African Episcopal Church of St. Thomas* (Philadelphia, 1862), p. 125.

31. The congregation size and value of church property for the various black denominations in 1837 are given in *Present State and Condition*, p. 32.

32. The history of the black Presbyterians in this era is recounted in William T. Catto, *A Semi-Centenary Discourse, Delivered in the First African Presbyterian Church, Philadelphia, May, 1857* (Philadelphia, 1857), pp. 69–88.

33. Mechal Sobel, *Trabelin' On: The Slavery Journey to an Afro-Baptist Faith* (Westport, Conn., 1979), pp. 270, 273; Census of 1837.

34. Catto, *Semi-Centenary Discourse*, p. 106, says the church was founded in 1816, but it was listed in Arthur Donaldson's survey of black churches in 1813, published in his *Juvenile Magazine*, no. 3 (1813). The size of the congregation in 1837 is derived from the Census of 1837.

35. Christopher Rush, *A Short Account of the Rise and Progress of the African Methodist Episcopal [Zion] Church in America . . .* (New York, 1843), pp. 52–54, 59–62; Census of 1837.

36. Daniel Coker, *Sermon Delivered Extempore in the African Bethel Church in the City of Baltimore . . .* [Baltimore, 1816], cited in Charles H. Wesley, *Richard Allen: Apostle of Freedom* (Washington, D.C., 1935), p. 150.

37. Daniel Payne, *History of the African Methodist Episcopal Church* (Nashville, 1891; reprint, New York, 1969), pp. 13, 20; Carol V. R. George, "Widening the Circle: The Black Church and the Abolitionist Crusade, 1830–1860," in Lewis Perry and Michael Fellman, eds., *Antislavery Reconsidered: New Perspectives on the Abolitionists* (Baton Rouge, 1979), pp. 75–95.

38. Daniel Payne, *Recollections of Seventy Years* (Nashville, 1883), p. 64; David W. Wills, "Womanhood and Domesticity in the A. M. E. Tradition: The Influence of Daniel Alexander Payne," in David W. Wills and Richard Newman, eds., *Black Apostles at Home and Abroad: Afro-Americans and the Christian Mission from the Revolution to Reconstruction* (Boston, 1982), pp. 135–136.

39. Lee's career is discussed and her famous *The Life and Religious Experience of Jarena Lee* reprinted in William L. Andrews, ed., *Sisters of the Spirit: Three Black Women's Autobiographies of the Nineteenth Century* (Bloomington, Ind., 1986). Also valuable is the essay on Rebecca Cox Jackson, another female visionary at Bethel in the 1830s, by Jean M. Humez, "Visionary Experience and Power: The Career of Rebecca Cox Jackson," in Wills and Newman, *Black Apostles*, pp. 105–132.

40. Wills, "Womanhood and Domesticity," pp. 138–139.

41. *Present State and Condition*, p. 31.

42. *Acts of the General Assembly of the Commonwealth of Pennsylvania, 1817–1818 Session* (Harrisburg, 1818), pp. 124–130.

43. *Ninth Annual Report of the Controllers of the Public Schools of the First School District of the State of Pennsylvania* (Philadelphia, 1827), p. 3.

44. Prince Saunders, *An Address delivered at Bethel Church . . .* (Philadelphia, 1818), in Aptheker, *Documentary History*, pp. 72–73.

45. "Account of Schools for Coloured Persons in the City of Philadelphia," Mathew Carey Papers, Manuscript Correspondence on Internal Improvements, p. 114, HSP; in 1816 six schools were taught by black teachers, according to Benjamin Johnson; Johnson to Stephen Grellet, May 5, 1816, Grellet Papers, I, 217, HSP.

46. Annual reports of the Controllers of the Public Schools (Philadelphia, 1823–35); Census of 1837.

47. *Tenth Annual Report of the Controllers of the Public Schools* (Philadelphia, 1828), p. 155.

48. The libraries and literary societies are detailed in *Present State and Condition*, p. 30.

49. *Report of the Committee Appointed at a Town Meeting of the City and County of Philadelphia . . . to Consider the Subject of Pauperism . . .* (Philadelphia, 1827), p. 7.

50. Mathew Carey, *Letters on the Condition of the Poor . . . Containing . . . Instances of Intense Suffering in Philadelphia, Nor Exceeded in London or Paris . . . ,* 2d ed. (Philadelphia, 1835), pp. 6–7.

51. *Juvenile Magazine*, no. 3 (1813), 21–22; *Freedom's Journal*, Feb. 22, 1828; a list of forty-four societies was compiled by a committee of black leaders and published in "To the Publick," *Hazard's Register of Pennsylvania*, 7 (1831), 163–164.

52. "To the Publick," pp. 163–164; James Forten, "To the Honorable the Senate and House of Representatives of the Commonwealth of Pennsylvania," January 1832, in Aptheker, *Documentary History*, pp. 126–133 (data on poor relief on p. 131); Census of 1837.

53. *Present State and Condition*, pp. 24–28. The number of members was 7,448 in 1831, and aggregate membership grew to 9,298 by 1837.

54. The official report on the riot is in *Hazard's Register of Pennsylvania*, 14 (1834), 200–203. Other reports, taken from newspapers, are in ibid., pp. 126–128, 264–266. See also John Runcie, " 'Hunting the Nigs' in Philadelphia: The Race Riot of August 1834," *Pennsylvania History*, 29 (1972), 187–218; and Lapsansky, " 'Since They Got Those Separate Churches,' " pp. 54–78. For the outbreak of racial violence in New York City in the summer of 1834 (a season of violence in many northern cities), see Paul A. Gilje, *Moboc-*

racy: Popular Disorder in New York City, 1763–1834 (Chapel Hill, N.C., 1987), chap. 6.

55. In its report on the 1837 census of black families, the PAS noted that, of Philadelphians admitted to the almshouse, blacks were far more temperate than whites; the report observed further that "in our streets . . . it is uncommon to meet a colored person intoxicated; while on the other hand, to see a drunken white, is an every day occurrence"; *Present State and Condition,* p. 14.

56. Watson, *Annals of Philadelphia,* II, 261.

57. Newspaper clipping from an unidentified Philadelphia paper, Mathew Carey Scrapbooks, Miscellaneous, X, 31, LCP. J. Thomas Scharf and Thompson Westcott, *History of Philadelphia, 1609–1884,* 3 vols. (Philadelphia, 1884), I, 624, give the date of the riot.

58. "Memorial of the People of Color of the City of Philadelphia and Its Vicinity," in Aptheker, *Documentary History,* p. 128.

59. Samuel J. May, *Some Recollections of our Antislavery Conflict* (Boston, 1869), p. 287; quoted in Ray Allen Billington, ed., *The Journal of Charlotte Forten* (New York, 1953), p. 10.

60. These riots are most fully detailed in Sam Bass Warner, Jr., *The Private City: Philadelphia in Three Periods of Its Growth* (Philadelphia, 1968), chap. 7.

61. James Forten to William Lloyd Garrison, March 21, 1831, Black Abolitionist Papers, microfilm ed. (New York, 1980), reel 1.

62. May, *Recollections of our Antislavery Conflict,* pp. 83–84.

63. James Forten to James McCune Smith, Aug. 9, 1835, Black Abolitionist Papers, microfilm ed., reel 1.

64. Warner, *The Private City,* pp. 131–137; the official report, which excused the arson and violence by claiming that citizens were understandably maddened by the sight of white and black abolitionists walking arm in arm through the streets, is in *The Public Ledger,* July 18, 1838.

65. Reprinted in *The Colored American,* Aug. 18, 1838.

66. "Memorial of the People of Color," p. 128.

Index

Abercrombie, James, 128
Abolitionism and antislavery, 3, 4, 24–27, 31, 33, 42–43, 45, 55, 60–65, 90, 137, 187–189, 246, 275–277; free blacks' involvement in, 44, 59–60, 64–65, 95, 103, 183, 185–189, 238, 240–243, 275–277; Society of Friends' involvement in, 17, 27, 29, 38–40, 42–44, 50, 59–60, 88–93, 99, 105, 108, 139; women's involvement in, 89–90. *See also* Gradual Abolition Act; Pennsylvania Abolition Society
Adams, John, 175
Adams, Samuel, 102
Africa, 7, 128; perceptions of, 101–102, 108, 115, 128, 210, 235. *See also* Colonization
African Baptist Church of Philadelphia, 201–202, 263, 267
African Church of Philadelphia (St. Thomas's), 1, 113–114, 119–121, 125–126, 128–129, 139, 172; affiliates with Episcopal church, 126–127. *See also* African Episcopal Church of St. Thomas
African culture, persistence of, 11, 13, 16, 18, 36, 79–80, 82, 94, 222. *See also* Cultural life of free blacks
African Episcopal Church of St. Thomas, 88, 127, 130–133, 139, 148, 169, 182, 189, 191–193, 210, 219, 222, 238, 244, 261, 265, 266, 267; and education, 205, 209; schism in, 192, 261. *See also* African Church of Philadelphia

African Fire Association, 226–227
African Friendly Society of St. Thomas, 210
African Independent Grand Lodge, 219. *See also* African Masonic lodges; Freemasonry
African institutions, 236
African Masonic lodges, 210, 218–219, 222. *See also* Freemasonry
African Methodist Church. *See* African Methodist Episcopal Church (Bethel); Allen, Richard; Methodists and Methodist church; St. George's Methodist Church
African Methodist Episcopal Church (Bethel), 88, 117, 130–133, 148, 167, 169, 182, 188, 191, 192–199, 219, 223, 237, 238, 243, 244, 260–265, 267; Articles of Association (1796), 197–198; burning of, 227; and education, 204, 205, 209; established as separate denomination, 227–233, 263–264; secedes from white Methodist church, 193–199, 227–233, 242, 264. *See also* Allen, Richard; Methodists and Methodist church
African Presbyterian Church, 23, 199–201, 202, 236, 244, 245, 251, 262–263, 274
African Repository, 246. *See also* American Colonization Society
African Supplement, the (1807), 198–199, 228–229
African Union Methodist Church (Wilmington, Delaware), 231